For students of Presbyterian history, Machen is always a stop along the timeline. We consider his scholarly role and applaud his supernaturalism. It is even commonly known of his international travels to study under men like Hermann. Now we have access to the humanitarian Machen. In the context of the Great War, these personal letters open up a new side of him. From his own pen, often in the midst of uncertainties, we are able to know him better. I can't commend this book too much.

—**C. N. Willborn,** Pastor of Covenant Presbyterian Church, Oak Ridge, Tennessee; Adjunct Professor of Historical Theology, Greenville Presbyterian Theological Seminary

What a treat Barry Waugh has provided for those who love Machen! J. Gresham Machen with the YMCA reveals Machen the perfectionist, the theologian, the servant, and the son. But, these letters to his family also reveal the changed man, having seen firsthand the horrors of war.

—**Danny E. Olinger,** General Secretary, Committee on Christian Education, Orthodox Presbyterian Church; Editor of *A Geerhardus Vos Anthology*

Doughboy accounts of their experiences in World War I are fairly common, but it is unusual to find the stories of those who offered assistance behind the trenches. J. Gresham Machen served in the YMCA in France for over a year and was always near the frontline. Whether helping the wounded or working in the canteen, he ministered to the men as best he could. Machen's letters reveal the frustrations and boredom that so many soldiers felt as well as the ⅂.
Machen's compassion is truly amazin ⅃
wonderful glimpse of the service of c ,
Dr. Barry Waugh, deserves commend 7
and footnotes provide essential guic ⌡
Machen's service and ministry during the war.

—**David Snead,** Chair, Department of History, Liberty University; Editor of *George Browne: An American Soldier in World War I*

J Gresham Machen is a fascinating, complex, and controversial figure, well known for his role in the church conflicts of the 1920s and '30s. What is often forgotten is that he was also a member of the generation of young men whose lives were forever changed by their exposure to the horrors of trench warfare in the First World War. This volume contains the letters which the young Machen wrote home as he served as a YMCA volunteer in the war. As such, they offer both important first-hand accounts of the conflict but also give us insights into some of the darker experiences which shaped the mind of the future church leader.

—**Carl R. Trueman,** Paul Woolley Professor of Church History, Westminster Theological Seminary, Philadelphia

J. Gresham Machen played a key role in the theological debates of the 1920s and 1930s. His work has been studied and evaluated from many angles. What is less well-known and less well considered is his service in the First World War. Although he objected to American involvement, he participated as a volunteer in the YMCA. From these rare letters the reader can see a fresh side of the great scholar. On the battlefields of France he was simply known as a compassionate soul who brought solace to scores of suffering soldiers. For those who only know Machen the polemicist, this volume will showcase Machen the caregiver.

—**William Edgar,** Professor of Apologetics, Westminster Theological Seminary, Philadelphia

LETTERS FROM
THE FRONT

LETTERS FROM
THE FRONT

J. GRESHAM MACHEN'S CORRESPONDENCE FROM WORLD WAR I

TRANSCRIBED AND EDITED BY BARRY WAUGH

PHILADELPHIA, PENNSYLVANIA

PUBLISHING

P.O. BOX 817 • PHILLIPSBURG • NEW JERSEY 08865-0817

Westminster Seminary Press, LLC, a Pennsylvania Limited Liability Company, is a wholly owned subsidiary of Westminster Theological Seminary.

This book is a copublication between P&R Publishing and Westminster Seminary Press.

Cover images are used courtesy of Westminster Theological Seminary.

Cover design by Cause Design Company and P&R Publishing.

Printed in the United States of America

Library of Congress Cataloging-in-Publication Data

Machen, J. Gresham (John Gresham), 1881-1937.
 Letters from the front : J. Gresham Machen's correspondence from World War I / transcribed and edited by Barry Waugh.
     p. cm.
 Includes bibliographical references.
 ISBN 978-1-59638-479-8 (pbk.)
 1. Machen, J. Gresham (John Gresham), 1881-1937--Correspondence. 2. Presbyterians--United States--Correspondence. 3. World War, 1914-1918--War work-Young Men's Christian associations. 4. Americans--France--History--20th century. 5. World War, 1914-1918--War work--France. I. Waugh, Barry G. (Barry Grant), 1954- II. Title.
 BX9225.M24A4 2012
 285'.1092--dc23
  [B]
                      2012011181

CONTENTS

CONTENTS

FOREWORD

THE NAME OF J. GRESHAM MACHEN is synonymous with high theological scholarship, unswerving biblical fidelity, and theological orthodoxy. His outspoken defense of historic Christianity has had a substantial impact on students, pastors, and scholars. Christians in the Machen tradition have even been called "Machen's warrior children."

So it may be a surprise that in the First World War Machen chose not to fight as a warrior. Instead he regularly risked his life in embattled France as a humanitarian non-combatant serving with the YMCA. The confrontational theologian of Christianity and Liberalism had previously been an agent of grace and compassion in the midst of danger and death in the Great War. This volume rounds out our understanding of Machen the brilliant scholar by also revealing him as a servant of Christ to needy and suffering soldiers.

Moreover, January 1, 2012 was the seventy-fifth anniversary of Machen's untimely death. Thus it is fitting that we remember his role with the Young Men's Christian Association in preserving lives of young men in military service. This publication also celebrates Machen's importance for the history of Westminster, as well as this largely overlooked aspect of his ministry for Christ.

It is with pleasure, then, that Westminster Seminary Press publishes Machen's letters home from the battlefields of France. I hope in the coming years we will be able to offer other books that highlight Westminster's heritage, and in the process, help to advance the gospel and the growth of Christ's Kingdom.

Thanks for reading!

Sincerely in His Service,

Peter A. Lillback
President Westminster Theological Seminary
January 2012

PREFACE

THIS YEAR MARKS THE SEVENTY-FIFTH memorial of the death of the
founder of Westminster Theological Seminary, J. Gresham Machen,
who succumbed to pneumonia, January 1, 1937, and it is the bicen-
tennial of the founding of American Presbyterian seminary education at Princeton, New Jersey. It is fitting that these two land mark
remembrances occur this year given Dr. Machen's leaving Princeton
Seminary to found Westminster Theological Seminary. His reputation
as a New Testament scholar, theological educator, and churchman
are all recognized, but his involvement with the Young Men's Christian Association (YMCA) in the Great War is not so well known. The
following collection of letters written to his family provides not only
a picture of several months of his life but also a recounting of some
of the horrors of the final days of what is now most often called the
First World War. When the United States entered the conflict it was ill
prepared for the logistics necessary to move and supply hundreds of
thousands of troops overseas. President Woodrow Wilson's efforts to
keep the United States out of the war and pacifist sentiments among
Americans contributed to the slow process of getting troops abroad
and into action. Not only was troop mobilization slow, but providing recreational activities, refreshments, toiletries, snacks, and other
aspects of the soldier's life in Europe had to be mobilized. The non-
military aspects of life abroad were provided by interdenominational
and religious organizations such as the Salvation Army, Knights of
Columbus (Roman Catholic), YMCA, and others. It is the desire of the
transcriber and editor of the letters that the following collection of
correspondence increases interest in the life and labors of J. Gresham
Machen, the Great War, and the war work of the YMCA.

I have been aided greatly by many people, but the most important
person has been my wife, Sandy, who has read the manuscript, followed

the progress of the project, and always been there to encourage me and give her opinion when asked. Our daughter, Heather, inquires regularly about the progress of this project and has encouraged my efforts. My mother and father, and Charles and Pat, have always supported my labors and the current project is no exception.

Early in the project, the Historian of the Orthodox Presbyterian Church, John Muether, reviewed a draft of the transcribed letters and encouraged me regarding pursuing publication. Also, my pastor, Rick Phillips, commented helpfully on some of the letters in the early days of the transcription process. Laurie Thomas of Mitchell Road Christian Academy read some of the letters to her middle school classes and confirmed my hope that the correspondence would appeal even to children. Most recently, C. N. "Nick" Willborn and Danny Olinger have reviewed the manuscript, and I appreciate the help provided by both of them. I am also grateful for the review of the manuscript by David Snead, Professor and Chair, Department of History, Liberty University, whose expertise in the Great War provided unique insights.

With respect to the French language and culture I must thank Westminster Theological Seminary's resident Francophile, Bill Edgar, for helping me with some French translating and explaining some aspects of French culture. Special thanks go to Kristi Wetzel of France by Design, LLC, for her translation of the Montí letters and advising me regarding translations of other French passages.

I have been helped greatly by several other people at the seminary. The manuscript letters have been lovingly guarded for many years by the archivist, Grace Mullen. It seems that almost anything I write requires her assistance with resources in her care. Once again, I must thank gracious Grace for her courtesy and willingness to help with this project. Her biographical knowledge of the members of Dr. Machen's family and friends was invaluable for the glossary. I would also like to thank President Peter Lillback for taking on the publication of the book for the seminary, Dick Dabney for aligning all the jots-and-tittles to complete the project, and Abbie Daise for her courtesy, patience, and direction of communications.

To those who helped but whose names I have forgotten goes my apology, but I am thankful for your assistance and hope that my porous memory has not diminished my appreciation for your assistance.

Finally, currently conflicts rage on many parts of the earth and in recent years the United States has seen many of its soldiers die for freedom. My final thank you goes to the many that have served and died—whether carrying weapons, serving refreshments, or driving an ambulance—to maintain freedom from oppressive regimes. Remembering J. Gresham Machen's labors with the YMCA reminds us that war requires many behind-the-scenes workers that are often described as "non-combatants," but it will be seen in this collection of letters that those serving behind the trench-lines also faced danger and contributed in their own way to the successful end of the Great War. As Jesus sat on the Mount of Olives teaching his disciples about the things that will take place he said, *you will hear of wars and rumors of wars. See that you are not alarmed, for this must take place, but the end is not yet.* With great assurance, the Christian looks to the reign of righteousness ending sin, war, poverty, false teaching, and megalomania, as believers of all generations gather before the throne of God.

Barry Waugh
March 27, 2012

INTRODUCTION

A BRIEF BIOGRAPHY OF J. GRESHAM MACHEN

John Gresham Machen was born in 1881 and raised in the family home on Monument Street in Baltimore, Maryland. His father, Arthur Webster Machen, was a respected attorney, and his mother, Mary (Minnie) Gresham, was born to a prominent family in Macon, Georgia. Gresham had two brothers, Arthur (Arly) Webster II and Thomas. Arthur followed in his father's footsteps and labored in the practice of law, but Thomas chose a more artistic and visual vocation working in architecture. The Machens were faithful members of the Franklin Street Presbyterian Church and exercised their gifts in its ministry in Baltimore.

Gresham's undergraduate degree was granted by Johns Hopkins University, 1901, where he also was a graduate student, 1901–2. He continued his education at Princeton Theological Seminary in New Jersey receiving the BD in 1905 while also studying at Princeton University where he received the MA in 1904. The hub of biblical studies in the early twentieth century was in Germany, so Gresham went there as a New Testament fellow at the Universities of Marburg and Göttingen, 1905–6. Following his studies in Germany, he returned to Princeton Seminary to be an instructor in New Testament, 1906–14, and then he was appointed Assistant Professor of New Testament Literature and Exegesis serving until his resignation in 1929. Due to the influences of theological liberalism at Princeton and the reorganization of the seminary, Machen and several other faculty members left the seminary to organize Westminster Theological Seminary in Philadelphia, which opened its educational doors in the fall of 1929. In 1936, he was the leader of those involved in founding what would become the Orthodox Presbyterian Church. J. Gresham Machen died of pneumonia in Bismarck, North Dakota, on January 1, 1937, while on a speaking trip. He was never married. His remains are interred in the Machen family plot in Baltimore where his grave is marked with "Faithful unto Death" written in the Greek language that he studied and taught so vigorously.

Dr. Machen wrote several books including *Christianity and Liberalism* (1923), *New Testament Greek for Beginners* (1923), *What Is Faith?* (1925), and *The Virgin Birth of Christ* (1930). These titles have been published in several editions. One of the emphases of his writing was defending the supernatural nature of the Christian gospel against the anti-supernatural or naturalistic foundation of the theological liberalism of his era. After his return from France, he delivered the 1921 James Sprunt Lectures at Union Theological Seminary, Virginia, which were published that same year as *The Origin of Paul's Religion.*

For those interested in learning more about Dr. Machen, *J. Gresham Machen: A Biographical Memoir,* by Ned B. Stonehouse, a faculty colleague of his and fellow minister in the Orthodox Presbyterian Church, provides a personal biography penned by a close friend.[1] Stonehouse's pages 206–54 provide background material leading up to the war and information regarding Machen's service in the war, which may prove helpful to set the scene for the transcribed letters that follow. *Defending the Faith: J. Gresham Machen and the Crisis of Conservative Protestantism in Modern America,* by D. G. Hart,[2] presents an intriguing intellectual portrait of Dr. Machen's life. Stephen J. Nichols has written a guided tour of Dr. Machen's life and thought for a more popular audience, which includes several photographs of him and of artifacts from the archives of Westminster Seminary. For a perspective on him as a New Testament scholar, one should read the work by Terry A. Chrisope, *Toward a Sure Faith: J. Gresham Machen and the Dilemma of Biblical Criticism, 1881–1915.*

THE MACHEN CORRESPONDENCE

If one spends some time reading through the letters of J. Gresham Machen it becomes clear that he was collecting his correspondence for the future. He organized his letters according to the way he thought;

---

1. Ned B. Stonehouse, *J. Gresham Machen: A Biographical Memoir* (Grand Rapids: William B. Eerdmans Publishing Co.; reprint, Willow Grove: Orthodox Presbyterian Church, 2004).
2. D. G. Hart, *Defending the Faith: J. Gresham Machen and the Crisis of Conservative Protestantism in Modern America* (Baltimore: Johns Hopkins, 1994).

his collection is organized chronologically but sometimes also by subject matter within the chronology. His collection of letters written to his alcoholic friend, Richard Hodges, spanned many years and all were meticulously stored just as he did his other letters. The letters he sent home during his YMCA service in the First World War are no exception. In a letter to his brother Arly, December 28, 1918, he commented, "I am enclosing the English *résumé* of *L. Aiglon* enclosed in the theatre program. Let Uncle see it if it is convenient and give it to Mother to put into the archives of my letters. I really think it is something of a gem." What Dr. Machen was concerned to have in his collection was a summary in English of Edmond Rostand's play, *The Eaglet*.[3] Why this bit of paper was important enough for Machen to mention it for inclusion in his correspondence is not known, but what is significant is that long before the ecclesiastical controversies of the 1920s, J. Gresham Machen was storing his correspondence for succeeding generations to read. In his January 17, 1919, letter to his mother, Dr. Machen mentioned he was delighted that she

> and the members of our circle have liked the letters that I wrote. It would have given me satisfaction if, as Arly and others wanted, extracts from the letters could have been published, but the instructions that we received some time ago were so explicit that I was obliged to write on the subject as I did. I suppose the regulations would not be so strict now, and I rather think it was a Y.M.C.A. regulation only that forbade the publishing of censored letters. At any rate, no doubt it was well enough to be on the safe side.[4]

Now, as the centennial of the composition of the Machen war correspondence approaches, the interests of Arly and the other family members regarding their publication are being fulfilled. The narrative provided by the nearly 100,000 words of text is at times intense, in other places there is great sadness, while at other points his New

---

3. This item was not found in the Machen collection.

4. The editor wishes to comment that these letters have been transcribed as Dr. Machen wrote them; the only corrections made are those deemed necessary to clarify the intent of what he wrote. The reader is reminded that many of the war letters were written in difficult situations and in a hurry.

Testament interests take the stage, in some correspondence his concern for the soldiers' spiritual welfare shows his intense desire that the supernatural gospel be brought to them, and as in any letters, there are bits and pieces of the family life of Machen that are mundane and routine. This letter collection provides an additional perspective on the life of a man who is known as a New Testament scholar, churchman, apologist for supernatural Christianity, and theological educator.

THE HANDWRITING OF J. GRESHAM MACHEN AND TRANSCRIPTION PROBLEMS

Any hand-written letter presents challenges concerning paleography and the script of J. Gresham Machen is no exception. When he had time to sit down at a table and write, his letters were legible, but due to aircraft attacks, chemical gas dispersions, artillery shells, and his many duties as a YMCA worker, his writing was sometimes scribbled yielding a cryptic scrawl. At one point, Dr. Machen was using a pen that he described as "a watering can" because the ink flowed too freely. So, there were good reasons for the unclear characters of Machen's script. Since this volume of Machen's war letters may encourage other people to dig into his vast collection in the archives at Westminster Seminary, it is appropriate to point out a few of the lessons learned by the editor during his transcribing in hopes of easing the interpretive task for future readers.

One transcription problem early on was the identification of Machen's upper case "N." A word kept appearing "_ena," where the blank designates the character in question. The mysterious letter looked like a shark tooth with its point at the top. After repeated occurrences, the letter was found to be "N," so that the word was "Nena." "Nena" was his sister-in-law. The editor also found it difficult to differentiate a "T" from a "t" due to the horizontal line not always being precisely located. Generally, Machen's uppercase letters are written a bit differently and they require some getting used to as one reads his handwriting. One aspect of his script is his practice of attaching his first person singular personal pronoun ("I") to the following word. For example, "Iremember," "Iwent," "Isaw," etc., is the way he wrote anything preceded by an "I." This habit becomes more confusing as the rapidity of his writing increases; the "I" gets closer and closer to the following word so that this quirk requires the reader to take a moment to decipher the word. Another situation requiring deciphering of his writing is his lower case "n" sometimes looks like his "u," which looks like his "v" that sometimes could be an "o" or an "a"—the letter finally selected by the editor was interpreted by context and previous uses, but there may be some transcribed words that are errant due to confusion of these letters. Machen had a tendency to start a letter with a clear handwriting and then as he progressed, the script deteriorated in quality. It is almost as if he was thinking, "I know my handwriting is not always clear, so I am going to do a better job in this letter," but then as he progressed in his composition in a less than irenic environment, the spirit was willing but the flesh was weak.

His use of a fountain pen—the most common type of his era—contributed to some of the difficulties faced in the transcription process. One of his practices most destructive to the clarity of his script was his correcting errors by writing *over* the mistake. It would have been helpful if he had lined-out the error and written the correction above, below, or after the mistake, but unfortunately, this is not the case. His use of a fountain pen increased problems because if he corrected his error as he wrote, then the original and the correction bled together, but if he corrected the error later, there was not so much bleeding and the word can sometimes be deciphered. Whether done during his writing or as post-completion editing, the overwriting makes some words totally indecipherable and in the cases where one finds "bi___" or "___ed" or "___" in the transcriptions, it may be due to overwriting. The length of the underline may or may not indicate the number of letters in the word or words; in some cases the script is so poor that the editor could not decipher the number of letters.

The recent article by William D. Dennison, "J. Gresham Machen's Letters Home from Marburg, 1905–1906," *Zeitschrift fur neuere Theologiegeschichte/Journal for the History of Modern Theology* 16 (2009): 241–75, provides transcriptions of several letters. An examination of these transcriptions will show how clearly Dr. Machen could compose a letter when he had the time and the convenience of a desk and did not have to be concerned about gas, "Y" responsibilities, enemy aircraft, sleeping, eating, and attacking troops. The letters included in this article were written to Machen's mother, father, and his brothers Arly and Tom; the content is more theological in nature due to his learning experience studying New Testament in Germany. Just as Machen complained in his war letters about his poor acquisition of the French language, so he complained about his inability to grasp German in the 1905–6 correspondence; he had the bar held high with respect to his own expectations.[5] Machen's sympathies for the Germans and their involvement in the war would have been built upon his experiences living with the nationals during his studies in their country.[6]

As for Machen's French, for someone who complained often about how little of the language he had learned, his errors of spelling, including the accents, were rare; undoubtedly his expertise as a New Testament scholar drove him to render the language as accurately as he could (he often refers to "LaRousse," which was the French-English dictionary that he used). Despite his being hard on himself regarding his acquisition of French, it would seem that he instead did remarkably well considering the pressures of his work with the YMCA. As the letters are read it will be found that during his time in Paris, he often attended French plays, some of which dated to the seventeenth and eighteenth centuries. This means that he would have acquired not only a substantial vocabulary but also a vocabulary covering three centuries. In addition to the dramatic performances, he sometimes mentions reading the play in French before attending its theatrical presentation.

The letters are arranged in simple chronological order. The vast majority of the correspondence was sent by Dr. Machen to his mother, but there are some letters to other members of his family and a few friends. The letters vary in length from two or three pages in the original manuscripts to over twenty.

LOCATING CITIES AND GEOGRAPHICAL CHARACTERISTICS

Most of Dr. Machen's work with the YMCA in France was situated around Soissons, northeast of Paris, but other areas include Paris; several locations around Roeselare, Belgium; towns between Troyes and Dijon; villages around Baccarat; towns to the northwest of Nancy; and

---

5. See page 256 of the article for Machen's complaint regarding his grasp of the German language.

6. Hart, 45-46.

the cities west of Paris—Tours, Angers, and Le Mans. He said of the locations of his service, "To sum up, I saw something of five sectors of the front—Aisne, Lorraine, Argonne, Woëvre & Belgium."[7]

It is suggested that if the reader is interested in following Dr. Machen's journeys, the purchase of a copy of Michelin's *France: Tourist and Motoring Atlas*, 2007, which contains 350 detailed regional maps and an extensive index will be helpful. The editor, after wasting his money on some lesser maps, found this atlas by Europe's premier mapmaker to be ideal for locating even the smallest villages.[8] It was also found that Michelin's inexpensive pocket tourist map of Paris was helpful for following Machen's movements while in the grand city of lights.[9] Dr. Machen went to great trouble to add village and city names in marginal notes in his letters after his return to America. He could not include the names of geographical locations when he wrote the letters due to censorship concerns.[10] The editor has provided footnotes locating the various towns and villages mentioned by Machen by means of their distance from larger towns and these accompanied with the atlas of France will allow the reader to follow his trips. In addition to these resources, his letter of January 5, 1919, to his mother provides a narrative of his early movements. The reader is referred to the section of maps provided in this book for an overview of his locations of service.

Another source that may prove helpful for those who want to walk in Dr. Machen's shoes is the Internet service provided by Google Maps, which proved especially helpful through use of its *satellite* and *street* views. The satellite view allows one to get a sense of the size of a battlefield or village, or the route of a street, river, or railroad. In some of the footnotes, the editor has used the Google street view to describe buildings as they were at the time the street view was filmed by Google. Many of the buildings in Paris mentioned by Dr. Machen

7. See his letter to Mary Gresham Machen (in suceeding citations abbreviated as MGM) 1/5/1919 for his mention of the regions he labored in for the YMCA.

8. *Michelin France: Tourist and Motoring Atlas* (Clermont-Ferrand: Michelin, 2007).

9. *Michelin New Edition Paris Plan with Street Index* (Paris: Michelin Maps and Guides, n.d.).

10. The censors were concerned that if mail in transit fell into enemy hands the location and strength of military units could be discerned from information in the letters. In the case of Machen's letters, it seems that the most touchy information included geographical locations, division names, and details about battles. In one case, Machen mentioned a secret installation and the material was snipped from the pages by the censors.

are extant and can be viewed using the street view feature. The editor found the street view helpful in locating the churches Machen attended for worship and some of the Paris sites that he visited. The opportunity to walk in the steps of historical figures in grand old cities like Paris, London, or Rome, is facilitated by some of the tools offered by Internet sources. However, it must be remembered that it has been nearly a century since the First World War, so one should keep in mind that geography, street names and routes, new highways, buildings destroyed by war and fire, and other modifications may have affected current geography, topography, and buildings.

THE FIRST WORLD WAR UNTIL THE ENTRY OF THE UNITED STATES INTO THE CONFLICT

On Sunday, June 28, 1914, in Sarajevo, the spark igniting the flames that erupted into the Great War occurred when the Serbian anarchist/terrorist Gavrilo Princip shot the heir to the Hapsburg throne, Archduke Franz Ferdinand. The first shot fired from Princip's automatic pistol entered the Archduke's wife, Sofia. It was the second cartridge fired that propelled the round into the Archduke near his heart. Both Franz and Sofia died before they arrived at the hospital. By July 6, the tension created by the assassination led to the German government's support of Austro-Hungary's desire to take reprisals against Serbia. As the events continued their domino-like results, Austro-Hungary and Germany allied, while France, Russia, and England united as their opposition. By the end of August, the Austro-Hungarians had invaded Serbia, the French had moved into Lorraine, the Germans had invaded France, the Russians invaded East Prussia, and the Germans surrendered to Anglo-French forces in Togoland, West Africa. The shots fired by the anarchist Princip ignited a catastrophic war involving many nations in conflict on battlefields scattered all over the globe.

As the war intensified and involved other nations, the United States followed an isolationist plan under the leadership of President Woodrow Wilson. Though isolationist with respect to declaring war, the United States was a supplier of arms and materials for the European war effort. The sinking of the *Lusitania*, the sabotage of a munitions plant in Delaware, the sinking of United States freighters by German

U-boats, and Germany's clandestine encouraging of Mexico to invade Texas all contributed to the United States declaring war on Germany, April 6, 1917. By the time the United States entered the war, the conflict had killed multitudes and destroyed property throughout the world. France suffered a particularly heavy burden of death and destruction. New technologies such as the airplane, tank, poisonous gas, and more powerful ordnance had increased the maiming and destructive power of war. The Germans were hoping that their spring offensive in 1918 would enjoy success due to the Bolsheviks having seized power in Russia in November 1917. The Russian Revolution allowed Germany to shift troops gradually from the Eastern front to the trenches in France. As Dr. Machen entered France to serve with the YMCA in January 1918, he would see the final German spring offensive, the *Kaiserschlacht* (Kaiser's Battle) or Michael Offensive, begin in March.

THE WORK IN FRANCE BY THE YOUNG MEN'S CHRISTIAN ASSOCIATION (YMCA)

Once the United States committed to enter the war, J. Gresham Machen wanted to contribute his labors to the effort. He thought of serving as a chaplain, as a secretary of a YMCA in France, or with the ambulance corps. The chaplaincy had no openings and service with the ambulance corps was abandoned when he was informed that he could be reassigned from an ambulance to a munitions transport. He was concerned to work with an organization that allowed him to befriend the enlisted men while providing noncombatant services.

When the choices were assessed, the YMCA became his field of service for the war effort. He believed that the "Y" was not the ideal organization for service, but he also thought he could serve effectively without seriously compromising his theological principles. He was particularly concerned about possible disregard of the Sabbath by the YMCA due to its commitment to a generic Christianity. In September 1917, he had the opportunity to speak in some YMCA meetings in Newport, Rhode Island, which helped him to understand the work of the "Y" better. As Dr. Machen learned more about the service he would be giving as a "Y" secretary, he said that it "seems to be just the kind of work I *dislike* most, but that is no insuperable objection to my going into it. It consists largely of selling postage stamps and 'mixing'."[11] Despite his reservations about the "Y," he believed there was great need for its work with the soldiers and it was the best and least compromising opportunity he had available to him for service.[12]

When Dr. Machen began his work with the "Y" in France, he was initially stationed near the front in a cooperative effort of the Americans and the French named the *Foyer du Soldat, Union Franco-Américaine*. The huts operated by the cooperative program were prohibited to have any political and sectarian propaganda and were not allowed to serve alcoholic beverages. Each hut was to maintain a library of 200 books that had been approved by a committee appointed by the Minister for War. As will be seen in the letters that follow, one of the major services provided by the foyers was selling snacks, toiletries, money orders, stationery, postage, and distributing refreshing beverages such as hot chocolate. When the war was over, it was determined that 1,452 foyers had been opened of which 130 were captured or destroyed by the enemy (Dr. Machen narrowly escaped a foyer that was seized by the Germans). It should be noted that the USO (United Service Organization) was not organized until 1941, and the YMCA huts served to fill the need for a place of rest, entertainment, and refreshment for the war-wearied troops.[13]

11. Stonehouse, 213; one of the weaknesses of Stonehouse's book is the lack of documentation. However, since the book is written chronologically, this quotation was probably taken from a letter written between Aug. 25 and Sept. 19, 1917.

12. This paragraph is a summary of Stonehouse, 211-15.

13. *Summary of World War Work of the American Y.M.C.A.*, The International Committee of the Young Men's Christian Association, 1920, 55.

Conventions Used in the Letter Transcriptions

Dr. Machen mentions several people, literary works, authors, plays, and other items that are identified for the reader. A glossary of people, plays, literature, and other terms considered uncommon has been included at the end of this book. It is suggested that the reader examine the glossary before reading the letters to be familiar with the glossary contents. Some common names of great fame, such as Robert E. Lee, have been left out of the glossary due to their identities being common knowledge. Readers of this letter collection will vary in interest from the skim-and-spot-read tactic to those who want to know every jot-and-tittle, so the glossary was used to reduce the amount of material to be included in the footnotes.

As Dr. Machen learned French, he used the language in his letters. French terminology is translated in the footnotes. In most cases, the translations are of a few words or less, but some of the translations are longer.

There are some references to web addresses in the documentation for information regarding Machen's letters. For example, the footnote describing "Dover's Powder" was taken from a website. Thanks to the web entry the reader can understand what Machen meant when he said, "a thing wrapped up like Dover's Powder," as he described the writing ink he was using (MGM, April 5, 1918).

Each chapter title includes the beginning and ending dates of the chapter. That is, the dates are those of the first letter in the chapter and the last date of the last letter. Some of the letters were written over a period of more than one day, so the last date in the title is that of the latest date given by Machen in the last letter of the chapter.

At the beginning of each chapter, following the title, are a few lines of italicized text. These sentences provide a summary of what is to follow in the letters of that chapter. This summary will give the reader a sense of what is to follow and provide continuity from one chapter to the next.

Many of the letters have notes in their margins that were added later by Dr. Machen. The notes are included in the footnotes of the transcriptions. These notes mostly provided the names of cities and towns that Machen could not mention in the letters due to censorship.

Please note that the letters have been transcribed, as much as possible, as Dr. Machen wrote them. In some cases, the reader will find some of the sentences cumbersome, over or under punctuated, or a bit difficult to comprehend, *but* this is how he wrote them amid the pressures of his YMCA service and the distractions of war. In a few cases, the editor felt it necessary to adjust the structure of the sentences because the original was too difficult to follow.

1

"OVER THERE"[1]

Following a safe and U-boat free voyage across the Atlantic, J. Gresham Machen would enter France. While waiting for his YMCA assignment in Paris, the Princeton scholar will seek to immerse himself in the French language through conversation, reading literature, and enjoying the theater. He will find the widow of a local Protestant pastor who will converse with him in French as they enjoy the meals she prepares. Dr. Machen expresses his frustration with his fellow Americans over their failure to try and learn to speak at least some French.

[This letter was written on letterhead that reads, "Cie Gle Transatlantique, A Bord."]

le 22 Janvier 1918 (Tuesday)

My dearest Mother:

Although we are not expected to get to port until about Friday, it is time for me at least to begin my letter home. Preparation for one or two Y.M.C.A. exercises in which I have taken part on board, though it has not taken much actual time, has served to occupy my thoughts and prevent me from doing anything else with a perfectly clear conscience.

1. "Over There," is a war song published by George M. Cohan in 1917. The relevant portion of the lyrics is, "Over there, over there, Send the word, send the word over there—That the Yanks are coming, The Yanks are coming, The drums rum-tumming Ev'rywhere . . ." etc.

I went aboard the ship on Tuesday afternoon, January 15, at about four o'clock. After passing the last barrier near the gang plank I was at once cut off from my native land, for the regulations prevent passengers who have once entered the ship from going ashore again. Since I was wearing my overseas uniform, which is not supposed to be worn in America, I was unwilling to be seen about town, there was therefore no use in remaining off the boat. It is true, I forgot a small detail of my equipment, and in order to supply the lack went up to Y.M.C.A. headquarters on that Tuesday afternoon when I found the boat was not to sail at once. But I made the trip both ways in a taxi. On the return trip to the boat, I stopped at a little stationer's store and sent you a farewell word, & also tried, before I went aboard, to get Jessie on the phone, but failed. With Cousin Saida I was more successful.

The only time I have felt cold since coming was in New York harbor before we left the dock. Leaving the porthole open right above my berth, I found the air a little chilly. This fact is noteworthy not at all because it involved any serious discomfort, but only because it serves to bring out better by way of contrast the surprising fact that during the rest of the trip we have been as warm as toast.

Rather to my surprise, the ship set sail almost exactly at seven o'clock on Wednesday morning, in accordance with the announcement posted the day before. We slipped down the familiar harbor in quite the usual way, and had pleasant smooth weather when we reached the open sea. Steamer chairs and rugs were secured in quite the usual tourist way, and everything ran on just about as we are all so well accustomed to it until nightfall. Then the first striking evidence of war-time appeared in the careful way in which every possible chink is closed to avoid allowing any light to be seen from outside. The main stairway is darkened, so that there is no appearance of light outside when passengers go out on deck; the lights in the salon and smoking room are so reduced that the skylights cease to be a cause of danger; and passengers are strictly forbidden to smoke or use flashlights on the deck. How you would revel in these regulations! They could give you a magnificent opportunity of observing the stars. Only, no stars have been visible on this particular voyage. The first night or two were black as Egypt[2] on deck, so that really it was difficult, after one had ventured out, to find the door again. There was one evening when the sky was clear, but on that evening things would have been spoiled for you by a bright moon.

On Saturday the sea began to rise, and during a considerable part of Sunday, passengers (or at least for some hours) were altogether prevented from going out on deck. Since the windows were not only closed with glass, but also battened down by metal covers, it was rather a gloomy morning. I did not know, however, that the sea was any higher than I have seen it once or twice on my summer voyages. Something was wrong in a minor way with the machinery of the ship—one report was that the steering-gear was out of order—and so for some ten or twelve hours she was kept with her bow headed back toward New York, not under way but simply kept facing the wind by the use of the port engine. During Sunday afternoon, however, we turned around and got under way again, with a sea and wind from the northwest that gave her a good roll. The sight from the upper deck forward at night was particularly grand. At times the big waves seemed to stand out above the highest deck, and from a point where a good part of the ship could be seen the whole thing seemed just like a chip in comparison with the waves. The gloom added to the impressiveness of the scene. Only the port and starboard lights and one light at the foremast are kept showing. Really I have seldom been as much impressed with a sight at sea—in fact perhaps never. Since it was a following wind, we shipped comparatively little water, and it was possible to be out and enjoy the sight.

Sleeping in the latter part of the night from Saturday to Sunday was a weak effort, especially after a metal pitcher (fortunately very light) surprised me by falling from the washstand on the top of my head. Movable things generally have displayed a tendency to slide—both in the rooms and in the dining room. But "they don't call this cold in Quebec." In other words it is considered by no means a particularly rough winter passage—even for January,

2. Machen is referring to the plague of darkness that God brought upon Egypt to encourage Pharaoh to release the Hebrews from bondage (Exodus 10:21-29).

which is one of the best winter months. The surprising thing to me has been the warmth. Ever since we got well away from the coast the temperature has been delightful. Yesterday, for example, an overcoat was not really needed on deck, and today is similar. I have never been so comfortable, so far as temperature is concerned, on a summer voyage. People lie out in their steamer chairs just as they do in summer. I keep out of mine pretty much all the time—also just as in summer. Of course I have been in somewhat warmer clothes than I want to wear on summer voyages, but, even absolutely, I believe many of the days have been warmer than very many summer days that I have experienced on the sea.

Sunday was pretty rough, but yesterday gave us a gradually diminishing sea. Last night, however, a strong wind and sea sprang up from a new direction—south—and the boat is continuing a healthy roll. As yet I have made no contribution to the fishes, and have not come even as near it as I sometimes do.[3] Since I have had a good deal to do in connection with the Y.M.C.A., I have not been on deck so much & have had my mind occupied. I believe these circumstances, though they might seem rather trying, have been good for me. That "mental condition" idea of seasickness is not correct, but there is just a modicum of truth in it.[4]

About forty Y.M.C.A. secretaries are on board. One of them was appointed head of the party, and there has been a regular schedule of classes and other activities. The head of the party happens to be a physical director, and in accordance with the natural bent of his talents has appointed "getting up exercises" on the promenade deck at half past six in the morning. I have attended these exercises twice. It is something of a struggle to get out at that hour of the morning.

At nine o'clock in the morning we have had a course of study on the history and principles of the Y.M.C.A., and at half-past ten a course, conducted by the leader of the party, on methods of the Y.M.C.A. army work. In the afternoon there are various French classes. The advanced class, which is attended by your erudite

3. He is alluding to seasickness and the "contribution to the fishes" would be vomiting over the ship's rail.
4. Presumably, if one thinks one is going to get sick, then one does.

son, meets at half-past two. It is conducted by a Mr. Upson, who
is engaged in Red Cross work. His French is very distinctly of the
American variety, so far as intonation is concerned; but his method
is really very good. He tells us a little anecdote in French; then asks
us questions about it (of course questions & answers are in French);
then asks some member of the class to tell the anecdote over. Also
M. l'Abbé—a very delightful and angelic Catholic, who looks exactly
like that good, good man in Les Misérables—comes in and gives
us little talks. When I tell you that I am by no means one of the
worst members of the class—though also some distance from the
top—you will understand that the standard is not extraordinarily
high. Among the Y.M.C.A. men my erudition, so far as French is
concerned, is considered extraordinary! Only a very few of the men
of the party have any considerable knowledge of French. Linguistic
opportunities aboard the ship are exceedingly limited, since the
vast majority of the passengers are Americans. I have talked with
stewards now and then, and had one very pleasant conversation
with the Abbé. But I feel rather discouraged. I believe I could get
there if I had a chance, but I am afraid there will be no chance
this time in France, if I am working with the American forces, as I
suppose I shall be.

On Sunday morning I made a very brief talk at the morning
service in the saloon or reading-room. I was not feeling any too
certain of my ability to get through with this duty—in view of the
condition of the sea. The first hymn was "How Firm a Foundation."
We needed that hymn. Apparently I got through fairly well, since
what I said seemed to be pretty well received by the Y.M.C.A. men.
Yesterday morning I gave a little informal lecture to some of the
Y.M.C.A. party on "Christianity and the World Crisis." In it I took
occasion to trace briefly the course of New Testament criticism, &
say what I think the big question is. My preparation was exceedingly
imperfect, since the rough weather had not been stimulating to the
operation of my mind. But on the whole I think I got along better
than might have been expected. Some of the men seemed to be
interested. At any rate I am glad of the opportunity.

One of the members of the Y.M.C.A. party is Judge Pollard,
former Attorney General of Virginia, who knows Lewis very well.

Another is a young Episcopal clergyman by the name of Lee, who is, if I got the thing straight, a grand-nephew of General R. E. Lee & a descendant of "Light Horse Harry." He knows Cousin Kensey, and seems to be a very pleasant fellow. Aunt Bessie may be interested. My two room-mates are both Y.M.C.A. men. We have an outside stateroom, on the bottom deck. The "outside" feature is not a very great deal of use, since during the night and all during the roughest weather even in the daytime a metal covering is kept over the port-hole. I have the sofa berth immediately under the port-hole. It is not a bad arrangement. The room has the great advantage of being almost immediately amidships.[5] That was greatly appreciated on Saturday and Sunday nights, and if the present weather continues it is going to be greatly appreciated again to-night.

The distance traversed by the ship is posted daily, but not the noon position.[6] At noon to-day we had about 1,150 miles more to run. We ought to be in port about Friday. Of course the most exciting times are ahead of us, when we run through the war zone, but the ship has made many runs through without having any trouble at all. A formidable looking gun is mounted on the forward deck & there is another one aft. Some days ago we had a boat drill. All the passengers put on life preservers & took their stand on the deck next to the life boats to which they have severally been assigned. Before going aboard in New York I hired a safety suit which is a big rubber affair, weighted at the feet, which is supposed to keep you dry and warm in the water, and enable you to support five other persons. It is certainly very ingenious. Lots of passengers have such suits.

Wednesday, Jan. 23, 1918

Little remains to be added to-day. The run of the ship up to noon was 363 miles, being about the average.[7] We are 790 miles

---

5. The closer one is to the center of the ship, the less one feels the roll (side to side motion) and pitch (bow to stern motion) of the vessel due to one's proximity to the center of gravity. For someone susceptible to nausea, this would be especially beneficial.

6. That is, the latitude and longitude are not posted at noon, but at that time the distance traveled during the previous twenty-four hours is given.

7. The speed would have been just over 15 nautical miles per hour, or about 17.5 knots.

from the mouth of the river to which we are going.[8] The ship, it will be observed, is not fast; but it is said to be the fastest of the French Line ships now in ordinary trans-Atlantic service. The tonnage is about 14,500. I understand the ship used to ply between France and Mexico. Certainly she has given us a very comfortable passage. The air down in our stateroom is somewhat inclined to be stuffy, since the porthole has had to be kept closed the whole time, but in general we have gotten on very well indeed. I can hardly get over my surprise at the continuous warmth of the air at this time of the year. To-day is rainy, with a considerable south wind and sea, but it is not at all cold.

Yesterday at the French class we had really a most interesting talk, made by an Italian "count," who has spent much of his life in France, seems to be a thorough Frenchman. He gave us anecdotes of his journeys in various countries of Europe, his glimpses of famous people, etc., all in a most entertaining way.

When we land the plan is to go at once to Paris, where we are to be assigned our duties. I dread this part of the business, especially since if I am asked what I want to do I do not know exactly what to say. My knowledge of the conditions of the European work is too slight. It would be more restful to be under definite military orders, where there would be no use wishing or planning. I have begun to wonder whether my knowledge of French may not be put to some use, since there seems to be so few who have gotten even as far as I. The very large group of Y.M.C.A. secretaries who went over in the boat just before ours will no doubt many of them still be waiting to be assigned. This will add to the confusion & make the work of assignment, I should think, very hasty & hap-dash. But the result may be better than I anticipate. At any rate, I am most fortunate to get a chance at the work.

Of course you have been in my thoughts and my prayers have been with you & and with Arly & Helen & Tom & Nena & Uncle and all those at home. Geographical separation seems to bring

8. It is noted in the letter margin that the river was "The Gironde," which is an estuary on the W. coast of France formed by the confluence of Garonne and Dordogne rivers near Bordeaux. The river extends about forty-five miles into France.

us all the closer together.[9] I hope to be able to add to my letter to-morrow, and so will not close as yet.

January 25, (Friday)

At noon today we were just fifty miles from the mouth of the Gironde and may expect to land at Bordeaux very early to-morrow morning. Little remains to be told about the closing days of the voyage. We have had a number of most interesting lectures in the French class by a French naval officer who, I understand, was a member of some mission in the United States. At one lecture he read a good deal of French poetry—a most discouraging feature to me, since I get very little of the poetry. The weather has been rough part of the time, but to-day we have a smooth sea. The chill of the land climate is making itself felt in comparison with the warm days that we have had in the ocean, but even yet it is not at all cold.

The war zone is being crossed altogether without excitement. Five men are now constantly on watch by the gun forward, and I believe the ship's lights are not lighted at night, but there seems to be no real expectation of seeing a submarine. Nobody on board, so far as I can see, has lost the slightest sleep about the matter. Certainly I have slept very well. Some passengers, I believe, slept on deck, but that was not advised by the ship's authorities or considered necessary. I did sleep in some of my clothes last night, but made myself thoroughly comfortable. There was a big benefit auction sale in the reading room last night. A glass of beer brought $100 etc. etc.[10] It is now nearly one o'clock, and since we were only fifty miles from the mouth of the river at noon, it will be seen that the voyage is nearly over. The customs police authorities are to come aboard at the mouth of the river. A minor discomfort of travel just now is the difficulty, amounting almost to impossibility, of securing French change. Brown Brothers in New York could give me some, and diligent pestering of the purser, buying of useless bottles of ginger ale, buying of stamps

9. Absence makes the heart grow fonder?
10. Yes, it is $100 and not 1.00.

etc. has only brought me a few francs in silver.[11] I have plenty of five-franc notes, but they are too big to give a porter. We hope to get the Saturday morning train to Paris. It is pretty nearly time to mail the letters; so I say good bye for the present and send lots of care to all.

Your loving son,
Gresham

[The following letters were written on the letterhead of the "Hotel Beaulieu, 8, Rue Balzac, Champs-Élysées—Paris, Despouys, Prop^{re}".]

January 29, 1918

My dearest Mother:

It seems a long time since I wrote to you from the steamer, and I am afraid it will seem longer still before the present letter arrives. Mail, I am informed, especially on account of the censorship, is necessarily very irregular. It is really hardly worthwhile for me to begin expecting anything from home just yet, but I shall inquire this afternoon when I go to the Y.M.C.A. office. Needless to say I am eager to hear from you and all of those at home.

After passing through the submarine zone without the slightest interest on the part of anybody, so far as I could see, we arrived at the mouth of the river on Friday afternoon.[12] The passage of the bar, which on account of thick weather conditions was out of sight of land, was rather curious. On account of comparatively shallow water the ocean swell became remarkably regular and powerful. The great surges really looked to me about

11. He is referring to what is currently, since 1931, Brown Brothers Harriman & Co., which is a commercial banking and investment company. Brown Brothers opened its first office in New York City in 1825. In Machen's time, the business was known as Brown Brothers Bank (from: www.bbh.com). It would seem that Machen did not like ginger ale and only wanted the change.

12. A note in the margin designates the river as "The Gironde," per his comment in the January 22 letter.

an eighth of a mile long and yet quite steep at the crest. When
they caught the vessel sideways they made her roll fully and deeply
(though not as quickly) as in the stormiest weather that we had
had in mid-ocean. The weather was fair and beautiful, the fog-
banks only adding to the beauty of the scene. After the police and
customs and railroad officials came aboard we had the hardest
night of work that I ever spent in my life. Passports had to be
examined, railroad tickets bought, baggage passed by customs
officials and checked for Paris. I worked from about nine o'clock
until 3 a.m. Then I turned in for three or four hours of sleep.
At that time, the dock was reported to be only two hours distant
and the ship was proceeding merrily on her way. But alas when
we awoke in the morning we discovered that a sudden fog, which
had disappeared as quickly as it had arrived, had caused us to
miss the tide necessary for getting up the river. Accordingly we
had to wait all the morning until the afternoon tide permitted
us to proceed. But we felt repaid by the daylight ride up the river,
which was interesting in itself, as the approach to Europe always
is, but doubly interesting this time because it gave us our first
vivid impression of France at war. And I cannot begin to tell you
how vivid the impression was. We landed on the dock at dusk,
and were taken at once in a very efficient way by a Y.M.C.A. man
(or by Y.M.C.A. men) to a hotel where we got supper and thence
to the station.[13] At this point I may remark that all the Y.M.C.A.
management of our party of about seventy people was a model
of efficiency. All the efficiency in the world, however, could not
save us from the very tiresome night trip to Paris in ordinary
second-class compartments. The very few of the party who had
secured berths relinquished them to the ladies. We left the port
at 10 P.M. and got to Paris at about 8 A.M. There were five in the
compartment where I was, and for my part I got very little sleep.
This made the second night's sleep even more important, but we
all still felt a little needy the next day. Fortunately the weather was
warm, and we hired blanket and pillow—the latter being of very

13. A note in the margin clarifies that this dock was in "Bordeaux."

little use to me since I had no room to use it—so that we had no taste of serious discomfort.[14]

On arrival at Paris Sunday morning we were taken in a body to the Hotel Wagram for breakfast, words of welcome, and instruction.[15] Then the party was distributed among various hotels. I drew the Hotel Lord Byron, out near the Etoile,[16] but not finding a separate room there am settled at a small hotel affiliated with the Lord Byron.[17] The quarters are fairly good, and since this hotel is even smaller than the Lord Byron, which itself is not large, there is some opportunity to talk French in a routine way. Of course there are some Americans here as everywhere. The hotel is in a pleasant quiet neighborhood just north of the Avenue des Champs-Élysées, and quite near the Etoile. The métro station is not far off.[18] That is a great advantage since the métro, when one learns to use it, is enormously convenient.

I did not go to church on Sunday, since getting into my room, about which there was a little delay, and sending my cablegram home took up my time. I had been much troubled about not getting the cablegram off from the port of arrival, but that was absolutely impossible, and if it had been possible I am informed that it would not have been any quicker. At any rate, I do trust you got either the Y.M.C.A. message or my own cablegram or both without undue delay. I had both sent to Arly since I thought receiving the cablegram directly might have been too exciting for you, and since I knew he could be trusted to give you the information at once. Probably you would open the message if he happened to be away.

On Sunday I met Birdie, who had come over on the boat preceding mine, but had not yet gotten started for the field. The

14. That is, Machen rented a blanket and a pillow but due to space restraints, he could not use the pillow. However, it did not matter because he was fairly comfortable despite the lack of a pillow.

15. The spelling was difficult to decipher and this may not be the correct name for the hotel. "Wagran" may be the name.

16. The "Etoile" refers to the traffic circle and area in which the Arc de Triomphe is located.

17. There is currently a Lord Byron Hotel in Paris that is located at 5 Rue Chateaubriand, which puts it near the Etoile and just N of the Avenue des Champs-Élysées, as Machen notes later in this paragraph. It may be the same hotel that he is describing in his letter. The smaller hotel where Machen stayed would be the Hotel Beaulieu named in the letterhead.

18. The "métro" is the Paris subway system.

meeting was exceedingly pleasant. We had lunch together on Sunday. I was glad to get the advantage of Birdie's experience.

On Sunday afternoon we had the first of a series of conferences at the Y.M.C.A. office. Mr. Carter, the general director, and Mr. Davis of the French work were the two principal speakers. They are both of them evidently able men. The impression made upon me by the Y.M.C.A. leaders generally with whom we have come into contact is that they are doing a large work in a large way.

Wednesday, Jan. 30, 1918

(It is hard to begin a letter under present conditions, but even harder to finish it—here I am continuing on a new day.)

Naturally, after two sleepless nights, sleep was very much in order on Sunday night. On Monday, our conferences, which provide us with information of various kinds were continued, and they have lasted until to-day. One of the leaders turns out to be Bobby Freeman, who graduated two years after me and lived over me in Alexander Hall at the Seminary during the winter of 1906–1907. He has really been just as good to me as he can be—not only in having me in to dinner, but also in saying that he is sure that sooner or later he will want me for the religious work. I was pleased at his cordiality, since I did not know what his opinion of me was. You may remember my having spoken of his career. Even during his Seminary courses he was in charge of a large Buffalo church from which he finally went to Pasadena. He has made a tremendous success, and is much looked to as a speaker over here as well as at home.

On Tuesday we had each a five-minute interview with Mr. Carter. I told him frankly how I felt. You may be interested in knowing how that was. It may be summed up under two contrasted heads:

(1) I have some start in French, and as far as my own personal preference I would greatly prefer to go into the French work. Just think of what an interesting experience that would be, and what a broadening affect it would have on all the rest of my life! But I was afraid it was selfish. For—

(2) All my training is for Bible teaching and the like which is not done in the slightest among the French troops, and indeed for certain reasons must be carefully excluded.

I also talked to Mr. Davis, head of the French work. The decision was reached by the leaders independent of my will. It is as follows: I am assigned to the French work temporarily, with the possibility of a change later on. I must say I am delighted with the decision, though I would not have taken the responsibility of making it myself. In the French work I am to be connected with the "Foyers de Soldats." It is a glorious chance, it seems to me, humble as the functions of the secretary might to some people seem to be. We are to provide recreation, not amusement for the men, and serve in a number of little ways. I am greatly in the mood of the thing.

Don't take a gloomy view of my turning aside from what now as always I regard as my life-work. A preacher who is preaching all the time is oft to run dry. There are many kinds of preparation that I need; and the kind of thing that I am going into now, just because of the academic life that I have been leading, is perhaps a thing that I need most of all. That does not mean that it is to be looked upon as new preparation for something in the future! On the contrary, it is a most glorious opportunity to render service where service is most deserved. I only hope I can make good. Certainly I feel inadequate enough in various ways.

Of course, I could not say where I am to be stationed even if I knew. But as a matter of fact I do not know as yet. Two other men of our party were assigned to the French work. We shall probably be in Paris at least five days more.

You will notice that my letter has been of a personal kind with out effort at describing the looks of things over here. The latter kind of letter of course cannot be expected in war time except within certain restrictions. Probably, however, it will not offend the censor to say that Paris in general seems perhaps a little more nearly normal than I had expected. At night war-time appears in the dark streets. It is really at times almost difficult to find your way around, if the names of the streets at the corners are not near lamps. There is illumination of the streets, but it is kept very dim. Of course soldiers are every where, but there is perhaps a larger proportion of civilians than I had expected to be. Yesterday morning we experienced the Paris fog. I wonder if a London fog is any thicker. Certainly this was much the thickest fog that I ever saw; you could often not see across the street. The effect was weird. But the weather (even yesterday after the sun got its power) has been uniformly warm and clear—day after day of almost spring-like weather.

My letter is very inadequate for various reasons. I do not know whether I am right in being so sympathetic to what takes one away from work with our American boys & from the kind of work that I have already been doing. But the decision was not mine. I am to obey orders. And I do so gladly. If I am in the wrong place I have faith enough to believe that I may be put in the right one hereafter. I have not been able to let you understand all the ramifications of the situation.

Love and then more love,
Your affectionate son,
J. Gresham Machen

Tuesday, Feb. 5, 1918

My dearest Mother:

My last letter, if I remember correctly, was written last Wednesday. Since that time I have been very busy getting nothing done. A lot of engagements during the former part of the time left little bits of mornings and afternoons which were just enough to begin things but not enough to finish. Having determined that I had to have another uniform, one of those that I secured in America being very unsatisfactory and in particular quite impossible for Paris use, I have spent a good deal of my time with a tailor having the new uniform made and the old ones repaired and altered. It would be stupid for one to attempt to say how many other little things I have had to do, and in particular how many remain to be done. However, it is not these trifles that have delayed my getting out of Paris. That is due to a delay about the necessary military pass. Such delay does not at all indicate a hitch anywhere, but is quite a frequent occurrence. In all probability I shall be detained for days or so still. Of course I feel exceedingly useless and ridiculous loafing around here after my companions on the voyage are nearly all engaged in the work for which they came. But if it were not for this feeling I should really be having a most delightful time. That is what gives me a twinge of conscious. The idea of having a delightful time in the midst of the misery of this war when whatever work I may be able to do has not even been undertaken, much less accomplished! However, the thing is not to be helped, for the idleness is enforced.

And it is not all idleness after all, for to say nothing of the constant labors about my equipment, I have now seriously gotten into the job of learning French. As soon as I could snatch enough time away from shopping, I looked up a French widow lady, Madame Lalot, who lives on the Rue Vaugirard, not far from the Luxembourg, and desires to take American boarders.[19] The two other Americans who are to go into the French work with me visited Mme. Lalot, but decided that the time was too short and her room too unsatisfactory for them to move into her home. The negative decision at once awakened my interest. I could not imagine anything more deadly than living in close intimacy with two Americans who speak little or no French, and seem to have very little gumption about learning. The chance to learn French under such conditions! But when they decided not to go to Mme. Lalot, I at once made an opposite decision. I had a very pleasant conversation with the lady on Saturday afternoon and arranged to take lunch and dinner with her every day beginning with Sunday. Because of washing that I had sent out, bundles that were to come from stores, a tailor in the vicinity etc.—a lot of things that centered around my old room at this hotel—I decided not

19. The "Rue de Vaugirard" currently runs from the Palais du Luxembourg, S.W., to the Palais des Sports.

to move my numberless pieces of baggage. So I am sleeping here and getting my breakfast near here, but taking lunch and dinner at Mme. Lalot's apartment. Since up to now I have been the only boarder, the arrangement has been a magnificent success. It really makes me feel like an utter fool to realize that all these years a fairly satisfactory working knowledge of French was all this time a thing that could have been grasped at any moment. After two days in a real French environment, I feel altogether different with regard to the language. Conversation with Mme. Lalot seems to proceed perfectly well, and I am having the time of my life. Of course you must not exaggerate the degree of my progress; I don't mean to say that I have yet by any means attained the degree of proficiency procured by the rest of the family. But my progress has astounded me. I really believe too—such is the enthusiasm of my first steps— that if I had a chance I could speak French with a less hopelessly Broadway intonation than that which is exhibited by most of the Americans over here.

Mme. Lalot is a dear old lady, I should say well over seventy. She is the widow of a Protestant pastor, and engages with great enthusiasm in ministering to the poor and to wounded soldiers. She is living all alone just now with an amorous pussy-cat and one servant. I keep her company, and ostensibly take one French lesson a day. But the "lesson" is just salve for my conscience for getting a free lesson the best part of the day. I joined Mme. Lalot at the Oratorre on Sunday morning. M. Alfred Monod preached a long sermon on "give us this day our daily bread," à propos of the loyal use of the bread-ticket system. I was disappointed. It was all perfectly good in its way. But it was not at all the bread of life. After Church, Mme. Lalot and I had lunch together and then went out to visit a poor family. With the necessary peregrinations, métro and electric car rides, etc. this took all the afternoon. Then dinner and on to bed. On Monday I spent the morning at the tailor's, then took lunch with Mme. Lalot, had a French "lesson," went to the tailor's again to have an overcoat shortened that meanwhile I had burned along the bottom on the stove, then went way back to Mme. Lalot's to dinner, and then took her to the Theâtre Français, where we saw the "Tartuffe" of Molière. I had a bump so far as my linguistic aspirations are concerned. I cannot understand French poetry, even when I have read it beforehand. After the theatre I took Mme. Lalot home & then made the long journey back to my own domicile. Since the métro stops running at 11.30 P.M., and electric cars at that hour or before, and since taxis are rare birds at that time of night, I had to hoof it. Fortunately I had taken the same walk in the day time. Otherwise I might well have lost my way in the dark streets. A walk of three quarters of an hour like that is quite impressive in its gloom and lonesomeness. To-night I am going to take Mme. Lalot to the Odéon to see Victor Hugo's "Marion de Lorme," but since the Odéon is near her apartment, I shall no doubt be able to catch the métro.

After such pleasant and profitable experiences as I have had with Mme. Lalot you can imagine my disgust when a rather-commonplace American fella appeared on the scene to-day. He knows scarcely any French at all, and converses with Mme. Lalot in English. He expects to become a regular boarder to-morrow & to take a room. Well, I knew the bully time I have been having was too good to last. I feel as though I were let down with a bang. Most of these fellows seem to have absolutely no gumption about them, no shame about using English. I do hope that whatever place I get in the French work I get a place where there is no other American. There is absolutely no way to learn French & be really useful in a French environment except to eschew English for twenty-four hours out of the twenty-four.

When I said, in referring to last Sunday night, that after dinner I went to bed, I forgot the talk that I made to the American boys at the American Army and Navy Y.M.C.A. at 31 Ave. Montaigne.[20] It was a fine little crowd to talk to. I had a good time, & hope I may have been useful. The Y.M.C.A. has splendid quarters some people think almost too splendid.

Last Wednesday night we passed through an air raid. Since it is ancient history now, and has no doubt been reported in the American papers, there is I suppose no harm in my telling you where I was when it occurred.

20. This is less than half-a-mile, as the crow flies, from Machen's hotel.

I was just returning from the theatre on Wednesday evening. When I got out of the métro I noticed a good deal of confusion on the avenue, but paid little attention to the matter till a little later, when I discovered that the confusion was due to the running of fire apparatus through the principal streets with their sirens that act as a danger signal. For an hour or so I stayed out in the streets and "rubbered."[21] There were the moving lights of French airplanes here and there, also little flashes which I suppose indicated aerial battles with German airplanes. One brilliantly lighted plane passed directly over our heads, and very near. This was about all that we saw. As to what we heard, that might have seemed to untrained ears to be anything. I thought it probably came for the most part from anti-aircraft guns. Finally there were two explosions louder than the others, after which most of the people near me, including myself, went indoors. After a time I went to bed, before the signal was given announcing the conclusion of the raid. Somehow, I did not feel enormously excited most of the time. But really I had no idea of the seriousness of it. When I heard after wards that nearly fifty people had been killed and many others wounded I was quite astonished. The whole thing, though it lasted with intervals perhaps nearly two hours, passed off so very quietly. The next day I observed the damage here and there in the city. It was all most interesting and of course most distressing. The crowd took it in a very matter-of-fact way. An occasional mild "Cochons!" was all that I heard.[22] But you just ought to have seen the crowd at one place on Sunday viewing the ruins. It was really a show in itself.

Next time I shall not, I think, promenade about the streets. The truth is that this time not only did my natural curiosity get the better of me, but also I did not realize how much protection it is to stay in the house. I had a sort of notion that a safe a place as any would be in open spaces where houses cannot fall on you. This is about as silly an idea as can be imagined. Not only the papers, but also a personal examination of the way the fragments scatter, convinced me of the fact. Stay in the house and keep away from the windows, and the risk is very slight. Of course, if a bomb strikes the

21. The term one might use today would be "rubber-necked."
22. A French epithet meaning "dirty pigs," "swine," or "beasts," referring to the Germans.

very house where you are, you may get hurt, but you are protected from flying fragments. Also cellars & métro stations, I believe, are to be utilized.

The astounding thing about Paris just now is the normality of life. Those who think that France is at the end of her strength have another guess coming. The vast machinery of life in this city is going on without interruption. In many respects we in America have been much more disorganized on account of the war. Of course I am not speaking about the spiritual side of the thing. The sacrifices have been tremendous. But that does not prevent a marvelous efficiency in the conduct of life.

Good-bye for the present, and nobody knows how much love to all— your loving son,
J. Gresham Machen[23]

February 10, 1918

My dearest Mother:

My last letter was written in the exuberance of my first experience of life in a French environment. That exuberance has now run its course, and I have come to the sobering conclusion that my efforts at learning the French language are utterly footless. Until Friday evening inclusive, I kept up the arrangement by which I slept here and took my lunch and dinner with Mme. Lalot, near the Luxembourg.[24] Since there was some chance of getting away on Saturday and since in the midst of the preparations for departure it would have been highly inconvenient to try to live in two places at once, I bade farewell to Mme. Lalot. The farewell was attended with somewhat less regret than you might have supposed from my last

23. The last three lines of Machen's letter were forced into a small space as he concluded his thoughts.
24. The "Luxembourg," refers to the Palais du Luxembourg (Palace of Luxembourg) and its large gardens.

letter. Mme. Lalot is a very good lady, but her intellectual interests are not extensive and a tête-à-tête with her day after day proved at times to be somewhat wearisome.[25] Fortunately, the American fellow of whom I wrote did not put in an appearance as early as I had expected, so that I was not hampered in my efforts at learning French.

You may think that the servant problem is bad in America. Well, so it is bad in America, but you just ought to see the pitiful tyranny under which Mme. Lalot is groaning. Her "Marie" is afflicted with moods. One day she is "charmante," and the next day she is horrid.[26] She was particularly horrid during the latter portion of my stay. It seems that Mme. Lalot has occasionally taken her to the Cirque or to the movies, and that she became horribly jealous at the frequency with which Mme. Lalot went with me to the theatre. The last time we went (to a matinée at the Odéon) we had to walk around the block in order to conceal our destination from Marie who was thought to be watching from the window!

On Tuesday afternoon, I accompanied Mme. Lalot on one of her visits to a hospital where she takes delicacies to the wounded soldiers. At the hospital that we visited, many of the men were convalescent, so that not a very great many stayed in the wards on a beautiful afternoon. However, the hospital is an immense place; the number of men that we saw was small proportionately rather than absolutely. In one of the wards a big negro (it seems queer to hear them talking French) was trying his wooden leg for the first time. He (and everybody else) seemed to regard it as great fun. After leaving the hospital we visited a poor family, and then went home to dinner.

During my two weeks in Paris I have taken a perfect debauch of going to the theatre. I shall not attempt to give you a catalogue of all the plays that I have seen. During last week I took Mme. Lalot a good many times. Once I had to go with her to the "Cirque," where there was an acrobatic exhibition which bored me stiff. She had complementary tickets. Taking her to the theatre was a tiresome business, since the performances finish just about in time to get

25. A "tête-à-tête" is a chat or casual conversation.
26. The word "charmante" means charming.

Behind the three soldiers and horses is a YMCA Foyer du Soldat similar to those Dr. Machen operated while at St. Mard and Missy-sur-Aisne.
Photo courtesy of Kautz Family Collection, University of Minnesota

people home before the métro service is stopped. After leaving her at her house, I had to run for it to get my way back here. But I had to walk only once.

Among the notable plays that I have seen were "Marion de Lorme" of Victor Hugo at the Odéon, and also at the same theatre a play of George Sand, "Le Marriage de Victoriae" and a little play of de Musset. The matinée where these two were given was preceded by a conférence.[27] At the "Antoine" I saw a poetic and patriotic play which is having a great success. It is called "Les butors et la Finette". "La Finette," the princess, represents France. "Les butors" are rough people, thought to be hopeless for their frivolity, who rally round la Finette at the out break of war. It is an elaborate performance, and in parts seemed to be quite fine. I already mentioned "Tartuffe" in my last letter. Last night at the Française I saw a modern play by Bernstein called "L'Elévation," which represents the elevation of

27. A "conférence" is a lecture.

a man's character at the devotion called out by the war. I did not think the "elevation" was quite as high as it might have been. Most of the plays that I have seen—indeed practically all—have accorded with the standards of taste which we are accustomed on our English speaking stage. Indeed they are superior morally to many of our plays.

Yesterday afternoon I attended a great patriotic celebration in the large auditorium of the Sorbonne.[28] The President of the Republic was there and other notables. There were many speeches, and finally a scene from "Les butors et la Finette." Unfortunately, I did not arrive early enough and had to stand up very far from the speakers. I did not understand many of the speeches very well. But the occasion was interesting.

Yesterday I met an Abbé who was at the office of the Franco-American work looking for somebody with intellectual interests who would exchange French & English conversation with him.[29] When he discovered that I did not want to bother with the English, he took it very good-naturedly, and spent a good part of the afternoon (rather middle of the day) with me talking about theology & other subjects. I felt rather mean about it, but my companion seemed to be willing.

My final "permission" to go is expected daily, but if it comes to-morrow I cannot get away before Tuesday. Of course, I have enjoyed my stay in Paris. It has not been my fault that I have had to wait, and all my theatrical entertainment has been one way of learning French. There have been no more airplane raids. It is simply astounding how normal the life of the city is. Here we are only a hundred miles or less from the enemy's lines, and yet everything is going on almost as smoothly as in time of peace. Theatres are open all the week; food is plentiful, though with some restrictions (I should enjoy a Washington pie).[30]

I find the U. S. uniform most horribly inconvenient. One of the regulations is that all buttons must be kept buttoned. Well, when I get into my overcoat I feel as though it were a worrisome job to get all those buttons and hooks unfastened, so as to get

28. The "Sorbonne" is the University of Paris.
29. An "Abbé" is an abbot, which is the superior of a monastery.
30. Is this a cherry pie?

at the pockets of my inside coat or "blouse." Each pocket has its button which must be fastened and unfastened every time. And the pockets seem very inconvenient to the untrained civilian. Leather leggings, further more, are an awful nuisance.

For the first time in my life almost I have been oppressively warm in winter. I am warmly dressed, and nearly roasted half the time. The weather every day without exception has been warm, the temperature day after day, being almost uniform. The winter will be almost over before I get to camp. I wish I had not loaded myself down with such elaborate preparation for cold weather.

No news from home as yet. None can be expected, probably, for another week. In the midst of all delays in mail, I hope that you for your part will always bear in mind the fundamental fact that no news is good news.

You don't know how much love goes with this letter to you and all the folks at home.

Your loving son,
J. Gresham Machen

2

AT LE FOYER DU SOLDAT,
ST. MARD

February 14 to March 2, 1918

Dr. Machen's first assignment with the Foyer du Soldat program of the YMCA would be in the once quaint village of St. Mard. As with much of the environs east of Soissons, St. Mard suffered devastation from the war. The new "Y" worker would learn quickly that the "cooperative" aspect of the American-French program would require some patience on his part. During this time of service, he would have the opportunity to wander in a battlefield and see a sample of the horrors of war, but he would find comfort reading the Psalms in his French Bible.

[The following letters are written on "Le Foyer du Soldat" letterhead.]

14, Février, 1918

My dearest Mother:

Your two splendid letters, one postmarked Jan. 20, and the other Jan. 22, arrived in Paris just in time to catch me before I left for my post. I was really surprised to get them so soon, and you can imagine what a thoroughly delightful surprise it was. Your account of the arrival of my clothes touched me very much because it indicated your loving care manifested even in details. Please be sure to express to Betty my appreciation of her skillful labors with which she assisted you. I was surprised at your compliment about my care of my clothes. They certainly did seem to me to be in a horrible mess. As for your account of the use made by the family of my S. S. lessons, I was delighted at it. The new edition, which will present the lessons separate from the graded system (which has now been abandoned) as an elective course, and which will embody many corrections and revisions in detail (including one or two which you made at Seal Harbor) and also one re-written lesson (on Ephesians, in the Students' book), ought to be sent before so very long.

Of course I was most deeply interested and concerned at the news about Nena. I believe it is a thoroughly good thing that she is getting a thorough medical examination, troublesome as it may seem. Modern methods did me lots of good, and I hope they will do as much for Nena. I do hope to get good news before long.

Last but not least, I was deeply concerned about the little that you said about yourself. I am sorry to hear about your cold lingering on. Bed is no doubt the best place until you reach a certain point in your recovery. How I wish I could know that the recovery had been completed long before now! I was glad to hear that Tom is again out and about, after the very trying time that he had had.

Up to late Saturday afternoon my military permit had not yet arrived. The Y.M.C.A. office was closed on Sunday. Hence, although the permit arrived on Monday, I could not get-off till Tuesday, since the only train leaves Paris rather early in the morning. On Sunday I attended the French Protestant service at the church near the Etoile in the morning, and in the evening went to the McCall Mission at 8 Boulevarde Bonne Nouvelle. The McCall Mission was interesting. In the afternoon I took my first extended walk in Paris. It was intensely interesting. I visited among other things the curious "Place des Vosges."[1] On Monday I took in a most delightful presentation of de Muset's play, "On ne badine pas avec l'amour" at the Odéon.[2]

1. The "Place des Vosges" is a square in Paris that is about a quarter mile N.W. of the more famous Place de la Bastille.
2. The Théâtre National de l'Odéon is located on the Place de l'Odéon in Paris. The theater is across the Rue de Vaugirard on the N. side of the Jardin de Luxembourg (Garden of Luxembourg), which is the grounds of the Palace du Luxembourg. Machen attended several performances at the Odéon.

During the incidental music, which was evident by a great feature and a large part of the performance, a party of Americans just back of me kept up a continuous running conversation. They seemed to think it was like the perfunctory playing of the orchestra between the acts in America!

On Tuesday I went out from Paris to the town that is the seat of the regional director of the "Foyers du Soldat," under whom I am to work.[3] It was his duty to assign me to a definite post within his "region." I was in the town Tuesday night, all day Wednesday, and Wednesday night. At present the place is perhaps ten or twelve miles from the front in a direct line, but at an earlier stage of the war it was immediately back of the front and under severe bombardment. Not a house in the town, so far as I could see, or scarcely one, has escaped serious injury, and many houses are smashed entirely to pieces. In those houses that have been rendered habitable, window glass is usually conspicuous by its absence. Light colored paper takes the place of glass, as is the example in my room in the hotel. The houses have been patched up in all kinds of ways. There are great sections of the town where roofs are altogether lacking. The finest of the churches—a very fine one indeed—has lost its roof, one of its towers and of course lots besides. The repairing of the choir has already been begun, but the nave is entirely roofless still. No enumeration of details can possibly produce any adequate impression of the desolate state of things that prevails in such a place. In many quarters it is like a city of the dead. Of course such a population as it now has is almost altogether military. Just outside of the town, I saw the old French trenches which were occupied before the retreat of the enemy.

At eight o'clock at night, hotel dining rooms, etc. are closed by military order. The streets of course are dark with a darkness that can be felt (to guard against air raids). In order to find your own door if you are out after dark, an electric pocket light is not a luxury but a necessity—also to prevent collision with pedestrians coming in the opposite direction.

3. There is a marginal annotation here "Soissons," which is located 58 miles N.E. of Paris and 33 miles W.N.W. of Reims.

To-day I was brought by a Ford out to my post. It was a trip of some fifteen miles. Many interesting things were to be seen—trenches, "abris," etc.[4] It may amuse you to know of the benefit of my Ford experience last Summer. In the village where I am now located, but before we had gotten to the exact place where we were bound, "Fordy" refused to start.[5] Crank as he could the driver could not make the engine go. At last your humble servant made the brilliant suggestion that she might be shoved a little down the grade, and thrown into gear. The thing worked like a charm. Brilliant wasn't it?

In this village we are probably about six or seven miles (estimates vary from eight to twelve kilometers) in a direct line from the nearest part of the German line. Before the enemies' retreat, the village was completely battered to pieces. The French troops are simply quartered in the ruins, which have been patched up here and there. Most of the houses, or remains of houses, are still entirely roofless. Of course there is no civil population here or, so far as I can see, in the whole countryside. I am occupying a house whose roof is entirely or almost entirely gone. But the ceiling of the first story remains. One fairly large room, which is to be our cantine, seems to be solid.[6] The room where my French colleague and I are to sleep has a patched-up ceiling. Daylight is to be seen through it here and there, but I am informed that the water does not come through in the rain. Why not, I do not know exactly, but I am cheered by the news. We intend to have another room fixed up after a time. We take our meals at a "popote" or room for non-commissioned officers. It is really very good fun. The cooking is done over a wood fire in the same room where the eating also goes forward. The cook is good friends with everybody. And I must say that despite the informality of the whole proceeding, the grub itself is quite good. I have been most cordially received.

In the afternoon we called on the captain who is now in command of the post. He received us very kindly indeed, chatted a while, and invited us to lunch for day after to-morrow.

4. An "abri" is a shelter.
5. A notation in the margin designates the village as "St. Mard," which is about 69 miles N.E. of Paris and about 25 miles N.W. of Reims.
6. Machen most often uses the French "cantine" but he also uses the English "canteen."

My French colleague, who has been here about a week, is exceeding kind and thoughtful—so much so that I feel like a very useless piece of baggage. The only possibility of trouble is that I may prove to him such a good associate that I myself may not be able to do anything at all that requires initiative. I am to run the cantine. Arrangements for it have been made and are being made. At present there is a "Foyer"—simply a meeting place for the soldiers where games can be played & letters written. Another "Foyer" is soon to be made habitable, in addition to the projected canteen. Of course everything is done in the makeshift way which is the only practicable way under such conditions as these. I have had great fun talking to the soldiers. One week in the trenches, one week somewhere near the trenches, and one week back here in the program. Most of the men have been through the thick of the great battles of the war, and so far as I can see the great majority have been wounded—some a number of times. My colleague in the Foyer work has been in the army for several years, and is now discharged (temporarily at least) on account of wounds. It all makes an able-bodied man feel a little queer to be so near the fight and never in it at all. But the experience is tremendous. I feel very happy at the privilege which is mine. It is hard to realize that the sound of distant firing that we hear from time to time is really part of the greatest war in history.

Living conditions, I think are going to be all right. My folding cot has been put up; I have the greatest abundance of blankets, and even a pair of sheets. The complete absence of sanitary arrangements, and the difficulty of getting good water are the greatest discomforts of the situation. But I am in first-rate health, and happy. I am delighted to say that my colleague does not speak English much, though he wants to learn. As for my own French, it is quite poor. Conversation at me I can usually grasp in time, but conversation around me is too much. Of course there are many who want to use their English on me. But on the whole, linguistic conditions might be worse than they are here. For example in the town where I spent yesterday, there were lots of Americans.

Love to all. The light is poor, and it will be more comfortable in my cot. Fortunately the weather, judged by American standards, is still exceedingly mild, to say the least. But there is lots and lots of mud. I am happy, and I wish I could know that you are happy too. You certainly have more than your share of trouble.

Your loving son,
Gresham

18 Fevrier, 1918

My dearest Mother:

My last letter was written last Thursday on the evening of my arrival at my post. A few words will probably suffice to give you the news of the following days. But first I want to say something that I forgot in my last letter. You mentioned, namely, your intention of writing to me twice a week. I was simply delighted. But knowing the burdens that rest upon you I just do not see how I can accept such a sacrifice of your vital strength. You know just exactly how I feel—our days together at Seal Harbor let you see exactly what my double attitude toward your letter writing is. To make a long story short, if you do not write so often I shall understand and approve—and indeed surely I do not see how you can write so often. It is entirely unnecessary to say, on the other hand, that the arrival of every one of your letters is a supreme joy.

By the way I received just the other day a letter from Bobby, forwarded from New York. It informed me more clearly than before (though in an incidental way) that he was feeling really very badly when in Baltimore. He thinks his preaching was poor—and it may well have been so—for him. But that is not saying that it was poor absolutely.

My post is not altogether satisfactory. My French associate is a rather capable fellow, and just as kind as can be. But I am afraid that my part in the work is not going to be worth very much. One evening I did have a heart-to-heart talk with my associate about his use of the first person singular in connection with the Foyer, and we are excellent friends. But I do not like the situation altogether. I have insisted at least on knowing what is going forward in connection with the installation of the Foyer but that is perhaps all that I have attained. The duties of the work are as follows. The French director has charge of the activities of the meeting place—books, concerts, cinema, etc.—and the business management etc. The American director has charge of the cantine and of out door efforts. But these divisions are not intended to be absolute, the constitutional instructions declare that the two directors are to labor in common. It is simply that the lead in certain things is to be in the hands of the American & in certain things in the hands of the Frenchman. Each director, as I understand it, has a part in all parts of the work. My associate agrees that I am to be welcomed in the meeting place, but I think he is inclined (or was inclined at first) to minimize my rights then.

One trouble is that the cantine is not to be in the same building with the men's work of the Foyer. Constantly I see myself shoved aside in a rather uncomfortable way. I wanted to be constantly at the main work where there would be opportunities for meeting the men. Up to the present there has been practically nothing for me to do. The cantine has not yet been installed. I am a fifth wheel on a waggon.[7] And I am a little afraid there is not going to be a tremendous amount of work for me even after the cantine is established. In short I am having a very pleasant and a very interesting, but also a very useless time as yet.

Just after my arrival here it turned really cold, and it is cold now. I certainly do need all those numberless blankets and war clothes that I thought were entirely useless. One thing that has helped enormously is that my French colleague with his usual kindness rustled around and got me a real good iron cot and mattress. The mattress makes an enormous difference so far as warmth is concerned. In general it is astonishing how well even I get sleep (with warm clothing) in these patched-up and unheated houses. Our room is a refrigerator; yet I seem to thrive in it. Writing letters is a little hard because of the coldness of one's hands. Of

7. Machen uses this double "g" spelling consistently.

course the cold is very mild compared with American standards, but it is quite enough. If we had an American cold snap, we should suffer. But it will not come. The present cold seems to be all that need be expected here. If you see Mrs. Buchanan or Miss Marie please say that the sleeveless sweater is as though made for my present situation. I wear it night and day. So far as day is concerned, nothing else would do. I am also grateful for the wristlets. I cannot remember whether it was Miss Marie or Mrs. Buchanan who gave me the sweater. One gave me the sweater & the other wristlets.

On Friday afternoon I went with a non-commissioned officer to a point about one mile or a little more from the front-line French trenches, and perhaps about two miles from the Germans (the distance behind the hostile trenches is much greater here than at most places on the front—indeed at many places French & Germans are only a few feet apart). We made our "promenade" forth on foot & partly by a little train that carries supplies. While my companion was at work, at one point I had a fine opportunity to explore the old French & German trenches used at an earlier stage of the war when the fighting in this sector was especially fierce. It is needless to say that the whole thing was most intensely interesting.

Feb. 19

During the latter part of our trip we passed through a little lateral valley running up toward the heights upon which the French line is now established.[8] Words can give no idea of the desolation of the scene. Our own village is entirely in ruins, but many walls at least are standing; the villages nearer the present front were in

8. In the margin is written the location as "Chemin des Dames" (The Ladies' Road). The Second Battle of the Aisne, also called the Chemin des Dames Offensive, involved the attack by French forces on German positions along and in the area of the Chemin des Dames between Soissons and Reims in April of 1917. This French assault was a disaster that led to mutiny among the French troops; see "Aisne, Second Battle of the," in Stephen Pope and Elizabeth-Anne Wheal, *Dictionary of the First World War* (New York: Macmillan Reference Books, 1995; reprint, Barnsley, England: Pen & Sword Military Classics, 2003). The Chemin des Dames route runs East beginning about halfway between Laffaux and Chavignon on the current N2 highway, along the S. side of the Forêt Dominale de Vauclair, and ends at Corbenny on the D1044 highway. The visitor's center at the Chemin des Dames historical site location has a website at: http://www.chemindesdames.fr/.

the very midst of the previous fighting and are now simply heaps of stones. Forests too are destroyed. The straggling remnant of the trees are eloquent witnesses to what went on some months ago.

Airplanes are much in evidence. The course of a German plane is marked by numberless little patches of white smoke in the sky caused by the bursting of anti-aircraft shells. In general this sector is considered extraordinarily quiet, though to a tenderfoot the noise of desultory firing seems quite interesting enough.

On Saturday I was invited to lunch by the "Capitaine Adjutant Major," who was in command of that part of the regiment then quartered in our village. There were present a number of the officers. The roughness of the surroundings served only to set in greater relief at the perfect courtesy and real kindness with which I was received. My host seemed much interested in the affairs of the Y.M.C.A. and of the Foyer. At present he is at the front. The routine for officers and men is eight days here, then eight days at the front "in reserve," then eight days in the front line. So we have practically an entire new set of men to deal with every eight days. Yesterday (Thursday) we said good-bye to those who were going to the front, and supplied them each with four sheets of letter-paper. Every body is very cheerful. Despite the roughness of his equipment & the frequent smallness of his stature the poilu is every inch a soldier.[9] I like the crowd very much. It is quite touching to see the appreciation with which small services are received.

The pomp of war is entirely lacking. No bugles, no bands, no large bodies of troops. There is no time for anything but real business.

Although I have seen none of the real horrors of war, I am impressed with the repulsiveness of the thing. This cold-blooded firing of a few guns here & there in order to pick off an occasional man who is thinking about something else seems in some way more repulsive than the carnage of an attack, when the element of self-defense, though perhaps not more real, is at any rate more evident.

You may be somewhat surprised when I tell you that I organized a game of quoits on Sunday afternoon—my first efforts

9. The word "poilu" was used for French soldiers in the war as "doughboy" was used for Americans.

as athletic director.[10] There is no Sunday at the front. My idea is that this is war, and also it is France. I just have to do the best I can in my own life, and not altogether destroy my usefulness in the place where God has put me. Of one thing you can be dead sure, this experience will never destroy my own devotedness to the Christian Sabbath. On the contrary it will make me feel all the more profoundly the inestimable blessings of it.

On the whole I count myself exceedingly fortunate in my post, for various reasons:—

(1) I am somewhere near the front, where although I am not making the full sacrifice required of a soldier I am at least sharing some of the hardships and deprivations of the destruction, and incidentally am able to get some idea of what is going on.

(2) I am in a French environment with all the educational advantages involved. My associate does not speak English, as I was definitely afraid he might do. Although my host of the other day speaks English well he was gracious enough to converse with me most of the time in French. I must confess, however, that I do not seem to be making much progress in French. Most of the conversation at the popote is lost on me.

(3) I am appointed to the French work "temporarily" and Bobby Freeman told me that ultimately he would want me for religious work among the American boys. That opens up the possibility for change if I do not seem to be useful here; and I should be much better fitted for religious work among the American boys because of my present experience near the front.

(4) My French associate is really an enviably good man. I am getting along better with him every day. For instance yesterday I think that I was really useful at the Foyer, and that my services were really needed. Of course when the cantine is installed I shall have much greater opportunities. We are to have a small "salle de reunion," a "hut," and a cantine.[11] Only the latter is my special province, but I think I shall be welcome in the other two. At the

10. The game of "quoits" is a traditional lawn game that is most popular in portions of the United Kingdom. It involves the throwing of a metal or rubber ring over a set distance for the purpose of landing it on a stake (called a hob or mott). It is similar to the American game of horseshoes.

11. The French "salle de reunion," means meeting room.

cantine, we shall sell hot chocolate, cigarettes, candles, and a good many other things. Of course it is the incidental personal side of the thing that is interesting to me, and I think it is going to be very interesting. I have no great talent for "affairs," but even a small talent may be developed under the stress of necessity.

I am reading the Psalms in a French Bible. The Psalms are the best reading in general for Army life. They seem just to fit the needs of the soul.

Love to all. I wish I could write to all directly. But conditions for writing are not favorable, on account of the cold.

Your loving son,
Gresham

February 24, 1918

My dearest Mother:

Your letter of January 27 (No. 3) has just come to hand. To say that it was welcome would not express my feelings about it at all. It is a brave and splendid letter. I treasure your quotations from the Psalms all the more because of the non-religious atmosphere in which I am living. Never before have I felt quite so keenly, I think, the value of the Christian Sabbath. Here every day is exactly like every other day. In the monotony of the schedule one feels oppressed almost to suffocation. I wish I could hear the church bells ring. As for your choice of a quotation, it is a striking coincidence that in my last letter I spoke of the peculiar fittingness of the Psalms here amid the destruction of war.

Your idea of numbering your letters is splendid. The only reason why I did not adopt it—or the chief reason—is that I do not know how many letters I have written. What I shall try to do is to note in every letter when the preceding letter was written. This time, however, I am at fault. I think I wrote about five days ago, but

one day here is so much like another that I am not certain. For the
future, however, I shall try to jot down in my note-book the days
when I write. I was touched by your sending me that miserable
postal card from Fat Axford, which I am afraid, because of my folly,
caused you pain. I threw it away, and kept only the thought of your
patience and love and care.

The news that you had gone down to dinner brought me a ray
of comfort. But what a time you have had and are still having! I wish
I could give you a share of my good health. If you see Aunt Bessie, I
hope you will tell her how deeply thankful I am for her kindness to
you. It cheers and helps me even more than any direct service to me
could possibly do.

Now about Nena. Of course you did right to tell me how
things are. I feel absolutely helpless even about experiencing the
real depth of my sympathy. Like you, I love Nena, and hope she
may know it. Like you also, I take refuge in prayer. In my present
surroundings, without privacy, it has been hard to pray. But God
is always with us. Your letter was just like a word of prophecy to me
to-day. And I never needed such a word more sorely than now. You
do not know how I have been strengthened and helped.

One day is very much like another, and as yet none of the days
is very satisfactory. The truth is that I have been placed in a post
where there is not enough work for two men. My French colleague
does not need my help at all in the installation of the various
activities of the Foyer, and even when the cantine and all has been
installed I think the post could get along with one man. There was
some thought of starting an annex in a neighboring village, but
for the present the director in charge of our immediate district is
opposed. I am intending to make representations to him and to
the authorities above him. Yesterday I looked in incidentally at a
Foyer about four miles from here.[12] A considerable plant is there
under the charge of an American director, who does not know a
word of French! The French director has gone to Paris to attend
a conference. It seems a little tough that I who have sufficient
knowledge of French should be put in a place where there is

12. In the margin is written the location of the foyer, "Bourq-et-Comins," which is about
71 miles N.E. of Paris and about 19 miles N.W. of Reims.

absolutely no chance to put such modest qualifications as I possess to practical use. Our schedule is about as follows. A little before eight o'clock, I get up. My French colleague stays in bed an hour or so longer. About eight o'clock I get my breakfast; after which I wash. At about 11.15 A.M., lunch. At twelve o'clock opening of the salle de réunion. Often my colleague does let me take charge of that. About eight or ten soldiers at a time show up in the afternoon. Sometimes the room is practically empty. We have a soldier assistant who is capable of doing pretty much everything that needs to be done in our absence. However the afternoon at the salle de réunion is at least more like definite duty than anything else that I have to do. The room is closed at four o'clock. The hut is open at six o'clock and continues open till eight. I usually take charge of it while my colleague takes his dinner, and then he takes charge of it while I get dinner. There is more of a crowd in the evening. I give out letter paper, attend to the lending of a few books, sell an occasional package of candles, and talk to the soldiers as much as I can. A little after eight o'clock I go to bed. My colleague sits up till late, and of course the light has to be kept burning. It is acetylene and smells often like fury. My colleague is a great enemy of fresh air, and now that the chinks in our room have mostly been patched up, the closed window gives us an atmosphere that is a might oppressive. After long sleepless hours last night I did get up & open the window. My colleague snores terrifically & suffers with catarrh.[13] I wish I could sleep somewhere out in the cold and wet. That kind of hardship, which is the kind I expected, is healthy hardship. But I don't know about closed windows. You know I am no "fresh-air fiend." But there are limits.

Idleness, however, is my chief complaint. I could stand any discomfort cheerfully if I were only useful. Probably I ought to manufacture my functions—for instance in the organization of sports. As yet my efforts in this line have met with only slight success.

Last night I met with such a severe disappointment that I could not sleep. The thing kept turning itself over, & over, in my mind. You will remember my speaking about an officer who invited

13. The illness "catarrh" is an inflammation of the nose and throat.

me to lunch and was generally kind. The biggest thing he did for me to speak to the colonel about getting me permission to visit the trenches of the sector held by the soldiers of the regiment quartered here. The colonel was perfectly in accord, but on condition that I get the permission of the officer of the division. In order to get it I walked yesterday over about four miles or so to headquarters.[14] From all indications I did not expect the slightest difficulty. But in the evening I received a refusal. I cannot possibly let you know how disappointed I feel. If I could see the life of the soldiers, even though I could not have it, I could feel comparatively content to labor here in the rear. But as it is I feel my job to be the job of a pretty poor kind of camp-follower. I have not given up ultimate hope. But my chances of seeing the front are slim, I am afraid. I wish I could have gotten into that American ambulance work, though that too had its disadvantages.

Night before last beginning at about eleven o'clock and again at six o'clock in the morning there were terrific bombardments at the front. Even at this distance the houses shook. The result I am told was the taking of twenty-three German prisoners! I was impressed with the terrific amount of ammunition it takes to carry on the war. Really it seemed as though the end of the world had come—so awe-inspiring was the sound. Yet the "corps-de-main" was not so great or so unusual as things are judged here.

I am finishing this letter in the salle de réunion, which is much better filled on Sundays than on week days because on Sundays the soldiers have more leisure. This afternoon I had at least one interesting conversation with a soldier. And I feel a little less gloomy about the situation. At any rate I am afraid to complain too much to the central authorities of the Foyer. Suppose they should post me far in the rear, and at some post where the French director knows English. Perish the thought! Patience is what is in place. Things might be far worse. Perhaps you may even detect a bright side in my disappointment about going to the front. But as a matter of fact a day such as I had hoped for could not have meant any appreciable danger of getting hurt. And it would have been right interesting. At any rate it is out

14. In the margin here again is written "Bourq et Comins."

of the question now. In the afternoon I have read classical works contained in the little library-box of the Foyer—"Les Fourberies de Scapin" of Molière & "Horace" of Corneille. I am attending the university of the western front. It is rather an unlikely place for acquiring a knowledge of the classics. But one must adapt one's self to circumstances.

Love to all. And don't forget to give my love to Tom and (directly or indirectly) to Nena.

I forgot to tell you that Arly remarked in his last letter that he had evidently done himself proud. His opinion coincides with mine exactly. Of course Helen herself may disagree, but her opinions are ruled out.

I also forgot to tell you a trivial matter that may be added to a rather rambling letter. It worried me a little. Just before I sailed from America Mrs. Magee of Princeton, Mr. Tar Hodges' sister, asked me to write a letter to New Jersey congressmen & senators in opposition to the woman's suffrage amendment. I did so amid the rush of getting off, and spent a pretty penny for typewriting it at the Vanderbilt. It did no good as far as the vote was concerned. But to-day there arrived a letter from one of the congressmen to the effect that my letter was one of the best that he had received, that it coincided with his own sentiments & that he had incorporated it in the Congressional Record. I can hardly say that printing in the Congressional Record is a very high literary honor. Indeed although that letter was written hastily I might venture to assert that there are even worse things in the Congressional Record. But at any rate I was pleased with the honor & glad there is one congressman from New Jersey whose sentiments coincide with mine.

Love to all once more. And lots of love to yourself. I hope to be able to answer Uncle's farewell letter to New York, which has just arrived & was fine.

Your loving son,
Gresham

February 28, 1918

My dearest Mother:

My last letter to you was written on Sunday, Feb. 24, just after I had received a letter from you. And I might say in passing that the good that that letter did me has not been lost. Since Sunday, I have not very much to report. The work on the rooms for the cantine is progressing a little better just now. It is being directed almost altogether by my French colleague. The only part that I have in it is an occasional expression of my desires. I do not like to insist upon my ideas, since my inexperience might lead to mistakes. For instance I did want a brick wall instead of a door to be put between our room and the kitchen, but did not feel sure enough of my position to insist. The soldier who is to make the hot chocolate and generally assist in the running of the center is to sleep in the kitchen. A flimsy door between our room and his will take away what remnants of privacy and quiet I now possess. I certainly do envy the director of the foyer in a neighboring village who has a room to himself. To me any old hole in the ground, no matter how uncomfortable, is preferable to the most magnificent apartment at the Waldorf if the latter has to be shared with another person. But I am afraid there is nothing to be done here, I have cast envious eyes on that kitchen, but I am afraid it must be occupied by our assistant. His present quarters, I understand, are highly undesirable, and of course in the ruined state of this village every bit of room has to be used.

The other day I wrote letters to the American director of our "region" and to a local superior of our immediate district expressing in both letters my opinion that even when our installation is complete the work at our village will not require two full time directors, and I expressed my desire that annex work of some kind be established. As yet I have received no reply. During the last few days I have felt somewhat more encouraged about the opportunities of the work here. Our present little room has been overcrowded in the evenings, and I have found it exceedingly interesting to talk to the soldiers who are fresh from the front. Of course it does seem a little ignoble for an able-bodied man near the front to do nothing but talk, but in the French army even much more than in the American army we are regarded as hopeless civilians and we might as well put it in our pipe and smoke it.

On Tuesday I went over to the "intendance" or quartermaster's office of our division to see about chocolate and other supplies for our cantine. Afterward I went on a little expedition in search of an American notary in order to have my income tax declaration witnessed. I have been granted an extension of time until March 30 to get my declaration in to the collector's office at Camden, N.J., but of course unless I can find a notary at once such extension will be insufficient. I cannot leave my post here. Even to get to the town of which I spoke in the first letter that I wrote after leaving Paris, I should have to secure the permission of the regional director. That would be a long business, since we cannot get into touch with him by phone. These restrictions of my movements are not mere rules of the organization of the Foyers, but are military orders. My search for an office with a notary's seal the other day resulted in failure. However, I found some American soldiers and had rather an interesting time when I got to the camp of the American company where a Y.M.C.A. secretary (traveling around in a Ford) was just making an address. Although I may be over estimating my ability I do think that that kind of circuit work is what I ought to be doing. All my training has been in that direction. I am emphatically not a business man or a physical director. But I think I can interest the boys in greetings of the kind that I saw the other day. However, I suppose it is not for me to say so.

The young captain in command of the company was a very pleasant fellow. He thought that I should seek my notary in the dug-out of the Americans up in the second line.[15] I might incidentally get a chance to go to the front. Unfortunately I did not go about the thing just right, and missed an opportunity which otherwise could have been easy enough to secure. Also the hour was late. I went to the dug-out in question which is a regular underground city—an old quarry (or we would perhaps say a mine) being used for war

15. The "dug-out" refers to the underground or semi-underground habitation of soldiers in the trenches.

purposes.[16] Americans and French are housed in it far underground
in great security. The place represents a magnificent opportunity
for Y.M.C.A. work. I understand that a Y.M.C.A. secretary was there
a little while ago. But at present they are very anxious for Y.M.C.A.
assistance. Entering the abri was rather exciting to the novice. Just
before I got to the entrance the German shells began to whistle
around my ears in a most disconcerting fashion. I ducked into
whatever hole in the ground I saw—an American soldier afterward
told me not to be afraid to duck no matter who saw me, since
everybody does it when a bombardment begins. Only two or three
shells came while I was outside. Within thirty seconds I was safely in
the abri. The shells could not even be heard except right near the
entrance. In returning I was required by the sentries to wait until
the intermittent bombardment had stopped for five minutes at a
stretch. You can bet I was not particularly anxious to disobey the
order. Then I made the first part of the return trip with a mighty
pleasant American lieutenant. Things were absolutely quiet. It was
a long walk home for me. I arrived about half past eight or so.[17]
Getting into that abri under shell fire seemed exciting to me. But
it is astonishing how few people get hurt by that kind of fire. Going
merely to the second line that way—even repeated trips back and
forth—is regarded as a slacker's job. As far as a bombardment of
our village is concerned, it is regarded as very very unlikely. The
first shells might happen to do some execution, but everybody
would at once take refuge in the cellars before the range could be
gotten and an enormous expenditure of ammunition would there
after do comparatively little harm—the houses having already
been destroyed. The Germans are exceedingly unlikely to waste
their ammunition in that way. So we can construct our "foyer" hut
without fear of its destruction. The astonishing thing to me is the
prodigious amount of ammunition that it takes to kill one man

16. In the margin is written, "Near the Ferme de Froidmont." This is probably the "Cavern
du Dragon" located along the "Chemin des Dames." This excavation was liberated from German occupation late in 1917. Machen's designation of it as a "quarry" or "mine" matches the
description of the "Cavern du Dragon" at http://www.caverne-du-dragon.com/en/decouvrir
-musee/history-caverne-du-Dragon.aspx.

17. A marginal annotation reads, "Past Ostel." Ostel is 69 miles N.E. of Paris and 25 miles
N.W. of Reims.

by shellfire. Trenches and dug-outs provide astonishingly good protection.

It is highly interesting to get the opinion of the French soldiers about the behavior of the Americans who took part in the "coup de Main" of which I spoke in my last letter (In my last letter I did not venture to mention the fact of American participation, but that I am now sure is an excess of caution).[18] The Frenchmen think the American boys did mighty well, they are a little inclined to smile at the ardor of the new soldiers, which takes the thing as a kind of "sport." Especially the American artillery which accomplished the "tire de barrage" has evoked universal admiration.[19] Everybody chuckles at its manifest superiority to the German artillery which it is facing just now. The "bataillion" (French, of course) which is here just now in our village is composed of younger soldiers than the other two that I have seen, and the younger fellows describe happenings at the front with more gusto. The schedule is very simple. Our regiment is divided into three battalions. One battalion remains here eight days, then is replaced by another battalion, and goes to the second line (reserve) for eight days; then, being replaced there by the battalion that has just left here, goes to the front line. Every eight days for twenty-four days we see a new crowd, then the cycle begins again.

On Wednesday I walked about six miles to a centre of supplies to get things for the cantine. Success was only relative.[20] It is hard to get the chocolate, which is to be one mainstay. I must go again to-morrow. Of course one cannot hire waggons in an ordinary way in the zone of the armies, but the military conveyances are put at our disposal very generously.

Continued March 2

For instance, on the trip of which I was just speaking I was given a special waggon to bring my chocolate (33 kilos was all I

18. A "coup de main" is a swift surprise attack.
19. A "tire de barrage" is shelling the enemy with artillery or anti-aircraft fire.
20. The note in the margin reads, "Oeuilly," which is about 72 miles E.N.E. of Paris and about 17 miles S.W. of Reims.

could get), cigarettes, tobacco, etc. back to our village.[21] To-day I have just walked again to the same centre of supplies to purchase some little ginger-snaps that I was doubtful about.

In wet weather like yesterday the dampness surpasses anything that I ever saw. This letter-paper that I left on my table is so wet that the pen is in danger almost of sticking through it at every stroke. Books and every thing become moist to the touch. My equipment is good. Especially the good high boots that I bought in Paris (American make) and had fitted with hob-nails are worth the 160 francs or so that I paid for them. Shoes certainly do cost money in war time. But good shoes are unquestionably the kind to get. My little candle-lantern, which I was advised to get on the basis of Army's friend's experience, is another magnificent success. It cost a matter of fifty cents or a dollar or so, if I remember rightly, and over here it is absolutely worth its weight in gold. Candles are the one thing that can be secured everywhere. An oil lamp would probably be useless, because of difficulty about oil; electric lamps, absolutely indispensable as they are, are in danger of going out. But the little old candle, encased in a glass cover that can be folded up, has come into its own in conditions like ours.

At times I feel a longing for a land of peace and for home. I feel as though it would be a relief to the eyes to see a window pane once more, and a relief to the ears not to hear at intervals the noise of the guns and distant shells. There is one little baby in our village. In the midst of the military surroundings it is refreshing to see the little face. I wonder what its first impression of life will be in the midst of all this ruin.

Most of all I wish I could see you and the members of the family circle. Glad as I am that I am here, there are times when the longing for the whole miserable business to be over becomes very strong.

I enjoy ever so much the mess of non-commissioned officers where we take our meals. The exchange of opinions at the table is to me intensely interesting when I can follow it. This would be

---

21. A "kilo" (kilogram) is roughly 2.2 pounds, or in this case about 72 pounds of chocolate.

a fine chance to learn the angst of the trenches.[22] My progress is slow. Some of the men are men of education & literary tastes. One gave me a copy of De Vigny's poems, which I have read with only a moderate degree of comprehension & appreciation. My French associate does not like the "popote" (because of inconveniences about hours, etc.) and says we must make arrangements to get our meals by ourselves. My wishes are not consulted in this matter. If the change is insisted upon I think perhaps the worm will turn. This does not mean that my associate is unkind, but only that he has a way of going ahead in his own way. When I especially request it he will open the window at night, but since he goes to bed after I do I sometimes suffer from the badness of the air. Sleeping in a closed room is certainly a bad habit, even when one does not smoke bad cigarettes. I am glad to say there is still a little chink in the ceiling, but in repairing a part of the roof they found a dead cat in what had been the upper story. The upshot of it all is, however, that I am enjoying about the best health I have had in years. This letter has not been as full of love as my heart is, but I must not limit myself to saying over & over again the same things.

Love to all.
Your loving son,
Gresham

---

22. The word "angst" is German and it refers to anxiety related to the human condition or a general fear of life and its experiences.

3

ADJUSTING TO THE WAR,
THE "Y," AND MONSIEUR PIA

As the work of the American-French duo continues, the American would find his participation in the Foyer difficult due to the domineering manner of his French colleague. The tension in the Foyer would increase Machen's frustration with his limited opportunities to minister the Word of God. He hopes to be placed in a situation where he could better use his theological education and gifts. However, the Princeton professor finds himself, at least for the time being, in the hot chocolate manufacturing business.

March 7, 1918

My dearest Mother:

I really believe, though I am not quite sure, that my last letter was written a whole week ago, on Feb. 28. One reason why I have allowed the days to slip by without writing is that there is really so little definite news to give you. Naturally life over here is always interesting to the person who is actually experiencing it, but in my case just now one day is very much like another. My last news from home was your letter of Jan. 26 or there abouts. I have received so little since I wrote to you the last time. Such gaps are altogether to be expected, as are also all kinds of irregularities like the arrival of letters before those that were written several weeks earlier. I dare say I may receive a regular bunch of letters some day before long. The mail-carrier who is the one that serves us "directors," arrives once a day, at about nine o'clock in the morning. His arrival is eagerly awaited.

This morning he brought me a copy of the "Presbyterian" of Feb. 7, which contains my little article on "The Minister and his Greek Testament." I was unable to see the proof. The editor has left most of the article unchanged, but has ingeniously spoiled the one thing that could possibly have made any pretences to being worthwhile. It did provoke me that the editorial artillery should have hit that one particular spot when it would have been comparatively harmless elsewhere.

The other day I visited an American Y.M.C.A. secretary who is inhabiting a dug-out a couple of miles from here.[1] He returned the visit the next day and incidentally got us to help him out by letting him have a few of our packages of candles which we sell to the soldiers. He is an episcopal clergyman of Newark, N.J., formerly of Baltimore. One of his wife's best friends is a daughter of President Gilman. They are now together in Paris. The name of the secretary in question is Johnston or Johnson.

I continue living under a benevolent despotism, which consists in not allowing me to do anything at all for myself. My colleague's characteristic expressions are "Attendez," which is used whenever I try to do anything great or small for myself, and "Ça n'a pas d'importance,"[2] which comes in when I make any suggestion. I am supposed to have charge of the cantine. But as a matter of fact I have had nothing whatever to do with it so far. I could stand on my rights in the matter, but that would be exceedingly unpleasant, and would probably not be for the benefit of the work. My inexperience, especially if further hindered by ill-will on the part of my colleague, would lead me to make mistakes. In some matters I absolutely

1. The "dug-out,"according to the marginal note, was "near Chavonne," which is 70 miles N.E. of Paris and 22 miles N.W. of Reims.

2. "Attendez" is an imperative form instructing Machen to "wait," and "Ça n'a pas d'importance," coming from the mouth of Machen's French associate, meant "it is not important."

In his letters Dr. Machen mentions his loaning library that provided books for the soldiers to read. Pictured here is what his portable library might have looked like. *Photo courtesy of Kautz Family Collection, University of Minnesota*

require his assistance. Accordingly, I am helpless. It is a pretty tough experience, I can tell you, but I am just going to try to stomach it. Every now and then I do protest, as when my companion in his monthly report wholly used the first person singular in describing the installation of the hut and the cantine, and merely remarked that I was to take charge of the cantine. It is rather strange, under such treatment, to observe that the constitution of the Foyer ascribes an absolute equality to the French director and American director. About the only thing that has kept me from feeling absolutely useless is the routine work of handing out letter papers and selling candles in the salle de réunion, which has been permitted while my colleague is engaged in watching the workman outside. Also I have usually some hours of stealthy freedom in the morning. Fortunately my colleague often does not get up till ten o'clock. But when the other day I ventured before his levée to give some directions to the workman who is engaged on my cantine I was rebuked for it later on.[3] Some days ago I was forbidden to open the window of one room at night. As the chinks have now been filled up and as my colleague has the habit of lighting a fire in the stove just at my bed-time and sitting up till 2 A.M. or so, suffocation or a fight was imminent. I escaped by moving my bed out into the room to be occupied by the cantine. There are objections to that room too, which are serious objections which are going to be more serious still when the cantine is started, but it affords some relief for the time.

But how long my patience is going to hold out I do not know. I live in an atmosphere of suppressed irritation all the time. The calm assumption of proprietary rights over me and all my surroundings makes me good and hot all the time. If it were not for one or two hours of comparative freedom in the morning and also the pleasure of the popote in the evening; I don't think I could stand it. My companion has to get his dinner first and then relieve me at the salle de réunion. I then make my way to the festive bunch and thoroughly enjoy myself from about seven o'clock till about eight or a little after.

March 8

I must bring my letter to a brief close if I am to catch the one and only mail this morning. Yesterday we received a visit from the French director of a neighboring Foyer. He suggested that we go ahead and start the cantine even though the room is not fixed up. It was a bully suggestion, and rather to my surprise my colleague was very nice about it.[4] I got busy yesterday getting the kitchen a little bit cleaned up. Maybe I have completely misjudged and misunderstood my colleague here. At any rate, I feel much more cheery about things.

Last night, at the popote, we had rabbit. It was perfectly delicious, something like terrapin only lots better. Everything is

---

3. The word "levée" means getting out of bed in the morning.

4. The word "bully" means "excellent" or "splendid" and it was one of President Theodore Roosevelt's favorite words. Dr. Machen used this popular term from his era several times in his war letters.

done to a turn by that Parisian cook. Macaroni au gratin under his treatment is a dish fit for a king.[5] I am having the best board (of course with the exception of home board) that I have had for many years. Coffee, for example, is grand. What in the world do they do to coffee at swell Paris hotels to make it so absolutely useless? Here near the front it is a mainstay of life.

Love & lots of it to all. You still know just how anxious I am to hear about Nena, & how I long to see you & Arly & Helen & Tom.

Your loving son
Gresham

March 8, 1918

My dearest Mother:

Your letter number 5 has just come to hand—by the same postman who took my letter dated March 6, 7. Letter number 4 is still missing. As the Y.M.C.A. authorities warned me, these irregularities are only to be expected. No doubt in letter number 4 you told me about receiving my cablegram from Paris and also the message of the arrival of the ship that was to pass through the New York office of the Y.M.C.A.

Fumigating your room seems to be a fine idea. I trust it will prove to be the means of overcoming the stubborn attacks that you have had in the spring. I am delighted to hear that Summerville is in prospect—or rather was in prospect, since now the Summerville stay ought to be well underway. For Uncle too it will be a fine thing. Give my best love to him & to Aunt Bessie. I have been trying to answer his letter which was forwarded to me from New York.

The news about Arly's success for the Safe Dep. & Trust Co. is most satisfactory. Be sure to congratulate him heartily. The news cheers me up a lot. I am happy also at the news that Helen has been

5. "Macaroni au gratin" is macaroni and cheese.

received into our church. As for Nena, of course I can only join you in your anxiety, but also in your prayers & in your faith.

You seem to have been having some weather this winter in the U.S.A. Here things have been comparatively mild, but the kind of life we had makes warm weather welcome. A nice sweater arrived from Mary Robinson to-day. It was just barely too late to catch me in New York.

I am afraid I did my colleague great injustice in my last letter. Every now & then I get into rather a sour mood. There is certainly another side to it all. My companion is the prince of kindness. It is only a possible excess of a good quality which has embarrassed me at times. I think things are going to work out all right. To-day I hope to be busy preparing to start our cantine.

Love to all. In haste,
Your loving son,
Gresham

March 9, 1918

Dear Arly:

For some time, despite my frequent letters to Mother, I have been intending to write directly to you. You and Helen have been very much in my thoughts ever since I left, and the news that I received about you both from Mother is very much cherished. The latest news is in Mother's letter for Feb. 1, which tells me about your little dinner of the night before. Mother was delighted about it, since she is a little afraid that her being laid up so long may make things gloomy for Helen.

Before I forget it, let me say that I am enclosing a letter of Jan. 31 from the Citizens National Bank. I am sorry to say that I remember nothing about the letter of Dec. 31, about which they are inquiring. Perhaps I thought it was merely a request for proxies or the like and threw it away. I am now informing the cashier that I am sending his frequent letters to you. Perhaps you will know what was contained in the letter of Dec. 31, or rather the letter "forwarded" Dec. 31. I hope I have not been guilty of a serious mistake about that letter.

Please tell Mother that her letter No. 4 arrived the day after No. 5, No. 4 was of Feb. 1. I wrote to her just before and just after receiving No. 5, No. 4 contains lots of news in which I am intensely interested. I am glad I wired direct from Paris, instead of trusting exclusively the Y.M.C.A. I wanted at least to have two strings to my bow.

Mother's interest in the way Paris looks under changed conditions is very natural. But the truth is Paris looks very much the same as ever. Of course there are differences. There are more uniforms, and in greater variety, to be seen on the streets, most of the women are in mourning; the streets are kept very dark at night. But the wonder is that the differences are not far greater still.

After some very wet weather it is now clear again. The mud is gradually drying up, and the letter paper and books no longer feel as though they had just been dipped in water. One of the men at the "popote" where we board remarked this morning how I have improved in healthy appearance since I arrived here. Certainly the life seems to agree with me. Good well-cooked food, and lots of air form the basis of health.

Yesterday afternoon I worked hard scraping off the encrusted dirt from the floor of what is to be our cantine. We hope to get things started before very long. I shall be happier if I can be engaged in somewhat more definite work. Probably you will think it is not the work that is fitted to me, and I do not think it is myself; but I want at least to make good in my present situation before I ask for a change. After some months, I dare say I may write to Bobby Freeman and remind him of the desire that he expressed to have me engage ultimately in religious work for the American boys. In a way which seems to be exceptional I was put with the French work temporarily. It has been a great experience for me. Just at present however, I am discouraged about my French. I do not seem to have improved one bit during the past three weeks. Excellent as the opportunities here might seem to be. I was simply delighted to hear that you had gained the case for the Safe Deposit & Trust Co. in the Court of Appeals. In the words of the immortal "Teddy" that is "bully." By the way I should be glad to get news of Mr. Williams' health. I hope to hear that both he & his wife are better this winter.

The two or three streets in this tiny little village are named after the first men of the present time. Our salle de reunion is on the Rue Roosevelt, whereas the cantine and our living quarters are on the Rue Wilson. I am glad I struck the Rue Wilson. The Rue Roosevelt is only about a hundred yards or so long.

Our village is prettily situated on top of a little hill. It is much the most picturesque village in the environs. The church, now in ruins like everything else, is ancient. The bulk of the edifice is still standing, though dilapidation is of course everywhere apparent.

As for my impression of the war situation—if I should undertake to unfold them in full I might, though with the best intentions in the world, say something that the censor might think unwise. One thing, however, I can say—American aid in the present war is absolutely essential if there is to be a satisfactory conclusion. That may seem to be a matter of course. But I for my part was not nearly so sure of it when I left home as I am now.

I long for congenial work. That is my chief need. The sense of adventure; the chance of learning French, etc. made me glad when the authorities decided to put me into the Foyer du Soldat. But I wish I were doing something for which I have special training. One thing is certain—if I do get into the work of preaching the gospel to the American boys it will be with a new sense of the privilege of it.

I am grateful in the thought of your care for my business interests in America. As I told Mother I formally sent my income tax return, possibly in time to arrive at Camden, N.J. before the expiration of the 30-day extension allowed to me. I hope there is no serious trouble about the Cit. Nat. Bank.

Give my very best love to Helen, & of course to Mother too. I hope soon to answer her "No. 4."

Your affectionate brother,
Gresham Machen

March 12, 1918

My Dearest Mother,

Since sending my last letter on March 8, I have received the two splendid letters from you—the belated No. 4, which arrived after No. 5, and No. 6 which is dated Feb. 15. The former was partially answered in my letter to Arly of a day or so ago, but it will do no harm to tell you again how grateful I was when I received it, and how deeply interested I was in the news that it contained. I am distressed indeed to hear about the death of your old friend, Mrs. Campbell of Macon, both for your sake and for uncle's. Loy's call, or prospective repetition of a call to Hampden-Sidney, is interesting and gratifying. I am so far away that I am afraid whatever I might say would be heard only after the decision had been made. All I can say is that I am so profoundly impressed by Loy's work in the pastorate that I do not see how he could possibly do any better anywhere else, though perhaps the chair in question might offer an opportunity for something like pastoral work. As for Nena, as I intimated in my letter to Arly, my concern is too profound for words.

But here is No. 6 at hand in remarkably quick time. My letter from the ship to which your letter is an answer also must have made mighty good time, judged by present standards. I am glad you are feeling a little better, but do wish that that "little" could be changed into a "lot." We look to Summerville to do the job both for you and for uncle, about whose illness I feel very deeply distressed.

I am glad you liked my article in the "Presbyterian." Unless I am mistaken I ordered extra copies to be sent to 217 Monument St., but cannot be perfectly sure after this lapse of time.[6] The editor's emphasis upon the extreme youth of the author may possibly be an answer to an impression which I understand prevailed in one of our Presbyterian colleges to the effect that none of the professors in Princeton Seminary is under seventy years of age. Sometime I will look up for you the place in the Congressional Record, which contains my letter on the subject of woman suffrage. I could give you the page now, but it would not do to put you to the trouble of looking it up.

6. "217 Monument St." refers to the street address of the Machen family home in Baltimore where Gresham was raised.

Somehow your being able to answer my letter, even though the letter is a long way back, makes one feel less absolutely lonely in my European experience. I never felt so lonely in my life. As you will remember, loneliness on a foreign visit is not at all one of my failings. But here in this desolate environment things are different, to say nothing of the continual irritation caused by my relations with my colleague. I feel as though I should give in a lot just to be able to relieve my mind. And when here, on the bare outer edge of war, I feel an intense longing for peace. Last night after supper I had an experience unique during the time after my arrival at this post—namely an hour of quiet. It was a beautiful starlit night, absolutely without wind. For a considerable time there was not a shot or the buzz of an airplane. What an inestimable blessing! The great blessings of life are those that we often appreciate least. And one of the greatest blessings of all is quiet. It did not last long here. At nine o'clock or so, the anti-aircraft guns were making night hideous again, reinforced by the sinister buzz of the German planes on their way to some work of destruction, I suppose for the cities of France.

If this war is ever concluded in a really satisfactory way, I am going to be an active worker for peace. And the kind of work that I believe might really be effective is the work of moral education in all the languages of the world. War is righteous when it is conducted as in France for the delivery of women and children and the repelling of an invader. But how any human being can have the heart or the absence of heart to continue this war for one moment merely for conquest reveals to my mind as nothing else in the world the abyss of sin. After the war is over, providing that its over in the right way, I do believe that there is going to be a spiritual rebellion of the common people throughout the world which if taken as the flood may sweep away the folly of war. I only hope that other things of a different character may not be swept away at the same time.

Last Friday night I had what might seem to be a pretty serious passage of words with my colleague. He took occasion before our workmen directly to contradict my order about a matter concerning the little department which is my peculiar concern here, namely the cantine. Before the same public I told him plainly that I wanted him to know that it was I who was to give orders about the cantine. I do not see how in the world I could have done otherwise, but at the time I very naturally supposed that after such an occurrence one or the other of us would have to leave. Nothing of the kind! After some soft words on my part, which followed a rather acrimonious discussion in our room, it was not five minutes before my colleague was bossing my affairs very much as before. His bad-nature seems to have returned. The truth is I am just determined that I will get along with that fellow—I regard it as a part and the hardest part of my duty. I am just determined to make good right here in my present post before I do anything else.

My colleague, M. Pia, has lots of good ideas, and I simply could not do without him. But he does not seem to see that the way to help me in the cantine is not to give orders to my assistant, but to make suggestions to me that they might then be transmitted by me to the assistant. At least he did not see it until the other day. Things have been going a tiny mite better the last day or so. What a blessed day of freedom I had the day M. Pia went to a neighboring town on the business of the Foyer! It was as though I had escaped from prison. I could do things in my own way and in my own time without fearing every time I returned to the cantine to find that things had been going along quite independent of me. And when I ran up against difficulties I could go ahead and surmount them in some sort of way without being stopped at every turn by M. Pia. M. Pia is not a bad fellow at all, and he has ability. But the first person plural does not exist in his particular dialect of the French language.

We have begun making the hot chocolate, M. Pia serving as a very efficient instructor the first time. First you shave up two kilos of sweet chocolate. This is a job of an hour or so if, as is the case here, you have no mortar and pestle. Then you boil two liters of water, then you mix in the chocolate, then you add eighteen liters and boil, then add condensed milk & boil again, then you remove the chocolate from the fire. The chocolate is ready for use any time you desire to warm it up, and it is very good. Unfortunately the French custom is to take the chocolate in the early morning. So for the present I am opening the cantine from seven to nine in the morning, the most inconvenient hour that could possibly be devised. After three hours of work I get my toast and coffee, both being apt to be cold. How different life was when I got that good coffee and toast right after getting up! It made me feel like a different man. Déjeuner comes at eleven o'clock.[7] I used to have a magnificent appetite for it when I got my coffee at a reasonable hour. At present we are serving only about forty cups of chocolate or less in the morning, but after our cantine is fitted up and advertised I think we shall be useful enough. The chocolate is sold for four sous (20 centimes, as of course you know, but it takes me some time to compute by mental arithmetic).[8] Every soldier brings his own tin cup or "quart" as it is technically called. This custom saves a lot of trouble so far as the washing of dishes is concerned. In addition to the chocolate we have little crackers (delicious), tobacco, cigarettes, matches, candles, condensed milk, anchovies & sardines. A brisk sale of candles has been going on all along in the sale de reunion. Light is one of the most precious commodities in the zone of the armies. The arrangement of the cantine is as follows:—[9]

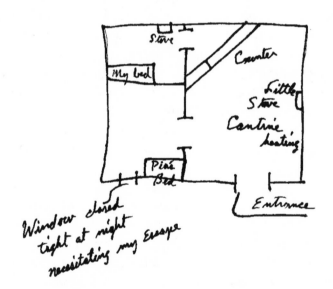

7. The French "déjeuner" means "to have lunch."

8. The "sou" is an older French coin. A "sou" was 12 deniers, which equals 5 centimes, which is as Machen calculated it in his letter. Four sous would have been equivalent to four cents in American money at the time of the war.

9. The sketch was copied by the editor from Machen's original.

Do not suppose that the various stoves indicated in the above plan give any heat, except just enough to heat up the chocolate.

We have a soldier detailed as "cantiniér" to assist us in cantine & other matters of the Foyer.[10] He is a good fellow, but very slow. Since he experiences the same difficulty that I experience about getting up at 6 A.M., it is difficult for us to get the fire lighted in time to serve chocolate at seven o'clock. Heating up 20 litres takes some time.[11] One thing is sure, I just have to get to bed at about eight or half-past. When I get into a discussion with M. Pia and then the anti-aircraft guns have a little séance, some of which are only about a kilometer away, the night's rest is badly broken up for me.[12] M. Pia frequently sleeps till nine or ten in the morning after being awake a good part of the night. You will begin to understand why I moved my bed. I do feel badly about it, however, since our cantiniér, instead of sleeping where I now sleep has to sleep in quarters with an earthen floor. The poor fellow has a bad cold, and makes me feel very guilty. But for reasons mental as well as physical, I just don't see how I can sleep in my old place. I enjoy those few blessed hours in the morning when I can paddle my own canoe! But you will observe that the arrangement of quarters is not helpful to my independence in the cantine.

Yesterday I took a pleasant little walk in the woods with two of the men at the popote. The green things are beginning to sprout a tiny little bit. At times we could almost forget we were in the war zone, though ancient Abris were not long out of sight. From the top of a hill we had a good view. By the way our village seems to be further from the Germans than I thought it was at first. It is said to be some twelve kilometers distant from the worst part of the enemy's line, though the information is not authoritative, & I do not believe it is quite accurate.

Americans look in on us here every now and then. Five very nice-looking boys came to the sale de reunion last night.

10. The French "cantiniér" means "canteen man."

11. A litre is about 33.9 ounces, so twenty litres is about 5.3 gallons.

12. Here, the French, "séance," means a performance or session, not an attempt to contact the dead.

I wish I could write to the servants, for I know they are good friends of mine. But I don't see how I could write to one without writing to all. Remember me to them most cordially.

The best of love to all. And do get well, my dearest Mother, & thus make me supremely happy.

Your loving son,
Gresham

March 17, 1918

My dearest Mother:

I am ashamed to say that I carried around my letter of March 12 and 13 a day or so in my pocket before I finally gave it to the postman. At any rate it is high time to write another, especially since it is a custom of the family for me to write on Sunday. Of course after my riches of a few days ago I am not expecting a letter from home just yet. But I did get the next thing to it in the shape of a perfectly lovely letter from Miss Marie, dated Feb. 5.

Even before I sent my last letter to you my relations with my colleague here had begun to improve, and now I regret the harshness of my language. Our difficulties no doubt reside in my own character as well as in that of M. Pia, and especially they reside in the very nature of the work that the "Union Franco-Américaine" is trying to do. How would we like it if a crowd of foreigners were dumped down on us suddenly to help us do our work? I am afraid I have not been as considerate as I ought to have been. Certainly I have been in the wrong sometimes. On the other hand I will say that I have tried to exercise self-control, and that certainly I have safely gotten over some very, very thin places in the ice. Just now I am having very much my own way in the cantine, perhaps more than is good for me. I must say that I have profited at every turn by M. Pia's experience. I should seek his advice oftener if I were not

afraid of being put again into the position of having everything
done for me.

One thing that seems strange in the zone of the armies is that
money often will not expedite things at all. When we have need
of a lock for a door, or that greatest of luxuries a door-latch, or a
little bit of paper for the walls, my first impulse is always to say: "In
order to hustle things up I will not bother to requisition the central
organization of the Foyer but will just pay for the trifle myself."
As a matter of fact, the little things are often just the things that
cannot be bought. They can often be secured far quicker if they are
not bought, but obtained as part of the assistance rendered by the
military authorities to the Foyer du Soldat. Money is no good where
the goods desired are strictly limited in quantity.

The other day in order to secure a number of little things, I
walked to a town about four miles from here, which has not been
demolished (but only injured here and there) and where there is
some population.[13] I did secure some things, but when I mentioned
lock, hatchets, door-latchets, and the like—nothing doing. That
town made a gloomy impression on me, even though it is not in
ruins. It has an appearance of being a real town with ordinary
people in it, but it does not really succeed in being one. Some of the
people in the stores seemed to be listless & without desire to show
the little that they had.

Every morning at six o'clock, our assistant, the "cantinier,"
knocks on the door to wake me up in order that I may let him in.
He then lights the fire to heat up the chocolate & I pull on my
clothes, get my table ready for the opening of the cantine, & usually
try to shave. The cantine has not been very well attended as yet.
About sixty was the largest number of cups of chocolate that we
served, and often we have been as low as twenty-five or thirty. An
excellent carpenter (with a young assistant) was assigned to me at
the beginning of the week. Unfortunately about the middle of the
week it was his time to return to the trenches, but I went to see the
officer in command, who was the man who has been so kind to us
right along, and got his permission to have the men remain three

13. In the margin is written, "Braisne," which is about 50 miles N.N.E. of Paris and about
56 miles W.N.W. of Reims.

extra days. They (or rather I should perhaps say "he" since only one is really an expert carpenter) have constructed the counter for the cantine, a door with a little wicket for passing the chocolate from the kitchen, and a set of shelves for our merchandise. Other workmen are to finish the installation.

Monday, March 18

Two important events have taken place since I began this letter. In the first place, your letter "No. 4," postmarked Feb. 21 arrived this morning. It was a lovely letter. You don't know how much I appreciate your goodness in writing to me so often in the midst of all your troubles. The news that this last letter contained is only fairly good, but you are not responsible for that. I am deeply distressed at your continued suffering and with you distressed at the slowness of Nena's progress. Before so-very long I hope to hear that you have at last gotten to Summerville. Thank you very much by the way for the copy of my article which arrived this morning with your letter.

The other event that has happened since I began this letter was the arrival of a regional director of the Foyers du Soldat to inform me that I had been transferred to another post. His coming indeed interrupted me in the actual writing of the letter, and prevented me from mailing it yesterday. My feelings about the transfer are mixed. In the first place I did have my back up to make good right here, and get along with my colleague. Since my colleague evidently (or at best probably) wanted me to go, and on the night of our tift was rather inclined to hold up before me the prospect of my departure, I can't help feeling as though my departure is a kind of defeat. On the other hand it is I who have said (rather unwisely & tactlessly, I am afraid) that the present post is not large enough for two directors. Certainly my new post seems to be (though I really know nothing whatever about it) in the nature of a promotion, since I am to be the only director, at least for the present. A hut is said to be already erected and ready for opening. The post is about twelve kilometers from here, about half-way between this village

& the town which contains the regional headquarters of the organization of the Foyer.[14] The new post is further from the front than my present post. In going to it, I do feel sad at having missed the opportunity of seeing the front—as others in my situation have had no difficulty in doing. However, I am here to be useful & not to see things that will be worth telling about at home.

What makes it hard to leave here just now is that the period of waiting is over & really our Foyer is just getting started. To-day was our best morning in the cantine. Also all kinds of unbearable conditions may meet me in my new post—worst of all a lack of opportunity to learn French, English-speaking associates & companies & the like. The place is said to have lots of Americans in it, and I believe an American Y.M.C.A. director. I do wish I could transplant the most excellent "popote" where I have had the best grub & congenial French companionship. The bright side of the situation is that my experience here has done me good & fitted me to start out in a more independent way.

Frequently in the afternoon I am visited by American soldiers. One of them, a big New-Englander, chatted with me an hour or so the other day while I engaged in the mechanical job of shaving the chocolate up fine preparatory to putting it in the pot. His simple faith in God did me good. He seems to have made up his mind not to worry about the shells, since his life or death is in God's hands & he is satisfied with that. I know I can receive lots more than I can give from many of the American boys, who are going into the battle, than I can give to them. Certainly I need from my dearest Mother just the help that her letters are giving me.

The greatest love to all.
Your loving son
Gresham

14. That is, Machen's first Foyer was located in St. Mard, or "this village," and the town where "the organization of the Foyer" was located was Soissons, which is located 58 miles N.E. of Paris and 33 miles W.N.W. of Reims. There is a notation for "Soissons" in the margin of Machen's letter.

March 18, 1918

My dear Miss Marie:

Just at the moment I find myself up against an absolutely impossible task—namely that of telling one how much I appreciate your lovely letter of Feb. 5, which arrived just the other day. Really I had just better give it up. Your letter did me good right down to the bottom of my heart, and I just can't begin to tell you how grateful I am for it. As for the things that you and Mrs. Buchanan gave me, they are great, as I hope Mother has already told you. I wear that sweater, for example, all the time, and the wristlets are also of the very best.

It was a lovely thought to give me news of my Mother. Of course she has been faithfulness itself about writing, but since she naturally as always tries to put the best face possible on her own troubles, the opinion of a true and observant friend is of the greatest possible value. I do hope Summerville may set her up. The news of Charlie was also mighty interesting to me. Wherever he may be sent, I am dead sure he will make a bully good officer. Mr. Kent McCay's enthusiasm over ships is exceedingly encouraging. Tell him to keep things stirred up all the time. It is revealing no military secrets to say that people over here have use for everything that Uncle Sam can put across. By the way the American boys, that I have seen sure have the real stuff in them.

Mother will give you what news you may desire. I am just being transferred to a new post. It is a little farther from the front than my present post. But it has the advantage of greater independence. I understand I am to be the sole "director" or secretary of the "Foyer," though there is an American secretary near by for the American boys.

Airplanes have sure been busy recently about here. Yesterday for a change, the French men were more in evidence than the German. I counted about ten or twelve not far apart & at one time. The expert can tell the French from the German planes by the sound of the motors, but I do not seem to have enough of an ear for music for that. I have to depend on noticing whether or not the French anti-aircraft guns take a shot at the planes.

Everything is demolished in our village and the neighboring places. The cellars are the chief resource in the way of living quarters, though I have been living above ground in a patched-up house. Some of the neighboring villages are still more utterly destroyed, so that little more than the foundations and shapeless heaps of stone remain to show for the picturesque villages of France.

Give my very best love to Mrs. Buchanan. It's a great help to me to think that Mother has such good and loving friends always at hand to give her sympathy & help. And I am mighty glad to get the same myself.

Affectionately yours,
J. Gresham Machen

4

A New Assignment at
Missy-sur-Aisne

March 23 to April 7, 1918

Dr. Machen's next "Y" assignment will move him from St. Mard on the south side of the Aisne, due west 6.7 miles to the north side of the river in Missy-sur-Aisne. The new location is just outside the embattled city of Soissons. The work would continue with the selling of toiletries, snacks, and hot chocolate to the troops. The new Foyer was located along a road that would provide a better opportunity to see the movement of troops and supplies.

March 23, 1918

My dear Mother:

My last letter, I believe, was sent on Monday, March 18. If I am to seize an opportunity of mailing a letter to-day I must write at once although there is little time & my hands are so cold that I can hardly hold a pen. Unlike my last post, the post where I now find myself has absolutely no civil population & consequently no civilian mail-box. I shall have to send my letters to be mailed in a neighboring town by the man who brings the newspapers. As for incoming letters I am afraid there may be delays & difficulties.

My new post is in a village about ten miles from the present post, which is even far more completely demolished than the village from which I have come.[1] The hut destined for the Foyer is not quite complete & there is a Frenchman in charge of the work. So I have not yet arrived at a state of perfect independence. I have been sleeping most of the time in a very nice dry cellar deep down under the church, to which I was invited along with my French companion by a non-commissioned officer. Sleeping underground is no doubt an excess of caution, but the place is very comfortable indeed & I rather hope to continue my right of access to it.

This post is very much more on the main lines of travel than the little place from which I have come. It must be confessed that hardly anybody showed up yesterday after we opened the building at 11 A.M., but no doubt the existence of a Foyer is not yet known. Also we are not yet prepared to offer very much to the men.

I am again boarding at a mess of non-commissioned officers— not quite so attractive as the one from which I ran, but still very good.

The formal opening of our Foyer took place on Thursday in the presence of some French officers & an American colonel. An American band furnished the music. In the afternoon I witnessed the presentation of the "Croix de Guerre" to three American soldiers.[2] The noise of a neighboring gun added to the impressiveness of the ceremony.

Good bye & lots of love. There is just time to catch the newspaper man.

Your loving son,
Gresham

1. At the top and in the margin of this page of the letter there is a note, "Missy-sur-Aisne," which is a village about 5 miles E. of Soissons.
2. The "Croix de Guerre" is a French medal awarded for heroism.

March 25, 1918

My dearest Mother:

My last letter, written about three days ago, was exceedingly brief and unsatisfactory. The present effort, I am afraid, will be of the same character, but perhaps the two letters taken together may convey some news.

The French director who was charged with installing the Foyer here is a man of somewhat more savoir-faire than my colleague at my first post, but displayed very much the same bossy character. The attitude assumed by these men has to be observed in order to be understood; I have never in all my travels run across anything exactly like it. However this time I said to myself that my time would come when I should finally be left to my own resources. Since Saturday I have been by myself.

The hut is practically completed, and makes a very fair appearance. It is quite a large roomy affair, with no floor except sand; and of rather flimsy construction, but still adequate, & tastefully fitted up inside with flags. We have better paper, games, newspapers, and a place to sit. Soon we hope to make hot chocolate. But as yet absolutely, or almost absolutely no soldiers have turned up. I feel absolutely useless, as I have felt a good deal of the time since I have been in the French work. During the past three or four days I have been at the point of writing to Bobby Freeman to remind him of his idea that ultimately he would want me for religious work with the America boys, I am at present having an interesting but useless time, which hardly justifies the tonnage required for my transportation. Yet I do not like to be impatient just after they have put me in sole charge of a new post.

On Wednesday my French colleague (or Superior) and I went to the neighboring town on business for the Foyer.[3] It was an interesting ride through a ruined country. The town itself, which

3. It is noted in the margin that the town was "Soissons," which is located 58 miles N.E. of Paris and 33 miles W.N.W. of Reims.

seemed to me the abomination of desolation when I first saw it six weeks ago this time seemed comparatively built up.

Our own village is utterly ruined—mostly by French guns. It was in the hands of the Germans for over two years, the French being perhaps a half a mile off. Not a very good position for architectural intactness! One lovely portal of the church remains, though most of it is a sad heap of stones. German trenches are every where in the vicinity; also splendid deep abris throughout the village. You see signs everywhere such as "abri de bombardement, 40 hommes."[4] Those abris to which you descend by long flights of steps produce a feeling of perfect security. I have been sleeping in one at night, which has the additional advantages of being far drier and freer from rats than my little chamber in the Foyer's basement. Yet I am a little afraid that I might by some be regarded as over cautious. Most people sleep above ground here. But also most people know a good deal better than I when to beat it for cover. When the German planes buzz overhead at night as the shells begin to fall on a neighboring village, I confess that that twenty odd feet of earth and masonry under the ruins of the church is a great help to repose.[5] And yet no shells or bombs have fallen in our village. Even if they do the peril is not as great as it might seem. There were lots & lots of shells fired into a neighboring village the other day without killing a soul, even though many were required by their duty to pass along the road.

Yesterday afternoon I took a most interesting walk with two of the non-commissioned officers who are my companions at table. We went up to the crest of the hill above the village. It commands a fine view of the neighboring river valleys and in the distance a wooded ridge which is in the hands of the Germans. I am not quite sure whether this is not the fist time that I have seen enemy territory, though of course, I have been far closer to it. The ridge of which I speak was some ten miles off. The German front line (invisible) is down somewhere close in front of it. On the heights we saw the bones of several unburied German soldiers. The German positions

4. That is to say in English, "a bomb shelter for forty men."
5. Machen noted in the margin that the neighboring village was "Condé" (short for "Condé-sur-Aisne"), which is about 1.2 miles N.E. of Machen's village of Missy-sur-Aisne.

on the heights were mighty interesting.[6] We entered into their
abris, "postes de commandement," etc.[7] To-day two other obliging
non-commissioned officers took me on a stroll through the former
German first line trenches which run right along the back of a river.[8]

I forgot to say that on Thursday my French colleague and I
visited a neighboring Foyer.[9] Two American directors were there (one
from a near-by place), and we got a chance to exchange experiences.
I certainly enjoyed the chance of relieving my mind before
sympathetic ears. The Americans differed from me in that they know
even far less French, but their experiences in important respects were
similar to mine. One is left, just now, in a desert as I am left, though
his Foyer was very full some weeks ago. What seems strange to me is
that the Foyer authorities seem to go right ahead with the installation
of their Foyer whether or not there are any soldiers to be served by
them. Sometimes opportunities can be made, however. For instance,
when a battery of heavy artillery, which was located about a hundred
yards from the American director's room in the rear of the Foyer
of which I spoke, began firing after midnight at intervals, he seized
the opportunity of spending the night distributing hot chocolate to
the gunners. I am afraid that kind of thing would not have occurred
to me. It is not put down in the official instructions, but it is the
kind of thing perhaps most worth while. And it is really, I hope,
characteristically American.

My position here on a great road gives me an impression of the
tremendous engines of this war that I did not get at my last post.
A regiment or two of soldiers rushing along the road at breakneck
speed in heavy, brute trucks is an impressive sight.[10]

6. A marginal note here comments that this was "Near the Fort de Condé," which is a fort
in Condé-sur-Aisne that was built in the 1870s and 1880s and decommissioned in 1912 (http://
www.cheminsdememoire.gouv.fr/page/affichelieu.php?idLang=&idLieu=4611).

7. The French "postes de commandement" means "command posts" in English.

8. A notation in the margin of the letter describes this river as the "Aisne." The area
around the river Aisne was the scene of three major battles. Machen was working in a hotly
contested part of France. The land between Amiens and Reims provided access to Paris for
the German advance from Belgium, but the Germans were unable to capture the national
capital ("Aisne, Third Battle of The," *Dictionary of the First World War*).

9. This Foyer, according to a note in the margin, was in "Vregny," which is about 4.5 miles
N.E. of Soissons and about 1.5 miles N. from Machen's post in Missy-sur-Aisne.

10. A marginal note comments that, "At time of German drive against the British. It was a
lateral road—i.e. parallel with front." Machen's note is describing the route taken by troops

I am afraid this is a hard, hard place to get letters since there is no civil mail at all. The greatest of love to all. Alas! I have lost my fountain pen. I can do almost nothing with the Foyer pens.

Your loving son,
Gresham

March 28, 1917[11]

My dearest Mother:

My last letter, if I remember rightly, was sent on Monday, the 25th or Tuesday the 26th. It is perhaps about time that I were writing again since leisure is not quite as easy to obtain as it was some weeks ago. Since I arrived at my new post nine days ago I have not received a single letter. Even the soldiers have been cut off for several days. The thing is painful for me not only because of the absence of news from home, but also because I am in great need of funds and am eagerly expecting the proceeds of a check that I sent to Munroe and Co. There are no banking facilities at the front. I have just used up twenty-five francs of my dwindling funds for a fountain pen. The pen proves to be a perfect terror. It is ingeniously fixed so as to do everything that a fountain pen should not do. The loss of my own pen was little short of a calamity. At every turn I miss the loss of that one thing that would really work.

Encouraged by the "planton" who is aiding me in the hut, I started the sale of hot chocolate on Tuesday.[12] The program was

and equipment through his village moving from one portion of the trenches to another. On March 21, 1918, Germany began its Kaiserschlacht, also known as the Michael Offensive. By March 25, the date of this letter, the whole British Fifth Army front had retreated some 25 miles W. while the right wing of the British Third Army moved back as well ("Kaiserschlacht," *Dictionary of the First World War*). What Machen saw on the road was the reorganization and shifting of the Allied Expeditionary Forces (AEF) troops due to the German advance.

11. No, it was actually 1918. The rush and confusion of war is not always conducive to thinking clearly.

12. A "planton" is an orderly.

for me to wait for the coming of a "cantinier" to help me, but I am tired of waiting. To my great surprise the sale of chocolate proved to be an immediate success, despite the very small number of soldiers who frequent the baraque.[13] The first day with twenty litres we did not have nearly enough. The second day we sold about 150 cups. Unfortunately our vessel is not large enough to make over twenty litres at a time, and our tiny little stove heats the twenty litres so slowly that some three hours or so is necessary for the making of twenty litres. We performed the operation twice yesterday. Add to our difficulties the fact that the conceited fellow who had charge of the installation of the Foyer—despite all his cocksureness planned the thing very badly, and you could see that I have my difficulties.[14] The "planton" does fairly well, though since he is very deaf and seldom takes a cigarette-end out of his mouth when he talks communication with him is a little difficult. At least he takes an interest in the business end of the job, and seems to be quite honest. He is also engaged in the work on the completion of the baraque. I don't know what the "installer" of the baraque would say to my taking up so much of the planton's time for kitchen work, but I don't much care. Fortunately I have not yet received the threatened visit of my colleague, though I think he regards himself (quite unwarrantably) as a kind of inspector of a number of Foyers. I am deadly afraid he may show up any time, and when he does I don't know when he will leave. He has a way of lingering.

My pleasure in the sale of our chocolate is spoiled by the fact that we have chocolate for only about four days more. There is a prospect of getting "cacao" at a neighboring Foyer, but "cacao" is awfully poor stuff, and besides I don't know how to make it. It requires the adding of sugar, which chocolate does not. Our chocolate receipt makes the most delicious drink of the kind that I ever tasted.[15]

13. A "baraque" is a shed, stall, or place.
14. Regarding the "conceited fellow," Machen added in the letter margin that he was named "Lecorq (and he has some good qualities)."
15. The word "receipt" has evolved into our current "recipe."

To-day I went to the neighboring large town of which I have often spoken.[16] I did not want to go. The town has been vigorously shelled for some days past—that is, until yesterday when only a few shells, I believe, fell in the town or vicinity. My enthusiasm for such neighborhoods, I confess, is not great. But I have a "permission" to go only on Thursdays, & the needs of the Foyer required me to make the trip. It went off altogether without untoward incident, and without the witness of a single "arrivée."[17] Shell holes were to be seen along (and right in) the road. Especially in one dangerous part. We returned by a safer route. Business was going on as usual in the town. Nobody thinks that a trip like ours is particularly dangerous, & of course lots of men make it every day. The strange thing is how very, very few people get killed by that kind of shell fire. Last night I could plainly hear the German shells passing over us at a great altitude. You could plainly hear their passage through the air, but there was not the slightest sound of their arrival.[18] They must have fallen a long way off. As yet we have been altogether undisturbed, except for noise. A very large gun has started firing at intervals to-day, perhaps a mile off.[19] Even at that distance the concussion of the air is terrific. To call the hideous sensation a "noise" is not to do it justice. It is rather a brutal violation of the two elements, earth & air. I hate it, as I hate the whole business of the war. But I am convinced that in the interests of peace the allies have simply got to win. And I pray that they may be given their righteous victory.

Much love to all. I can't begin to tell you how my heart is with all the loved ones at home, and how anxious I am for news.

Your loving son,
Gresham[20]

16. The marginal annotation says that the town is "Soissons," which is located 58 miles N.E. of Paris and 33 miles W.N.W. of Reims.

17. An "arrivée" is an incoming artillery shell from the enemy.

18. Machen's note in the margin comments, "They were rather probably 'duds'."

19. Machen wrote in the margin that, "One battery of big guns was three-quarters mile off near Condé; another was a half mile off, near Missy."

20. The handwriting of this letter is particularly unclear. It is obvious that, as Machen said at the beginning of the letter, he was very busy and the letter was hastily written.

March 28, 1918

Dear Arly:

Despite my letters from Mother I have been so anxious to hear directly from you and Helen that I am going to drop you a line, in the hope that it may bring a reply. Since I arrived at my new post ten days ago I have not received a single letter from anyone. I am afraid there is some difficulty about the address, there being no civil post here. A registered letter from Munroe and Co. would be exceedingly welcome since my funds are getting scarce. But this is war, and I suppose inconveniences and anxieties of this kind are only what is to be expected. Every day brings me new hope, always followed by new disappointment. I long to hear from home. This is certainly a lonesome life that I am leading. Long before this letter arrives the papers will have told you what an exceedingly anxious time this is in France. Even so insignificant a civilian as I share in the general inquietude.

If anybody wanted to make me really happy just now he could do so by supplying me with about 200 kilos of sweet chocolate. There is a big demand for our drink treat that warms and cheers but does not inebriate. Yesterday for example three captains came in and after partaking of two cups a piece informed their men (who were at our village in passing) of the advantages of our Foyer. The consequence was that we were absolutely swamped with customers, and had to refuse a crowd in the evening. This morning I worked unusually hard, and with our little store succeeded in making forty litres in a little over three hours. You can tell just about how far that will carry us if you remember that the soldiers' tin cups (or "quarts" as they are always called) contain just a quarter liter apiece. Our hut is right on an important road, so that in addition to the men stationed in our containment (now mostly workmen of one kind or other) we receive the visit of passing troops. Not those, however, who pass in autos at high speed, as was the case with the regiment that I knew so well at my last post. In their case all I could do was to wave my hand to old acquaintances as they passed. I wonder how many will return. I certainly am glad that the kindness of a non-commissioned officer has provided me with a nice deep dry cellar or crypt to sleep in. Aside from the greater security, the freedom from rats and the dryness are both highly welcome. The hut of the Foyer is simply reeking with moisture even in the places where the drops do not actually fall during a rain. And the rats are perfectly terrific. I hate to go into our little kitchen after dark, so little do I enjoy the feel of the loathsome creatures on my feet. And even in the daytime they sometimes make themselves thoroughly at home. Our cellar, on the other hand, has not the feel of a cellar at all. A nice flight of stone steps leads directly down to it, and there is plenty of air and even light. I am grateful to my French associate, much as he provoked me in other ways, for putting me on to this opportunity.

For the first time since I arrived in France I really feel as though I were now performing a service, small and humble though it be. The only trouble is that I have enough chocolate for only about two or three days more. Then what? It will not be a pleasant business turning away the crowds. I am afraid I am not much of a manager. If I had enough money of my own to buy some chocolate altogether on my own responsibility I might possibly be able to find it. But my pocketbook is very slim, and Munroe and Co. are far away.

Tell Helen that I am thinking of her, and drop me a line if you can.

Your affectionate brother
J. Gresham Machen

April 2, 1918

My dearest Mother:

My last letter if I remember rightly, was sent Friday March 29 or Saturday March 31. I have received no letter at all since arriving at my present station, except one letter from Mr. Hodges, which came via my old post. Certainly so far as news from home is concerned I am living in a lean and hungry land. But France has other things to think about at the present than the delivery of one poor civilian's mail. The worst of it is that I am afraid my letters to you may be similarly held up. It is useless for me to say how full of love my heart is for you and for all, and how I long to hear that you and Nena are both getting along better.

My life here has been proceeding very much as described in my last letter. After a comfortable night in our "abri" down under the church, I get up at about half past six or seven, get breakfast at about 7.40, and then put in the morning making forty liters of hot chocolate. The chocolate has to be made in two installments, since we have no vessel to contain the whole; but I have now, with the help of my energetic "planton," got the thing reduced to a science, so that not so much time is consumed. The afternoon I put in minding the desk while my planton is at work finishing the interior of the hut and afterwards at five o'clock getting his supper. Incidentally there is time for keeping up my accounts and for writing letters, to say nothing of the opportunities of talking to the men who come in. Lunch and dinner at our popote come at twelve and six-thirty—just the hours when we have the biggest crowds in the hut. I do not like this, since I should greatly prefer to keep the service of the counter more in my own hands. Even when I arrive, my planton does not want to leave his position behind the counter, and since he is a very good fellow I do not want to run too much contrary to his way of doing things. Unfortunately the counter was made so absurdly small that the service cannot be divided, as it ought to be when possible, between two persons.

On Easter Sunday we served 249 cups of hot chocolate.[21] Our ordinary week-day average is apparently going to run over 200 if we can manage to make that much chocolate. So far I have been able to get only little 5-kilo packages at a time. At present I have chocolate only for three more days. This is certainly living from hand to mouth. I am getting nearer and nearer to the point of absolute chocolate famine. In addition to the partaking of the

---

21. As mentioned earlier by Machen, the cups held about 8 ounces, so if each cup was full 249 cups consumed about 15½ gallons.

chocolate the men play checkers, cards, etc., and write letters. They
are not nearly such a checker-playing crowd as the men of our last
post—fortunately so since we have only a few checker-boards. The
Foyer has to be closed at nightfall, since we have neither means
of lighting nor camouflage for the windows. I am personally
rather glad of the early closing, though light would no doubt
be appreciated by the men. Some weeks ago the clocks were all
changed an hour in France in accordance with the daylight saving
plan. It does not get dark, therefore, till about 7.45 o'clock just now.
As for me I sleep well, and enjoy the best digestion that has been
mine for some time. For digestive trouble let me recommend the
battle-front of France! The food is good, and the habit of eating
slowly & sitting around after meals adds to the wholesomeness of
the regime.

Last Saturday night there was considerable excitement. The
Germans fired some fifteen shells into our village or rather the
immediate environs. I was in bed in our abri. About twenty soldiers
joined my "sous-officier" friend and myself, and they did not stand
on the order of their coming.[22] They waited till the bombardment
had ceased for a reasonable time and then left us to continue our
slumber. Most of the men were solid middle-aged fellows, very sleepy
& very bored—just the kind of men who ought to have been living
quietly in the bosom of their families. The war is a horrid, unnatural
kind of thing even in its least horrible aspects. In perfect safety in
our abri we could plainly hear the discharge of the German gun,
then the increasing whistle of the shell in its fifteen or twenty mile
passage through the air, then the explosion. A considerable number
of the shells, however, did not explode. Nobody at all got hurt, and
there has been no continuation of the bombardment. Very different
is the lot of the men, women and children in the neighboring large
town which is bombarded every day.[23] It is comforting to know,
so far as our Foyer hut is concerned, that the Germans are very
unlikely to aim at its immediate vicinity. Their objectives would be
some distance away on either side. This is not going to prevent your

22. A "sous-officier" is a non-commissioned officer.
23. The "neighboring large town" was Soissons, which is located 58 miles N.E. of Paris
and 33 miles W.N.W. of Reims.

This man in a Y-Hut is wearing a gas mask to protect himself from poisonous gas, which was the latest tool to improve killing efficiency. Dr. Machen's mask may have looked like this one, but there were several styles available in the final months of the war. Gas masks were also made for horses and some soldiers adapted human masks for dog mascots. Note that the sign behind the man's head reads, "Our Motto—The Best for the Man in the Mud."
Photo courtesy of Kautz Family Collection, University of Minnesota

humble servant from getting underground as soon as the first shell arrives anywhere near. At any rate I am, I think, far safer here than I would be in Paris. The other day I received a visit from a neighboring American Foyer "director." It was an enormous relief to relieve our minds about the bossy manners of our associates. His words were even more emphatic than mine. My position as professor of theology prevented me from doing full justice to the situation. Evidently my experience is by no means unique. The personalities of the case were partially the same as between this particular American & my self. Perhaps my knowledge of French makes the thing a little harder for me to stomach, because bossing me around is not at all necessary in my case. I say "my knowledge of French" in a relative sense. I am almost the only American Foyer du Soldat director whom I have yet seen who can speak more than a few broken words of the French language. I sometimes think my linguistic attainments are almost useless, as far as my work is concerned, though they are an immense advantage to me personally.

The Colonel dropped into the hut the other day. He was very gracious, and expressed himself as much pleased with the American officers, especially with their lack of false pride and their willingness to profit by the experience even of men of inferior rank.

My lack of news from home seems to keep me—without mere meaningless repetitions—from telling you how deeply concerned I am about Nena's health & about yours and how full my heart is of love for you all. I do hope that the blockade of letters may be lifted before long, or that the hitch may be discovered & removed. Of course you know I am not for a minute hinting that you have not written often enough. The lack of letters is general. At my last post I was getting a letter from somebody or other almost every day.

Your loving son
Gresham

April 4, 1918

My dearest Mother:

Your letter number 10, of March 3, arrived yesterday, and you can be sure that I was glad to receive it. It is the first bit of mail that has come to me here except by way of my old post. And it came in the most curious way, being delivered in quite the wrong village and picked up apparently more or less by chance by

APRIL 4, 1918   81

a messenger of the camp there. Letters number 8 and 9 have not
appeared. At any rate, I have news from home, and that is enough
joy for the present.

Of course I am too deeply concerned about Nena's operation
to be able at all to tell you how I feel. It is an immense relief to
know that the operation seems to have been successful and without
complications. I hope and pray it may prove to be the beginning of
an entirely new era in Nena's health.

As for your own journey, you know how delighted I am to think
of you under the trees at Summerville. May Summerville prove
to be a place of real recuperation! I was going to send a special
message to Uncle & Aunt Bessie on the ground that they were the
only members of the family now with you. But of course you may
have left Summerville before this letter arrives. At any rate do give
my love to Uncle and Aunt Bessie and tell them how glad I am to
know that you either are or have been with them at Summerville.

Oh, what a misfortune to have lost my pen! The ink of the
Foyer is absolutely unusable, so that I cannot employ an ordinary
pen, and this fountain pen is more like a watering-can than a
writing-implement. My last letter, I believe, was sent about Monday,
April 1, though for the life of me I cannot seem to remember to put
down the date of my letters in my note-book.

At any rate, things have proceeded very much as before. I
continue to make about 40 liters of chocolate in the mornings, and
to sell about 200 cups of chocolate in the afternoon and evening.
The Foyer is justifying its existence, and as long as I am let alone I
think I can be fairly useful in a very humble way. I know that I have
not the initiative, gumption, and mix-ability necessary for a real
Y.M.C.A. man. But I can at least plug along with my hot chocolate,
until I am stopped by the arrival of unneeded assistance.

The French director of a Foyer about two miles from here,
who visited me a few days ago, was kind enough to phone me about
the presence of chocolate at an army cooperative store which is
closing out.[24] I purchased 60 kilos, but in order to do so had to

24. A note in the margin designates the village "two miles from here" as "Ciry-Salsogne,"
which is about 65 miles N.E. of Paris and about 25 miles N.W. of Reims. There is no note
regarding the location of the "army cooperative store."

borrow 100 francs of the money from the director in question. The whole thing was a bit of genuine kindness on his part—helpfulness without dictation. He seems to be a different type from those of his colleagues that I have met so far. He is perhaps forty-five or fifty years old, but has the "Croix de Guerre" and seems to be a genuine soldier. I did hate to borrow, but no doubt the money came from Foyer funds and might be repaid by the central office if not by me. My financial condition is precarious. I found that I had by an oversight not sent the check to Munroe and Co., when I thought I had. So it has not yet been a week en route now, and I am doubtful whether the money will ever reach me. Since the funds given me for the Foyer were insufficient, I have had to make advances from my own little store in order to buy the chocolate which keeps us going from day to day. Of course the sales will help to get my money back, but it is a miserable condition to be in. The "direction régionale" or some colleague will help me out if it comes to the worst, but that is humiliating and my pennilessness is most worrisome under the trying and unsettled conditions that prevail now. The move from my old post came just at the worst time—when I was about to replenish my funds.

We have had no return of the shelling of about five days ago, thus being much more fortunate than neighboring villages and towns.

Love to all.
Your loving son,
Gresham

April 4, 1918

Dear Tom:

Mother's letter of March 3, telling of Nena's operation, has just come to hand. I can't begin to tell you how deeply concerned

I am, and how glad to learn that the operation seems to have been successful. My prayer is that it may prove not only to have removed danger, but also to be the beginning of a real recovery of health. I wish I knew whether to write to Nena. But I think I shall, on the chance that she will be well enough to receive letters. The only thing is, I don't know whether I can make her understand that an answer is not to be expected. You can always answer for her. But you too must spare yourself. Mother says you have been heroic under all the care that has been resting upon you. I am glad to hear that the kiddies have at least done their part so far by keeping well.

Lots of mail sent to me recently seems to have been held up somewhere or gone astray. But such things are to be expected. At the present critical time in France, the only wonder is that business is able to go as well as it does. The fate of the nations has certainly been hanging in the balance during the last week or so.[25]

My acquisition of the French language seems to have reached a kind of dead point. I seem at last to have gotten into a rut. Since arriving at my new post I am not sure but that I have gone back rather than improved. Nena would be ashamed of me. Perhaps my mind is too much stuck-up with hot chocolate as my fingers are. But I at least have something to do that seems to be useful so far as it goes. The soldiers that are here at present are for the most part middle-aged men, who are workmen. I am glad that at my last post I had the opportunity of knowing those who were constantly on the firing line.

Since you probably get the news contained in my letters to Mother it is useless for me to write more. I just want to tell you again how deep is my affectionate concern for you & for Nena.

Your affectionate brother,
Gresham

25. Machen here again refers to the Kaiserschlacht offensive that began March 21 (Germany's final spring offensive of the war). On the day that Machen wrote this letter, the Germans directed their final offensive assault towards Amiens ("Kaiserschlacht" and "Chronology," *Dictionary of the First World War*).

April 5, 1918

My dearest Mother:

Your letter no. 8 arrived just after I had answered no. 10. No.
8 is postmarked Feb. 26. It is very sweet, and the fact that I have
already heard of your safe arrival at Summerville reassures me as
I read about the fatigues of packing. Your letter no. 8 arrived with
a considerable batch of other letters, which are not only welcome
in themselves but also reassure me as to the practicability of the
address which I have given to the Paris office and to Munroe and
Co. I have some hopes of hearing from the letter in a few days. It
will be an immense relief. I shall not again let myself get into such
financial straits.

One of the letters was from Bobby Robinson. It told me of
the safe arrival for Harold M. A. Robinson, Jr., and of the happy
way in which all is progressing in the family. I feel very happy over
the good news. Bobby is exceedingly busy writing Sunday School
lessons for Faris—with more success than I had—and also plans to
do Y.M.C.A. work in the camps. Of course he envies my chance to
be in France. I have told him that the opportunities are not always
greater here than they are at home.

Brooke's services are much needed in France. It is interesting
to hear of his safe arrival. I hope he and his comrades may soon
give us a decisive superiority in the air.

I have just gotten the first hair-cut that I have had since leaving
Paris, "Je me suis fait couper les deuilles." There is some "argot" that
you can make out if you like. But really I don't have confidence in
the grammar of the verb part of the sentence. I am not very strong
on reflexive verbs.[26]

If there is one rule of modern hygiene which we do not break
in making and distributing our chocolate, I don't know what it
is. In the first place to my mind I make the vessel out to be of
earthenware instead of metal. In the second place the water that
we have been using is only "eau passable." That is better than "eau

26. In this paragraph, Machen is experimenting with his use of French. His meaning has
not been determined.

mauvaise," but I should prefer "eau potable," despite the incidental boiling.[27] In the third place, although the men are supposed to bring their own "quarts" with them, as a matter of fact many of them do not, so that we have to use a few of our own over & over again with a purely perfunctory washing in the same old water. And so forth, ad infinitum. To all this there is but one answer: "Ou'est-ce que vous voulez? C'est la guerre."[28]

I think I have exhausted the possibilities as to pen and ink since I lost my fountain pen. I have tried to write with the ink of the Foyer, which I made by mixing with water a thing wrapped up like Dover's Powder.[29] As well try to write with water without the Dover's Powder. I have tried to write with the fountain pen purchased at a neighboring town. This is the most clearly impossible of all. That pen is more like a watering can than a writing implement. Finally I have tried the Foyer's pen dipped in what remains of my fountain pen ink. This is the best yet devised, though some of my letters written in accordance with it look like the Codex Ephraemi rescriptus.[30]

Saturday, April 6

The chocolate problem having just been solved for about two weeks I am in desperate straits as regards condensed milk. To my consternation the cooperative here announced to-day that all their milk was gone. I do not have enough even for the chocolate of to-day. So this afternoon immediately after lunch I went on a

27. Tolerable water is "eau passable"; "eau mauvaise" is bad water; and "eau potable" is drinkable water.

28. "Ou'est-ce que vous voulez? C'est la guerre," means "What would you expect? This is war."

29. "Dover's Powder" is named for Thomas Dover, who developed this opium-based medication in 1732. It was commonly used in the United States and Europe. It was taken as a non-prescription pain medication for over two hundred years. Excessive use, as with any opiate, led to addiction (see "Dover's Powder," at: http://www.bookrags.com/research/dovers-powder-edaa-01/). Machen's comment about "a thing wrapped up like Dover's powder" alludes to the wrapping of a dose of the powder in a small waxed paper envelope similar to that used for B. C. headache powders. The "thing" in the wrapper was most likely carbon black powder, which if it had been mixed with thinned linseed oil would have provided a suitable ink that has been used by writers and printers for centuries.

30. This is the last in the group of the four great uncial manuscripts of the Greek Bible. It is known for its obliterated and nearly indecipherable writing.

search to a neighboring cooperative. Alas twelve cans was all that I could obtain. That will not even carry me through to-morrow without skimping. There is some chance of getting more from a neighboring Foyer du Soldat, but the uncertainty is alarming. The shortage seems to be general. Everybody is on a search for lait condensé.[31] I am certainly weary after lugging the twelve cans three miles or so to-day.

Yesterday was a bigger day than usual at the Foyer; we sold over 300 cups of chocolate, and we could have sold more if we had made more. I should enjoy the increase in our work more if I had the lait condensé. Of course there were special reasons for the crowd yesterday—"troupes de passage"—but even on ordinary days we are going to have to hustle to supply the demand.[32] I have just got to skimp the milk for to-morrow. I hate to do it, but nobody may notice the difference and I want to do my best to satisfy the crowd.

Spring is sharing itself a little. The blossoms in the midst of ruined villages seem to express the contrast between the goodness of God and the wickedness of man. Even before I left my last post the violets had begun.

Love to all.
Your affectionate son
Gresham

April 7, 1918

My dearest Mother:

Since my letter sent yesterday I am made very rich by receiving, not only your no. 9 (thus making the series complete up through no. 10), but also a letter of March 9, which, though not numbered, is probably no. 11. No. 11 (or March 9) is especially fine. It is in

31. The French "lait condensé" means "condensed milk" in English.
32. The "troupes de passage" are "passing troops."

answer to my first letter after I left Paris and it gives me a most encouraging and most refreshing account of your life under the trees at Summerville. You can have no idea how much good that letter has done me. I just love to think of you as chasing a blue-jay, listening to the mocking-birds and regaining something of the health and strength which you need for the benefit of all of us.

The news about Nena encouraged me greatly. Of course I know that an anxious time remains before the good effects of the operation may be expected to appear, but at least it is an immense relief to hear that the operation itself has been undergone successfully. I certainly sympathize most deeply with Tom.

It is also good to hear that Helen and Uncle are recovering from their recuperative troubles. Evidently it has been a hard winter for all of our family circle.

Yesterday was a Sunday of hard work for me. We sold 378 cups of hot chocolate, and I can tell you both the making and the selling kept me busy from morning till night. A crowd of soldiers from a neighboring village who were employed here for the day on some special work added to the rush. To-day the same crowd was on hand in the morning long before our formal hour of opening (11 A.M.), and we did our very best to hustle up the making of the chocolate in order to satisfy them. The weather has been cold and rainy, so that on that account something hot, I suppose, was doubly welcome. However, the complete absence of water makes something or other to drink essential at all times, and the chocolate was nearest at hand. The worst of it is that I was afraid this useful work may have to stop for lack of materials. The central organization of the Foyer seems not to have succeeded in establishing any regular system of supply. The consequence is that the individual Foyer director has to be chasing around the country and do the "direction régionale" work seeking letter paper, chocolate, condensed milk, and other necessities.[33] Obviously this method is enormously wasteful. It is highly important that I for example should stick to my post. I am working hard all day right here. The worst of it is that if I should go to the "Direction regionale" there would be no assurance that anybody would be in the office when I got there. They have no

33. The "direction régionale" is the regional office of the YMCA work.

phone unless one has been installed very recently. And they will not write letters. It is not the fault of the director, I think. But they are under manned. The individual "Foyers" are often over-manned, and the central offices under-manned. That is my capital criticism of the organization. There should be a regular weekly supply system. It would save the time of the directors and also waggon-space in the end.

I wish I could hear from Munroe & Co. But since a communication of theirs dated March 22 has just recently come to hand I suppose I shall have to wait long for the all-important letter.

The patter of the rain is not a very cheerful sound when the roof leaks in a hundred places. That's been our situation for several days of wet and rain. My, but it is wet and miserable to-day. At night, our cellar is dry. But one of the two new "sous-officiers" who are now occupying it with me carefully stuffed a sock or other article of clothing into the one air-hole that made respiration possible in the little 8 x 6 foot apartment! The enmity of the French people to fresh air beats everything I ever saw. The only wonder is that that apartment is as habitable as it is. I think there must be chinks communicating with some more extensive crypt.[34] At least there are no rats. The rats in our baraque are terrific. We have suspended our bag of sugar from cords, and at night I place the box of chocolate on top of a tin basket. But I do not know how long these measures of protection will be efficacious. The production of rats in the ruined villages of France and in the trenches is appalling. After the present strife is over I believe the entire human race will have to unite in a war on the great German army of rodents.

Love to all.
Your loving son
Gresham
(Finished April 8)

---

34. The "chinks" refer to cracks in the walls or gaps between boards. The "more extensive crypt" would be another room beyond the "chinks."

5

A River of Hot Chocolate Flowing at Missy-sur-Aisne[1]

April 12 to May 6, 1918

As the routine duties of the Foyer worker continues, Dr. Machen enjoys serving as the director without the personality conflict of his previous post. He finds his hardworking helper and friend, Montí, a competent, self-starting, and dedicated laborer. The two would make and distribute gallons of hot chocolate daily to the cold, damp, and war-weary soldiers. The new post would allow Machen freedom as the director, but his labors will be hampered due to dental problems, a defective phonograph, a leaky roof, and intermittent shortages of supplies.

April 12, 1918

My dearest Mother:

My last letter, I believe was written about April 8, in answer to your No. 11. Since then the days have been slipping by very much as before. Monday, Tuesday and Wednesday were big days for the salve

1. "Missy-sur-Aisne" means in English "Missy on the Aisne."

of chocolate; on Tuesday, for example, we sold nearly five hundred cups. I think the simple service that we perform is appreciated by the men. Fortunately I now have a fair provision of chocolate and of condensed milk, though after about a week or less the problems will again become acute. Yesterday, the man who installed the Foyer here sent me (in addition to a little chocolate, which was very welcome) a big box of sugar. When I saw that sugar arrive I was pretty nearly in despair. Almost three weeks ago the same man sent me a perfectly enormous bag of sugar. For this big stock I have absolutely no use so long as the supply of sweet chocolate lasts, and it makes me just sick to see so very scarce and valuable an article put where it will do no good and is in imminent danger of being reported. I have tried every means within my power to keep the rats out of the sugar, but without avail. At last some obliging men got some heavy wire and hung the thing from the central beam of the roof. This may be efficacious so far as the rats are concerned (though they seem to be able to jump), but I am afraid the sugar will get wet when it rains since the roof leaks terribly. Every night we put the chocolate-box on top of a metal bucket, but one night the rats got into it there. They also jumped from above into the chocolate that we put on top of the oil stove. You can imagine my dismay when I saw a heavy and useless box of sugar arrive yesterday. We have put it (most inconveniently) on top of the metal vessel that contains our oil. I do wish that fellow would leave me alone. The American regional director tells me that the fellow's connection with my Foyer is "merely nominal" & that I alone am director here. But the trouble is that the man in question does not regard his position here as merely nominal. If he arrives again and tries to take complete charge even of details as he did before it will be unfortunate for my relations with everyone in the cantinnement. The thing needs further cleaning up. I am not the only one, by the way, who has run up against the difficulty. In contrast to the bossy ways of the young fellow of whom I have been speaking is to be put the considerate kindness of a French director of a neighboring foyer who has given me genuine help in a number of ways.

One of the mistakes of some of the Foyer directors is in supposing that an American gets along better with the military authorities if he is trailed around like a baby in a go-cart.[2] Nothing could be further from the fact. The kindness of the French officers is called forth just exactly by the fact that it is a foreigner who is trying to help the men. Yesterday for example I applied to an "intendant" (who holds the rank of "commandant," corresponding to our major) for some coal for the Foyer.[3] Nothing could exceed his kindness to make an official trip with me in his automobile to our village to see our building, then he said he would fill out the necessary procés-verbal himself to save me all possible trouble.[4] All I had to do was to sign a simple paper, and the coal is mine any time I call for it. All this special kindness was shown me entirely without solicitation on my part. I don't believe the officer would have thought it worth while to do as much for one of his own countrymen. Yet he didn't seem to think it a nuisance at all.

Our "direction régionale" has just been moved in order to escape the constant bombardment of the town where it has been located up to the present.[5] The new location is nearer to us. In securing the "lait condensé" which was left for me at the neighboring Foyer of which I have already spoken, I made the trip on a borrowed bicycle.[6] Although the place is only two miles or so from here it is very different in appearance—not being much demolished—and contains a considerable civil population. At the moment when I arrived the good French director was running the phonograph in the Foyer for a crowd of children. It was quite refreshing to see them, after the depressing atmosphere of a military camp. I also visited the civil post-office to replenish my stock of postage stamps. Everybody else here in the cantinement of course possesses the "franchise militaire," so that postage stamps are not to be obtained.[7]

2. Today, a "go-cart" is a small, engine-propelled sporting vehicle, but what Machen describes is what we would think of as a child's wagon or a carriage.

3. Machen's marginal note commented that the coal was obtained at "the Gare de Missy-Condé." A "Gare" is a station and Machen must be referring to the railroad station in the village of Missy-Conde, where coal would be stored for trains.

4. The "procés-verbal" is a requisition form.

5. The marginal note comments, "From Soissons to Braisne." This was a move of about 4.7 miles to the E.S.E. of Soissons.

6. According to the marginal note, "the neighboring Foyer" was in "Ciry-Salsogne," which is about 65 miles N.E. of Paris and about 25 miles N.W. of Reims.

7. The "franchise militaire" is the military's exemption from having to pay postage.

Bobby's letter of Feb. 24 has just shown up long after letters which were written weeks afterwards. So you will understand that there are irregularities in the postal service. I have not yet gotten the all-important letter from Munroe & Co. Fortunately my personal expenses here are at most nil. But I should like to be more independent.

I have worn one uniform ever since leaving Paris. And it is now all spotted up with hot chocolate. The washing that I have had done here has served to leave the cloth rather wet, but not very clean. My effort to secure a regular bath has not been crowned with success, but I still have hope. I am not sure whether the baths that I took at my last post were much in the interest of cleanliness. Clean water is rather a scarce commodity in these ruined villages.

As yet I have not been as successful as I should like to be in getting really acquainted with individuals among the men. I have conversed some with one user of our library who admires Poe very greatly. He says that the French translator of Poe is a very distinguished writer. I have now forgotten his name. That shows me up all right! Also I have helped out another man in his English studies and incidentally talked to him a little on serious subjects. But for the most part I am a cook and nothing more. And I like it for a change. More, perhaps, than for years, I feel a desire for New Testament study. I certainly did need a change. The hand of a good providence may perhaps even now be detected in the decision of the Paris authorities. If God wills I may return to the preaching of the gospel with new appreciation of its privileges just because for a time I have been engaged in a totally different kind of work.

You know how full of love my heart is for all at home, and how I long to receive good news.

Your loving son
Gresham

April 15, 1918

My dearest Mother:

Although I cannot remember when I wrote my last letter, I feel quite sure that it is now high time to be writing another. After the riches of a week or ten days ago when letters from America arrived in regular packets I have been without news for some time. The worst of it is that these irregularities make themselves felt just as much, no doubt, in the case of mail going in the appropriate direction.

One very welcome letter, however, has arrived from Munroe & Co. My slight financial embarrassment (which really only amounted to a risk of future embarrassment) has now been removed. The embarrassment was the less because my personal expenses here are almost nil.

On Sunday, April 14, our sales of chocolate amounted to 476 cups, and even on week days they run now generally well above 400. I take a childish pleasure in watching the business grow. At my last post I thought I was doing well if I sold 60 cups; at the beginning here it was 150 to 180; and now just look at the magnificent figures. The worst of it is that my little stock of lait condensé will last only through to-day and chocolate is also almost gone. This afternoon I must go on a hunt for more.

The success of this Foyer, so far as it has any, is due very largely to Montí. Montí is my planton. He is not much to look at, and he is hard of hearing, but he has turned out to be a perfect treasure. In the first place, I am convinced that he is perfectly honest. In the second place, he has a genuine interest in the work of the Foyer and seems to like to work. For instance he objected that I did not get him started early enough. So now I give him the key of the baraque so that he can enter while I am at breakfast. He is hard at work at 7.20 A.M. and does not finally knock-off till about 8 P.M. He does more work in one day than the regular "cantinier" whom I had at my last post did in ten. In the third place, that boy has got brains. He not only uses them in practical ways in keeping the place in order and running the business, but alas he actually plays

A quaint village that has not suffered the destruction of some of the towns in which Dr. Machen worked. Some YMCA workers are shown giving soldiers a tour.
Photo courtesy of Kautz Family Collection, University of Minnesota

a good game of checkers. We play sometimes in the afternoons when business is slack. French checkers is a much better game than American checkers. I hope to introduce it to America. It has something of the variety interest of chess without being so long.

Two things are to be feared. In the first place, they may take my Montí from me. They have a perfect right to do so at any moment, since he is just a "detail" and not a cantinier.[8] In the second place the Foyer authorities may put another director in here with me.

Two days ago I got in a new stock of coal. The place where I had arranged to get it, about a half or three-quarters of a mile from here having been under rather serious bombardments (or

8. Montí, a French soldier, was assigned the task of assisting Machen at the Foyer as part of his military duty. A "detail" is one assigned to a specific task or duty. A "cantinier" is a canteen worker.

near to bombardments). I was told that all the provisions for the cantinnement were to be sought at another station. But when I presented myself there with a waggon, three men informed me that the coal was still at the old place. So we had to go to that rather evil spot after all. Fortunately the weather was rather thick, and the Germans did not start bombarding at all that day. But I was glad when that coal was safely in the bin. It will last me for twenty days.

You know how much love every one of my letters carries to all, & how I long to get good news.

Your loving son
Gresham

P.S. Excuse chocolate on first page. Please regard it as a souvenir. I am spotted with chocolate from head to toe. J.G.M.

April 19, 1918

My dearest Mother:

Again I forgot to note the date of my last letter, but I know it was about three or four days ago. The absolute dearth of letters from America is still continuing here. When news does come at last, I trust it will be good news, as it was after the last long period of silence.

On Tuesday I made a trip on a borrowed bicycle to the Direction régionale, which had recently been moved from the town which has been subject to bombardment to a small town which is a little closer to my post.[9] My conference with the authorities was most satisfactory. The American director who

9. A note in the margin comments that the headquarters was moved "From Soissons to Braisnes." From Machen's Foyer in Missy-sur-Aisne to Braine (the editor could find no village named "Braisnes" that was closer to Machen's Foyer than Soissons) is a distance of about 6.5 miles.

is in charge of the material for the cantines expressed himself
as interested in my work, and desirous of helping me out in the
victualling of my Foyer. A plan has been instituted by which the
American director of a neighboring Foyer is to make weekly
trips in a waggon to the Direction régionale in the interest of
my Foyer as well as his own. A beginning was made this week
by bringing me a box of chocolate and five boxes of condensed
milk, which will last me about a week. Next week I am to have a
phonograph, more letter paper, more checker games, a big sign
for the outside of the Foyer, and last but not least a Norwegian
"marinite." A Norwegian marinite is a big vessel containing, I
should say, fifty litres, which is placed inside of an outer covering
of metal—thus forming a sort of gigantic thermos bottle, which
is said to retain the heat of the contents for twenty four hours. At
present, what forces us to say "All served," so far as the chocolate
is concerned is the lack of room in our vessels. At six o'clock,
all our available vessels, even a little bucket and a little pitcher,
are full of chocolate. But this supply is often insufficient for the
evening rush; and after the vessels are half emptied, it is too late
to make more. With our marinite we ought to be able to make
adequate provision not only for the evening rush but also for the
early hours of the next morning. Although the official hours of
opening are from eleven till seven-thirty, we are usually, thanks to
the energy of Montí, able to serve chocolate before nine o'clock in
the morning, and we do not close in the evening till the light of
day deserts us.

The most encouraging thing about my trip to the direction
régionale was the discovery that really there is now some hope
of a steady and sufficient supply of the necessities—chocolate,
condensed milk and letter paper. We need per day nearly ten kilos
of chocolate and 20 cans of condensed milk—which are necessary
to make one hundred litres of our hot drink.[10] Yesterday we sold 470
cups of chocolate, and would easily have surpassed our record of
476 cups if we had sufficient room in our vessels to make provision
for the evening rush.

10. A "kilo" is about 2.2 pounds, so Machen needed 22 pounds of chocolate every day.

Sunday, April 21.

Two days have elapsed since I began my letter, there being
many interruptions. I am afraid there may be a considerable gap in
your receipt of news. Yesterday a batch of papers arrived for me, but
the letters that accompanied them, with the one notable exception
of a belated letter of Uncle's of Feb. 22, were uninteresting.

Things have run on very much as usual. I have some slight
hopes of getting the holes stopped up in our roof, but as yet
nothing has been done. The weather has been very cold and often
wet. We had a little snow the day before yesterday. I have come to
the conclusion that summer is colder than winter in France.

Yesterday I saw a "sausage" burned much closer to me than I
had seen the night before. A "saucisse" is a captive balloon.[11] The
German airplane could be plainly seen to approach the saucisse,
which was moored only a mile or so from us. The saucisse at once
burst into flames & descended. The "observer" in it however had
had time to take refuge in his parachute & descended, it is to be
hoped unhurt. In the escape of the German some thought he was
hit by an anti-aircraft shell. This is very doubtful, though he did
descend at one point of his course rather suddenly.

Conversation at the "popote," so far as I was concerned, was
in danger of languishing, until a few days ago when a JOKE was
developed. This joke is capable of infinite development—far more
so than the Wright & Dutson joke and even more than the spinach
joke. The joke consists in the fiction of a battle between the good
cheer on the one hand & the health of the company on the other.
It began by an attack of indigestion in my case begun by épinards
& confitures bordelaises.[12] Every time those preserves come on the
table I can now remark on the time of the communiques—"Coup
de main assez vigoureux des confitures bordelaises. Journée calme
___ le reste du front." And so on "ad infinitum." You have no idea
what a help this joke has been.

11. The word "sausage" is English for the French word "saucisse." This slang term for
observation balloons was adopted due to their elongated shape.

12. The French word "épinards" means "spinach," while "confitures" means "jams." However,
how "bordelaises"—a red wine based sauce—relates to "confitures" is not clear to the editor.

But if I am to catch the "cycliste" who carrries my letters I must close abruptly & not launch ____ upon the boundless sea of confitures bordelaises joke.[13]

The best of love to all. And how I wish I had news.

Your loving son
Gresham

April 25, 1918

My dearest Mother:

After having addressed my mail correctly for a time, the Paris office of the Y.M.C.A. has suddenly and without rhyme or reason begun sending my things again to the address which I abandoned some four weeks ago. Fortunately the two places are close together, and the "direction regionale" acted as an assembling point. Indeed the mail addressed wrongly has apparently reached me more quickly than that which was addressed according to Hoyle.[14] At any rate I am wonderfully rich in the possession of three new letters from you—namely Nos. 12, 13, and 14 of March 16, March 24, and March 28. I have just given myself the refreshment of reading them all three over once more. They are sweet and lovely letters. The news they contain is partly good, partly bad. The bad is contained in the last letter, which tells of the cold which you caught just before starting for home. That was most distressing, but I am glad at least that you did not have the horror of a journey in such a condition. The good news concerns Helen, who seems

13. The French "cycliste" refers to a bicyclist, which in this case is the mail carrier's conveyance.
14. "According to Hoyle" refers to the published works on gaming by Edmund Hoyle (1672–1769). Thus, Machen's use of "according to Hoyle" was a common saying that meant according to the rules of the game.

to have gotten well over her attack of grippe, and Nena.[15] The
news about Nena in the first letter (and in the enclosed letter
of Tom which I appreciated greatly) was most encouraging;
and although in the last letter the "good" is lowered to "fairly
good" I feel somewhat reassured and cheered. I do wish I had
more time to write to Arly, Helen, Tom and Nena; for although
I mean to write to them through you I am afraid they all get the
impression that I am not thinking of them every one with special
and individual affection. The conditions under which my letter
writing is carried on here make me think of your expression at
home where constant interruptions double and triple the labor.
Every few minutes I have to stop to serve a cup of chocolate or
give out a pack of cards or a library book. The library is the
biggest interruption of all, since by the bad judgment of the man
who arranged the hut the director is obliged to have the counter
entirely in order to reach the cup-board that contains the
books. The whole thing was planned just about as badly as could
possibly have been imagined. That conceited fellow certainly has
a lot to learn. But he is too conceited ever to learn it. Meanwhile
I am the sufferer. But, to return to pleasanter subjects, I must
mention the perfectly splendid long letter that I have received
from Loy. It is one of the most truly Christian letters that I ever
received—not in the sense that there is any preaching in it, but
in the simple and modest recital of Loy's own attitude toward the
work to which God has devoted him. He gave me a full account
of what he is doing in the Salem church.[16] It is just splendid, and
I am sure that it possesses far more value from the divine point
of view than many more shiny achievements. There is not a bit of
wood, hay or stubble about it.[17]

15. The word "grippe" was used to describe influenza and/or diseases with flu-like symptoms.
Beginning in 1918 and into 1919 there was a horrible influenza epidemic that killed about
30 million people worldwide including roughly 550,000 Americans ("Influenza,"*The Oxford
Companion to United States History*, Paul S. Boyer, ed., Oxford: Oxford University Press, 2001).

16. Rev. Leroy Gresham would serve as the pastor of the Presbyterian Church in Salem,
Virginia, from 1909 until he retirred in 1946. See E. C. Scott, *Ministerial Directory of the Presbyterian Church, U.S., 1861–1941* (Austin: By Order of the General Assembly, 1942); and E. C.
Scott, *Ministerial Directory of the Presbyterian Church, U.S., 1891–1941 Revised and Supplemented
1942–1950* (Atlanta: By Order of the General Assembly, 1950).

17. Dr. Machen alludes to 1 Corinthians 3:12 when he uses "wood, hay, or stubble."

Last Monday, a day earlier than was expected, supplies arrived from the "direction régionale," including our phonograph and our "marmite norvégienne."[18] Both proved to be big disappointments—especially the "phono," which broke the spring that runs it in the evening of the very first day.[19] There are plenty of mechanical experts in camp, and the machine was patched up. But it soon broke down again, and was evidently defective. Since the phono had doubled the attendance in the hut the breakdown was a disappointment. But we hope to have another (second-hand) in a few days. The "marmite norvégienne" also was disappointing, though to a lesser degree. I hope the marmite is going to be all right as a marmite, but as a marmite norvégienne it seems to be a disastrous failure. Montí and I were happy that first evening; for we thought the difficult problem of providing hot chocolate in the morning was at last solved. But we discovered that the novice in the kitchen has a lot to learn; the thermos bottle qualities of the marmité, which are supposed to retain heat for twenty-four hours, proved to be a delusion and a snare. When we opened the marmité in the morning the odor that greeted us was awful, and the taste was worse than the odor. Montí and I retained the effects of both all day. At my last post I kept chocolate perfectly good even for three or four days, but I have now discovered that it must be allowed to cool overnight. To-day we are boiling water with potatoes & carrots in it in that marmité. It seems that is the way to get the metal taste out of a new vessel, and it will also, I hope, remove the vestiges of that awful chocolate.

It is going to be impossible to have the whole of our roof repaired. But I hope to keep the rain out of that end of the hut that is to house our letter-paper and phono and other supplies. The cook at the popote proves to be a professional flower-nursery gardener, and he is at work preparing the ground in front of the Foyer for the reception of some seeds. A little beautification is certainly needed, since the hut is situated in the midst of a muddy

18. The "marmite norvégienne" is a Norwegian designed cooking-pot used to make the hot chocolate.
19. The word "phono" is short for "phonograph." The phonograph was powered by a spring that was wound up with a hand-crank.

piece of ground well plowed-up by horses' hoofs. A little touch of color in front will be much more suggestible of a real "foyer."

The attendance at the Foyer has not been quite so good as during the previous week, but this is probably due to the fact that there have been fewer men passing along the road or fewer workmen near at hand. Yesterday we sold only 399 cups of chocolate. Montí thought we might have taken an extra cup ourselves & paid for it to make 400 cups for the day; but I did not want to juggle the figures. In addition to the games of cards and checkers we have a little library. I have never yet made the catalogue or covered the books as advised by men of experience. But the books are fairly well in use. I am adopting the rash policy of lending the books without requiring a deposit. A neighboring French secretary has this policy, and his example has emboldened me to do an unorthodox thing. I also abandoned the two franc deposit required by my associate for use of ink-well, blotter, and pen-holder. We retain a deposit for checker-games and games of cards. The dinner-hour at our popote represents a great difficulty for me, since it comes just at the time when we have the biggest crowd at the Foyer. But I have now secured a second poilu to help for the evening hours. He will run the "phono" for example after we secure it. My regular assistant, Montí, is just splendid. I don't know when I have seen a boy with whom I get along better, and so far as the work goes he is a tower of strength. The other day he told me a little about his experiences in the war. They would put the trials and sufferings of epic days far in the sheds. Every now and then the pathos of the whole business strikes a person. Here is this boy with almost his whole time of youth spent in the rough and unnatural life of the front, and his hearing if not his health in general has been sacrificed. It is no wonder that these fellows have a longing for the ordinary life of boys. Night before last they got up a game of "association football" (which the French play much more than Americans do).[20] The whole eleven came in after the game & drank a couple of rounds of our chocolate. They were as full of that game (against some other unit) as a crowd of Americans would be. The captain, especially, is a nice-looking fellow, very much like one of our American boys. What I would like to know is, "Where in the world is the France of caricature." I have seen

20. "Association football" is what Americans would call "soccer."

nothing of it. Far from being over-sentimental I find the French an exceedingly reserved people, with whom it is not in place to be too effusive on short acquaintance. And these boys are surprisingly like our own boys at home. But the larger part of the men here are not boys, but middle-aged fellows, who, I think, might be designated by the term pépère.[21]

Yesterday (or day before) I made a satisfactory trip to our direction régionale, which seems to be working well. They are going to give me not only all the chocolate & condensed milk that I want, but also some good games—a kind of bowling game and the frog game, where you try to throw something into the frog's mouth. Montí being an expert on sports I anticipate no difficulty in getting these things started. He will have no difficulty enlisting the fellows of his own "unité" first & others will follow.[22]

My deadly fear is that the threatened visit of the "installer" will come off. It is threatened for next week. If he gets to giving orders to my assistants here & generally legislating for me as he did before, my temper is going to be seriously tried. As it is I am having a busy and correspondingly satisfactory time. I do hope present conditions may continue. Good hard work all day—that's what I came over here for and that's what I am getting at last.

Love to all.
Your loving Son
Gresham

April 29, 1918

My dearest Mother:

Lots of letters ought to be answered to-day, but the most pressing duty is my letter to you. My last letter, I believe, was sent

21. The French "pépère" means "grand dad" or "grandpa."
22. The English "unit" translates the French "unité."

on Thursday, April 25, and it was an unusually long letter in answer to three lovely letters of yours. I have not had much time to write letters during the past three days.

Thursday, April 25, was our record day for the sale of chocolate; we sold 510 cups.[23] But the next two days we fell below 400 cups—a thing that Montí and I regard as a disgrace. A new "phono" replacing the broken one arrived the other day. It is rather a cheap, poor instrument, but it does seem to give pleasure to the poilus. The sound does not carry very well in our large hut, with its dirt floor. As Montí remarked, our "phono" is "aphone."[24] Still, the crowd gathers around it and seems to have a good time. Yesterday our chocolate figures attained the fairly respectable mark of 490.

To my surprise, no less than four carpenters got busy in the hut the other day and put in some very necessary shelves and a door for a little cupboard.

Yesterday, while I was at lunch at a popote to which I had been invited for a meal, the three regional directors—one American and two French—appeared on the scene. Fortunately one of my assistants was able to find me. The exalted personages seemed to be satisfied with the way the Foyer is running, and promised to seek the help of the "génie" for all the changes that I need in the baraque.[25] The worst of it is that the moving of the door—which is a necessary step in almost any changes that might be made—will necessitate the breaking up of the nice little flower-beds that have now been made by our obliging gardener on either side of the present entrance. At any rate the génie, I trust, will be able to repair the roof. The rain which fell last night certainly did play billy with the inside of our hut.[26] I was rather tickled when the American regional director agreed with me that the present arrangement of the cantine is about the most footless thing ever seen. I like that director. He encouraged me, & is going to try to get me a new grate for our stove. We

23. This would be 32 gallons if the cups were 8 ounces, but that seems like a great deal of hot chocolate.
24. The word "aphone" is French for "voiceless."
25. Here "génie" refers to an engineer or administrative person.
26. To "play billy" is to cause trouble.

broke the old one the other day. These little mishaps are serious in our present environment.

Last night and this morning we had a series of mishaps:

(1) The rain played billy with the hut, and the moisture spoiled lots and lots of our envelopes, which can no longer be opened.

(2) The rats ate our chocolate despite the fact that it was suspended by a wire from the roof.

(3) Our coal is running low. Montí says I will soon have to look for more. Fortunately the coal station is not bombarded.

(4) Twenty litres of chocolate spoiled over night. Defective condensed milk caused this mishap; the same thing has been happening at a neighboring Foyer. We could not serve the morning crowd to-day, and were altogether late and deranged about all our business.

(5) A filling which has fallen out of a tooth, will cause the death of the director of this Foyer unless a dentist can be found pretty soon. Montí thinks that this will be a far less serious loss than the loss of the chocolate. I differ with him there.

And so it goes. The Boches are now not dropping anything at all our way and we are generally having a busy, humdrum, chocolaty time.[27] My companion in the cellar where I sleep reports that in my sleep the other night I spent a good part of the night crying, "Monsieur, vous a'avez peu votre quart?"[28] I am proud to know that I talk French in my sleep, but wrong to disturb my associate in the hut.

I am not learning any French at all, despite wonderful opportunities. It is a marvel to me how you and Arly, without opportunities have learned to understand the language. I really believe I am going backwards instead of advancing. Yet here I have been in France for three months.

April has been almost uniformly rainy and cold, in contrast to March, which was warm and sunny. Flowers and fruit blossoms

27. "Boches" is a slang and derogatory term for the Germans.
28. In English, Machen's question reads, "Sir, would you like to have some in your quart?" The tedious and time consuming job of making and serving chocolate was getting the best of him.

are coming out in the midst of the desolation. Also there are birds with strange plumage—not catalogued in the North American bird book.

Love & lots of it to all. How I long for good news.

Your loving son,
Gresham

May 4, 1918

My dearest Mother:

The pile of letters that I ought to answer is still waiting for my attention, but again my first duty is to maintain my correspondence at the most important point of all. My last letter, I think, was written about the beginning of the week, and here it is Saturday already. All I have been able to do about my other correspondence is to write a line to Dr. Patton expressing my sympathy for him on account of the death of his son "Jack" of which a letter from Army has informed me. I always did get Dr. Patton's sons confused—you know my deficiency about such matters—but this son, I suppose, was the one that has been sick so long. He was buried at Princeton, Mister Hodge conducting the service. Dr. Patton was in Bermuda, but there is some chance of his being in America at about the time of present writing.

On Tuesday I went to the dentist at a big military hospital about four miles from here. A big amalgam filling had gone to pieces. The dentist put in something hot temporarily—the only temporary filling, I believe that I ever had really stay in—and I am to go again to-day to have the tooth refilled. It is rather disappointing after the hundreds of dollars that I expended in America before leaving and the large force of specialists that was required to put me in proper condition for departure.

Just as I was turning in to that hospital I met the "installer" of my Foyer, who was on his way to visit me. I pled dental necessities instead of returning with him. I certainly am glad to have escaped his visit. On the same trip I visited the direction régionale & got some more phonograph records. Our phono is now running all right.

Montí helped me a little with my monthly report in French. One sentence had to be cut out—though it contained one of the most important things that I had to say—because Montí thought it made no sense whatever. My report is very concise—quite on the "veni, vidi, vici" order.[29] It shows an average daily consumption of 358 cups of chocolate during April (or something like that), and a maximum of 510. My financial report is not yet made—the necessary blanks not having arrived. That financial report is going to be "quite a chore," or, to translate, a "lourde corvée."

The attendance at the Foyer is displaying a tendency to dwindle; yesterday we sold only 294 cups of chocolate. Montí is disgusted and I am a bit disappointed too. But these are big variations. Every now and then we have a big day, though the tendency during the past two weeks is downward. I wish I could start some singing, but I regret to say that my knowledge of the language seems not to be sufficient for me to exercise the proper control. The other day I thought I understood a song, and approved it, whereas as a matter of fact it ought not to have been approved at all.[30] Seldom have I felt more like a fool—which is saying a good deal. I have now learned caution. If, however, we are lacking on the musical side, we keep the Foyer always open for other activities from about 7.30 A.M. till nightfall. Most other Foyers are less generous in this respect, but our position near an important road in my opinion makes long hours desirable. And since we have to be at work making the chocolate it is not much additional labor to keep the door open, though of course it makes epistolary labors subject to constant interruption.

I had a bath before I left my last post six weeks or so ago. That bath is a very pleasant memory.

This sector is now very quiet. The Germans were not sending us any more shells during the past three weeks. An air raid night

29. This is the Latin original of, "I came, I saw, I conquered."
30. The songs to be played on the phonograph had to be approved for their decency.

before last was a brilliant affair, but we were not the object of the German effort. Most of the planes were friends anyway. The signals were brilliant & interesting.

The chocolate has begun to boil & Montí has gone to lunch. So I must stop, in order to mix in the condensed milk—a sticky job that I dislike.

I wish I could hear from America. The wrong address seems to be more efficacious than the right one.

Love to all.
Your loving son
Gresham

May 6, 1918

My dearest Mother:

The long waits between letters, which are necessary in wartime correspondence, make the letters all the more welcome when they do at last arrive. This was the case especially with your letter of April 4, which came to hand last night and with a splendid letter from Uncle that arrived at the same time. It was an immense relief to hear that you had stood the journey to Baltimore, hard as it was, and that your condition at home was better than during that last trying attack at Summerville. Apparently the good of Summerville is going to appear more after the holiday is over than while it was actually in progress. This is perhaps not so surprising as it may seem. A change was what was needed, and a change enables you to appreciate all the more the comforts of the home to which you have returned. Those comforts are due to your own loving care—during the years gone by—for all the members of the household.

I am mighty sorry to hear about the death of Mrs. Clements. Sometimes a blow like that, about which you get little sympathy, is harder to bear than sorrows which to an outsider seem more serious.

The news about Tom and his new clothes is very funny. He seems to be different from your humble servant. The very thought of Franklin or Best and Co. makes me shiver yet.[31]

It is natural for you to wonder where I am, especially in view of the present danger of a few weeks ago. I can at least tell you that for about three weeks we have been having a very peaceful time here. The delicate attentions of the Boches, as far as we are concerned, have altogether ceased. A hostile airplane every now and then is about all we see, or even hear, of enemy activity. And since the weather has been almost continuously thick and rainy for three or four weeks, even airplanes have been rare birds.

Speaking of birds, some of the European varieties, which are now beginning to appear, are very pretty; and in the morning the songs are also cheery. I wish I had somebody who likes the birds enough to point out at least a sky-lark to me. A little earlier in the season I found the magpies amusing—especially an inquisitive tame one which would peck around inside the house. My pleasure in the latter, however, was spoiled after I heard that in order to make pets of the birds they have to clip their wings. At any rate I wish you could enjoy the pretty song-birds with me. I don't think that for beauty the birds of this region compare with Princeton, but that impression is perhaps due to the fact that I am not well situated for observation. The spring here is very beautiful when you can get away from the scars of war, but the leaden weather has dulled even the beauty of spring-time. We have not had a really pretty day for three or four weeks.

Last Saturday, on my way back from a visit to the direction régionale, I stopped in at the dentist's. To my disgust he would not fill my tooth, on the ground that there was still danger of infection; but imposed upon me the inconvenience of temporary protection for another six or seven days. At the evacuation hospital, where I found the dentist, just as I was leaving I met an American ambulance-driver, whose ambulance had broken down. Since he

31. Presumably, these were either stores for men or department stores. Most often, Dr. Machen had his suits tailor made, so maybe these were tailoring businesses.

spoke no French, I was able to act as interpreter, in order to get the
necessary telephoning done. Even a slight knowledge of French is a
rare thing among the Americans over here.

At the "direction régionale" I had to wait a long time, while
some other directors were having a conference, and then I secured
my report-blank from the financial man and tried to find out how
the financial report is to be made. The "Foyer" account has to
be kept separate from the cantine account since normally there
are two directors at every post—and it is not always easy to see
what belongs under Foyer and what under Cantine. Like the hero
in the "Mikado" I unite various functions in my self. As Cantine
director, I am filled with awe of myself as Foyer director. Also my
merchandise account is not in as good shape as it will be next
month. If I keep this up I shall become a regular business man.
Y.M.C.A. work, you see, is a great experience. Army said, when I
went away, that I would no doubt come back such a "mixer" that my
friends would not know me. I am afraid not, however. It is not easy
to make a mixer out of me.

One of the chief reasons for going to the "direction régionale"
is to get rid of money. Since there is no good place here to keep the
proceeds of the cantine, and since the 2300 odd francs for April
came in chiefly in five-franc notes ("billets de cent sous," as they
are always called), you will understand that the bulk of the money
in an envelope in my pocket soon becomes considerable. What is
hard to get is small change—there is usually a "crise de monnaie"
in the zone of the armies.[32] But even without being too disobliging
to those who present their "billets de cent sous," I have managed to
keep ahead of the game. There is scarcely anything that provokes
me more than to have a little change refused me when I try to buy
anything, and now that I am running a buffet I try to apply the
Golden Rule.

You ought to see our flower garden. About a month or so ago
the "direction régionale" sent me some seeds. It seemed to me to
be a joke; since the surroundings of our baraque looked absolutely
hopeless—a sea of ugly mud ploughed up by waggon wheels and
horses' hoofs. But I happened to mention the thing in the presence

32. A "crise de monnaie" is a currency crisis.

of our cook at the popote. This cook is a professional flower-gardener or flower-nursery man from Rouen. Without any prodding he got busy in his leisure hours until now the ugly embankment made by the earth from the drainage ditch in front of the baraque has been transformed into an artistic flower-bed, most tastefully bordered with green-sod. In addition to the planting of the seeds, the gardener has transplanted from the neighborhood the plants which his expert knowledge has dictated. Back of the baraque I am going to get him to lay out the ground for a "jeu de boules," which seems to be a sort of out door ten-pins.[33]

During the past week or so I have been much discouraged about the Foyer. The attendance has been declining rapidly, until yesterday we sold less than 250 cups of chocolate. A few weeks ago we were keeping quite regularly above 400, and in the evening at least the hut was full. Yesterday was the most meager day since the very first days of the Foyer's existence. And even on Sunday we only attained the pitiful figure of 365, despite the fact that there was no cinéma that evening. Cinéma is run by the army in another hut, and of course cuts into our attendance.

Also I am sorry that the men whom I am serving here are not the fighting men who need the service most. And yet, these good old fellows, living year after year away from their families, in this gloomy, though not overly uncomfortable environment, have my sympathies along with the younger men of the infantry. I certainly cannot find it in my heart to regret rendering them service. All that I mean is that I am not doing such war service like two American Foyer directors whom I have seen recently, who have the full confidence of high officers & are engaged in establishing Foyer work in the lines, where such work is most needed & most appreciated.

At any rate I have a lot to be thankful for here—and the greatest blessing is my independence. If I don't do the work nobody is here to do it. That is the thing that makes me feel a little as

33. Machen's use of "ten-pins" refers to American bowling, but the "jeu de boules," or "bowling ground" may have been used by the French soldiers to play pétanque, which is a lawn game that vies with wine-and-cheese as France's national pastime. The throwing balls are about 3 inches in diameter. These balls are rolled on the ground, with back-spin, at a smaller target ball. The bowled ball closest to the target ball is the winner.

though I were worth while. And who can tell? Changes in the army are very rapid. Infantry might be put in here any time. And if it should be put in, I would be too busy even to get the blues.

Montí thinks that hot chocolate will not go in warm weather, and that something else ought to be substituted in summer. But to get something else we shall have to employ the "Système D." You might ask Aunt Bessie if she knows what the "Système D." is. It is the "système débrouillard," and is most important in all work in the zone of the armies.[34]

To-day the sale of chocolate seems to be going a little better. Montí thinks that is because the weather is not good, but I am rather inclined to think that the fluctuations are due principally to differing arrangements of the corvées of the men.[35]

Recently I have been letting Montí do more of the actual work of making the chocolate, in order to permit me to get out in front of the counter and get acquainted with my guests. Lending the books sometimes gives me the opportunity for brief conversations about literary subjects. The popularity of Poe in France is remarkable. It seems he has been very ably translated. One intelligent fellow the other day commented that the translation of "the Raven" is so beautiful that it must be as beautiful as the original, so far as the music of the language is concerned. To prove it to me he recited the first verse. I was somewhat inclined to adapt the remark that somebody made to Pope about his translation of Homer: "It's a pretty poem, Pope, but it's not Homer." Imagine the job of translating the "Bells"![36] However, the keen appreciation of

34. The "Système D." is the abbreviation for, as Machen defined here, the "système débrouillard." It is a French idiom best rendered as "resourcefulness." One might think of the resourcefulness of the film characters played by James Garner in *The Great Escape* and William Holden in *Stalag 17* to get an idea of how "Système D" worked. This "resourcefulness" involved utilizing venues of purchase that were not officially sanctioned but may not be illegal either. As Machen's letters to this point have shown, he had to be resourceful for some of his cooking supplies and for his coal.

35. The French word "corvées" means "duties" in English.

36. Machen is referring to Poe's, "The Bells," which is a poem composed of four stanzas of increasing length. Each of the four stanzas describes milestones of human experience—childhood, youth, maturity, and death. Each stanza is a complex study of bells as descriptive of those four stages of life ("Bells, The," in *Merriam Webster's Encyclopedia of Literature* [Springfield: Merriam-Webster, 1995]). Machen's point is that if "The Raven" did not come out well in French, then imagine how difficult it would be to render such a complex poem as "The Bells" in French. Machen might have agreed with Robert Frost that, "Poetry is what gets lost in translation."

the French for Poe is gratifying. I really believe he is not only the best known American writer, but one of the English authors most read in France. It is not merely the stories that attract the French; on the contrary they consider Poe a great poetic genius.

The shower baths are working today! I am now off for my spring cleaning.

So good bye and lots and lots of love for all.

Your loving Son
Gresham

6

WAR IS DECLARED
ON THE RATS

May 14 to 26, 1918

The routine work of the Foyer continues in Missy-sur-Aisne as the war rages on. There is no lack of evidence that the Foyer is near the front because the drone of the military aircraft reminds Machen day and night. Hot chocolate distribution declines due to the warmer weather, but the unceasingly increasing rat population faces extermination by Dr. Machen.

May 14, 1918

Dear Helen:

The fact that my letters home have been addressed almost exclusively to Mother does not mean that the other members of the family have been out of my thoughts. In particular I followed with deep sympathy the news of the attack of grippe which you passed through earlier in the spring. I hope it may be ancient history long before this letter arrives. It was a pleasure to me to think of you being in sole charge of 217 during Mother's visit to Summerville; for it makes home still homelike, as it can never be when "mere man" is in charge.[1]

---

1. The number "217" refers to Machen's family home on 217 Monument Street in Baltimore.

My letters to Mother just about exhaust my stock of news, and indeed I fear I am but a poor-letter writer. One would suppose that my situation would give me lots and lots of interesting things to say, but then there is such a wealth of experiences of the war just now that my observations can possess only a personal interest—especially since I have succeeded in getting only as far as the rear of the armies. Life in a place like mine is not as much different from life at home as one might suppose. One soon becomes used to the ruined villages and the ancient trenches and shell-holes until they seem to be the most commonplace things in the world. When I get back to the world of window-glass and solid roofs I suppose it will be difficult to accustom myself to my environment. At any rate the life that I have been leading involves no serious discomforts except those (like trouble with one's teeth) which belong to peace as well as to war. As for the military character of the environment, that is not so troublesome to a raw civilian as I had supposed it might be. After four years of war, military etiquette does not occupy the large place in camp like it does in the days of preliminary training.

The routine of life here is so humdrum and everybody seems to be so thoroughly accustomed to it that it is hardly to be realized that only a year ago our village was in the hands of the Germans. Everything is going on so smoothly here now that I feel as though these men must have been born and raised right here. As for my own work, chocolate has to be made and sold, library books given out, etc., day after day just about the same. Unfortunately the dreadful time is approaching when my admirable Montí is to go on his "permission" for ten days.[2] What shall I do? I feel almost as the household would feel if Betty had to be given up! The work of the Foyer has devolved more and more upon Montí. He is a very independent young fellow, but despite his independence of spirit he and I get on together fine. I wish I could get him some good clothes—and indeed this afternoon I intend to see what a neighboring town possesses in the way of shirts.[3] An unusually

2. The "permission" is a military leave.
3. "In the margin is written, "Braisne," (Braisnes) which is about 50 miles N.N.E. of Paris and about 56 miles W.N.W. of Reims.

intelligent boy whose father's business has been ruined by the war, and who himself has spent a good part of his youth in the rough life of the army! Montí and I have some great old discussions now and then.

Yesterday I called on the Colonel, who is to be here only for a day or two. He was not visible, but promised to drop in at the Foyer later on & say "Bonjour." Well, Montí and I sure did get busy. We wiped up shelves that have never been wiped up before; we arranged the old newspapers of the "pays invalis";[4] we swept up the floor as well as a sand floor can be swept up. At least Montí did these things. One of Montí's peculiarities is that if he does a thing he has to do it all. The worst of it is that the Colonel did not appear. He will probably appear to-day at some moment when we are in the most disreputable condition. Why, yesterday, I put on my only remaining presentable collar, and I had not put on a collar for months. Alas for that collar! It is in a sad state now. Also I used up practically my last bit of shoe-polish. High boots sure do take a lot of polish. Cleaning them is like starching collars for a giraffe.

You will hardly think that so silly a letter as this one deserves an answer, and indeed I don't want to put a burden on you. But I should certainly like to get a line if you did happen to feel like it some day. I don't venture to ask you to make Arly write. That would be too big a job. What are the plans for the summer?

Affectionately yours
J. Gresham Machen

May 16, 1918

My dearest Mother:

The days drag along without any news; I heard some time ago indirectly that some of my mail, which had arrived at a neighboring

---

4. The French "pays invalis," means in English, "disabled country."

town, had been returned to Paris. A civilian in a camp which has no civil post office is an anomaly; apparently I am not allowed to use either civil or military address. Probably I shall have to come to the plan of having my letters sent to the "direction régionale" of the Foyers and then trust to occasional visits to get them. But I certainly hate that plan. A registered letter from Munroe & Co. in Paris, which was mailed in March just came to hand two or three days ago! This is the kind of thing that forces me to the "direction régionale."

At the time of my last letter which was written on Sunday, May 12, I was feeling rather blue on account of indigestion and headache.[5] That trouble, I am glad to say, has now passed off, and my cold also proved to be much lighter than colds usually are. The weather has at last turned warm and dry. What in the world I am to do for clothes I do not know; I have nothing but the very heaviest of winter underwear and shirts. In America I wear summer underwear winter, as well as summer; apparently in France I am to be condemned to wear winter underwear summer as well as winter. I much prefer the former plan; though I must confess that warm clothes are necessary in the kind of life that I have been leading here. On principle the directors of the Foyers du Soldat are given a six-days leave once every three months, but they must provide for the proper care of their posts in their absence. The qualification is prohibitive in my place. For if I should ask for a substitute, the substitute would probably become an associate or a boss; my cherished independence would be gone. I am too lucky in being sole director to think of spoiling things for the sake of a holiday. It must be admitted however, that a trip to the shops of Paris would not be a mere holiday, but an affair of the utmost utility both to me and to my work.

Monday night my tooth began to give me trouble again, and I thought surely the large filling would have to be removed. But on Tuesday the dentist at the hospital where I have been going told me that the root of the trouble was not in the tooth that he had filled, but in the neighboring one. He applied something apparently red-hot to the gum, and gave me a prescription to be filled by the

5. If he was right about the May 12 date of this letter, it is not extant.

pharmacist here. I have had no more serious trouble, except that my teeth generally seem to be "loose."

I have secured from the "direction régionale" twenty-five more books for our Foyer library. The books are in constant use. Some for the collection—notably some religious and philosophical books—I do not like, and I am even keeping a few from circulation. Since books in favor of Christianity are excluded from the library (such seems to be largely the case) I do not think it is fair to circulate books against Christianity.[6]

The other day, at the town where our "direction régionale" is located, I got some underwear, shirts, etc., for Montí. With respect to such things he seemed to be in the most utter destitution, his father's business having been largely ruined by the war. I was glad to have the opportunity of helping out in that way, since so far such opportunities have not somehow presented themselves. My own expenses are almost nil—my bill for the last two weeks of excellent board was thirty francs! I regret very much that I did not do what many Y.M.C.A. men are doing and waive my salary. Of course I could return it every month but the trouble is that my letter of credit, which is in my pocket, is useless here away from banks, so that the Y.M.C.A. salary is my only means of subsistence except for a small deposit at Munroe. I should have left my letter of credit with Munroe & Co., who have a way by which payments can be made in the absence of the holder; but I thought there might be opportunities of using the letter here.

Montí was taken sick with grippe yesterday. To-day I have had to get along without him. Fortunately he has a friend who has already been helping out at the Foyer at odd times. The man is now acting as Montí's substitute much to my satisfaction.

Hot weather does not help in the sales of chocolate; our business is much smaller than it was some weeks ago—under just about half of what it was. I expect to try the experiment of selling tobacco & matches. These things will not take the place of the chocolate since the consummation of the hot drink causes the men to linger in the hut and so braced up our business in general.

6. It should be remembered that Machen was working with the Young Men's *Christian* Association.

I confess I am getting tired of my job. It was really a foolish thing to put such an academic person in a place like this when there are perhaps not many who could do my proper work among the American boys. But such consideration must not be allowed to prevent me from doing my very best in the place where I now find myself. If there is other service for me to do I believe it will come my way without too much special effort on my part.

I feel disgusted with my lack of progress in French. What splendid use you or Arly would have made of my opportunities. The truth is, I am intellectually lazy. I suppose, I am too old to learn a language. The job takes all the enthusiasm of youth if it is to be done right. I was really astonished that I got along so well at first in French, but also astonished now that having gotten along so well at first I do not get along better now. Fortunately my lack of progress is not sufficient to hamper me very seriously in my work. Compared with the attainments of most American Foyer directors that I have seen (I think I can say it without conceit) my French is simply magnificent.

The best of love to all. You know how much love there is given from your affectionate son
Gresham

May 22, 1918

My dearest Mother:

Last Saturday the day after my letter was sent to you, I received your fine letter of April 11 (No. 16). It was an unusually long letter, and the quality was fully equal to the quantity. A letter like that, when one is particularly blue, seems like a message straight from heaven. In general the news that the letter contained was good. Your own improvement delighted my heart, and also the favorable impression that Tom had received from his visit at Atlantic City. It is just lovely for Helen to be with Nena, though I know it means self-sacrifice on the part of Arly. As for Carrie, she is evidently just what she has always been—a comfort in the hour of need.

I am greatly pleased at your interest in Mr. Hodges. He has had a most painful attack of shingles, but is now gradually recovering. Dr. Beach of Princeton writes to him every week, and thus faithfully takes my place. I write occasionally. Mr. Hodges seems rather below par physically, his spiritual condition, judging by his letters, seems to be excellent. The church and Mr. Ranigan who prays for me constantly (according to Mr. Hodges), and other such matters are the things that interest him the most. Uncle will sympathize with anybody who has suffered with shingles.

Since my last letter the weather has been hot—real American heat too. The paper said that the thermometer the other day was 30 at Paris, which if my calculation is correct, is 86° Fahrenheit. The subsequent days, at least here, have seemed to become warmer and warmer. And I am wearing an immensely heavy woolen undershirt, a heavy flannel shirt, and a uniform that buttons up high around the neck. Summer, not winter, is going to be the time of discomfort here—heat, to say nothing of various enemies of repose.

The work of the Foyer has dropped down to practically nothing. During April, we had good attendance, but now our building nearly all the time is a perfect desert, and even in the evenings only a few drop-in. Instead of hot chocolate we now sell the chocolate cold—which seems absolutely nauseating to me, but is drunk with apparent relish by some. We also provide cold tea, which is not so bad, though to suit the taste of the majority we spoil it by putting in condensed milk. The best that can be said for it is that it is "not half so nasty as it looks." Of course "cold" as applied to these drinks does not mean really cold, but only that degree of coolness which can be attained by allowing them to stand in the tepid atmosphere of our hut. The total receipts for the chocolate and tea yesterday were Fr. 16.40. During April they were Fr. 80.00–100.00 a day. At present the work here is scarcely worth while. It is not as though the soldiers were in the cantinnement only for limited periods as at my last post. They have been here for months & have been able to make themselves so much at home that the Foyer du

Soldat is scarcely necessary. Y.M.C.A. work without the spiritual side of it is rather a limited business anyway. But I am exceedingly lucky to have an independent post, instead of being one of two men put in to do a half a man's work, as at my last place. When my independence is taken from me, as it well may be, I shall ask for leave (as is my due after three months of service) to go to Paris. There I shall see Bobby Freeman, if possible, about getting into the work with the American boys. Meanwhile I must be as faithful as possible here, and hope for the large opportunities, which may, indeed, come at any time by unexpected movements of troops.

As yet I have not been very successful in fixing up the hut and its surroundings. The neatness of a neighboring Foyer makes me envious. I suppose I am a pretty poor Y.M.C.A. man.

On Saturday I went no less than twice to the Direction Régionale to see about supplies of tea and other things. Also I went to the neighboring Foyer of which I have just spoken to see how the ground must be fixed for a "jeu de boules."[7] All this was accomplished on a wheel.[8] And I can tell you my heavy clothes in the heat were stifling. To-day, however, is the real scorcher. I would never have thought such heat possible in Europe in May.

In our hut the airplanes keep me awake to such an extent that I have taken to sleeping in the crypt again, at least on clear nights. It has become rather crowded down there, and since I lost possession of my straw mattress when I deserted the quarters temporarily, I have to content myself with hard slats to sleep on. The rigor of the slats, however, is somewhat mitigated by the admirable thick sleeping bag that I brought from New York. A number of my almost numberless blankets serve the comfort of my companions in the cave. I lend the blankets to one man, & then when I arrive some fine night I find another occupying the bed on the blankets of the first man. And so on. Blankets are needed in that crypt on warm nights just as much as in cold nights.

At last I have declared war on the rats, but as yet have not stemmed the tide of their advance. Their holes began to appear

7. A note in the margin designates the village as "Vregny," which is 4.5 miles N.E. of Soissons and about 1.5 miles N. from Machen's post in Missy-sur-Aisne.
8. A "wheel" is a bicycle.

not only around the edges of the baraque and all around my
room (they have their headquarters, I suppose, under that room
because it contains the only floor that we have), but also in front
of our counter & else where. There is something loathsome about
the appearance of a rat-hole. Monday night I caught one rat in a
spring-trap, and three in a large trap. Not liking the customary
method of killing the rats in a trap, I took them myself down to the
river to drown them. I drowned them all right, but unfortunately
I also drowned the trap. My foot slipped on the muddy bank and
away went the trap. The water is about twelve feet deep right near
the bank. Finally the man that had lent me the trap attached a
pitchfork to a long beam & fished the thing up. But we had some
fishing before we succeeded. My troubles naturally caused some
amusement, & even I myself was able to see the joke. Next time I
was determined to attach a string to the trap. But, alas, the rats now
disdain the nice cheese that we have provided for them. As I have
been writing this letter they have been sniffing around that trap
within a few feet of me. But without entering. I did catch one by my
spring-trap last night.

Montí is as discouraged as I am about the Foyer. He thinks that
our popularity is finished unless fresh troops arrive.

I have been reading Lamartine with a great deal of
satisfaction. The first poem in the book, "L'isolement," arrested my
attention.

The other day I actually took a little stroll. It was beautiful.
I wish you could have been along to see the lovely flowers—so
different, many of them, from those that we have in America.
Unfortunately, in the evening, just when the nightingale is
singing in the thickets along the river, I have to be listening to the
phonograph instead. A phonograph is all right in its place, but I
prefer the nightingales.

Love and more of it to all & to you, my dearest Mother
Your affectionate son
Gresham

May 25, 1918

My dearest Mother:

Your letter number 17 of April 20 was waiting for me at the "Direction Régionale" this morning. It is a sweet and lovely letter, as all of your letters are. Of course I share to the full your disappointment at the failure of Nena's visit to Atlantic City. Evidently Helen was lovely about the whole thing and a great comfort to all concerned. Let us hope and pray that rest and patience will finally bring about a recovery. I wish I could make Tom feel, as well as you, how very, very deep is my sympathy. As for my understanding of your own feeling, you know how complete that is. It is these deeper troubles that make us feel the need of the Searcher of hearts.

The news about Arly's case was most gratifying and interesting. The newspaper clipping, interpreted by what you said, gave me a good idea of the story.

I am glad you feel an interest in my letter on woman suffrage which was published in the Congressional Record. Somewhere in my trunk I have preserved the congressman's letter in which he mentioned the place in the Record where the letter is to be found. So sooner or later you may expect to find it. But I am afraid you will be disappointed since the letter was brief & quite hastily written.

I am glad Miss Marie let you read my letter to her. I am still wearing, at this moment, that sleeveless sweater which either she or Mrs. Buchanan made for me. It is about the most useful thing that I have.

At the same time with your letter I received an invitation from Mr. Will Moody to make addresses at the Ministers' Meeting at Northfield once a day for a week, during the conference in August. You will remember that I conducted the meeting twice last summer. I was much gratified at the invitation of this year, and am sorry not to be able to accept it. The ministers' meeting is not a showy affair like the "platform meetings," but perhaps it offers just as good an opportunity in its way.

When I hear the buzz of the allied air squadron at night as they are on their way to German territory I can now wonder whether Brooke Bird is among them. Probably he isn't, but then again he might be.

But now it is perhaps time to take up my narrative of life in the Foyer du Soldat. The worst of it is that I do not know where to begin. When did I write my last letter—was it Sat. May 18, or was it Sunday May 19, was it Monday, May 20, I cannot say. At any rate up to Thursday, May 23 the weather was hot, and hot weather was not good for the attendance at the Foyer. Tuesday was the poorest day—we sold on that day 16.40 francs' worth of cold chocolate and cold tea, and 4.05 francs worth of tobacco etc. On Thursday, with the change of weather, the attendance improved, and we were able to go back yesterday to the sale of hot chocolate. But the figures are only about one-third to one-half of what they were in the paling days of April. Something ought to be done to brace the work up in the summer. The "direction régionale" thinks that perhaps some bottled drink may be secured, but that is as yet problematical. Meanwhile I have handed out tobacco, cigarettes, and matches.

On clear, still, moonlit nights I sleep in my crypt. I must confess that the "avions" are serious enemies of repose.[9] Even the good French ones make a lot of noise. At times, when a considerable squadron is passing, it seems as though earth and heaven were one gigantic Jew's-harp—so general, so un-localized, so pervasive is the sound. When the Boches pass you can hear the explosions of the numberless anti-aircraft shells, an occasional bomb, and once in a great while the whistle of a falling part of an anti-aircraft shell. Though despite all this the chance of getting hurt is very slight, I cannot help listening to the proceedings with such interest as to be kept awake. Those twenty feet of earth and ruined masonry over our crypt look mighty good to me. And as there seems to be room enough for all in the cantinnement & no imperative duty requires me to sleep in my baraque, I think I shall continue to descend when the night is clear.

The war upon the rats is going on fairly well. The first night I caught five, the next two nights one each, the next night none, and the next night one.

9. The "avions" were, using the English spelling of Machen's time, "aeroplanes."

Sunday May 26

Here it is Sunday again, and I am still behind with my letter. Montí writes to his mother every day. That rather puts one to shame.

As a censor of phono disks I am a dismal failure, for I can't understand the songs to save my life. Some of the disks, that I have been running with perfect contentment (one at least) proved to be the reverse of what Foyer du Soldat disks ought to be. I received what the Direction Régionale gave me with out question. But unfortunately the disks were not examined before they left Paris. More care will be exercised in the future.

Love to all, my dearest Mother. In the midst of all your troubles my thoughts and my prayers are always with you.

Your loving son
Gresham

7

THE GERMANS ARE COMING—
SUDDEN EVACUATION FROM
MISSY-SUR-AISNE

May 29 to June 13, 1918

As the third phase of the German spring offensive begins on the Aisne on May 27, Machen will find himself in the midst of a dangerous situation. A gas attack, shelling, and the death of a man nearby bring the realities of war closer. Machen would flee with the Germans at his heels and in the process lose some of his personal luggage. After working his way back to Paris, he would await new orders from the "Y" leadership because Missy-sur-Aisne was in the hands of the Germans.

May 29, 1918

My dearest Mother:

The impressions of the last few days have followed one another in such rapid succession that I despair of being able to produce anything like an adequate narrative.

On Sunday afternoon, all was peaceful at our little post. In the slack time at the Foyer I even took a little stroll with the "planton" that I like so much, leaving another assistant, who helps me on

125

Sundays, temporarily in sole charge. Little did we anticipate the convulsion that was to follow. At five o'clock there was "alerte"— that is the order was given that everything should be packed up and the waggons made ready to depart at a moment's notice. Sometimes such an "alerte" proves to be a precautionary measure merely as it was on one occasion some time ago. Consequently I was not greatly disturbed. My planton being unable to come to the Foyer because of military orders, I was particularly busy during the evening serving chocolate and receiving the library books that were hastily returned. This was one thing that prevented me from making my own preparation for departure more carefully. How glad I should be now if I had packed a little bag of necessaries that could have been carried on my shoulder! Instead I depended on a suit case that would have to be put on a waggon. Also I expected to be able to carry my small army locker.

In the evening I descended into my "abri," and got an hour or so of sleep. At one o'clock a violent bombardment began; a number of non-commissioned officers entered the abri and I sat up the rest of the night. The bombardment surpassed anything that we had experienced before. Shells hit right in the village as well as in the environs. One which struck a point a couple of hundred yards from our Foyer killed a man, who however was not one of the men of the "cantonnement" but a soldier who was passing along the road. At the beginning of the bombardment there was some gas— fortunately of the "lachrymogene" variety instead of one of the deadlier kinds.[1] I thought I had merely a slight attack of "snuffles" until those who came from outside reported that things were worse there. We stopped up the chinks in our door and put on our masks, at least for a moment or two. One of the non-commissioned officers was kind enough to bring me a better mask than the little one which I keep always with me. Fortunately the gas was not continued, and the little that I experienced of it could scarcely be dignified even by the name of discomfort.

1. *Lachrymogene*, benzyl bromide, was used by the French and Germans for gas warfare. This agent irritated the eyes causing tears, pain, and even temporary blindness, while irritating the skin and mucous membranes. Benzyl bromide was one of the earliest gases used in the war beginning in 1915. See Simon Jones, *World War I Gas Warfare Tactics and Equipment* (Botley, Oxford: Osprey Publishing, 2007), 3.

Early in the morning we were ordered to vacate our abri
in order that wounded men might be put in it if necessary, but
another abri near by was assigned to us. A non-commissioned
officer took me to inspect a pleasanter cellar some distance off, but
profundity and proximity appealed more to me. The noise of the
bombardment was terrific; though shells were not actually falling
in the centre of the village. While I was standing at the door of my
abri near the centre of the village they brought in a man who had
been killed near by.

Still I rather expected that we were to stay. Meanwhile I did
not know exactly what to do. The Foyer evidently could not be
kept open in the ordinary way. Perhaps I might have been there to
receive library books, but for all I knew that might be accomplished
at a more propitious time later on. Certainly I might also have gone
to get my suit-case. But I anticipated time to do that and other
necessary things after the order to depart should be actually given.

At about nine-o'clock the troops began moving to the
bridge. One of the men that I had known well at the Foyer
called out to me something about the Boches being two
kilometers away. This, if I understood it aright, was of course a
great exaggeration. But everything began to move, and move
quick. So in order not to miss the chance of putting my suit-
case on a waggon I rushed to the Foyer and got it. The non-
commissioned officer in charge of the waggons told me, since
I was unattached, to get across the river at once and let the
suit-case follow. I was glad to do so. The bridge was only a few
hundred yards away, but, to adapt a remark of Mark Twain, the
time required to get across it was one of the longest weeks that
I ever spent. A solid train of wagons and men was moving across
the bridge and along the road. A terrific cannonade was going
on, and fresh shell holes could be seen along the road, but for
some reason the Germans did not seem to be trying particularly
just then to cut that bridge. Thus I got away from a place to
which I had really become attached. I saved nothing, not even
a clean shirt or a tooth-brush or a clean handkerchief. And I
did hate to leave my Foyer. Perhaps I might have stayed a little
longer. But you see I was on the wrong side of the river—the

bridge might be cut at any minute—and I did not want to make hot chocolate for the Boches.

After getting across the bridge I decided not to wait for my suitcase, but to beat it at once to a place where I could get in touch with the authorities of the Foyer. A soldier informed me that the town where the Direction Régionale had been was under particularly heavy bombardment. He advised me to get away from the main roads. This I did, particularly since it enabled me to pass by a neighboring Foyer where I might get instructions. The village of that Foyer had been bombarded; the place had a very empty appearance.[2] The Foyer was closed, but fortunately I met the directors. The French director is a man of years, has had military experience and possesses the "croix de guerre." Thus he was a man whose advice was worth having. His advice was that we spend the rest of the day and the following night in a neighboring "carrière" and await developments.[3] So we took a little chocolate, a can or so of sardines, some bread & some blankets about a half a mile up the hill to our abri. The carrière in question extended underground for a hundred feet or so, but rather too close to the surface for perfect safety. It served our purpose very well, especially since a few steps from the entrance there was a fine view of the valley & the heights beyond where great doings might be expected. There were three of us, the French director of the Foyer, the American director, the French director of a neighboring annex, and myself.[4] The afternoon was full of interest. Huge clouds of smoke could be seen ascending here and there where buildings or materials were on fire. My Foyer, which I could plainly discern, still seemed to be untouched. The German air-planes added to the interest; they came close to the ground in order to mow down the troops on the roads with their machine guns. One German plane, I believe, was brought down by a French machine-gun close to the entrance of our "carrière." But I did not witness the event. The rattle of a

2. The "village" was designated by Machen in his marginal note as "Ciry-Salsogne," which is about 65 miles N.E. of Paris and about 25 miles N.W. of Reims.

3. Machen is using the French "carrière," which means "pit" in English, to describe an air-raid shelter.

4. The "and myself" was added by him during his proof reading, but he missed the disparity between the four persons named and "the three of us."

machine-gun, close at hand, is not an encouragement to staying out in the open.

About five or six o'clock the American director & I went down to get something to eat at his Foyer. I appreciated the dinner very much, since I had had almost nothing all day, but I did not see the use of lingering after dinner merely for the sake of lingering. As it turned out there was an opportunity of serving coffee to some men who had returned from the thick of the fight, so that my colleague may congratulate himself.[5] But this was not anticipated, and at the time, the thing was put on the ground for the additional comfort of his own room. In general the gentleman in question was inclined to take an optimistic view of the situation, which was not based on knowledge. Deliver me from a Christian scientist at such times— entirely too cranky for me![6]

The ground in the carrière was hard and the night was cold. I had no overcoat, but the two blankets that my comrades were able to lend me from the stock of the Foyer enabled me to snatch a few minutes of sleep. During the night a medical officer dropped in and said that he might need the part of the carrière where we were sleeping for the wounded, and also if there were many of them he might need our help. Needless to say we placed ourselves at his disposal, but no wounded men arrived. I forgot to say that during a part of the afternoon & early evening the carrière was occupied by some five hundred men of French primary troops, & also by the men of a "saucisse" which was raised immediately over the carrière. But toward morning all had gone. I cannot say that [7] the night was pleasant—much too chilly to suit my taste.

You can imagine the interest with which at early dawn I took my first look at the valley. The surprising thing was that the appearance of the scene was so little changed. There were the puffs

5. That is, the American director patted himself on the back for his bravery as he served coffee.

6. Machen's disdain for the "Christian scientist" may reflect the teaching of the Christian Science cult regarding the reality of matter and one's perception of it. Says Mary Baker Eddy, "Through immortal Mind, or Truth, we can destroy all ills which proceed from mortal mind" (*Science and Health with Key to the Scriptures* [Boston: First Church of Christ, Scientist, 1971], 374).

7. The letterhead of this sheet and all the following sheets of stationery read, "Hotel Beaulieu, 8, Rue Balzac, Champs-Élysées-Paris, Despouys, Prop, Téléphone Wagram 68-35."

of arriving shells here and there and the smoke of what I took to
be more of the fires observed the evening before. As a matter of
fact, the accordance with the communiqués that I read later on
the Boches must have been at or across the river at a point within
plain view. So far as I can make out they were only two or three
miles away from us at the time when we left the carrière for the
rear. But we had no idea at the time that they had advanced so far.
However, I did not take the optimistic view of my Christian science
friend, who returned to the Foyer for breakfast. The bombardment
became exceedingly intense, and we finally decided that there was
no chance of our being able to return to our respective posts & that
our duty was to get in touch with the Foyer authorities.

   The first mile and a half we walked. Then we got up on the
plateau back of our carrière and the appearance of things was
not encouraging. Great clouds of smoke were rising here and
there in the rear, and all the reports that we could get indicated
that the Boches had advanced in such a way as to risk cutting
us off. Loaded down with the blankets and the hand-bags of my
companions, we were glad when we reached the headquarters of
the "Dames Anglaises," who ran a concern somewhat like a Foyer
du Soldat in a neighboring village.[8] There through the extreme
kindness of the "Commandeur" who was attending the moving of
the "Dames Anglaises," we were able to load our belongings on
a waggon—at least the belongings of my comrades, since I had
none.[9] On the road the rattle of the German aviators' machine
guns was not pleasant; passing troops on a road are pretty much at
the mercy of an air-plane. But after something like a four or five
mile trip we got to a little town where there was a railroad station
of a branch line.[10] We just caught the last train that was to be
run. It was filled with women and children leaving their homes &
trying to carry some of their personal effects. Mighty pathetic that
train was, I can tell you. But you from personal experience know

   8. "Dames Anglaises," is French for "English ladies." A note in the margin of the letter
describes the village as "Serches," which is about 65 miles N.E. of Paris and about 28 miles
N.W. of Reims.
   9. A "Commandeur" is a female "commander."
   10. The "little town" is described in a marginal note as "Chacrise," which is about 60 miles
N.E. of Paris and about 30 miles N.W. of Reims.

what such scenes are like.[11] After a trip of ten or fifteen miles we
reached a station on a main line.[12] Since we had all afternoon,
or rather most of the whole day, to wait for the Paris train, I
seized the opportunity of inquiring at the Foyer du Soldat of the
town about the Direction Régionale.[13] I was informed that it was
established at a small city not very far from Paris.[14] So instead of
going at once to Paris I decided to get off at the city in question &
report to the regional directors. Arriving at nearly midnight I was
fortunate enough to get a room at a hotel. You may well imagine
that after two such nights as I had spent, the bed looked mighty
good to me.

The next morning the French regional director told me to go
to Paris, report to the Direction Centrale, & wait until it was to be
decided what should be done. So here I am at Paris, as the paper
upon which I am continuing my Letter will show. Life has to begin
over again. I have my skin, and the very dirty clothes with which it
is covered. But that is all. My letters, my thousand little cherished
knick-knacks, and my equipment are all gone. If I can locate that
suit-case I shall recover some things of importance. As for what I
left at the Foyer I suppose that is lost even if the Boches are not
actually in possession. And from my interpretation of the official
communication, I should judge that they are. It is interesting to
read that the Boches were attacking the height upon which our
carrière was situated in the course of the very day when we left.

May 30

Good bye to all my things, the Boches have swept over my
post. One of the Foyer directors of the region is removed to be a

11. Machen may be alluding here to his mother's experiences in Macon, Georgia during
the Civil War.
12. The town of Breny is about 53 miles E.N.E. of Paris and about 31 miles W.N.W. of Reims.
What Machen designates as, "Oulchy-Brény," is a shortened form of the "Gare d'Oulchy-Breny,"
which is a train station on the railroad in the town of Breny.
13. A marginal note names the town as "Oulchy-le-Château," which is about a 1.5 miles
N.E. of Breny.
14. "Meaux" is the name of the "small city" according to the marginal note. Meaux is
about 23 miles E.N.E. of Paris and about 56 miles W.S.W. of Reims.

The soldiers are gathered in front of a YMCA hut. The hut construction was simple, of questionable durability, and inexpensive. Notice the bow in the siding to the left of the first soldier's elbow.
Photo courtesy of Kautz Family Collection, University of Minnesota

prisoner; others had a very much harder time escaping than I had. My former post was the scene of hard fighting.[15]

I have been directed to wait here in Paris till to-morrow when instructions may be given me. Naturally clothes are almost my first concern. The prices are something terrific—for instance I paid 185 francs plus a war-tax for a pair of high boots. But I should not mind if I could only get the things that I desire. French underwear is cut in the queerest way imaginable, and the American variety cannot be found. But this morning I am at least fairly clean. I even had a bath! Still I am just about the toughest looking person in Paris. How other Foyer directors manage to look as though they had just come out of a band box when in reality they have been sleeping

15. With reference to "One of the Foyer directors," Machen commented in the margin, "He was not, I bet." The marginal note says, "St. Mard," which was Machen's first post.

in a carrière is beyond my comprehension.[16] I must think quick about my purchases, since of course to-morrow I may get the order to leave town at once. Without doubt I shall forget just the most important things, I think however, that I shall be here some days.

Let me say that nothing that the papers say about the "sang-froid" of the Parisians is exaggerated a bit.[17] The town is being "bombarded" again, but everything goes on just as unconcernedly as before. The city presents the same busy, bright, normal appearance, as at the time of my last visit, before the "grosse Bertha" had begun its deadly work.[18] Of course the risk to an individual is almost infinitesimal. Paris is big and there could be an explosion somewhere in its great area even every few minutes for a long, long time without getting around to you or me. Also the bombardment is only occasional. In general it is far less terrifying than I had anticipated. As for the much more dangerous air-raids, an admirable system for the opening of cellars to the public has been devised. There are placards, "Abri," where the cellars are good. Still, the bravery of the people of Paris is admirable. The Germans are never going to win the war by trying to play upon their feelings.

In one respect things have changed in Paris. The restrictions on food have become much more severe—no sugar, no butter, no meat (on many days), etc. The change from the great abundance of the army fare is striking, but certainly the army ought to get the best.

16. A "band box" was used to store a hat and/or its decorative band. Machen's point in this sentence is that the other Foyer directors seemed to enjoy cleaning and clothing privileges that he did not.

17. This literally means, "cold blooded," but here it is an idiom meaning "self-control" or "toughness."

18. The "grosse Bertha" or English "Big Bertha" was a term used to describe the large artillery pieces used by the Germans to begin the war with their assault on Belgian fortresses. The Allies tended to apply this term to any large German artillery piece and Machen's use here refers more precisely to the "Paris Gun," which was a massive cannon that could fire a 264 pound shell with a range of 75 miles. This monster of an artillery piece was used from March into September 1918 and it is believed that during those months between 320 and 367 shells were fired. The trajectory of the shell had to be adjusted for the rotation of the earth because the round was aloft so long and the range was so great. The 92 foot long barrel and its massive carriage were mounted on a special rail car for portability. In Paris, the shells would fall and explode with no warning because the noise of the great cannon firing the shell was too far away to hear. In today's terms, the "Paris Gun" was more of a weapon of terror than destruction ("Paris Gun," *Dictionary of the First World War*).

When I met Bobby Freeman yesterday, I found him hospitable to the idea of putting me into the American religious work. Nothing at all is decided; I am to see him again if possible before I leave Paris. There are two sides to the thing. On the one hand my training has perhaps fitted me better for the religious work. On the other hand, I do not want to desert the directors of the French work in an hour of need. It would be rather a poor business to have the appearance of being discouraged by the experience that I have just been through. If the Foyer du Soldat authorities think that they have special need for men of such experience as I have had in order to reorganize their work in the sector that has been destroyed, I do not see how I can honorably go back on them. On the other hand if they should want to put me where I could have no independence & not enough to do, now is the time for me to break away.

I do not feel at all satisfied with my failure to save more at my lost post. The emergency, I am afraid, found me lacking. Still, the loss in any case would have been serious. I hate to think of the Germans enjoying our stock of chocolate. And still less do I like to think of them nosing around in my trunk.

The above letter, I know, is very inadequate. The scenes that I have stressed can never be forgotten, but it is not so easy to make any one else realize what they were like. The refugees, I think, constituted the saddest part of all. The roads for miles and miles were crowded with the waggons containing household effects placed on them in direst confusion. On the train by which I arrived at Paris there was a middle-aged woman with an aged man—utterly infirm—who she told me was her grandfather! I helped with the bundles, and got an employee of the station to look out for the party. On arrival, it must be said, the government authorities are doing everything in the world for the unfortunate people. But it is terribly sad.

Probably some of my mail may be much delayed, if not actually lost. I wish all of you at home could be as well and as fortunate as I am.

A letter from Mrs. Wiley, Bobby's mother-in-law, informs me that the baby, who is now two months old, has colic very badly. Bobby has to take a hand in soothing him, along with his many other duties.

It is getting time to think of Seal. At least I suppose it may be
Seal, despite the absence of your boys. They are certainly not absent
in spirit. Your love, my dearest Mother, is what keeps us all alive, no
matter on what side of the Atlantic we may be.

Love loads,
Your loving son Gresham

June 3, 1918

My dearest Mother:

Your two lovely letters, Nos. 18, 19, of April 26 and May 3,
were saved by the Direction Régionale at the time of their hurried
departure. I received them yesterday. It was an unexpected joy in
the midst of this gloomy and anxious time. News rather bad as well
as rather good—but at any rate a little bit of home.

At Paris I busied myself getting the most necessary clothes and
other belongings. It was a hard job and an expensive one. At least I am
glad that I brought along an ample letter of credit. The Y.M.C.A. could
have refitted me, but I chose not to take my things free from them. If
I had had more gumption I should have saved more, and besides the
Y.M.C.A. has done fully enough for me financially already.

Paris life at present is marked by the bombardment and by the
air-raids. Nobody bothers about the bombardment at all, or tries
to take the slightest precaution even when there is a succession of
shots. Generally the shots are not very numerous, as a protection
against the air-raids there is an admirable system of alarm signals.
When hostile air-planes cross the lines headed toward Paris, fire-
apparatus is sent through the streets making an unearthly racket
with sirens. After this there is usually plenty of time to dress and go
down into an abri. The cellar of the house nearby across the street
from my hotel serves the purpose admirably. When all danger is
over, there is a signal made by bells and in other ways, this is a great

bore and a great interruption to sleep, but at the same time a very efficacious preventative of danger.

On Saturday, June 1, I was sent out here to the provisional headquarters of the Direction regionale, which is not very far from Paris.[19] Yesterday, with another American director I took out as much tobacco and cigarettes as we could carry on bicycles to a place about ten miles from here, where his Foyer is situated.[20] I had hoped to be able to engage in free distribution of tobacco to passing infantry along the roadsides. But there are official difficulties, and I am going back to Paris on the next train. The train last night was so late that I spent the night here instead of undertaking a midnight trip to Paris.

The long bicycle trip yesterday (we returned by a longer route) was most interesting. A smiling beautiful country under the imminent threat of war. The roar of the cannon could be heard in the distance, but that was all as yet. Life here is gloomy. The civil population is leaving and food for unattached travelers is consequently scarce. The scenes at the station are pathetic. It makes one's heart sick to see the aged and infirm in the midst of the interminable delays—leaving their homes and under the immediate menace of the German bombs.

The house where the Foyer directors live here was completely destroyed by a bomb Friday night. Fortunately they slept elsewhere that night—for the first time. If they had been in the house most or all of them would have been killed. At the same time it must be said that that house is perhaps the only one which has so far been destroyed here.

I have contracted the habit of descending into the cellar when hostile airplanes are passing.

My companion on the bicycle trip yesterday was an Amherst French professor originally from Virginia. He speaks French perfectly, as does another Foyer director here. So my disparaging remarks about the linguistic attainments of my colleagues will have to be modified on the basis of a wider generalization.

19. "Meaux" is the name of the city given in a marginal note. Meaux is about 23 miles E.N.E. of Paris and about 56 miles W.S.W. of Reims.
20. This place is noted in the margin as "Lizy-sur-Ourcq," which is about 34 miles E.N.E. of Paris and 50 miles W.S.W. of Reims.

Bobby writes frequently—I think every week.

I do not know what I shall do. But I rather think it is time to get into American work.

Love to all
Your loving Son
Gresham

June 7, 1918

My dearest Mother:

To save my life I cannot think just when I wrote my last letter, but I think it was nearly a week ago. At any rate, last Saturday I went out again to a town not far from Paris where the regional directors of the Foyers that have been dispossessed have their quarters. On Sunday I took a bicycle trip of twenty or thirty miles to carry some tobacco & investigate. This was in company with the American director of a Foyer of the region. Official difficulties against the kind of roadside work that I had desired emerged, and after consultation with the regional directors I returned to Paris. The civil population of the town was leaving, and it was hard to get meals. At Paris the Foyer authorities at the central office told me to await instructions. This I have been doing with great anticipation, since I need the time sorely in order to get some clothes. The other day I took lunch with Reid Dickson, one of the Benham boys who is in the Y.M.C.A. work. After various efforts I at last saw Bobby Freeman, who is in general charge of the religious work in the American Y.M.C.A. in France. He seemed to think that he wanted me to talk to the boys in the camps, and took up with the American head of the Foyers the question of my transfer. The most that has been granted so far is that until I am wanted in the Foyers I can do work to which Freeman may assign me. So I am leaving to-night on a rather long journey in order to work on Sunday. After a day or so

I am to return here to Paris. Sometimes I feel terribly lazy about doing any intellectual work—strangely dull and heavy. Perhaps this is partly due to lack of sleep last night. Just as I was returning in the Métro from a presentation of Corneille's "Polyeucte" at the Théâtre Francais, the "alerte" was sounded. Since the station at which the train stopped was not deep enough to be an abri, I beat it toward my hotel. On the way the "tiré de barrage" began, and I stopped in at an abri until after twelve o'clock, when I moved to the abri near our hotel.[21] The "berlogne," or signal for the end of the danger, was sounded soon after. These are the regular incidents of life in Paris. All along the street the houses that have good cellars are plainly marked. For instance Tom's Hotel du Danube is marked, as I happened to notice, "Abri, 100 places." The bombardment by canon has almost ceased for the present.

Of course I have been calling at the Y.M.C.A. every day for mail. I hope to get something to-day from home.

It rather looks as though there is going to be a change in my activities. Good bye learning of French and a lot of other fun! I cannot help feeling sad about it, and I wish I could continue in the French work. But perhaps the other will be more useful, if I can shake off the deadly lassitude that I feel at present. I just cannot get up enough energy even to write an adequate letter. But I send lots of love to you & all who are at home.

Your loving son
Gresham

June 13, 1918

My dearest Mother:

The weeks in Paris, which I thought would bring me into closer touch with home, have been on the contrary lean and hungry

21. A "tiré de barrage" is heavy artillery or anti-aircraft fire.

weeks as far as news from home is concerned. Such are the chances of war-time mails; letters seem to arrive just when they are least expected.

On Friday night I left on a long journey to do some speaking in an American camp. The trains were tremendously crowded and I had to change at about three o'clock in the morning, so that sleep was not much in evidence. In the morning I arrived at a beautiful little city where I had to wait all day until five o'clock for the only train to my destination.[22] In the morning I sallied forth with my Guide—Joanne (feeble substitute for the non-procurable Baedeker), and thoroughly enjoyed seeing the place.[23] The views from the citadel were particularly fine, the surrounding country being broken by lofty hills. I arrived at my destination at about eight o'clock, and spent the night in comfortable quarters provided for me by the Y.M.C.A.[24] It was a relief to be far enough from the front not to be wakened by airplanes. The camp is most comfortable and well arranged, and the Y.M.C.A. arrangements really splendid. Only, religion is given but an infinitesimal place in the program. In the morning there was a service conducted by the Episcopal chaplain. Almost seventy-five men were present. A ball-game was going on just outside, and every now and then the ball would knock against the side of the house where the service was being held. In the afternoon I addressed a group of colored men—not artificial colored men from New York but the genuine article from Virginia.[25] In the morning at 7.30 an "informal service" (in the main building) was scheduled. There was some difficulty about getting it started, because a ball-game was going on just outside the room where the service was to have been held, and was making more noise than the ball-game itself because of the presence of a large crowd of enthusiastic spectators. At last we moved over into the other compartment of the building—it

22. A marginal note says this city was "Besançon," which is about 210 miles S.E. of Paris.

23. "Baedeker" was a travel guide publisher.

24. The destination, according to Machen's marginal note, was "Valdahon," which is about 225 miles S.E. of Paris and about 15 miles E.S.E. of Besançon.

25. Machen may be thinking of the minstrel shows with reference to the New York comparison to Virginia. The minstrels were white men who blackened their faces and performed for entertainment. Al Jolson (1886–1950) was a particularly famous minstrel. Regarding Machen's racial terminology, see the footnote in his letter of Jan. 30, 1919.

is used for a reading-and-writing room—and after the leader had explained that nobody need stop his writing unless he felt like it, the service began. I did the best I could under rather discouraging circumstances, and got along better than might have been expected. The ballgames in question are more or less under the supervision of the Y.M.C.A. itself. The chaplain acquiesces with apparent contentment. I did not notice any Y.M.C.A. workers in attendance at the chaplain's service, though I believe one said after wards that he had been there. It is right to remark that the head-secretary, and the "religious-work-director" were both away. Since my services did not seem to be required further, I took the night train back to Paris.

To-morrow I am bound for another American headquarters, and may work there permanently.[26] The religious work director wants help, and I may become his assistant. Unfortunately the director in question is expecting to leave before long and another man is to be put in his place. Also Bobby Freeman is returning to America. I shall therefore be left more or less adrift. As yet I have not been given my release from the French work but am allowed to do American work for the present.

Paris is still an exceedingly pleasant place to be, despite the assaults of the Boches. I have been enjoying the Théâtre Francais. Also I have been getting some clothes and other equipment. But, oh how I miss the things I lost! The loss of check-books and other indispensable records is perhaps the worst of all—how shall I ever make out next year's income-tax return, for example?—but every now & then I think of something else that is gone.

I do wish I could get to work—this miserable uselessness is what gets on my nerves. If I only had some friend among the authorities here! But the only one who has been interested in me is leaving.

After weeks of waiting I was told to-day that an American mail is expected not for a week. It seems an age since I got a word from home. Most anything may have happened. My thoughts are with you all, you know.

26. The town is named, according to a marginal annotation, "Baccarat," which is about 210 miles E. of Paris, or about 31 miles E.S.E. of Nancy.

By the way I had my picture taken to-day. I have not seen my proofs, but the photographer reported the four negatives good. I am having three copies of each of the four pictures sent to you at the Baltimore address. They ought to get off in about two weeks. The photographer is Eug. Piron, 23, Rue Royale. Extra copies can be secured later if desired.

Is it Seal Harbor this summer?

I wish I were there with you.

Your loving son
Gresham

8

A "HUT" IN THE AMERICAN YMCA

June 20 to July 16, 1918

While awaiting a more permanent assignment, Dr. Machen is given brief duties involving travel to various locations, but more importantly he will be given the opportunity to lead worship services with the soldiers. With his escape from the advancing Germans he also enjoyed an escape from the Foyer du Soldat program. Now, he would be working with the American troops in the "Y" huts. "Camp de la Grande Voivre" ("Mud Camp"), will be his first post as an American "Y" director. He will find the labor strenuous in the midst of the noise and dangers of war.

June 20, 1918

My dearest Mother:

My last letter, I believe, was written Thursday, June 13, just before I left Paris. On Friday I reported to the divisional headquarters of the Y.M.C.A. in the region where I am at present writing. For several days I was put at the work of addressing meetings at various camps. I spoke on Saturday night, on Sunday morning, and Sunday night, on Monday night and Tuesday night. The necessary trips were made in the Fords that are operated by the Y.M.C.A. I also took a long trip in a Ford on Saturday with one of the secretaries who was on a sort of time of inspection. The country is perfectly beautiful, and although we were at one point only some two miles from the front line, the villages have not been devastated very much. There is plenty of excitement in the lines, but the rear is left pretty much alone even by air planes. The forests are magnificent.

The Y.M.C.A. "huts" for the most part are very remarkable quarters, in marked contrast to the terrible arrangement of the Foyers du Soldat.[1] But since the Y.M.C.A. men regularly move with the troops in the American army it is not worth while usually to provide very elaborate quarters in any one place. Certainly the services of the association are highly appreciated by every one. On Saturday night, I spoke in a tent, near a little village, and on Sunday morning, in another village, out of doors.[2] My congregation on Sunday morning was composed of Alabama men.[3] The village street, with passing motor-cars, etc., certainly was a hard place for speaking. On Sunday night I spoke to a big crowd in the cinema hall of the town where our Y.M.C.A. headquarters for the region is located.[4] The crowd had been attracted by a band concert, and it was a little hard to make a religious talk after that. On Monday night, in a little village near the lines, I had a much more satisfactory audience, though it was not so large.[5] After spending the night in the village in question, the secretary & I walked about a mile and a half to see another secretary, whose place is by a village within a mile or so of the front line.[6] Both of those men work right in the lines as well as in the villages, and sometimes they have very exciting times. On

1. For the account of one man's experience as a hut director, see William C. Levere (1872–1927), ed. Jenny Thompson, *My Hut: A Memoir of a Y.M.C.A. Volunteer in World War One*, Evanston: Sigma Alpha Epsilon Foundation, 2006.

2. Machen's speech in the tent is noted to have been in "Merviller," and the Sunday morning meeting was at "Vacqueville." Merviller is about 31 miles E.S.E. of Nancy, and Vacqueville is about 1.8 miles E. of Merviller.

3. Machen's note says these men were from the "42nd Division."

4. The town is named, according to a marginal annotation, "Baccarat," which is about 210 miles E. of Paris, or about 31 miles E.S.E. of Nancy.

5. The margin note designates the village as "Reherrey," which is about 26 miles S.E. of Nancy.

6. The village is "Migneville," which is about 30 miles E.S.E. of Nancy.

Tuesday night I spoke at still another village, and had a fairly good time.[7]

But now I am in utterly different circumstances. On account of the fact that many of the secretaries are leaving with their men, there is great need for secretaries to carry on the work here with the soldiers who are arriving.[8] So I have been drafted into taking charge of a hut in one of the villages. I arrived at my post yesterday. A more discouraging looking place, it must be confessed, could hardly be imagined. The village, which is some eight miles from the Germans, and entirely quiet, is small and rather dirty; the wood shack which has been used for the Y.M.C.A. is perhaps about the dirtiest spot that I ever saw, and the roof leaks nearly everywhere. There is scarcely any place at all to sit down. But all the merchandise that they sent out with me yesterday was sold in a very few hours. Early this morning I walked in to Y.M.C.A. headquarters, turned in over one thousand francs and asked for more goods. The goods came this afternoon, and to-morrow, when I am expecting a rush, still more are promised. You just ought to see the boys go for the canned pears. I also have little biscuits, chocolate (solid, not liquid), cigars, and tobacco.

June 21.

I have never had such a hard job in my life. There is not a moment to write or do anything for myself. The rush is tremendous. I must send this letter off unfinished to let you know that I am well.

Love to all
Gresham

7. Per Machen's note in the margin, the village is "Bertrichamps," which is about 34 miles S.E. of Nancy.

8. Per the margin note, the "secretaries leaving with their men" were "Leaving with 42nd Division."

June 23, 1918

My dearest Mother:

My last letter had to be sent off unfinished, I was just trying
to impart to you some of the impressions of the last ten days. The
first few days of my present job were among the very busiest of
my life. This American work is certainly very different from the
Foyer du Soldat. Every day, and sometimes twice a day, I went in to
divisional Y.M.C.A. headquarters (a long forty minutes walk) to seek
merchandise to sell. By making myself a nuisance at the warehouse
I managed usually to get stock for an hour or two of sales. Several
times my sales for a day amounted to well over 1,000 francs, and
they would perhaps have been five times as great if I had had the
goods. Sweet crackers were particularly popular. I limited each man
to one package, but even then four big cases of them lasted hardly
any time. As for bars of chocolate, I could not keep them at all.

But Saturday night most of the crowd moved away. This broke
up the plans for Sunday services—I had managed to get hold of
a chaplain for the evening service and was going to conduct a
morning service myself. All I was able to do was to read a chapter
from the Bible and offer a prayer with six or eight men.

When I got news of the move I at once walked in to consult
with the divisional secretary. He told me to stick to my present post
till matters could be settled. But now I am going to the neighboring
camp to which the men have gone.[9] It is going to be a very, very
big job. In marked contrast to our present quarters, a very large
wooden building has been set aside for the use of the Y.M.C.A.
Yesterday evening, when I walked over on a tour of inspection I
found a very large crowd of men in the building having an informal
entertainment conducted by local talent which was splendid. When
I get on the job I am going to try to put the entertainments on days
other than Sunday.

To-day the major, who has been very cordial to the Y.M.C.A.,
is going to send over a waggon and a squad of men to move me, my

9. A note in the margin designates this as, "Camp de la Grande Voivre near Brouville."
The village of Brouville is 30 miles S.E. of Nancy and 2.7 miles N. of Baccarat.

personal belongings and such slight equipment of the Y.M.C.A. as is to be found here.[10] Before the headquarters were moved from here I had begun taking my meals at the major's mess. The officers present seemed to be an unusually fine crowd of men. I think they will be real company to me, and I sure do need company.

The kindness of the non-commissioned officers and privates beats anything I ever dreamed of. They always seem willing to turn in and devote all their leisure time to helping the Y.M.C.A. In short, I have a big job and a job worth while at last. I only hope it is not too big for me.

It has been nearly a month since I heard from home, and I am afraid there is no immediate chance for a letter. The uncertainty about my address has added to the delay. I am not quite sure whether Paris Y.M.C.A. headquarters has as yet received my address. The system of mailing letters is some different from that which prevailed when I was with the French army. Mail, for example, has to be read by an officer of the post where I am staying, etc.

Love to all,
Your loving son
Gresham

[Beginning with the following letter, Dr. Machen used letterhead which reads, "American Y.M.C.A. (with its logo) On Active Service with the American Expeditionary Force"]

June 29, 1918

My dearest Mother:

After a month without news from home, you may imagine my delight at receiving your letters number 21 and number 22, of May 18 and May 23. No. 20 seems not yet to have arrived. Since I entered

10. There is a note in the margin that "the major" was "Maj. Powel."

the American service, my mail arrangements are entirely different; my mail, for example, has now to be censored by an officer, etc. As for my opportunities for writing, they are almost nil, since I am over-burdened with a bewildering mass of duties large and small.

The better news about Nena delighted me, even though I had your warning not to be too jubilant till the permanency of the improvement is established. I am glad you are going to Seal, and shall venture, I think, to address my letter there. Of course I feel a little dismayed, as you thought I might be, by your care of the babies. But maybe with the help of Betty you may get along better than might be expected and if the sleeping quarters be divided satisfactorily you may get some quiet, and even a little bit of company from the babies' presence. At any rate I am forcing myself to look on it that way.

The news about the church is good, since we have been in great need of elders and deacons. Mr. Ober's death is very sad.

I am delighted to hear that Arly and Helen are well settled for the summer, and also delighted at the news of Arly's good case and at the praise (well-deserved I am sure) of his lecture on "Law and Literature."

During this week I certainly have had some job. On Monday I moved to a camp away from town.[11] There is a large body of men there, and I am the only Y.M.C.A. worker. The demand for the things to eat and smoke is insatiable. Pretty much everyday I have had to go (often on foot) to a town about four miles or so away to stir up the Y.M.C.A. supply department.[12] The worst of it is that supplies cannot be sent direct to camp in Y.M.C.A. trucks or camionettes, because of bad roads, but can only be sent to the nearest point on the main road.[13] Thence they have to be brought in by army waggon. The process is long and difficult. It involves numberless pedestrian trips to two separate and distinct villages. The other evening I did succeed in obtaining 1000 packages of cookies, which we sell for a franc apiece. Limiting each man to one package, we sold the whole thousand in about three hours, in addition to many boxes of cigars, and other merchandise. Yesterday our sales amounted to about 1,900

11. Machen's note in the margin reads, "Camp de la Grande Voivre" ("Mud Camp").

12. The town is named, according to a marginal annotation, "Baccarat," which is about 210 miles E. of Paris, or about 31 miles E.S.E. of Nancy.

13. The word, "camionette," is French for a small truck or pick-up truck.

francs. There was a line extending out from our canteen that looked like the line at the ticket-window of a world-series game. Of course we could sell perhaps ten times the amount a day if we could only get the goods. I do not think the Y.M.C.A. divisional headquarters realizes the relative importance of this post. Other canteens serving one fourth the number of men are well stocked, whereas I am left in the cold. However the difficulties are great and the Y.M.C.A. is undermanned. I am able to get along here only because of the help of a sergeant & one or two of the men who have done the work at the counter as much or more than I. But we need a force of about three or four secretaries.

A big part of the routine work is the job of making out money orders for Americans. Their name is legion, and some of them are for substantial sums. In addition, I have been sending many more orders to Italy. This is a particularly troublesome job. For the American money-orders there is a regular Y.M.C.A. form, and the thing is done by Y.M.C.A. machinery, but in the case of the Italian orders I have simply to take the men's' money, give a purely personal receipt, and then buy the orders in my own name at the French post-office on my next trip to a neighboring town. But I am glad to do the work. The sending of money to relations seems to me to be one of the most important routine services that the Y.M.C.A. is rendering.

Sunday, June 30

Last night, after a great deal of trouble, I got in another little dribble of stock. Again there was a long line in front of our building. An accountant from the central office came in to make an inventory. I think he was impressed with the inadequacy of my stock & the need and importance of the post. Perhaps he will take the matter up at Y.M.C.A. divisional headquarters. We have a very large hut, placed at our disposal by the military authorities. There are scarcely any tables or benches in it as yet, but the regimental authorities have put a carpenter on the job. A stage has been constructed, & I hope to have a counter also and a place to look up my goods. At present the hut is being used as a guard house, & has therefore to be kept open all the time. All night the guard is coming in & out, and sometimes the prisoners make a good deal of conversing. Sleep therefore is very difficult, even aside from the noise of air-planes & an occasional gas-alarm. The danger of gas is very slight so far from the front, but the men have been awakened several times when gas has been signaled at a considerable distance.[14] When the guards become more experienced, no doubt these alarms can be avoided but it is well to be on the safe side. One can sleep the better if it is known that we shall be awakened in plenty of time to put on our masks.

This morning the chaplain of the regiment, who is a catholic, has just held a general service & is now celebrating mass as I write.[15] The general service was frankly supernatural—the loaves and fishes—and satisfactory. The reading of the Gospels was urged, & the moral exhortations were good. As hymns we had "Onward Christian Soldiers," "Lead, Kindly Light." I was pleased with the service. It was far, far better than what we get from the Protestant liberals.

One night during the week I held a little service, but had very few men in attendance.[16] This morning before service I had a little Bible study with about a half-dozen men. The chaplain's service, I am exceedingly glad to say, was well attended. To-night, I am going to try to hold an evening service.

I am still eating at the Major's mess, & find it exceedingly pleasant. About six officers are there. I like them & the major himself particularly.

Sleeping in a passage-way is not pleasant. What a soft life I had when I was with the French! I am ruffled by my failure to get what the men need. They are absolutely dependent for necessities as well as little luxuries upon the Y.M.C.A. canteen. And I have practically nothing for them; but I for myself have little sleep.

Love to all. And how glad I am to hear from you.

Your loving son
Gresham

14. Machen noted in the margin that his hut was "4 or 5 miles from the front."

15. A notation in the margin reads, "306th Infantry Col. Vidaner."

16. In the margin is written, "They nearly always had a roll-call of the men just at the hour of my service."

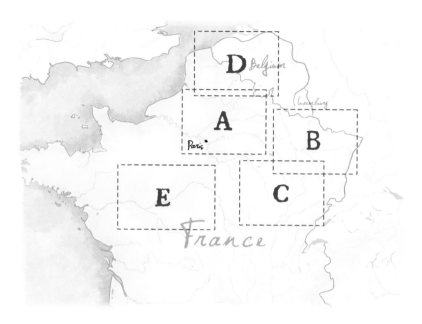

J. Gresham Machen's travels with the YMCA during World War I
January 1918 – March 1919

A

Where I barely escaped across the bridge from the Germans

I saw the devastation of the war from here.

The city where I saw the ruined cathedral and great destruction.

Chemin des Dames

This was my first post with the Foyers du Soldat.

Beauvais •

Missy-sur-Aisne • Ostel
Lemoise • Chavonne
Soissons • St-Mard
Chacrise • Cirg-Salsogne • Oeuilly
Serches • Braine • Bourg-et-Comin
Oulchy-le-Château • Breny

Lizy-sur-Ourcq •
Meaux •

Paris •

Luxembourg

Somme

Oise

Aisne

Reims →

Seine

Marne

France

Section A (see map above)
February–June 1918

Bois de Montfaucon
Avocourt
Verdun

The closest I got to an existing front was near here.

Germany

B

Jaulny
Thiaucourt
Doullonville

Bar-le-Duc • Commercy
Toul
Nancy

Mérviller
Brouville • Merviller
Baccarat • Badonviller
Pexonne
Bertrichamps

My first YMCA hut (of any permanency) was "mud-camp" or "camp de la Grande Voivre," near Brouville.

Chaumont

France

Section B (see map on preceding page)
June 1918 – January 1919

Seine

Marne

C

Bar-sur-Seine • Chaumont

I spent a week with the 80th division here.

Vertault • Molesmes
Dicey
Châtillon-sur-Seine

Ource

Langres
Buxerolles
Bussières-les-Belmont
Recey-sur-Ource
Grenant
Colmier-le-Haut
Coublanc
Prauthoy

I dined in the mess of the colonel of the 320th Field Artillery.

Doubs

I roomed in a home owned by a couple whose only daughter died the week before.

Dijon
Besançon

Saône

France

Section C (see map on preceding page)
January–February 1919

North Sea

Dunkerque • • Malo-les-Bains
Calais • Lichtervelde • Thielt
Ypres • Roulers • Deinze • Gent
Olsene • Synghem
Ejine
Oudenaarde

Schildt

Where the soldiers dug-in
in holes and there were
no trenches

Bruxelles

Lille •

France

D

Belgium

Maas

Section D (see initial map)
End of 1918

E

• Le Mans

Dourron-Marlotte •

Paris
76 km

Loire

The château made me
want to read Ivanhoe
over again.

Angers

Saumur •

YMCA headquarters
for me for over a week.

Tours

• Château-de-Chambord

Where the great central
warehouses of the U.S.
forces were located.

Gièvres

Vienne

France

Section E (see initial map)
Early December 1918 – January 1919

Address:—
Care of American Y. M. C. A.
12 Rue d'Aguesseau
Paris

January 29, 1918

My dearest Mother:

It seems a long time since I wrote to you from the steamer, and I am afraid it will seem longer still before the present letter arrives. Mail, I am informed, especially on account of the censorship, is necessarily very irregular. It is really hardly worth while for me to begin expecting anything from home just yet, but I shall inquire this afternoon when I go to the Y. M. C. A. office. Needless to say I am eager to hear from you and all of those at home.

After passing through the submarine zone without the slightest excitement on the part of anybody so far as I could see, we arrived at the mouth of the river on Friday afternoon. The passage of the bar, which on account of thick weather conditions was not in sight of land, was rather curious. On account of comparatively shallow water the ocean swell become remarkably regular and powerful. The great surges really looked one almost an eighth of a mile long and yet quite steep at the crest. When they caught the vessel sideways they made her roll fully as deep (though not as quickly) as in the stormiest weather that we had had in midocean. The weather was fair and beautiful, the fog-banks only adding to the beauty of the scene.

Soon after his arrival in Paris, Dr. Machen wrote this letter to his mother, January 29, 1918, telling her more about his sea journey from home and passing through "the submarine zone."

used to have a magnificent appetite for it when I got my coffee at a reasonable hour. At present

LE FOYER DU SOLDAT

UNION FRANCO-AMÉRICAINE

Y.M.C.A.

we are serving only about fifty cups of chocolate or less in the morning, but after our canteen is fitted up and advertised a little we shall be useful enough. The chocolate is sold for four sous (20 centimes, the price of course you know, but as it takes me some time to compute by mental arithmetic). Every soldier brings his own tin cup or "quart" as it is technically called. This custom saves a lot of trouble so far as the washing of dishes is concerned. In addition to the chocolate we have little crackers (delicious), tobacco, cigarettes, matches, candles, condensed milk, anchovies & sardines. A brisk sale of candles has been going on all along in the

This undated portion of a letter recounts Dr. Machen's experience serving hot chocolate to the soldiers at the front as he filled their "quarts" with the hot beverage.

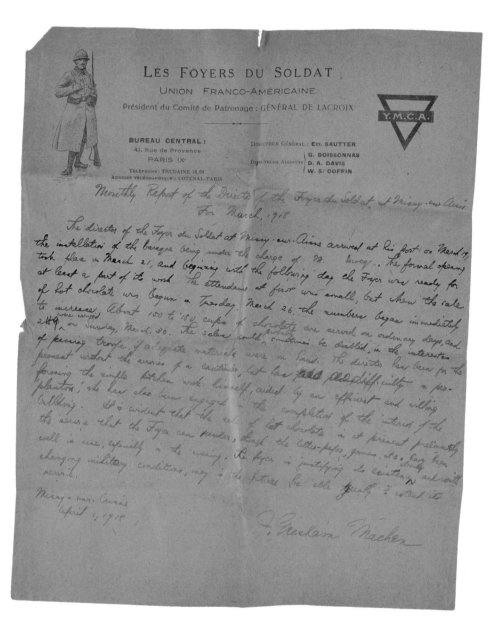

LES FOYERS DU SOLDAT
UNION FRANCO-AMÉRICAINE
Président du Comité de Patronage : GÉNÉRAL DE LACROIX

Y.M.C.A.

BUREAU CENTRAL :
41, Rue de Provence
PARIS IX·
TÉLÉPHONE : TRUDAINE 28,60
ADRESSE TÉLÉGRAPHIQUE : COTÉNAL-PARIS

DIRECTEUR GÉNÉRAL : Em. SAUTTER
DIRECTEURS ADJOINTS :
G. BOISSONNAS
D. A. DAVIS
W. S. COFFIN

Monthly Report of the Director of the Foyer du Soldat at Missy-sur-Aisne
For March, 1918

The director of the Foyer du Soldat at Missy-sur-Aisne arrived at his post on March 19, the installation of the baraque being under the charge of M. Buroga. The formal opening took place on March 21, and beginning with the following day the Foyer was ready for at least a part of its work. The attendance at first was small, but when the sale of hot chocolate was begun on Tuesday, March 26, the numbers began immediately to increase. About 150 to 180 cups of chocolate are served on ordinary days, and 249 were served on Sunday, March 30. The sales could probably sometimes be doubled, in the interests of passing troops, if adequate materials were on hand. The director has been for the present without the services of a cantinier, but has had difficulty in per-forming the simple kitchen work himself, aided by an efficient and willing planton, who has also been engaged in the completion of the interior of the building. It is evident that the sale of hot chocolate is at present preliminary to the service that the Foyer can render, though the letter-paper, games, etc. have been well in use, especially in the evening. The foyer is justifying its existence and with changing military conditions, may in the future be able greatly to extend its service.

Missy-sur-Aisne
April 1, 1918

J. Gresham Machen

Dr. Machen's concern for doing his job by the book is exemplified in this monthly report of his *Foyer du Soldat* work for March 1918.

AMERICAN
Y.M.C.A.

ON ACTIVE SERVICE
WITH THE
AMERICAN EXPEDITIONARY FORCE

June 23   1918

My dearest Mother:

My last letter had to be sent off unfinished, just dum trying to impart to you some
of the impressions of the last ten days. the first
few days of my present job were among the very
busiest of my life. This American work is certainly very different from the Foyer du Soldat.
Every day, and sometimes twice a day I
went in to divisional Y.M.C.A. headquarters
(a long forty minutes' walk) to seek merchandise to sell. By making myself a
nuisance at the warehouse I managed
usually to get stock for an hour or
so of sales. Several times my sales
for a day amounted to well over 1,000
francs, and they would perhaps have
been five times as great if I had had
the goods. Sweet crackers were particulary

Following Dr. Machen's hurried departure from Missy-sur-Aisne
with the Germans at his heels, he entered service with the American
YMCA program. In this page from a letter home he tells about his
busy schedule.

HOTEL LORD BYRON

CHAMPS-ÉLYSÉES · PARIS

DESPOUYS, PROP^{RE}

TÉLÉPH. WAGRAM 37-73

Address:
Y. M. C. A.
12 Rue d. Aguesseau
Paris

October 20, 1918

My dearest Mother:

Paris is evidently looking up; I could get only a tiny little uncomfortable cubby-hole of a room at that old place, the Beaulieu, and shall probably move over here to-morrow, the two hotels being under the same management. This place, I am sorry to say, is too English, and there are even Y. M. C. A. secretaries in the dining-room. You don't know what an immense relief it is to get into a different atmosphere even for a day or so. I do not mean anything derogatory to the Y. M. C. A.; it is the change that is desired. At any rate, the last time I was here there was no great need for rooms. It was in the darkest days of the great retreat, and the "grosse Bertha" was going full tilt. Now of course

In this letter written from Paris, October 20, 1918, Dr. Machen recounts for his mother his current living situation and comments on the preponderance of English speaking in his French hotel.

GRAND HOTEL DU PALAIS-ROYAL
4. RUE DE VALOIS
ADR. ☩ OTELPALROY
☎ CENTRAL 17-47

PARIS, LE 12 janvier, 1919

My dearest Mother:

Your letter of Nov. 30 was received considerably later than that of Dec. 8, and I am not quite sure whether I have answered it. At any rate it deserves a far better answer than I can possibly give it. I am glad you received my letter of Nov. 7, and that along with the next one, which was written shortly after the armistice, contained an account of things which in themselves, aside from my feeble account of them, were undoubtedly interesting.

Your account of Arly's defense of the two young Hagerstown fellows is highly interesting and gratifying. I wish I could congratulate the successful attorney in person, and in particular I wish I could have been

---

In this letter of January 12, 1919, Dr. Machen goes on in the pages that follow to ask his mother to find an earlier letter he wrote to her and remove critical comments he had made regarding J. Ross Stevenson.

January 3, 1918.

Dear Gresham:

I don't know how to write to you about your going away. You are more like my own brother to me than anybody that I have in the world, and I don't let myself stop to think how much it means to me to have you go. And yet I am glad and proud that you are doing it, and it is my firm belief

A letter from LeRoy Gresham, first cousin to J. Gresham Machen.

that God is going to bless and prosper you in the world to which you are going. I need not tell you that my heart goes with you. I am going to try to write to you regularly, if you will keep me posted as to your address through your mother. In the meantime I am sending you a little pocket Testament bound in pigskin to remember old Salem by.

Jessie and the boys send their love.

Affectionately,
Jay

A letter announcing Machen's return to Baltimore, dated March 12, 1919.

J. Gresham Machen's mother,
Mary Gresham Machen
(1849–1931).

J. Gresham Machen's father,
Arthur W. Machen (1827–1915).

The Machen family home, 217 Monument Street, Baltimore, Maryland. A note on the back in Minnie G. Machen's hand says, "This is an old picture of our house with Uncle ringing the bell—taken some years ago. But I thought you might like it now to remind you of home." "Uncle" is Thomas Gresham, Mrs. Machen's brother. Both pictures were sent to Machen while he was in France in World War I.

The interior of the Machen family home. On the left of the picture a piano can be seen, which may be the one on which Machen learned how to play. In a letter to his mother from August 5, 1918, he commented that he played the piano and was the "musical director" in the evening service he led.

Alexander Hall at Princeton Theological Seminary.

July 4, 1918

My dearest Mother:

Your letter of June 7, and Arly's of April 15, which came to hand at the same time, constituted bright spots in the midst of a trying and wearying time. The good news about Nena delights my soul, and I felt cheered by your joy at receiving my telegram. Existence over here is so desperately lonely that it is a comfort to know that somebody cares. You are very brave and good about the babies. As for Arly and Helen and their country home and Arly's good cases—all that is just splendid. Please let Arly know how much I appreciated his letter; which was simply packed with just the kind of news that I wanted to have. Even two and a half months late, such a letter is exceedingly interesting.

I have just received a communication from the Baltimore Country Club to the effect that my name had been posted some months ago for non-payment of dues. Since I explained by letter before I left the reason for my absence, I confess that I am just about as angry at the humiliation inflicted upon me as could well be imagined. I should be very grateful if Arly would straighten this out. By the same mail I learned that "Monti," my old associate in the Foyer du Soldat, had not received my long French letter, which cost me a deal of labor, nor had he received the costly uniform which I sent him from Paris a month ago. Also there is no news from my suit-case. Evidently the letter I addressed to the non-commissioned officer concerned has not arrived. These annoyances help to make life hard.

And life is hard in my present position—there is no question about it. We are supposed to be in a "rest-camp," but there is little rest about it—especially for the Y.M.C.A. man. Practically every night we have gas-alarms, which require us to put on our masks, although really there has been no gas near-by so far. Far worse are the air-plane visits, with the terrific noise of near-by machine guns. And then the guard was in the Y.M.C.A. building during last week. The changing of the guard and incidental noises filled up the intervals between more serious disturbances. I suppose I have had about an average of three or four hours of sleep a night. During the day-time, our building is about the busiest and the noisiest place I ever saw. The concourse of the Grand Central station at 6 A.M. on business days is the only place that might compare with it. When we have something to eat for sale, a line forms in front of our cantine like the line before a world-series game. In short there is no privacy and no quiet day or night. Day before yesterday I received an associate in the shape of a Y.M.C.A. secretary just come from America. He is a great help—an Episcopal minister by the name of Redint who came from Virginia who knows Cousin Kensey.[17] In his presence I count myself fortunate. In the midst of the crowd I really needed a little company.

Pretty nearly every day I have gone to the neighboring town—a brisk walk of about an hour, when some obliging auto truck or even an American Colonel's auto is not encountered— to see about supplies, send money-orders for Italians, make a hundred inquiries, and do other things too numerous to mention. Naturally the work at the camp is left loose ends, but there is plenty of volunteer assistance from the soldiers. Our business is large—day before yesterday for example our sales amounted to almost 3,200 francs, to say nothing of some thousand francs entrusted to me for money-orders. The problem is to conserve the stock. We have limited the amount of individual purchases to one thing of each kind to a man—for instance no one can buy more than one cigar—but to-day we have actually had to stop the sales off after an hour or so in the morning in order to have a little something for the rest of the week.

My efforts at evangelical work have not been successful. When the hour arrived for my evening service last Sunday, a crowd of men were playing rag-time on the piano, and it was evident that no one present was there for the purpose of the service. In general, all of the deeper things of life have been crowded out in the rush of business details. I might as well be back in the French work so far as any evangelical work is concerned. But opportunity may come when least expected. There are very few Protestants among the soldiers— that explains partly the difficulty in finding a starting point.

17. Both of these names are unclear and those written in the transcriptions are guesses.

What a peaceful luxurious life I had when I was with the French army! And what a toilsome nerve-wracking life here! But the value of one's life, I suppose, is in inverse proportion to the ease and comfort of it. Certainly the American job is the bigger job of the two.

I am forgetting what French I knew, my environment here being altogether American.

Amusements and athletic activities here are very largely managed by the regiment. I scarcely know what is going on.

Last night we were disturbed for a couple of hours by cannonading (mostly our guns) and by an order to get ready to move in case it should be necessary. But before and after I got the best sleep that I have had for some time. It was too hazy to be good for airplanes.

Love to all,
Your loving son
Gresham

July 8, 1918

My dearest Mother:

The missing letter, number 23, of May 31, arrived the other day, much to my delight. The letter is sweet as usual, and the enclosed pictures of the babies are among the best that I can ever remember seeing. I love to come back to those pictures again and again unless I feel particularly blue.

As usual I do not know where to begin in my narrative. Since I cannot remember when my last letter was written. The first considerable stock for our canteen was secured by the kindness of the Colonel of one regiment who took me with him in his auto to a neighboring town where he secured two large three-ton auto trucks for me to transport supplies from our divisional headquarters. The stock has not lasted very long, Indeed we could have sold practically all of it in a single day. As a matter of fact we have economized by opening up for the sale of popular "eats" only an hour or so every day. At present the stock is nearly gone.

My present position is one of the most discouraging I ever got into in my life. The great mass of the men that we see are Jews or Catholics; the Roman Catholic Chaplain has pre-empted the Sunday-morning service and two evenings during the week, and my efforts to unite some of the Protestant men have not met with much success. Last night I had a neighboring Protestant chaplain, formerly a student at Princeton Seminary, to address the little group of men that we succeeded in collecting. I am impressed, by the way, with the immense superiority of the opportunity offered by the chaplaincy to that offered by the Y.M.C.A. At the present post, particularly, the Y.M.C.A. secretary is a grocery clerk and nothing else. All deeper elements of the work are crowded out in one way or another. At least they seem to be. I have not yet given up all hope. This afternoon, for example, I hope to get two or three men together for prayer and Bible reading. We may find a comparatively quiet place at the edge of camp.

I get so tired of the constant loud ragtime in the hut that sometimes I feel as though I must simply run. Last night before the service I deliberately occupied the piano before the service by practicing some hymns to prevent it from being occupied. One hour a week is perhaps not too much for us to ask for the use of the piano for something other than amusement.

Last night I caught cold, and as I have gotten very little sleep for many nights past, you will understand that I am not feeling very exuberant. Living conditions are not particularly favorable in our "hut." The building is all in one piece. When the crowd leaves in the evening we have to put up our folding cots, and take them down again in the morning. There is no proper place to stow either the cots or the blankets.

A letter from a French non-commissioned officer, which has recently arrived about a month old, informs me that he had put my suitcase on a Y.M.C.A. automobile bound for Paris.[18] There is

---

18. In the margin Dr. Machen has written, "Sergent Aubé."

therefore a chance of recovering it, though if it arrived it is strange that the Paris Y.M.C.A. authorities have not communicated with me. I believe I told you that Montí had not received either the long letter or the uniform that I sent him from Paris a month or so ago. It is certainly provoking.

I can only live and do the best I can and hope that my present miserable and useless existence (or the present period of it) may be terminated in some way not now in sight. Apparently I am facing a closed door. However, it may be opened; and I suppose the acceptance of God's will means spiritual opportunity no matter how hard it may seem.

Perhaps I may go back with the French. It would certainly give me pleasure to do so, but I do not know whether I ought yet to give up all thought of getting evangelical work to do. Unfortunately Bobby Freeman has returned to America, so that I am altogether without a friend at court.

July 9.

Last night I had the first real good sleep I have enjoyed for two or three weeks; my cold seems somewhat better; and it is astonishing how much brighter things look. Yesterday afternoon two Christian fellows at the camp united with me in a half-hour of prayer & Bible study. I hope this may prove to be a beginning.

Your letter number 20 of May 8 has just arrived, after about three later letters. It is unusually sweet. The news about Helen & Arly is fine, and also about Nena, though I know her improvement must be slow. It is easy to understand your joy at Arly's happiness & I share it with you to the full.

To-day I am writing at a Y.M.C.A. hotel at the town where our Y.M.C.A. headquarters is.[19] Lots of money-orders for Italy have to be attended to—a tedious matter—as well as other business.

A reference in one of your recent letters to your desire for a picture of me reminds me that I had my picture taken by Euq. Pirou, 23 Rue Royale, Paris. The pictures—about three each of four different

---

19. The town is named, according to a marginal annotation, "Baccarat," which is about 210 miles E. of Paris, or about 31 miles E.S.E. of Nancy.

negatives were sent July 2. They were addressed to Baltimore. I hope Arly will get them for you & send them on.

Remember me most cordially to Betty as well as to Mrs. Kent (if she is with you) & to our other friends. The thought of Seal Harbor makes me homesick, but it is a comfort to me to think of you as enjoying the good air and the lovely scenes.

Your loving son
Gresham

July 13, 1918[20]

My dearest Mother:

Since my last letter the days have succeeded one another with little variation. The unsatisfactory features of the situation have been unabated; I have had almost no opportunities for any service other than that of selling tobacco and candles. We seem to be hemmed in on every side. The thing that gave me the most satisfaction was a little Bible class that I held for exactly five men, and that lasted exactly two lessons. The men were appreciative, and their appreciation showed me that what I have to offer is needed among the men in the army; there are lots of men, if we could only get at them, who would welcome not only Bible teaching but the kind of Bible teaching that I like myself. Unfortunately, however, neither my commanding officers in the Y.M.C.A. or anyone else is interested in bringing me into contact with such men.

Every other day or perhaps even more frequently, I have found it necessary to go, usually on foot, to the neighboring town where our Y.M.C.A. headquarters is situated. The cash is to be turned over to the treasurer, also American money orders, the money orders

20. The number is unclear in the original and it may be "July 10, 1918" instead of the thirteenth.

for Italy and Ireland are to be attended to; the supply department
of the Y.M.C.A. is to be nagged about giving us some stock for our
cantine; and Y.M.C.A. supplies are to be supplemented at civilian
stores. For example, there is the Gillette razor-blade supply, which
constituted a big problem. Every man among the troops who are
here now has been issued a Gillette razor for free before leaving
America; the demand for the extra blades is therefore insatiable.[21] I
drain the civilian stores and then re-sell to the men. And then there
are tooth-paste, tooth-brushes, shaving-brushes, pencils, paper, note
books, all of which are much in demand.

The Y.M.C.A. secretary at a neighboring post, who had
departed with his ten boxes of cigars en-route for us, coolly helped
himself to five of them. Afterwards he insulted my intelligence by
offering to pay for them! Ten boxes of cigars, sold at the rate of one
cigar to a man, would last only a few hours here. Yet here this fellow
whose place has been an offence to me by being so much better
stocked than ours (in proportion to the number to be served),
and who has sold freely while we have had to dole out our stock,
robs me in this fashion! It was a case of the poor man's lamb with a
vengeance.[22] Poor old Dassy! Everybody picks on Dassy!

There is an elaborate amusement program on foot for
our men at this post—rather elaborate theatricals, etc. It is a
bully thing, but has the disadvantage of crowding out valuable
features of a true Y.M.C.A. such as the opportunity of writing
letters & amateur singing.

Yesterday my pleasant Virginia associate was taken from me
to go into transportation work—a minister in transportation work
is an example of the faulty distribution of effort in the Y.M.C.A.—
and I have had associated with me another Episcopal minister
from Baltimore (by the name of Cook) who will take full charge
of the post in a few days. I am to be moved to another post—where
I do not know. The divisional secretary said he had an idea that

21. The safety razor was invented by King Camp Gillette (1855–1932) at the end of the
nineteenth century. Gillette headed his safety razor company from 1901–1932 (*Webster's New
Biographical Dictionary* [Springfield: Merriam-Webster, 1988]).

22. Machen here alludes to the biblical record of Nathan's confronting David regarding his
adultery with Bathsheba (2 Samuel 12:1–23). Nathan told a story about a rich man stealing a poor
man's lamb, thus in Machen's case, the rich YMCA director stole from Machen's limited wares.

I was not happy at my present post—which is usually a polite way of saying that a man is a failure, but in this case it is true in the strictest sense. I really think I should prefer a smaller post where I should have more of a free hand. Here we are in something of a gilded cage—a large building of which we have little control. My new associate will probably handle the situation well. He will probably make his presence felt before long. As for me, I am too bashful or too feeble, according as one chooses to use a soft word or a harsh one. I do not think I shall ever be a good Y.M.C.A. man, but I still think that there are places in the Y.M.C.A. where the things that I could do are needed. Whether I shall ever find such places is more doubtful.

It was a relief to see a secretary of a neighboring post with a Larousse under his arm.[23] Such intellectual alertness is rare indeed. No more speaking French for me, unfortunately. I might almost as well be in the U.S.A.

I have been sleeping much better of late. Our living conditions have been improved, since a place for our folding beds has been partially boxed in.

The other day I received another letter from Montí informing me that my long letter written a month or so ago had at last been received. Unfortunately he had to get off on his "leave" before the uniform that I sent him had arrived. It was for the purposes of that "permission" that the uniform was intended.

The 500 francs sent me by a Paris bank just before the crash of May 27 has at last come to hand. I was glad to get it. A letter of credit is pretty useless here. It would have to be sent away to some large town in order to be used. At my next visit to Paris I expect to draw on my letter of credit in order to make larger deposits in the bank. I can then cash my checks at my own cantine—as I am informed it is entirely permissible to do.

We have a good system of saving—book-keeping. A daily report of money received—and the form of the money—is turned in to divisional Y.M.C.A. headquarters. You just ought to see some of the French money in circulation now. We get a good deal of local

23. "Larousse" is a publisher of dictionaries and other reference works. The secretary must have been carrying a French/English dictionary.

chamber-of-commerce one franc and 50 centime notes. These and
the five franc notes are frequently in lamentable condition. Often
the disjecta membra of the bills have to be pieced together.[24] Worn
and wounded soldiers those old bills are. They have seen service
like the poilus in the trenches.

I am facing another important change. Perhaps it may give
me better opportunity. I wish I thought the divisional secretary had
some understanding of the kind of service where I might be able
to fill a useful little place. Unfortunately the leader to whom Bobby
Freeman originally commended me left the region shortly after I
arrived. I feel very friendless, and somehow I have not the Y.M.C.A.
faculty of making friends.

But enough of what might seem to be mere complaining. You
will know that it is not mere complaining, but nobody else would
place such a charitable emphasis on it, I am afraid.

I wish I had a little bit of Seal Harbor. Even a real bed & the
opportunity to settle down at night would be appreciated.

But most of all I should like to see the loved ones at home.

Your loving son
Gresham

July 13

My dearest Mother:

I am writing a little sooner than usual to-day partly because
there is some leisure before breakfast this morning, and partly
because I want if possible to repair the damage of an omission in
previous letters. Some time ago you spoke of knitting works, and
by some strange perversity I failed to jump at the chance. The
good time for knitting is already past, but if you have odd moments
of time before winter I should certainly be delighted to have the

---

24. The Latin, "disjecta membra," means scattered pieces.

socks, not only for their associations but also for their own sake. They will no doubt (if you do have time to make me a pair) be an immense comfort during the winter. My size, I may say before I forget it is 10. I hope you will be permitted to send the socks—you know regulations about this matter have become very strict. But my impression is that a package can still be addressed to 12 Rue Aguesseau. Perhaps you might inquire about this before knitting the socks.

Your letters have all been so lovely that when I have not the luxury of a new one, re-reading gives me joy. Yesterday I wrote briefly to Tom, in answer to his very welcome letter, but did not give him the brief chronicle of Sunday.

Sunday was the French holiday, July 14.[25] The Germans celebrated the day be sending over a few shells into a neighboring village (not very uncomfortably close) exactly at 6 A.M.[26] This did not dampen the ardor of the French and American celebration. At eight o'clock there was a service in a little village church about three quarters of a mile from our camp. A French chaplain spoke in French and one American chaplain in English. There, there was presentation of some flags. In the afternoon there were sports, and an allegorical representation—which I did not see. Our morning service was conducted by the Catholic chaplain as usual. He chooses "Onward Christian Soldiers" & "Lead Kindly Light" as the only hymns every Sunday, & the singing of them on the part of the Catholic congregation is even poorer than the hymns. In the evening our own service was attended by about eight persons. As is quite usual, many of the men were paid off on Sunday evening just at the hour of my service. I talked to the few that were present, with no apparent results.

My associate now is an Episcopal minister from Baltimore by the name of Cook, Mr. Redint of Virginia having been transferred. The change has no doubt been for the ultimate

25. Bastille Day is as significant for the French as the 4th of July is for Americans. This holiday celebrates the storming of the Bastille in 1789 during the French Revolution.

26. The "neighboring village" is named in Machen's marginal note as "Brouville," which is 30 miles S.E. of Nancy and 2.7 miles N. of Baccarat.

benefit of the work, since I think Cook will be successful. But I preferred the more retiring & even unselfish man. My present associate is not a bad fellow, however—I do not want to leave the impression that he is. Last night he never returned from a visit to the neighboring town. I was thus left a little in the lurch, but not particularly sorry to be left—except that I do want to go to-day to make a few purchases before being transferred to some post perhaps remote from town. Also I do not think my associate has quite grasped the situation between us here for the few remaining days of my stay. But in general he is all right & might be a friend if I knew him better.

Love to all, & to yourself, my dearest Mother.
Your loving son
Gresham

July 16, 1918

My dearest Mother:

Your letter of June 14 has just come to hand, and while I have a few minutes waiting for the car which is to take me back part way to camp, I am going to add a word to my letter of this morning, in order to tell you how dear and sweet your letter is. It is pathetic—your distress and loneliness on that Sunday night— but I am sure that God answered your prayer. No doubt you will obtain some true happiness, in the midst of a great deal of care and trouble from your loving service to the babies. If they were always what they are in their picture, all would be well, but I know well that love has to stand a good deal as far as babies are concerned—even if they are not bad ones such as the present writer certainly was.

My new post has been determined. It is not far from my present (or former) post, though somewhat nearer the front. I am to be a subordinate this time; evidently I was not found to measure up to the job of superintendent of a hut. After the first feeling of humiliation & failure is over, I rather think the new situation may offer me better opportunities of true Christian service, and I am going to try, with earnest prayer, to do my very best.

It is positively too warm for comfort to-day. I wish I were enjoying the breezes of Seal Harbor. But it is not the breeze that I really desire. Remember me cordially to Betty. I certainly am glad she is with you.

Your loving son
Gresham

9

THE "Y MAN OF PEXONNE"

July 22 to September 7, 1918

Pexonne will be the village location of Dr. Machen's next post. After a brief time serving under another secretary, he will take charge of the post as the director. In R. N. Johnson's book about his war experiences, he commented on the "Y" at Pexonne saying, "In one of the buildings in the central part of the village the Y.M.C.A. had established a canteen, and we wish to say that it was one of the best Y.M.C.A.s we ever had with us. Our hats are off to the 'Y' man of Pexonne." Johnson, who served with the machine gun company of the 145th US Infantry, was stationed at Pexonne Aug. 29 to Sept. 14, 1918. Machen was the "Y" secretary at Pexonne from late July through Sept. 14, so Johnson was praising Machen. Both the 145th US Infantry and Machen were reassigned on Sept. 14, it may be that the truck Machen waited for on that day was associated with the transporting of the troops of the 145th to their new assignment.[1]

[A portion of the following letter is missing. The missing text is marked in the transcription with elision points (. . .) followed by [ ] containing a description of the size of the missing portion. Machen became too detailed in his description and the militarily sensitive portions of the letter were cut out (the missing areas are not torn but cleanly snipped with scissors). Fortunately, he provided an extended annotation at the bottom of the letter at a later time: "I went from the ruined and deserted town Badonvillers to a post called 'P.A. 5'.[2] From that post trenches ran out further to advanced posts. We went to P.A. 5 above ground. A communicating trench could have been used if necessary. I was told that when

---

1. R. N. Johnson, *Heaven, Hell or Hoboken* (Cleveland: By the Author, 1919), 75–76.
2. Badonviller is 36 miles E.S.E. of Nancy and 7.7 miles N.E. of Baccarat. Machen writes "Badonvillers," but according to current mapping it is spelled "Badonviller."

the Germans made a raid, our men were withdrawn from P.A. 5 and even back of Badonvillers." "P.A. 5" was a secret, dug-out fortress near the front.]

July 22, 1918

My dearest Mother:

My last letter was written soon after it had been told me that I was to be transferred—or rather soon after the whereabouts of the new post had been disclosed. On Tuesday my baggage was taken from my old quarters. Since I was obliged to pack up while the camionette was waiting, it is not surprising that I left several things behind—an overcoat and a rubber blanket.[3] Apparently the overcoat is gone for good, since the one that was sent to me the other day was not mine; but I still have hopes of the blanket. Tuesday night I spent at the town where Y.M.C.A. headquarters for the region is situated and where I have been doing my shopping. I seized the opportunity of going out to the evacuation hospital, on Tuesday and again on Wednesday, and having a thorough test made of my gas-masks—the Americo-British mask that I wear ordinarily and the French mask that stood me in good stead in the night of May 26. Both proved to be thoroughly O.K. The chances are that I shall not have need of them, but if I do need them I shall need them bad. The American mask, which is modeled after the British, is very uncomfortable, and comparatively difficult to adjust, but it is thought to be the most efficacious. Every man is supposed to be able to adjust his mask in six seconds, though ordinarily a considerable longer time could be occupied. The masks give perfect protection if put on in time.

On Wednesday evening I came out to my new post, travel by auto in broad daylight being forbidden on these roads.[4] Apparently I am now situated about two miles from the American trenches, and about three miles from the Germans.[5] By the wise regulation of the

3. The "rubber blanket" would have been beneficial in the cold, damp French winters if Machen had to sleep on the ground.

4. Wednesday was July 17, 1918, per Machen's margin note.

5. The sentence as originally written reads, "I am now situated about two or three miles from the American trenches, and about three or four miles from the Germans." The "or three"

Y.M.C.A. authorities, I left my trunk in the town, and took only a shoulder-bag, a blanket-roll, a suit case and a folding cot. It is well to travel light near the front, as I learned to my cost two months ago.

My post proves to be even more of a step downward than I had supposed.[6] It is considered to be a beginners job, where a man is put for a week, or a few days, till he can learn the game preliminary to taking his own hut. After my three months or so of independence the situation is galling in the extreme. The secretary in charge of the post is a self-reliant, competent, methodical man who really does not need any assistance except of the most menial kind. I was put at once on the job of opening boxes and cleaning up the back yard, and I spent the day in strict obedience to orders. That is just exactly what I should desire of my own assistant, and I do not blame the secretary at all. But I do feel a little sore at being placed in such a position. It does not seem to me to be just, though I am thoroughly anxious of my defects.

Apparently the divisional secretary was considerably dissatisfied with my management of my last post, though he confesses that his dissatisfaction was based upon what I said myself rather than upon what others said of me. I never thought the distribution of goods for the cantines was properly proportioned to the size of the post, and I said so with such plainness and such persistence as to be a nuisance at headquarters. Somehow from the very start I never succeeded in standing in with the leaders. The man to whom Bobby Freeman commended me was fine, but he left soon after I arrived, and there arose a new king who knew not Dassy.[7]

July 24

The latter part of what I have just written might have been conceived in a different vein if I had known the change that was

---

and "or four" were crossed out by Machen at a later date.

6. Though not noted in the margin of this letter, based on his letter of Jan. 5, 1919 to his mother, the post was in Pexonne. He remained at this post for two months. The area was the scene of considerable heavy combat and destruction, as his description in the current letter shows.

7. Machen is alluding to Exodus 1:8, "Now there arose up a new king over Egypt, which knew not Joseph" (KJV).

soon to occur. Yesterday the divisional secretary appeared on the scene and announced that Mr. McQuaid, the secretary here, was to be associated with Y.M.C.A. headquarters, and that I was to be in charge of this post along with a new secretary by the name of Briggs who has just arrived from America. The arrangement will probably last only a few days. After that there is complete uncertainty as to my movements or lack of movements. I was able to express my very sincere admiration to Mr. McQuaid before he left. He has run the canteen in a peculiarly wise, orderly way, and I have learned a lot from him. Running a large grocery store is not a particularly easy task to be flung suddenly on a professor of New Testament Literature and Exegesis, and I do not want what I said earlier in this letter to be interpreted as indicating any exaggeration of my own business ability.

Having now said all too much about my own desires and feelings, I had better return at once to a little description of the place and of the work. The place is certainly most dismal. By a recent order the civilian population (or what had remained of it) was evacuated, and the great mass of the houses in the village are entirely open and empty. Intermittent shelling during four years of war has knocked things very much to pieces, without reducing the place to a mere heap of stones as was the case with many villages that I saw when I was with the French. The effect is depressing in the extreme. We have here the mere empty shell of a town. You can wander at will through the deserted rooms of the homes. Here and there a shell has entered and wrought havoc, or flying fragments have pierced holes. The floors are littered with the numberless odds and ends of family life that are naturally left out in a hurried departure. Old garments, dirty wine-bottles, pictures, baby-carriages, books, straw, dirt are everywhere, in inextricable confusion. It would take more than Hercules to clean the place up. The filth in the houses is terrific, and the flies beat anything I ever saw—certainly anything that I ever saw in Europe.

The Y.M.C.A. is situated in what apparently used to be a meat-shop. The floor is of concrete, also the ceiling; and the walls are solid. All this is of importance in case there should be any shelling of the town. We have our cantine downstairs, up stairs there is the kind of loft characteristic of the houses in this part of France. We use the loft for entertainments and meetings. Unfortunately the roof is none too solid, and it requires delicate adjustment to find a dry spot for the piano. At the rear of our establishment is situated what McQuaid called the pavilion—a kind of shed on top of a pile of manure and refuse. That pavilion is all right except for the smell.

We take our meals at an officer's mess. Unfortunately one of us has to be always at the Y.M.C.A. so that we are obliged to take turns eating a cold dinner or hurrying up the meal for the benefit of the one who is to follow. I do not know which alternative is most unpleasant. The first few nights we spent at what used to be the nunnery, but the lieutenant who acts as town-major very kindly arranged for our transfer to a safer place in a house more solidly built that possesses a vaulted cellar. So we are now established in the "chateau" (as we somewhat ambitiously call it)—a fairly large double house on the village street.[8] The house is owned by the proprietor of the large china factory which is situated here. He has recently come to town to get his stock away—or as much of it as possible—or at least to settle up his affairs. In order to get some lemonade-bowls I visited the warehouse the other day. The bowls, which were quite pretty cost me forty centimes a piece. The officers' mess has the luxury of real china, owing to the lucky presence of the stock left in the town.

In marked contrast to the conditions at my last post this cantine, under McQuaid, has been kept well stocked. Every evening a camionette arrives from Y.M.C.A. headquarters to bring and take mail, if there is any, and to bring merchandise. It is not nearly as large a post as in my last one, though by means of soldier messengers it serves a good many men in the lines. The regular system of communication is an enormous help. I still do not think they were right in neglecting that last post as they did, even though it was further from the front.

Under McQuaid, our day's work was as follows—At seven o'clock or a little after we arose. Before eight o'clock, we relieved the guard of three men who spent the night at the Y.M.C.A. Then came

8. The French word "chateau" means a "palace," "castle," or "mansion."

breakfast—one of us waiting for the other to be through. McQuaid then straightened up the cantine, and I did what I could under his direction. Then we opened up for sales, and remained open all day long till 9.30 at night. Selling went along at a healthy rate for him all day. McQuaid did most of it. I busied myself with trying to get a little ____ machine into operation, and with odd jobs. Probably the routine will be a good deal the same for the next day or so.

Yesterday morning, McQuaid told me that I could have the morning off—I am gradually coming to understand all the feelings of a twenty-dollar a week clerk or a house-servant. So off I went for a walk, McQuaid advising me where to go. First I walked up into a magnificent forest where there is another Y.M.C.A.[9] Then I went mostly through the woods to a town that is only about a kilometer or so from the front line.[10] Before the war it had about 2,000 inhabitants. Now it has practically none—not even soldiers. I walked through the entire length of the town without seeing a solitary living soul. Street after street of solitary, empty, open houses—in places barricades with holes for the guns. Of all the dismal sights that I have seen, that deserted town was about the most dismal. In the ruins of the region where I was with the French there was at least an appearance of life brought by the crowds of soldiers. But here death held undisputed rule. A complete ruin would have been less impressive and less dismal. But to wander through those deserted streets was enough to get on one's nerves. It seemed as . . . [about 3 lines missing] all such expectations were vain. There was not a living soul.

9. Machen penciled in the margin here, "Ker Avor." According to a comment from Hugh S. Thompson, "Camp de Ker Avor was in a dense forest. We were E. of Pexonne and about three kilometers behind Badonviller" (Hugh S. Thompson and Robert H. Ferrell, *Trench Knives and Mustard Gas: With the 42nd Rainbow Division in France*, College Station: Texas A&M Press, 2004, 68). Pexonne is 35 miles E.S.E. of Nancy and 6 miles E.N.E. of Baccarat. Badonviller(s) is located 36 miles E.S.E. of Nancy and 7.7 miles N.E. of Baccarat. The "dense forest" that Thompson mentions is probably the "forêt dominale des élieux."

10. According to his marginal note, the town he went to was "Badonvillers." (Johnson, 63) described Badonviller similarly. He said the town was "weird" and "dead." He and his colleagues named it the "Deserted City." Johnson also commented that, "Not a single building, not a single home had escaped; those that were not stricken by shellfire or aerial bombs, had been deliberately dynamited. The interior of the great cathedral had been thoroughly mutilated and the great roof had tumbled in." He went on to say that it was evident the people had evacuated the town in "a frenzy of haste" leaving behind many valuable items. The town, said Johnson, even "on the brightest and most sunny days was spooky."

Just near the end of the town I did find two or three American officers. One of them was very kind & would no doubt have let me walk with him into the lines if I could have waited for his own departure. But unfortunately duty called me back to replace McQuaid, and I had to content myself with being sent under the guidance of a "non-com" to a point . . . [about 14 lines missing] being modified in somewhat the same way. I do not think that you now often find regular French trenches within fifteen miles of regular German trenches, as you did earlier in the war. No man's land is tending to become broader & to become the place for advance posts & reconnoitering parties.

Mr. McQuaid was Y.M.C.A. secretary . . . [about 11 lines missing] it is astounding how very few people get hurt when a town is bombarded.

So far we have been having the most peaceful time, almost, that I have enjoyed since I came to France.

Give my very best love to all whom you may see.

You don't know how I long to see you my dearest Mother. Your love and the letters that express it are my stay and comfort. Of all the Mothers that the American boys have left behind them I have absolutely the best. I thank God for that inestimable gift.

Your loving son
Gresham

August 1, 1918

My dearest Mother:

When I give you a little outline of my daily life and at the same time tell you that I am now alone in charge of the post, you will understand how hard it is to write letters. At half-past-seven sharp in the morning I have to open up the "Y" for the men who clean it. Then I get my breakfast, and almost immediately after we

open for business. Business continues all day until about a quarter
past nine at night. With the close of business begins the job of
counting the money and getting the report ready for the office.
Sorting the ridiculously torn money is apt to be rather a tedious
job, and calculating the worth in French money of American bills,
money-orders etc. also takes time. So the secretary is lucky if he
gets to bed before ten o'clock. During the day I leave my post only
for meal time, and then only for about a half-hour. One of the men
has been good enough to keep the place for me while I am out.
It would be almost impossible to get the men out of it in order to
lock it up, and we rather take pride in keeping it open at all times.
During the day the stream of purchasers ebbs and flows somewhat,
but I do not suppose there is ever more than one or two minutes
without interruption. Even such intervals as that are rare. Despite
the confining, sedentary nature of the life, I like it better than when
I am associated with another man. It seems to put me on my metal,
and I get along better with myself than with any other associate!
The fellow that was with me for a few days after the departure of
Mr. McQuaid suited me only fairly well. He was too much inclined
to go his own way without consulting his senior. Also he seemed
always to drift in first at meals, leaving me to cold dinners and
malnutrition. I finally had to call a halt to this latter procedure.
McQuaid was just the other way—always wanted me to go first. But
I should not have liked to be McQuaid's assistant permanently.

Our supply is carried on by Ford camionettes which arrive
in the evening at about nine o'clock, day travel being forbidden
hereabouts. The stock has now been allowed to run down to almost
nothing—compared at least with the good stock that we had ten
days ago. At times I have sold some 1,900 francs worth of goods in
the course of a day. One important part of the work is the filling of
orders assigned by a sergeant or by an officer, for things to be sent
to men in the lines. The demand for goods, however, is not nearly
equal to that which prevailed at my last post.

On Sunday, we held two services, at both of which I talked
briefly to the men. My associate proved to be a singer, and was a
great help in the musical part of the day's exercises. The attendance
was not large, perhaps twenty in the morning and the same or

somewhat less in the evening. But in the evening, especially, I had the feeling that one meeting together was well worth-while. Owing to the initiation of my colleague, a Wednesday evening service was planned for, and it was duly held last night. I had the assistance of a Y.M.C.A. man who happened to be here in passing. It was rather hard to get the meeting started, since at the appointed hour an impromptu concert was going on, but despite the unpleasantness of appearing to be a spoil-sport I was resolved that the main business of our association should not be crowded out. The result, on the whole, was reassuring; the dozen or so men seemed to enter into the little service with cordiality.

In the midst of my discouragement of a week ago I wrote a letter to Reid Dickson, former Princeton Seminary student, who has done well in Y.M.C.A. work in France, asking him whether he could do anything for me. I should give a pretty [penny] if I could re-call that letter. It was a desperate measure anyway, and as things have turned out I am in no hurry to leave here; on the contrary I feel more as though I might be able to do worth while work than I have yet felt. The independence is refreshing, and as for the distinctly "religious work," although I have as yet been able to do little, I rather think the opportunities may increase. The confessional barriers between myself and the men who live here are no longer so serious. On the whole I do not want to be ordered away. It all depends upon what the new Y.M.C.A. director in the region may do with my post—whom he places here with me, etc. Perhaps I can work here as well as anywhere else. Meantime I am very busy, and fairly happy, though I do wish I had some clean underwear. Routine duty has some curative value—prevents undue introspection and depressing thoughts. Sometimes at Princeton, with all the liberty of academic life, I have almost envied the man who has to be at the office from nine until five.

The writing of this letter—about two lines at a time with intervals for business—has taken all day.[11] Just now I received a visit from the new director. I was delighted with him, and should give several hundred dollars if I could recall that wretched letter.

11. In the margin of this paragraph Machen has written, "the 77th had moved out, the 37th had arrived."

There is to be a conference of the secretaries who are remaining in this region. It will probably take place about five days from now. Meanwhile I am content, but dirty—no possible time to go to take a bath, and no clean clothes. I sleep in my clothes, or in most of them. McQuaid did not. But if there is something started I don't want to have to reach for anything except my gas-mask.

My recent letters, I know, have been very inadequate. Life over here, even in this quiet sector, is interesting enough till you get used to it. The road to this village, for example, smacks of war. It is thoroughly camouflaged by high brush-work fences on both sides, and numerous shell holes testify to the difficulties of travel at different times in the past. At times the noise of our guns is disturbing; seventy-fives certainly can make a racket when they are not too far away.[12] But so far everything has been going and nothing coming our way. Last night we had a gas-alarm and put on our masks. But there was really no gas anywhere near. My quarters are very safe—in the solidest house in the village with a vaulted cellar under it where one can descend and be in practical security. Even an air-plane bomb, unless it were an enormous one would likely be wasted on us because it would never reach that cellar. There is too much house above. Air-plane raids at night, I confess, do not add to the pleasure of the life for me. There is something nerve-wracking about the intermittent hum of the German motors, punctuated by the bursting of the anti-aircraft shells and by an occasional bomb.

Some Frenchmen have been bringing me French papers. But to-day they have dropped me again. These are certainly stirring times. It really looks as though the turning of the tide has come.

No letters have been coming through for some time. I hope they will come in good numbers when they do finally start up again.

I am sorry to hear that sub-marines have been operating off the American coast. Although there is really no danger at Seal Harbor, yet I can well understand that one's imagination might get at work. What I want for you is a good quiet summer. I do hope and pray that it may do you lots and lots of good. You can have no

12. The "seventy-fives" are artillery pieces that fire shells measuring 75 millimeters in diameter, which is about three inches.

possible idea how precious you are to me, my dearest Mother—more so now, if anything, than when I was in America. I don't think any of the other boys here begin to have such a Mother, although they no doubt think a good deal of theirs.

I am engaged in "mixing" with a lot of fellows at the same time when I am finishing this letter. So good-bye for the moment.

Your loving son
Gresham

August 5, 1918

My dearest Mother:

Your two letters, nos. 26 and 27, of June 25 and July 2, which arrived together the other night, are redolent of Seal Harbor—they make me see the little cottage with the pretty fringe of flowers in front, and feel the freshness of the northwest wind as though the whole thing were right before me here. Really it does seem to me that there is a new freshness and cheerfulness about the tone of those letters which makes me feel that Seal Harbor has already begun to do its work. Not that all the letters have not been cheerful and brave. But I feel encouraged by the good news, and I do think that these are about the two best letters that I have yet received. It is very, very good of you to write to me so fully. I know exactly what letter-writing at Seal Harbor means. These letters are just splendid at any rate, and I am grateful. Of course I cannot begin to say how thankful I am about the improvement in Nena's health, and the good health of the babies. As for Dr. Kirk and the fear of his leaving, I can only reflect on the storm that one church has already weathered.

I was delighted at the interest which was taken by Arly and others, as well as by yourself, in the letter that I wrote you some time ago with regard to publication, however, it is my duty to warn you all that publication of such letters is one of the things most strictly forbidden by the censorship regulations, and we are cautioned to warn correspondents accordingly. If I am to publish anything in America, the letter must pass through the publicity bureau of the Y.M.C.A. at Paris. As for the letter in question I was surprised of it amid our family circle and among such friends as Mr. Shriver. It did seem to me so inadequate. Also my own actions were so very inadequate to the emergency that I cannot feel very much satisfaction in those memories.

Since my last letter I have continued to be in charge of the Y.M.C.A. at the same post. In contrast with the rushing business that we did at the canteen a week ago, things are now very quiet. The men who are now with me have not been paid for some time, and are consequently "broke"—also there do not seem to be so many men here. Despite the slowness of business I have kept the place open all day, having received a very nice fellow (a soldier of course) to replace me at meal times. Yesterday, which was Sunday, we held two services. The one in the morning, which was attended by a little group of men, I conducted myself. There did not seem to be any very defined response, and yet I felt that the service was worth while. The more experience I have the more my conviction is confirmed that a religious service ought to be limited to a religious service and nothing else and that the music ought to be limited to real hymns. You may be surprised to know that I acted as musical director at both services yesterday, and officiated at the piano. But I was not very good at playing the "Battle Hymn of the Republic" at the evening service. For the evening service I make a very special effort to get the boys to attend, since the meeting was addressed by Dr. Anderson, the chief of our Y.M.C.A. work in the division. The result was very satisfactory, considering the number of men who were on duty in one way or another and so prevented from coming. For the afternoon I invited the men to come to a little half-hour or so Bible study. Only two appeared, and the thing was rendered a little difficult by the lack of knowledge of English on the part of one of the two, who was Italian. But I am going to keep on knocking, in case the door of opportunity should finally be opened. One great difficulty is that I am afraid I am not a "mixer." Years of Princeton I

Gathered at the door and entering this large Y-Hut are several American soldiers. The man facing the camera with his hand to his ear is involved in an activity that captures the attention of some of the men.
Photo courtesy of Kautz Family Collection, University of Minnesota

am afraid have made me love my own company too much. Not that I don't try to get acquainted with the boys, but twelve or thirteen hours a day of "mixing" is a bit too much for me. In general I like the post very much. I like the independence, for example, and indeed for the present, another secretary would be useless. Just now it is a small post. The life is sedentary, and some men might regret the lack of adventure. But as far as that goes, I rather enjoy the quiet. I sleep for more than I did at my last post. My relations with the officers at the mess where I get my meals are pleasant.

Wednesday, Aug 7.

To-day I am attending a conference at the headquarters town. It is the first time for three weeks that I have had a chance to get some washing done, have access to my trunk, and do a little shopping.

I have written to Dr. Kirk telling him to remain at Franklin Street.

This poor little letter bears lots of love. Your last two letters make me long all the more to be with you at dear old Seal.

Montí is all right. I had another letter from him the other day. The news from Mr. Hodges is splendid. He writes to me frequently, & Dr. Beach has stepped into my place by writing to him every week, I believe, and by taking care of the money.

By the way the collector writes me that I am penalized for not paying my income tax on time! This on top of the almost endless correspondence & entirely without fault of mine.

Your loving son
Gresham

August 15, 1918

My dearest Mother:

Your letter number 29, of July 16, which arrived last night, really rivaled in interest the two splendid letters that I answered about a week ago. The only thing that I regret is that you are not receiving regular news from me. I was very gratified, by the way, for your cablegram, which arrived in such a mutilated condition that it is hard to see how it could arrive at all. Still, it did arrive, and made me feel fine on account of the up-to-date news, though brief, which it contained.

The news contained in your letter is most reassuring, and I feel overjoyed at hearing that the burden which you assumed in the care of the kiddies is already having its compensations, and from the supreme compensation which always comes with the consciousness of a labor of love well done. You make me want to see those babies, and indeed the whole picture of Seal Harbor life would make me homesick if I were not able to enjoy it with you in spirit, even at this distance. What you say about Betty's help is exactly right. I hope you will tell her how very grateful I feel for her good care of you.

As for those trips to the dentist, I wish you could take just one jaunt to Bar Harbor without the little incident with Dr. Hinch; but still it is well to make the most of what is ordinarily thought to be a bad business.

It has been a full week since I wrote to you last—a tremendously busy week about which there is not a very great deal to say. Many of the American soldiers in this village having been paid, the business of the canteen has become more lively. I am leading a more sedentary life than ever before in my existence. With the exception of Wednesday's trip to the conference of secretaries I have not been more than two or three hundred yards away from my Y.M.C.A. for more than three weeks. Before eight o'clock I go to breakfast and get a detail of two men started in cleaning the place up. Although I try not to begin selling goods till nine o'clock, it is usually impossible to keep everybody out till then. Of course there is a lot of straightening up of the counter to be done, arranging of goods in the ware-room etc. At about half-past-twelve, after a busy morning selling goods, I am relieved in order to get my dinner. Fortunately I have a very intelligent and trustworthy soldier assistant just now.[13] He was formerly a paying teller in a Cleveland bank, and has even, I believe, had Y.M.C.A. experience. Sometime after lunch I take a little rest in my room but more often I have been at work all the afternoon as well as all the morning. The evening is apt to be the most strenuous time of all. In the first place there are services and entertainments to be arranged for; the cantine is apt to be crowded; and the supply camionette arrives with goods that have to be checked up. Some time after nine o'clock I try to get at the big job of making up my accounts. There is not only the cash of the day to be arranged and sent in, but also the money to go to America. Some days I do a considerable business in these money orders.

Incidentally I am learning something about cigarettes, cigars, chewing-tobacco, chewing-gum, and a lot of other things with regard to which I must confess that my knowledge has been

13. Machen's note in the margin identifies his assistant as "Davis, 112th Eng."

limited. To-day I started making a sort-of pink lemonade with a syrup that comes in bottles. Messy business! Since I did not have a litre measure handy I was obliged to guess at the quantity of the ingredients. It was something like Mark Twain's receipt: "Take a sufficiency of this, put in a sufficiency of that, etc." The result was undeniably sour, though the receipt expressly states that no sugar is required. Since the sugar could probably not be obtained it is comforting to know that it is not required. But, my, that drink was sour! The boys drank it anyway, and I am sick of seeing those syrup bottles leaking around the place.

About four days ago I started a French class and got a French "aspirant" or candidate for a commission, to conduct it. A non-commissioned officer continues the class since the departure of the original teacher, and it seems to go fairly well. It is of course exceedingly elementary, and naturally will lack continuity. But perhaps it serves to stimulate interest in the French language and give a start in the pronunciation.

My day in the headquarters town a week ago yesterday was very busy. In the morning we had a very instructive conference of the secretaries. The rest of the day I spent in much-needed shopping, inquiries about various matters connected with my work, arrangements for getting some clothes washed, etc. In the evening I was taken out to my post again, and the old existence recommenced. On last Thursday night we had a little concert by the American ladies and a male pianist. Who should one of the ladies prove to be but Miss Horisberg, sometime member of the Franklin Street choir? The boys were simply delighted at the entertainment. Not only was the music very pleasing, but they particularly enjoyed seeing some real American girls again.

On Sunday morning I conducted the service, which was fairly well attended. At night, a chaplain took the service, and after he left, the boys kept coming in to join in the singing of some old hymns, led by a good pianist. They would have kept up the singing for hours if the light had not failed. I had nothing to do with the thing; it really seemed to be quite spontaneous. One of the men spoke to me about the "Soldiers Prayer League," conducted by the men themselves. I did everything I could to cooperate, and we held one little meeting, but afterwards no one seemed to come. On Wednesday night I held a mid-week service, but did not seem to get much response from the boys. When you have to leave a crowd of men in the canteen and leave them discontented every time you want to hold a service, it is very hard to adopt just the right tone in doing the thing. Yet I am still determined that the canteen shall be closed during the three brief services that we hold during the week, even though there seems to be little cooperation about this matter. If I stay here long enough I hope the men will see that it is not mere neglect or stubbornness which leads me to take the stand. Meanwhile, it is very discouraging to see so desperately little interest in the deeper things of life. But the condition is the same over the whole world to-day.

To-night we had a little entertainment by local talent—prestidigitation—and music. It was very impromptu and not exceedingly successful—except the prestidigitation, which was all too soon over. A French officer also undertook to sing us some songs. The good will was thru the night, but even I could detect flaws in the music. The American music was excellent, but there was not enough of it.

When I came back from town I brought some maps and a few printed photographs of French news, with which I have decorated the walls of our "Y." The maps are very useful—a crowd of men often standing before them. I often have to explain to the boys that despite the great advances of the past few weeks the Germans are not quite driven out of France yet![14]

A good many more Frenchmen are appearing in the "Y" these days, and I am glad of it. It seemed too bad to be forgetting all the French I knew even before I get out of France. Of course even now I can talk French only occasionally. It is very difficult for me to be polite to Frenchmen who want to talk English with me, but I am very friendly to those who discuss the war with me in their own tongue. I can now usually get hold of the French papers. Tomorrow I am invited to lunch by a French officer. I have accepted though I do not yet exactly see how I am gong to leave the "Y" taken care of in my absence.

14. Machen is poking a little fun at what must have been an optimistic group of news reports regarding how well the French were doing against the Germans.

I have been taking my meals with a captain and a lieutenant. We have got the same grub as the men, but with the inestimable advantage of having our dishes washed for us. The other day I dined with the boys at one of the other messes. The grub was fine, but a little bit of dish-washing goes a long way.

What effect the proposed new draft legislation will have upon my continuing in Y.M.C.A. work I do not know. Fortunately I am so tremendously busy every day that I do not have a whole lot of time to worry. Probably the new legislation will make my position in the Y.M.C.A. less satisfactory to myself and to others even if it does not necessitate any change. I see there are to be a great many new chaplains.

No news, also, has come of my suit-case, though I have written twice to the Paris Y.M.C.A. people inquiring about it. As the months slip by the chances of recovering its precious contents become slimmer & slimmer. It is the personal papers that I want. I do think Paris might at least acknowledge my letters.

Several letters have come from Montí. He has never received the fine uniform which I had sent to him from Paris some two months ago.

It is after eleven o'clock, and I am tired through and through.

Your loving son
Gresham

P.S. Peace still reigns in our village—no shells, no bombs. One would not think that we are less than three miles from the front. Some would want excitement, but I get along very well.

On the whole I like the present job best of any that I have had. It is really a typically Y.M.C.A. job—much bigger than the French job. I think I am improving in my conduct of it, though I am conscious of how far short I fall of the opportunity.

Again, with much love,
Gresham

August 31, 1918

My dearest Mother:

The dreadful inventory for the month has just been made, and I am in the cellar. The soldiers in the next room have settled down to sleep; it is ten-thirty. A cheery candle casts a dim glow upon the reassuring concrete above my head. An airplane may or may not be buzzing around in the vicinity; those few scattering shots may or may not be German. My curiosity is less lively on these points than when I slept upstairs. The rats are astoundingly quiet; I never knew them to keep still as long at a time before. The air is bad, and I do not know what that is that is running around on the table. But I have slept bully down here for several nights, and I hope I shall sleep well to-night. Bold, brave men sleep in the upper air—for instance the town-major in the room next to mine. But at night I like to be already where I may have to get.

Apparently our bombardment is not continuing; the Germans sent us nothing at all last night and during to-day. We shall probably settle down again to peace and quiet. Not that I know anything at all about it.

During the month I turned over some 46,000.00 francs to Y.M.C.A. headquarters of which more than half was canteen receipts & the rest of the money was to be sent to America. Pretty big business, I call it. It is a lot of work, but I am awfully glad to be doing it.

The captain & lieutenant with whom I mess have certainly been good to me.[15] Among other things they have provided me with splendid men to help me out at the counter. The first one was a former paying-teller at the First National Bank of Cleveland, O. The present one is also thoroughly up to the job. That lieutenant proved to be (in civil life) a roofing contractor. It was great to see the way he had the holes patched in our tile roof. That roof looked absolutely hopeless. We were not so much worried about the water. But about how to keep the light on, when, with the shortening of the days, artificial light is becoming more & more necessary.

15. The note in the margin appears to read, "Cap. Gechler, 112th Eng."

Your letter number 28 arrived long after the two subsequent letters. It is a splendid letter, but I am glad to say that the later news is the better. Seal Harbor seems to have been great for the children.

I have just received a splendid letter from Arly—of July 8. Do tell him how much I appreciate it. I want to answer just as soon as I can. The news of himself and Helen is most welcome.

Your own loving son
Gresham

September 4, 1918

Dear Uncle:

Your fine letter of July 2 ought to have been answered long ago, but I have been so busy behind my counter that sometimes it takes me three or four days to finish a letter to Mother—a few lines at a time in the few slack moments that customers will allow me. Just now it is a quarter past eight in the morning. I was preparing my counter and wareroom for nine o'clock opening when the Germans began a little shelling of the environs. The shells are not falling in the town itself, and no one is running for cover. But I feel more tranquil in the cellar of my billet, and am seizing the opportunity for a little writing. It is quite comforting to be underground under such circumstances since underground one does not follow with such disturbing interest the whistle of the shells through the air.

Although I did not answer your letter I did at best what you no doubt preferred—I dropped a line to Dr. Kirk. Probably what I wrote arrived too late, even if it could have done any good anyway. But I should not have liked to miss doing me best. I hope that the decision will be the right one. And of course I join with you in affection for our dear old church. It looks as though we could plainly detect dime boding thus far, and I think therefore that we may reasonably have confidence for the future. But I fully appreciate the care and difficulty that rests upon you who are the mainstay of the session.

The good news from Maine cheered me up—both from Kennebunkport and from Seal Harbor. I hope no submarines broke up the good time!

After having turned in 46,000 francs to Y.M.C.A. headquarters during August, I feel as though I were making John Wannamaker look like a piker. Do you prefer Star, Horseshoe, or Battle Ax chewing tobacco? Just now I can supply you with all three. And then I have handkerchiefs, fountain pens, many kinds of cigars, cakes, cigarettes, candles, letter paper, jam, tooth-brushes, a library, etc. etc.

I unite with you in being glad that Loy declined the overtures of Hampden Sidney. Although the offer was a great honor to him, the raising of money, especially just now, would have been a false hope, and would have taken him away from that pastoral service where he is simply magnificent. Despite all his intellectual gifts, I don't think I ever want to see him out of the pastorate—unless there were something very, very special.

The shelling does not seem to be continuing, and I think I must open up the "Y." So good-bye for the present, with much love to Aunt Bessie.

Your affectionate nephew,
Gresham

September 7, 1918

My dearest Mother:

The days succeed one another so rapidly here, and there is such a similarity of detail among them that I hardly know where I left off my narrative in my last letter. No letter from Seal Harbor has arrived to break the monotony—of that I am painfully conscious. But I was especially fortunate in the riches of the previous days, and indeed have been exceedingly happy all through in the splendid letters that have been written to me with such faithful regularity.

The canteen has not been as crowded recently, but we are still, I am sure, quite useful. An important part of our work, always, is the supplying of men in the lines, who send for tobacco and other stock to be carried out by messengers. After the departure of the Captain and two lieutenants with whom I was messing, I was fortunate enough to get in with the medical lieutenant in charge of the dressing-station and the ambulance men. The food is excellent, and both officers and men are especially good companions. One of the boys helps me out at the counter, and also cleans up for me in the morning. Men are of course not detailed for such service against their will; but everybody seems delighted to help. The whole arrangement is delightful, and owing to the proximity of the dressing-station very convenient. I don't think I have ever been as well fixed since I entered the American army service.

About three mornings ago we had rather a lively time. When I came down to the "Y" in the morning about eight o'clock to get ready for nine o'clock opening, it soon became evident that a good deal of artillery activity was being displayed by the Boches, and I soon concluded to go back to my billet and write letters until the hour for opening should actually arrive. A little after nine I opened up, but after doing some selling of goods, I had no difficulty in determining that the shells were beginning to come far too close for comfort! So hastily locking the front door I led the way to the nearest cellar which could be classed at all as a dug-out or "abri." We did not get out of that cellar for an hour or so. When I did venture out, I was reminded of the logging-camp. There is a little lull in the downpour; you start out for the rest camp, and just then the rain may come down harder than ever. Several times I got only as far as the door of the cellar. But finally I was able to venture back to the "Y" to complete the sales that I had been making. Unfortunately I did not know that the "Y" had been hit. As a matter of fact a piece of shrapnel had put a hole in our roof directly over the piano. Formerly I used to examine the position of that piano & see that the key-board was closed, but since the roof had been so magnificently repaired I had put the matter out of my mind. A good concrete ceiling above the canteen fortunately protects the most important part of our building from the ordinary accidents of war. Well, it rained during the night and soaked that piano, swelling the cork of the keyboard so that the instrument cannot be played. And alas for our roof, of which I was exceedingly proud!

The bombardment has not been repeated, and life goes on very much as before. Such incidents are by no means so dangerous as the layman might suppose. I am happy on account of the concrete over our cantine. It is a big protection in many ways. A tent or wooden hut sometimes seems very frail. And in my cellar at night I am snug as a bug in a rug. A good night's sleep makes a big difference.

The other day I wore my gas mask for well over an hour—in a tent. It is nearly as uncomfortable as having dentist's rubber in your mouth for an hour or so. But the discomfort of the mask is not to be minded much when there is gas about. Neither are "cooties" minded in a dug-out when the shells are dropping anywhere near.[16]

I certainly do like my present post, confusing as it is.

Love to all, my dearest Mother, from your own loving son
J. Gresham
12 Rue Aguesseau
Paris[17]

16. "Cooties" is slang for lice.
17. At the bottom of the page of Machen's letter a note was added, "The roofing-expert lieutenant was wounded outside of town on the same day when the roof was spoiled. He had to be sent to America."

10

CONTINUING "Y" SERVICE
IN SEVERAL LOCATIONS

September 14 to November 6, 1918

Dr. Machen leaves his post at Pexonne to travel to several locations. During this time, he rediscovers the joy of reading his English New Testament in the absence of his Greek text. His service will involve helping the wounded in dressing stations and the usual distribution of hot chocolate to the active and wounded troops. His travels will show him more of the destruction, pain, and death caused by the war. He will also enjoy some time in Paris as he awaits a new assignment.

September 14, 1918

My dearest Mother:

Having received orders from the Y.M.C.A. to leave my present post, I have packed up my modest belongings and am awaiting transportation. How long I shall have to wait is quite uncertain, and the interval hardly constitutes a very restful time. Leaving a place to which I have been accustomed always gives me the blues, even if the place in question is only a ruined village. And here I have on the whole been better contented than at any previous post. Living conditions have been quite tolerable. At first things were altogether quiet; and since we have been having some attentions from the Boches a good cellar has provided restful sleep. In short the place is near enough to the front to make me feel that I am engaged in war service, and at the same time not terrific enough to spoil the equanimity of life. Best of all has been the hard work. At times it has been too hard, and at the end of it I am really tired out; but hard work is better than insufficient work. Unfortunately the routine has prevented me from getting closely acquainted with many of the men, but on the other hand the canteen service has been obviously necessary and I have been glad to be engaged in it. I have especially enjoyed the independence. When you are associated with another secretary somehow you never feel quite as indispensable as when you are alone. One thing that I have made it a point to do, despite the short-handedness of the post, is to keep the canteen open all day long—with the aid of a number of excellent fellows among the enlisted men. To-day, alone in my dismantled place of business, I feel very blue, and I eagerly await the truck which will take me to some new scene. The best way to chase the blues is to write a letter home—or at least that is the next best way to the most excellent way of all, which is to receive a letter with well-known and well-beloved handwriting.

There is very little to tell about the existence of the past few days, except to say that we have done a rushing business at our counter. On one day I sent more than 2000 francs to America by our system of New York drafts, and since it was divided up into many comparatively small amounts it involved a lot of working in addition to the ordinary salesman's work. I was tired out that night, after the last torn one-franc note had been pieced together, and all the accounts made up. So far as possible I have sent the money to Y.M.C.A. headquarters every day. At least I have made up the accounts separately for every day.

You don't know how I long for home these days. Home things acquire a new value. For many years, for example, I have read very little in my English New Testament, the Greek having taken the place of the English. But very often in the evening during the past weeks, my Greek Testament having been left at the Y.M.C.A., I have been reduced to the little pocket English Testament that Loy gave me. And the grandeur of our old English Bible has appealed to me as never before. The grandeur and the comfort too of the old familiar words, which had become almost unfamiliar through an over done erudition.

Orders are for Y.M.C.A. men to continue at their work despite the raising of the draft age, until some definite notice comes to the contrary. As long as I am as busy, and (I think I can say) as useful as I have been during the past seven weeks, I am not impatient for any change in my status.

By the way, I forgot to say some time ago that of course I am entirely in accord with what Arly has done about our family affairs—in connections with places or anything else.

Good-bye for the present, my dearest Mother. I want to get this letter addressed before I am interrupted. Love to all. Your affectionate son. Gresham

October 3, 1918[1]

My dearest Mother:

During the days just past I have altogether lost track of the passage of time; positively I could not always tell to within two or three days what day of the week it was. There seemed to be no opportunity either to read or to receive letters, and even now I have no idea how I am to get the present letter mailed. The opportunity for writing is of the very worst, but possibly there may be even less chance later on. My pocket is stuffed with important letters and papers of various kinds which have been reduced almost to formless hash.

Where did I leave off my narrative? I really cannot say. But at any rate we spent the first part of the time since my last letter in traveling. Or, no, I believe I am wrong. I believe I wrote you a line

1. The number was difficult to decipher and the date may be October 5, 1918.

when we had arrived or nearly arrived at our destination after our days of merry life on the rails. Our destination was a ruined village where the conditions of life are certainly not commodious. Almost our first job was to build up the entrance and roof of our dug-out with stones and prop it up inside. It must be confessed that it was not much of a dug-out, since it was more above than below ground, but at least it afforded some protection. There was bombardment the night before I arrived, but it was not repeated—or rather the shells did not come very close. The second night was a whopper as far as noise was concerned, since our own big guns were being worked vigorously in the near vicinity. The whole place quivered and shook during most of the night. Our Y.M.C.A. secretaries were crowded on the floor of the remnants of a house when we were not in the dug-out. There was hard work enough getting our merchandise up from the "rail-head" and selling it to the boys.

Finally we sullied out in the direction of the front. The place where we established ourselves was a picture of misery as bad as anything that I have ever seen. Until just a day or so before I had been within about a kilometer of the front.[2] The houses were entirely ruined, even the cellars for the most part being caved in, and walls and roofs being non-existent. The proximity to the lines during several years of the war, however, had occasioned the making of dug-outs, which are for the most part foul, damp, and smelly, but were better than the rain outside. The Y.M.C.A. dug-out was practically impossible as a sleeping place & the little wooden shed or passage-way in front of it was crowded to overflowing by Y.M.C.A. belongings & the belongings and persons of the secretaries. Accordingly I sought me out a dug-out in the vicinity where there were canvas bunks. Mine, since I was not lucky enough to secure an upper berth, displayed a rather lamentable tendency to sag and let me down into the ooze; but it did manage to hold out until I left.

The roads being absolutely blocked by the military traffic, it was difficult to get out even a little Y.M.C.A. camionette. Accordingly we could not hope to start a regular canteen. What we

2. Machen's annotation described this location as, "Avocourt," which is 130 miles E.N.E. of Paris and 52 miles E. of Reims.

did do was to distribute chocolate, cookies, cigarettes and especially hot chocolate to the wounded. One thing that made the thing more satisfactory to me was that I found myself again associated with the same ambulance men that I had known at my last post. They are certainly a splendid lot of men. And how finely these medical officers did work—day and night with practically no sleep at all. Sometimes I had a night shift at the dressing-station and sometimes a day shift. Our hot chocolate was especially appreciated—not only by the patients but also in a professional way by the doctors, who constantly called for it when badly wounded men were brought in. One German fellow said when I gave him the chocolate that it was "wie bei der Mutter."[3] It would have taken a harder heart than mine to keep from being a bit touched by that. By the way along with the hatred and bitterness incident to the war, there are some examples of the other thing which like fair lilies in swampy ground are all the more beautiful because of the contrast with the unlikely soil in which they grow. Thus at one of the dressing-stations near the front, I saw an American wounded soldier deliberately take off his overcoat and give it to a wounded German who was suffering a bit more than he.[4] When one reflects what that little act meant— the long cold hours of rain and damp on the long way to the rear and during the interminable waste—it becomes clear that magnanimity has not altogether perished from the earth.

The walk from our dug-out to the dressing-station which had to be repeated several times a day seemed almost interminable.[5] Hard rains made of the road a sea of mud which surpassed anything that I could have believed to be possible. Progress at times, even for a pedestrian, was almost impossible, the road being so crowded with waggons, automobiles and horses that you could barely squeeze along beside them. At times one was tempted to

3. The German "wie bei der Mutter" means "like a mother's" in English.

4. In the margin, the location of this dressing-station is given as "Bois de Montfaucon." "Bois de Montfaucon" means "Woods of Mountfaucon" in English. The use of "Bois" rather than "Forêt" seems to be the preferred designation for the early twentieth century per Lee, who uses "Bois" rather than "Forêt" and refers to the location as "woods" (Jay M. Lee, *The Artilleryman: The Experiences and Impressions of an American Artillery Regiment in the World War, 129th F. A., 1917–1919* [Kansas City: Spencer Printing Company, 1920], 287).

5. A reminder is in the margin that the dug-out was in "Avocourt," which is 130 miles E.N.E. of Paris and 52 miles E. of Reims.

take to the ruins on one side or the other of the road, but progress there would soon be blocked by caved-in cellars. My shoes gave-out completely under the strain. The heels wore down & left long nails sticking up inside. When I pulled the nails out—an operation which often had to be delayed—more and more of the heels would go. Of course my feet were wet all the time. But finally I "salvaged" a dry pair of socks. Do you understand that word "salvage"? It is a great word in the army. When you see anything good lying around and appropriate it that is not "stealing"; it is merely "salvaging." Well, I "salvaged" a perfectly good new warm pair of socks from one of the packs left by wounded soldiers at the dressing-station. Since there was not one chance in a million, probably, of the man ever getting his property back, and since I acted under the advice of an officer, my conscience is not troubling me very much. Needless to say I should be delighted to pay either him or the government twenty times the price of those socks if I ever had a chance. You may laugh, and think I am irreverent, but I can say in all seriousness that one of the most fervent prayers that I ever offered in my life was the prayer of thanksgiving that I prayed that night in my dug-out when I pulled on those warm socks to sleep in. I can feel yet the new warmth and courage that they put into me. Sleeping in cold weather with one little blanket is a cold business anyway, but wet socks are the worst of all.

On one day I walked out with some other secretaries toward the front. On the way we passed what had recently been no-man's land and the German lines beyond it. Right here all attempt at description would be vain. It was a scene of desolation so abominable, so unlike anything that could have been expected on our fair earth, that neither words nor photographs could bring any realization of it. For miles the forest had been reduced to a few straggling stumps. I have seen burnt and ruined forests before. But the effects of shell-fire are different. There was something indescribably sinister about that scene of ruin. Every where there were enormous craters caused by the big shells—at places running into one another. Along the road in one or two places the unburied dead were lying, enough to indicate the horrors which were probably concealed by that ghastly desert on either side.

At last we came to another dressing-station, where the wounded were lying in incredible numbers—of course unsheltered along the road.[6] We distributed some of the chocolate and cigarettes that we were carrying on our backs, and pushed on. Our objective was a recently captured town on a high hill. The fighting was going on perhaps a mile or so beyond. At last we reached the town.[7] But we were soon driven out. The Germans seemed to have our range, and after a shell burst a few feet from us, we beat a retreat, seeking the comparative shelter of ditches and shell-holes on our way. On our way back, as well as on the way out, we distributed our chocolate & cigarettes the best we could—chiefly to the wounded. Others of the secretaries had a more extended and a more adventurous life at the front—acting as stretcher-bearers, burying the dead, and spending the nights in shell holes. But most of my time was spent at our advanced base helping at the dressing-station.

At last, with the withdrawal of the troops to which we are attached, it became time for us to go. About a day was spent at the ruined villages of which I first spoke—selling goods to our men and living in a might crowded & uncomfortable way. Then, day before yesterday (I forgot to say that I am finishing this letter on Sunday, Oct. ___)[8] we came back here to the rear, chiefly by train. On the way we spent a night at a large town, where I just did manage to get a mattress and some blankets.[9] But last night we spent in a real bed, in a nice clean house.[10] After the misery of the past weeks it seemed just too good to be true.

Since I began my letter your two splendid letters of August 24 and 31 (Nos. 35, 36) came to hand. The account of Seal Harbor life and of the children was simply entrancing. How I wish I could be with you! I did not think I could be so homesick as I am now.

6. This dressing station, according to the note, was "In or near Bois de Montfaucon."

7. The annotation reads "Montfaucon," which is about 4.7 miles N. of Machen's post in Avocourt.

8. The date number is indecipherable. If the date at the opening of the letter could be clarified, then this would probably be the next day.

9. "Bar-le-Duc," is this larger town, according to the marginal note, which is located 133 miles E. of Paris and 45 miles W. of Nancy.

10. The home was in "Commercy," which is 150 miles E. of Paris and 26 miles W. of Nancy, or about 20 miles E. of Bar-le-Duc.

I was touched by Maggie's thinking of me. And of course I was profoundly interested in the letter from Tom which you enclosed.

What a splendid summer of loving sacrifice you have had! The children are lovely; but not nearly as lovely as their grandmother—of that I am sure. Nobody could be that lovely.

It is unbelievable that I have not written for two weeks. But what was the use of writing when there seemed to be absolutely no chance to get a letter censored and mailed. I have just sent a "safe & well" telegram to Arly. That might relieve the anxiety which you might have felt on account of the long gap in my letters.

Good-bye now. I must hustle after some bread-tickets or we shall have no bread for breakfast to-morrow.

Love to all,
Your own loving son
Gresham

Oct. 17, 1918[11]

My dearest Mother:

The week or so that has elapsed since my last letter has been a busy, unsteady, letter-less time. It is almost necessary for me to send you another cablegram. Our "rest" at the rear did not last long. After about two days in an unusually nice clean house at a moderate sized town some distance from the front we were soon on the move again.[12] Before we left, we got the trunks of the party

11. At the top of this letter, to the left of the return address and date is written, "Thiau-court in St. Michiel Sector." Thiaucourt is 160 miles E. of Paris and about 22 miles N.N.W. of Nancy. On modern maps this town is called, "Thiaucourt-Regniéville," to distinguish it from Thiaucourt-sur-Meurthe. According to *The New York Times*, Nov. 6, 1918, "Hailed Americans Entry," three American privates were the first to enter Thiaucourt as liberators from four years of German occupation. For four years the 700 residents of the village had not been allowed to leave except for extraordinary reasons such as family members dying in neighboring towns.

12. The town is "Commercy," which is 150 miles E. of Paris and 26 miles W. of Nancy, or about 20 miles E. of Bar-le-Duc.

up from the station to the left of our lodging-house, where they are now stored. It is out of the question to bring them with us to the front, where I content myself with a blanket-roll, a suit-case, and several small bags to hang over my shoulder. What I would give for an old-fashioned rucksack, such as the one I carried in the Alps! But they are not to be obtained on this side of the battle-front. Of course, during the hardest life such as we had two weeks ago the baggage has to be cut down still more, since it all has to be carried on one's back or in one's hand. The worst of it is that when we left our comfortable place we had to carry a lot of wet underwear along with us. In the army you never know when you have to move. Consequently the moment after the wash woman puts your clothes in the water always seems to be the moment when the movement order comes.

We got off on the five A.M. train, which left about seven, and got on to our junction point an hour or so later, though the distance was only a few miles.[13] The train which was to take us on a branch line to the front was to leave the next morning; so we had a full day and subsequent night at the junction-point. The junction-point, fortunately, was a rather interesting town, where we enjoyed seeing a fine cathedral and another ancient church. It was a restful change to walk around in the lovely garden adjoining the cathedral. At night there was an air-raid alarm, but in general we had a good time of it. I had a big job transferring and checking the baggage of fourteen people, since during the trip such labor fell to a considerable extent to me on account of my attainments in the French language. I felt greatly repaid by the appreciation of my labors which was expressed by my companions. It is indeed a joke getting thirty-six pieces of baggage moved and checked when conditions are what they now are in France, and I do not think I did so very badly. At last we were off on a little branch line, moving again toward the front. We detrained at a little ruined village and awaited army transportation to get to our final destination.[14] I got into lunch with French officers & men,

13. Machen noted that the "junction point" was "Toul," which is 165 miles E. of Paris and 12 miles W. of Nancy.

14. There is no annotation providing the name of this village.

who specially prepared us a lunch, in the very kindest possible way. Our ride in an army truck took us over the scene of recent fighting and into the territory long occupied by the Germans. German signs were everywhere and the solid products of German labor. Of course everything in the way of houses was ruined—alas, largely no doubt by the guns of our own side.

At the village where our Y.M.C.A. division ware-house was to be located, I found it comfortable to sleep in what seemed to be an ancient stone-quarry or small mine hollowed out in the side of a steep hill.[15] A light rubber blanket protects from the dampness underneath, and a few layers of blankets keep the ground or boards from seeming too hard. I have gotten so I don't mind at all this sleeping on the floor.

But after two nights I was moved out to a more advanced station about two and a half kilometers further toward the front.[16] On a "reconnoitering expedition" we went still nearer to the Germans. Indeed if it had not been a thick hazy day we might have been the object of undue interest on the part of the enemy. I am told that sometimes a considerable number of shells are aimed even at lone travelers on that road. One is sometimes obliged to make a portion of the trip in the ditch on one's stomach. But we got back without any unpleasant incident.

Five of us have been established here for about five days. The town had about a thousand inhabitants before the war, and many of them apparently were well-to-do. Everything is of course now dismantled and shot to pieces, but it is still possible to reconstruct in imagination something of the old life. Evidences of the German occupation are of course everywhere. It is the books & papers that are interesting to me; somehow I have no enthusiasm for general souvenir hunting. To-day I prowled around in a house which was evidently the abode of French people of culture. The books were scattered about over the floor, in confusion along with old clothes, bits of furniture and everything else you can think of. Somehow it

15. The marginal comment designates this village as, "Bouillonville," which is 165 miles E. of Paris and 25 miles N.N.W. of Nancy.

16. At this point, Machen is at "Thiaucourt" which is the village he mentioned in his note at the heading of this letter. Thiaucourt is 160 miles E. of Paris and about 22 miles N.N.W. of Nancy.

made me think of ____ & that will always be the war, I suppose, to us. I came away feeling very sad. If I had had time, & if it could have done any good, I should have loved to gather those books together in the hope someday of finding the owner. But I am afraid a lot of "salvaging" will go on before the owner finds any of them.[17]

The place is shelled every night, but for some reason the Germans let us alone in the daytime. We five Y.M.C.A. men sleep in a splendid deep cellar with vaulted roof, and we sleep well. In a really good dug-out the shelling of the environs has almost the same soporific effect as the patter of the rain above you on a good solid roof. It was a big-job cleaning our cellar out, since the filth was absolutely indescribable and the flies were (and still are) terrific; but the air is good and the place dry. We even have a little stove. I wish I could stay here all winter.

In the mornings we have been getting merchandise out here from our divisional ware-room, and in the afternoons we have been selling it with great rapidity. Yesterday we sold almost 4000 francs worth of goods in a few hours, & I also sent a lot of money home to America by our system of New York drafts. The head of our little party, whom I like very much, has made me treasurer.[18] We have boarded with the same ambulance company that I have been with at two other places. Everybody from the captain down has been unlimitedly kind. In short the life has been fine—a congenial Y.M.C.A. party, cordial cooperation on the part of the army, sufficient and useful labor (I have even carried on some New Testament study with our inquiring men), a good solid dug-out. But alas it is all over! We are on the move. The Y.M.C.A. camionette was to come for us to-day & will no doubt come to-night or to-morrow. All the work of getting started will have to be done no doubt again on some other front. Such is army life, and I tell you it is rough. In the Foyer du Soldat I knew nothing of it. Why, in those days I used to sit down at a table to my meals, instead of getting in line with my mess-kit in my hand and being served at the out-of-doors kitchen. And conditions generally

17. See Machen's Oct. 3, 1918, letter to his mother to understand how he is using "salvaging" here.

18. In the margin is written, "Wadmond," who must have been the "head of our little party."

were stable, & comparatively tidy. I used to shave every day, and brush my teeth! It is now evening, but I have not yet washed my face to-day. This confession may shock you! But I might tell you worse things.

Oh to get home & to get washed up!

Love to all
Your loving son
Gresham

[The following letter is written on letterhead that reads: "Hotel Lord Byron, Champs-Élysées—Paris, Despouys, Prop^{re}, Téléph. Wagram 37–73."]

October 20, 1918

My dearest Mother:

Paris is evidently looking up; I could get only a tiny little uncomfortable cubby-hole of a room at my old place, the Beaulieu, and shall probably move over here to-morrow, the two hotels being under the same management.[19] This plan, I am sorry to say, is too English, and there are even Y.M.C.A. secretaries in the dining-room. You don't know what an immense relief it is to get into a different atmosphere even for a day or so. I do not mean anything derogatory to the Y.M.C.A.; it is the change that is desired. At any rate, the last time I was here there was no great rush for rooms. It was in the darkest days of the great retreat, and the "grosse Bertha" was going full tilt. Now of course victory is in the air.

You are no more surprised to hear of me from Paris than I am to be here. After awaiting orders for some time at the town from which my last letter was written we were finally told to report for further directions at headquarters here. When the next move

19. The Hotel Beaulieu was where he stayed when he first arrived in Paris before he was deployed to his Foyer du Soldat station at St. Mard.

will come I do not know at all. Meanwhile I hope to be able to do some necessary shopping—heavy underwear, a respectable overcoat, shoes and other useful things. Also I may see Gardiner of the First Church of Princeton who seemed to think he might have special work to offer me. He is in charge of some department of the Y.M.C.A. work.

The long night journey on the train was no great pleasure. The express was packed to the scuppers. I was obliged actually to stand up nearly all the night, there not being room enough even to crouch down on the floor of the corridor. I had a few square feet of space, but relinquished it to a middle-aged French soldier who was evidently having a hard time of it. These old, old veterans are the ones that get me. Sometimes the pathetic side of the thing strikes me so strong that I could almost weep. At any rate I did accomplish something by rolling up my round French gas-mask in my waterproof-coat & giving it to that poor old boy to use as a pillow. '

Why do I always have to arrive at Paris on Sunday morning, after a sleepless night on the train? The Y.M.C.A. post-office was closed, & I could not call for my mail. It is hard to wait another night for news from home. So near and yet so far.

I went to church at the French Protestant Church on the Avenue de la Grande Armée, and I confess nearly went to sleep during service.[20] It was not the fault of the service.

There are big doings here in connection with the opening of the campaign for a French liberty loan. The Place de la Concorde & the Jardin des Tuileries are crowded with German canon, tanks & air-planes.[21] The planes are interesting—all nicely labeled. There was to be a parade, decoration of soldiers, etc., but I got tired of waiting for it in the rain.

My last letter I believe was written before we left for the rear. The trip to the rear was made in an army truck which with several others I was fortunate enough to catch. The truck-ride provided a cross section of the desolation of war—first the old no-man's land,

20. There is currently in Paris the Eglise Protestante de l'Etoile, 54 Avenue de la Grande Armée. The church architecture is similar to that of the Huguenot Church in Charleston, SC, which is the last active Huguenot congregation in the United States.
21. The Place de la Concorde and the Jardin des Tuileries are at the S.E. end of the Avenue de Champs-Elysées and the Eiffel Tower is at the N.W. end.

villages reduced to heaps of stones; then the gradual appearance of houses & smiling woods & fields. We spent about three nights at a town awaiting orders—then Paris, as above explained.

Love & then some to all & to you, my dearest, dearest Mother.

Your loving son
Gresham

October 25, 1918

My dearest Mother:

Since my last letter I have been made unnecessarily rich by five perfectly splendid letters from you—no. 37, of Sept. 7; no. 38, of Sept. 15; no. 39 of Sept 18; no. 40, of Sept. 27; no. 41, of Sept. 29. Never at one time have I received so much and on the whole so good news at one time. Of course the biggest item of all is the expectation of a son and heir for Machen aîné.[22] Another subject for prayer and for trust! As for the general good news from you, from Tom and Nena, and from Arly, it seems to surpass all possible expectations. God has done for me more abundantly than we could ask or think.[23] With deep thanksgiving I have just read the five letters over again once more. Really I do not know at what point to linger in my thoughts. Your improved health, Nena's recovery, the splendid development of the children, Arly's well-deserved professional success—it is all just too good for words. At every point we have been led through the valley of the shadow of death. But your prayers, my dearest Mother, never deserted us, and it is they and the divine answer to them that have led us through. Of course I know that trials lie ahead; I do not let my joy run away with me. But after such

22. A "Machen aîné" would be an "older Machen" referring to his older brother, Arly.
23. Machen is here thinking of Ephesians 3:20, "Now unto him that is able to do exceeding abundantly above all that we ask or think, according to the power that worketh in us" (KJV).

tokens of God's mercy I do not think that any path can look quite as dark again.

The greatest blessing to every single one of us, my dearest Mother, is now and always has been just you yourself. In short, I would not take all the gold reserved of the Bank of France for those five letters.

The enclosure of letters from Arly and from Uncle were also very ____. I do hope that Arly will not be called upon to break off his growing practice, but if he should have to do it I feel sure that even the interruption will not stop it now. It is impossible for me to express my delight in the tone of Arly's letters. How splendidly he deserves whatever professional success may come to him! But if I stop to linger over the many things in those letters that delighted and cheered me I shall never come to an end, and my own letter will never be mailed.

We are here in Paris just in passing, but when official papers etc. are to be gotten passing through Paris is apt to be more than a momentary experience. So we have been here so far nearly six days already. The time has been most welcome to me. As far as my equipment goes the shopping has been rather unsatisfactory. For instance there are no more long boots in the city to fit me. And worst of all I have not succeeded in finding the suit-case which was sent to Y.M.C.A. headquarters in June. Also Gardiner, of the Y.M.C.A., who wanted me to call at his office about religious work, is out of the city. The time has seemed to slip away through my hands.

But what a splendid debauch of French drama I have had! Yesterday, for example, I went to the matinée at the Odéon and to the evening performance at the Théâtre français. Molière was the order of the day at the Odéon—"La Jalousie du Barbouillé," "Les Précieuses Ridicules," and "Georges Dandin." I read over all three of these plays and also "L'École des Maris," thus improving my acquaintance with a great writer. But why do some people put Molière up somewhere along with Shakespeare? I have not yet succeeded in discovering. Perhaps I shall do so when you discover why Balzac is thought to be the greatest of all novelists. By the way I stumbled recently upon a most remarkable novel—"Le Disciple" by

Paul Bourget. It is a masterpiece, and the thesis of it is surprising. Dr. Patton would be interested in it.

The first two nights at the theatre I had a most painful experience. The offerings were most interesting. But alas I was so sleepy that the pleasurable anticipation that had sustained me during the annoyances of the days was sadly set at naught. Really I thought I should disgrace myself in my prominent position near the stage. My head simply would not stay up, and the actors seemed to be moving about in a haze.

Oh what a relief to be my own master, or relatively so, for a little while! I detest shopping, I detest getting a suit of clothes, I detest going to the Y.M.C.A. office for orders, I detest the failure to accomplish the things I had been longing for a trip to Paris in order to accomplish. But at least the evenings have been mine, and I have been able to eat, sleep and read in my own little way.

What a delight it is not to have to wash your mess kit after your meals. But the opportunity of reading is perhaps the best—in the Métro, at meals, between the acts at the theatre. Really it is hard to go back to work. But I shall be the better for a little holiday.

As I understand it we Y.M.C.A. secretaries are to wait for instructions from Washington before changing Y.M.C.A. work for army service. I rather think I shall just go quietly along awaiting developments. The work that I have been engaged in has been hard enough to keep me from feeling altogether like an "embusqué."[24] Paris is full. No more bombardments by day; a respite from air-raids; and more light allowed in the streets at night. The statue of Lille, in the Place de la Concorde, along next to that of Strassburg, is covered with flags, and liberty bows are being sold at the base of it.[25]

I wish I could send some little Christmas present—at least to you, my dearest Mother. As it is I have been able to send you some more of my photos—nine of the one that I think you liked, one of each of the others. Unfortunately the letter where you expressed

24. An "embusqué" is a shirker, one who hides from work and responsibility.
25. In the Place de la Concorde, Machen's comment, "along next to that of Strassburg," refers to the statue that represents Strasbourg, France, located along the perimeter of the area. There are eight statues representing the French cities of Marseille, Lyon, Bordeaux, Strasbourg, Lille, Rouen, Nantes, and Brest.

your preference was not with me when I ordered the pictures, but I think I struck it right. I have not seen the pictures myself.

Would it be too much trouble (if you have not already done so) to send a copy to Rev. W. P. Armstrong, D.D., Library Place, Princeton, N.J. and to Rev. Prof. Harold M. A. Robinson, Lafayette College, Easton, Pa.? I hate to put the bother upon you, but probably Betty & William will help.

By the way please be sure to remember me most cordially to all the servants. I am greatly touched & delighted by their interest in me.

And above all give my love to all the family. I can't begin to say how I long for more news,

Your own loving son,
Gresham

Oct. 31, 1918

My dearest Mother:

In case it may not be too late I am sending you the coupon which would permit the sending of a Christmas parcel. Possibly the socks could be put in. But on the whole I think I should rather have it kept quiet that space in a Christmas parcel is available. Those socks unquestionably would be bully.

Just before I left Paris I met Gardiner, late assistant pastor of the First Church of Princeton, who had returned to the city earlier than had been announced to me. He informed me that several weeks ago I had been ordered to report to Paris to enter into the specifically religious work. The order never reached me. As it was, my movement away from Paris with my division had already been arranged. Before I left I had a brief but satisfactory interview with President King of Oberlin College, who is now head of the religious work department.[26]

26. Oberlin College was the home of "Oberlin Theology" in nineteenth-century America. Asa Mahan, the first president of the College, published the *Scripture Doctrine of Perfection,* 1839, and in 1835, Charles G. Finney, became a professor of theology (Darrel Bigham, "Oberlin Theology," *The New International Dictionary of the Christian Church, Revised Edition,* Grand Rapids: Zondervan, 1978).

He says that he will have work for me in that department if I want it. Certainly I want it; but in my situation I do not know whether I ought to have the work nearer the front. Bible class work & the work of religious meetings are necessarily difficult at the front. If a truce should come, they would be much [needed] in places.

Nov. 8

The above letter never got mailed, I have just sent you a long letter to-day in which I said the coupon had already gone!

Your loving son
Gresham

Nov. 7, 1918

My dearest Mother:

Life has been so full during the past few days that I am quite at a loss as to how I am ever going to reduce the bewildering wealth of my impressions into anything like a semblance of order. The first part of the time since my last letter, it is true, was not particularly exciting, but Monday the 4th and Tuesday the 5th of this week, as I look back upon them, seem as though they must have been each about a month long.

 The journey from Paris was as usual rather troublesome. There was one pleasant day (Nov. 1st?) of waiting in a fairly large town, then we started out again in the search for our troops.[27] There was about a day, 2nd or third Nov.?, in another large town, where I think I wrote you a letter.[28] Then it looked as though I were

27. The marginal note designates the large town as "Dunkirk," which is in France, close to the Belgian border, and about 150 miles due N. of Paris and 93 miles W.N.W. of Brussels, Belgium.
28. The second large town was, "Roulers," which is located in Belgium and is about 145 miles N.N.E. of Paris and about 55 miles W.N.W. of Brussels.

side-tracked. Most of the men had succeeded in getting on, but I secured no transportation. Finally an officer's car took another secretary and myself on to a small place where two of our other men had succeeded in getting one car-load of canteen stock, which they had started to sell.[29] It soon became apparent however that we were not near enough to the front to render real service to the men of our division, and transportation consequently became the primary problem. There were no freight-cars, and no American army trucks, but the French authorities as usual treated me fine and placed three large trucks at our disposal. With these we moved our merchandise and ourselves (three secretaries) to a good-sized town which seemed likely to be our Y.M.C.A. distributing point.[30] By conference with the "town-major" or "major de cantonnement," I received a provisional ware-house, where we dumped our stuff and began selling it to the American soldiers. Five secretaries of our division were all that were in the region: I was, therefore, this time in an advance guard. It was determined that two of us were to push on toward the front, leaving two to run the canteen and watch for freight that might come in. One was already at the front. I was one of the two additional men chosen to push on. Our transportation was secured in ambulances, since we intended to work in the dressing-stations, as we had done several times before.[31] The ambulances of course go back to the front often nearly empty after having discharged the wounded men at the rear.

The first night was spent at a hospital some five miles from the front.[32] It was not a pleasant night for me. Wounded children made a pitiful noise, and the noise of German air-craft bombs and shells, some of them rather close, was more disturbing still. I confess that I slept hardly at all.

The next day two of us rode on an ambulance, with our little stock of powdered chocolate and cookies, to a dressing-station

29. In the margin, Machen named the town of "Lichtervelde," Belgium, which is located about 150 miles N.N.E. of Paris and 65 miles W.N.W. of Brussels.

30. This location is designated "Thielt" in the marginal note, which is located 150 miles N.N.E. of Paris and 45 miles W.N.W. of Brussels.

31. Machen wrote between the lines here "Saturday Nov. 2," and "Monday 4th?"

32. Machen's marginal note designates the location as "Dentergem," which is located about 153 miles N.N.E. of Paris and about 42 miles W.N.W. of Brussels.

about one mile from the front line.[33] There we proceeded to make our hot chocolate and distribute it to the wounded men. To my great delight I found myself again associated with the admirable ambulance company that I had been with several times before. But no amount of pleasant comradeship can conceal the fact that the twenty-four hours that I spent in that dressing-station was a strenuous time.

The small cellar of the house that we occupied was packed with some fifty civilians, mostly women and children, who had not been able to get away from the front after the Germans had left. The rest of us therefore stayed in three rooms of the ground floor, one of which was used for the wounded also. No one displayed a great enthusiasm for the upper floor; certainly it was much too far from the cellar to suit me. The house, though not large, was solid; its walls afforded considerable protection against the fragments of exploding shells. And shells in the immediate vicinity were not lacking, though while I was there only one came close enough to permeate the house with the odor of the high explosive. Fortunately there was work to do. We had two little stoves to make our hot chocolate on, in two separate rooms, and although my colleague was the leader in cookery I relieved him during a good part of the night. A little rest on some straw, with perhaps a snatch of sleep, was the extent of my repose. In the early part of the night I had my first experience in stretcher-bearing; a shell had struck a house some hundred yards or so away with disastrous results.[34] My services were accepted, though as it turned out there would have been enough to do the work without me. I made two trips to that house with men of the ambulance company. And I confess I was glad when the job was over, though nothing hit very close to us.

What in the world was to be done with the fifty civilians, including some twenty children and infants, and a number of pitifully aged and infirm men and women? It seemed cruel to make them try to walk away in the midst of the shell fire, but on the other hand there was no room for them where they were,

33. This dressing-station was "Near Eyne." Eyne is located about 148 miles N.N.E. of Paris and 32 miles W. of Brussels.
34. Machen's note comments, "two children killed, I think, and 2 American soldiers."

and they were in danger all the time. Finally, the lieutenant in charge determined to send away a crowd of the most needy in an ambulance. In view of my linguistic qualifications it fell to my part to choose the ones who were to go. Can you imagine a more pathetic task. It was like the last boat load leaving the Titanic. Finally with the help of one young fellow of superior intelligence among the civilians I got a good number of the smallest children with their parents aboard. We had to shove in one or two people ruthlessly when they wanted to get some bundles of clothes. It was some waggon-load, I can tell you. I am afraid they were not taken very far, since of course it is not possible to use ambulances ordinarily for such a purpose, but at least we got them started. Unfortunately the thing could not be repeated.

Before and after this departure I distributed some hot chocolate in that cellar. It was astonishing how they were cheered up, by the nourishing drink, and also by a few kindly words from someone in uniform. It was somewhat out of the line of the Y.M.C.A., but I must confess that no bit of service that I have been privileged to render since I have been in Europe has begun to give me the joy that I derived from ministering to those sweet little children in that hour of deepest distress.

Certainly it was a night that I am not likely to forget. Outside the whistle and roar of the arriving shells, and from the cellar the monotonous prayers of the frenzied women. In the morning the sight in the road outside was the most pathetic that I have ever seen. Nothing that I witnessed in the great retreat can compare with it. Tiny children and aged men and women, some of them loaded in wheelbarrows along with pathetic fragments of household effects, were all madly endeavoring to escape over the shell-menaced roads. I hope never to see another such sight; yet I think I shall always have a more tender and better heart on account of what I saw. Somehow I feel more certain that there must be a Father somewhere who cares for those little ones.

During the forenoon a medical major gave me the opportunity of going to a still more advanced dressing-station; located in a sort of convent about three hundred feet from the front line.[35] I did not want to go one bit, but duty seemed to call. Part of the way I went in an ambulance; then a detail of two men was given me to help carry my pounds of chocolate, my sugar, my condensed milk, & my little biscuits. We paused a number of times on the way in the shells of houses, & finally arrived at our destination without incident.

The dressing-station was in a large house occupied by some sisters of charity. Now I am a Protestant of the most uncompromising sort, and I do not believe a bit in nunnery; but I want to testify that those ladies were admirable. You should have seen the way in which they cared for the American wounded and doctors & ambulances as well as for the crowd of children that had fallen to their care. In fact it looked as though I would be rather useless. The sisters were far better cooks than I. But several people suggested that I might serve the soldiers in the line. This I did, on the day after the day in which I arrived. But on that previous day I had excitement enough. Just after I had been taken out by a captain to be shown the way to the lines, as I was returning a shell hit the street just at the door where I was to go in, and there were several direct hits in the house where I was to stay. The captain and I threw ourselves on the ground in the orthodox way, and after repeating the gesture when the second shell arrived got safely into a little cellar. Fortunately no one was hurt in the house where I was staying or in the house where I took temporary refuge—at least not hurt that time.

The next day I went twice out to the line carrying kettles of hot chocolate with the assistance of a fine young fellow among the men, who volunteered to help and guide me. There was a couple of hundred feet where one had to walk across a field in view of the enemy and be prepared to duck if the machine-guns opened up. But nothing happened. It must be supposed that the trip was especially dangerous; it was only the kind of thing that is done many times a day by the men in the army. To me it was most exciting, being my first experience in what may be called the front

35. The marginal note, once again, mentions the village named "Eyne." Eine is located about 148 miles N.N.E. of Paris and 32 miles W. of Brussels.

line. The service that I rendered was certainly most trifling, but it is a satisfaction to have made an effort at any rate.

Tuesday Nov. 5

That evening we were relieved. The night before I had spent in the cellar and had gotten some good sleep despite crowded conditions. The relief itself was satisfactory in its results, but rather nerve-wracking in the process of execution. Burning farms lit up the countryside for miles, and why the Boches planes which could be heard buzzing above us did not catch sight of us I do not know. But by the mercy of God they did not. On the way I looked in for my colleague at the other dressing-station; but the place was empty. It had finally been smashed by the shells.[36] My Y.M.C.A. colleague escaped injury.

My blanket and other belongings were badly arranged for carrying when I arrived at the stopping-place at about ten o'clock or so at night.[37] I was as dead tired out, I think, as I have ever been in my life. Imagine the feelings of the men when told that the place was crowded to overflowing and that there were no billets except, I believe, one little room for the officers & runners. I was inserted into that room, but to avoid the congestion found a cellar next door for a captain and myself. Practically no roofs were on the houses in that village, since severe fighting had taken place there a week or so before.

Nov. 6

The next day, I hiked back well to the rear, securing several welcome lifts. Just now I am in a town at the rear, enjoying the comparative peace and quiet, though there has been work enough to do.[38] When I arrived from the front dead tired out I did hope

36. A note written by Machen between the manuscript lines reads, "The man of the ambulance company who had helped us make the chocolate was killed in the doorway of the house," which refers back to earlier in the current letter.

37. The "stopping-place" was designated by Machen's note to be "Olsene," which is in Belgium and about 151 miles N.N.E. of Paris and 38 miles W.N.W. of Brussels.

38. The "town at the rear" was named by Machen in his later note as "Thielt," which is in Belgium and is located 150 miles N.N.E. of Paris and 45 miles W.N.W. of Brussels.

These women YMCA workers are involved in making hot chocolate. Hot chocolate making was one of Dr. Machen's duties while with the Foyer du Soldat program. In the lower left corner are containers of what may be condensed milk, which Machen often mentioned when he was making chocolate.
Photo courtesy of Kautz Family Collection, University of Minnesota

for a rest, but long lines of men were waiting outside the Y.M.C.A. canteen, and I just had to stop in and help as a salesman. Instead of sleeping somewhere on the floor crowded together with the Y.M.C.A. secretaries, I went to the French town major's office and got a sergeant in charge to find me a room, which he did in the most obliging possible way. So for two nights I have had the luxury of a room, a bed, and a quiet time. You can therefore, without worry, simply share my thankfulness for having been brought safely through dangers now past. God has been very good to me. That is the one great fact that stands out amid the confusion of the past days.

My landlady does not want to charge me anything for my room. She says that having had to house Germans for so long she is only too glad to house Americans on equally good terms. Of course we have taken pains to explain that I have no right to requisition a room, and of course I shall pay her a good rent; but at any rate her good will is significant and typical.

Your most welcome letter of Oct. 6 has arrived since I began the above. I am sorry to hear of Dr. Kirk's illness, but the good news about yourself, about Nena, and about Arly has cheered me beyond measure. You write about the socks just after I had sent you the label. I hope it may arrive in time, but if it does not, don't worry. The prayers that accompany the making of those socks will do me good in any case. I am thankful to-night for two great blessings—for the preservation of my life and for the possession of such a Mother.

Your loving son
Gresham

11

THE WAR IS OVER!

Following an exuberant celebration of the end of the war, Dr. Machen will review his movements in northeastern France and Belgium just before the war ended. The end of the war will result in a change in assignment for Machen and his hub of operations will be Paris. The new time of peace gives him the opportunity to travel to several locations and serve by leading worship and lecturing. He will enjoy French theater and literature in Paris as he has the opportunities between assignments, but he will also have hopes of going home.

Nov. 14, 1918

My dearest Mother:

The Lord's name be praised! Hardly before have I known what true thanksgiving is. Nothing but the exuberance of the psalms of David accompanied with the psaltery and an instrument of ten strings could begin to do justice to the joy of this hour. "Bless the Lord, O my soul."[1] It seems as though the hills must break forth into singing. Peace at last, and praises to God!

On the evening of the tenth of November I was again at the front. Little news had been coming through about the progress

1. Psalm 103:1.

of negotiations. Without a doubt you were far better and far more promptly informed in Baltimore. There were rumors, but they could not be definitely confirmed; other rumors have often disappointed us. Was there hope of an immediate peace? We did not know.[2]

I was to spend the night in a little house near a dressing-station where we hoped to serve the wounded with hot chocolate.[3] We were in the midst of our own artillery, which made the most infernal noise that I ever listened to.[4] There was absolutely no cellar or dug-out in which to take refuge, and I thought the German reply would blow us to pieces. Shells had been landing in the environs during the day; in the early part of the evening a man was slightly wounded just at the door of the house where I was staying. But although the whistle of the German shells could be heard from time to time, in general things became quieter as the night wore on. I got some sleep on the floor of our little hovel. Then rumors began to come in. The armistice was said to have been agreed on at 2.10 A.M. Desultory firing continued, but this was said to be usual even after an armistice is signed. At four o'clock the French could be heard singing in their quarters. When I poked my head in they said that the news was not official. But somehow there was a new atmosphere of hope. With the morning light the news was confirmed. Firing was to cease at 11 A.M.[5] Meanwhile there was quiet. A strange peacefulness pervaded the air. The walk to the Y.M.C.A. canteen, which the night before had been hideous with the flash and roar of the guns and arriving shells was now safe as though we were at home.[6] I shall never forget that morning. Perhaps, one might regret not having been at Paris when the stupendous news came

---

2. In parentheses following this sentence is written, "Spent a night at Deynze on the way to Synghem." Machen's "Deynze" is located in Belgium and is 150 miles N.N.E. of Paris and 37 miles W.N.W. of Brussels; "Synghem" is in Belgium and is 147 miles N.N.E. of Paris and 30 miles W. of Brussels.

3. This was "near Synghem," which is in Belgium and is 147 miles N.N.E. of Paris and 30 miles W. of Brussels.

4. The margin has the note, "Belgian & French," referring to the nationality of the artillery troops.

5. The actual time was 11:00 A.M. on November 11, 1918 (i.e. 11:00, 11/11).

6. The "Y.M.C.A. canteen" is noted to be "At Synghem," which is in Belgium and is 147 miles N.N.E. of Paris and 30 miles W. of Brussels.

in. But I do not think I regret it. We heard indeed, no clamor of joyful bells, no joyful shouts, no singing of the Marseillaise.[7] But we heard something greater by far—in contrast with the familiar roar of war—namely the silence of that misty morning. I think I can venture upon the paradox. That was a silence that could really be heard. I suppose it was the most eloquent, the most significant silence in the history of the world. About noon I took a walk out through the village to what had recently been the German position. Instead of the sinister appearance of a front-line town, with streets deserted or occupied only by men walking warily close to the walls, the place had almost taken on a holiday appearance. Of course the great gaping holes in the homes were still there, the pedestrian's feet would still crunch into the broken glass scattered by recent shells, but people were walking freely about as though life had begun. But joy should not be careless or exuberant, the dead were being brought in just as I passed, and along the road an occasional poor fellow was lying who would never hear the news of peace. It seemed almost impossible. On that exuberant joyful morning when the whole world was shouting, what possible place was there for death and sorrow? God knows and He alone. Meanwhile I felt more humble but not less thankful.

Across the river an American soldier showed me the German machine-gun emplacements which he had been trying to "get" with his own gun a few hours before. The cartridges were still strewn around.

But I must go back and bring my little narrative up to date, to explain how I happened to be near the front again after the relief of a few days before. First, however, let me say that I have received your sweet and welcome letter of Oct. 12. It is sweet and welcome even though not all the news in it is what I could have wished. I am sorry of course to hear about Dr. Kirk's severe illness (though my regret is tempered by the news of his passage of the danger-point), about the cook troubles of the "children," and (last but not least) about Arly's cold, which must have been very troublesome in the midst of his busy life.

7. This is the French national anthem.

After the two exciting days which I spent at the front about
a week or so ago, there was a period of about four days in a
considerable town in the rear, where I had considerable work at
the Y.M.C.A. cantine, but also considerable rest in a real bed.[8] I
had rather expected that our division would be given a long rest,
and was not overjoyed, I confess, when it became evident that we
were to go to the front again. However, I was encouraged by a little
word of praise that was handed on to me by one of the Y.M.C.A.
secretaries from the colonel of the regiment for which I labored
that day in the line. The colonel wanted me to know that he would
be glad to help me in any way, and that he appreciated what I had
done for his men. Such words of cheer have not been so numerous
in my experience as a Y.M.C.A. secretary but I enjoyed this one
considerably. As a matter of fact, I really just drifted along into
the service in question, indeed was almost forced into it (others
deserving what credit there was), but still I could not help being
pleased by the message.

The first night after leaving our Y.M.C.A. warehouse was
spent in a town about half-way to the front, where we had a busy
time selling things to the men.[9] Peace rumors had been coming
in, and the guns were phenomenally quiet. I confess that I thought
the war was over. The impression was reversed when we got out
near the front the next day. Shells were dropping around quite
frequently enough to suit me. A Y.M.C.A. cantine had already
been located in a village perhaps about a mile and a half from the
Germans. I worked a while selling goods there and then was sent
to a dressing-station perhaps a half-mile further to the rear. About
what happened there I have already told you. The opportunities
of service were so slight that after making our chocolate & having
it kept on the fire during the night, my companion & I returned
in the morning to the Y.M.C.A. canteen, where there was at first
a good deal of work to be done. Soon, however, our stock was
exhausted, & the next day was really a day of idleness. So yesterday

8. The "considerable town in the rear" was "Thielt," which is in Belgium and located 150
miles N.N.E. of Paris and 45 miles W.N.W. of Brussels.

9. It is noted in the margin that the town was "Deynze," which is located in Belgium and
is 150 miles N.N.E. of Paris and 37 miles W.N.W. of Brussels.

I came back to the Y.M.C.A. base, where I am now established in my old room.

I came to an important decision, which I hope may prove to be a wise one—the decision namely to ask for my movement order to Paris in order to report to the "religious work" department. You will remember that according to Mr. Gardiner of Princeton I was actually ordered to Paris, to engage in the work of that department, some weeks ago, though the order did not reach me. President King, head of the department, seemed to be able to find no record of such an order. But as soon as he found out who I was he received me cordially & told me very definitely that he would have useful work for me & that he thought my place was elsewhere than in a canteen. My movement papers away from Paris had, however, then already been made out, & besides I was not at all sure that I could feel justified in leaving my division as long as the fighting was going on. So President King agreed that I could go on with the division while at the same time having the way open to enter his department at the first convenient opportunity. That opportunity, I think, has certainly now arrived. For the present, there is no question of shirking the danger of war, that danger having been removed by the armistice. I could therefore work in Paris or anywhere in Europe with as good a conscience as with a moving division; and the opportunities for my kind of work would be enormously greater where life is a bit more stable. In general, the present situation offers an unparalleled opportunity both for religious & for educational work. If the truce is of long duration there will be millions of men over here relieved from the stress of war whose minds will be open.

Perhaps the safer procedure would have been for me to write to President King telling him that I would welcome a repetition of the order to report to Paris. But it would have taken weeks, probably, to get the reply, & meanwhile I am eager to get at my own work. It must be confessed that I feel a little like Esther in the presence of the king. If the golden scepter is not held out to me I shall be in a very embarrassing situation.[10] But although I have only

10. Dr. Machen is here referring to the historical account of Esther as recorded in the book bearing her name in the Old Testament.

oral answers, I think that if either Mr. Gardiner or President King is in Paris I shall be well received. And the heads of our Y.M.C.A. division appreciate my position. No one can say that I have shirked the simple, homely service of the canteen; for I have had some nine months of it. But I am not a business man. Others can do that important work as well or better than I. I am impatient now for my own work. And I am going for it with all my might, even though I am compelled to blow my own horn just a tiny little bit.

Meanwhile I am thankful to God for the preservation of my own life. Or rather, that does not just express what I mean, and I am not quite sure whether I can express it. I mean rather that I am thankful that God has not put upon me more than I could bear. It is obvious that other men are far braver and cooler than I am. I lose sleep when they seem to think nothing at all of the dangers that hover in the air. But out in the dressing-station, when the shells were falling close around, I somehow gained the conviction that I was in God's care and that He would not try me beyond my strength & that courage would keep pace with danger, or rather that danger (for I confess it turns out rather that way) would keep within the limits of courage![11] If for example a shell had hit within five feet of my head & I had been blown six or eight feet by the concussion, I am a little afraid that my nerves would have given way & I should not have been able to continue my service as coolly as before, as one of my Y.M.C.A. colleagues did under those circumstances. Nothing terrific like that happened to me, & I got through the trying days, though not at all with distinction, at least without distinct disgrace.

In short I believe I understand the eighth chapter of Romans better than I did two weeks ago.[12]

Oh, what a relief to enjoy once more the glory of a crisp autumn day or the beauty of a moon-lit night. I confess that during the last nine months I have longed for clouds and rain. There has scarcely ever been a time when I could stand under a clear sky without keeping my ear open for the nerve-wracking sound of a

11. When Machen wrote,"He would not try me beyond my strength," he may have been thinking of 1 Cor. 10:13.

12. This chapter of Romans is particularly concerned with the sovereignty of God, his providence, and his care for his people redeemed from sin and death by Jesus Christ.

German aircraft motor. Cloudy nights have sometimes brought me my only chance to sleep. No doubt such an attitude is very mean & wrong. Perhaps I ought to have been glad when it was clear; for if it gave the Germans a chance to bomb us, look what a splendid chance it also gave us to bomb them! But although reason might speak thus, feeling, I may as well confess never did.

And, oh, the joyful calm that we are enjoying now. Pray God it may not be interrupted again.

The best of love to all
Your loving son
Gresham

Wed., Nov. 21, 1918

My dearest Mother:

Great was my satisfaction, even after arriving in Paris, at receiving your letter of Oct. 25 (No. 44). Naturally I am distressed to hear of the siege that Helen has been through, but I am also relieved at her improvement now, and at Arly's recovery from his cold. The epidemic of influenza must have been terrible—in some way, fully as bad as the horrors of war. How thankful I am that all our family circle escaped the danger, which now happily seems to be on the wane!

Really I do not know exactly when I wrote you my last letter, but I rather think it was after my arrival at Paris. At any rate it gave an account of the last day of the fighting and of the way we felt when the firing ceased. That letter and the one immediately preceding it contained probably what were to me the most interesting items of news that I have had to tell since I have been in Europe. The journey to Paris was rendered pleasant and easy by the kindness of a medical major whom I met by chance on the station platform just as I was contemplating an all day ride of fifty miles or so in a "train de permissionaires," with the prospect of missing Paris connections at the end of it and sleeping goodness knows where.[13] The Major took me on a three-hour ride in an automobile (the train would have made it probably in fifteen) which in addition to the enormous saving of time enabled me to see the intensely interesting scenes of four years of battles. The desolation of the country near the former no man's land would beggar any description that I might attempt. After a pleasant afternoon in the town where the automobile landed us we actually secured sleeping-car berths to Paris. Think of it! Real berths with the most immaculate of sheets and bedding. At Paris I was most extremely lucky in securing a splendid quiet room with bath at a hotel where they do not insist on talking English. It is the Hotel du Palais Royal, a moderate sized place, in the Rue de Valois, just back of the Palais Royal.[14] The location is so exactly what I desire that the last time I was in Paris I took occasion to notice the hotel in passing. Without further recommendation, I tried it this time, and found it the puppy's eye.[15] Certainly it is the reverse of my previous quarters, which were inconveniently situated, expensive, cramped, and infested with Americans. I wonder now how I ever stood the tyranny of that landlady as long as I did. Certainly I should not have done so if I had known that anything like my present room could be secured in Paris. The quilt, the abundance of room, the convenience of a place that is only a few paces distant from the Théâtre Fràncais and from a métro station—well it is all just too good to be true. What a delightful time I have been having since last Saturday! How I wish it could last for weeks! Every night I go to the theatre, and during the day I read over the plays that I am to see—that is when they are classical plays and worth reading. There is also plenty of time for walks around Paris, and unfortunately there is a good deal of business to be transacted—a suit of clothes to be made, a lost money-order to be looked up, the search for

13. A "train de permissionaires" is a train dedicated to soldiers on leave.

14. Currently in Paris, there is an 81-room, three-star hotel named the Grand Hôtel Du Palais Royal at 4 Rue Valois. From its architectural appearance, it looks to be early enough to be the same building where Machen lodged. The "Palais Royal" was built by Cardinal Richelieu (1585–1642) in 1629 during the reign of Louis XIII (1601–1643) ("Plesis, Armand-Jean du, Cardinal and duc de Richelieu," *Webster's Biographical*).

15. Did "the puppy's eye" evolve into "the cat's meow" in the Roaring Twenties?

my suit-case to be continued, business letters to be written, teeth to be filled, and a lot of other things to be done too numerous to mention. But you may wonder whether my duty to the Y.M.C.A. has been altogether forgotten. To show you that that is not the case I must tell you about my situation with the "religious work bureau."

When I reported at that bureau immediately upon my arrival I was cordially received by President King, and especially by Mr. Edworthy his assistant. Mr. Edworthy plans to send me on a little speaking trip in the central part of France, and perhaps later in the "leave area." I was to have started to-day, but since Mr. Edworthy had received no reply from his telegram to the men in charge in the region in question, he thought it well to postpone my departure till Monday. Meanwhile I am to speak somewhere on Sunday near here. I am glad to have time to collect my thoughts, since only two nights in the week are to be given to religious services. On the other nights I shall have to talk on secular themes a task which is new to me. I do hope that the plan for itinerant work may not fall through. Meanwhile I am certainly enjoying my stay in Paris. After having done particularly no reading for months & months, you may well imagine what an immense relief & joy it is to have a little privacy & put a book into my hands again. Yesterday afternoon, at the Odéon, there was a splendid rendition of the "Carmosine" of de Musset, with beautiful "musique de scène."[16] I simply longed for you. The play was preceded by an interesting conférence by Funck-Brentano.[17] As for the play itself, I don't think anything more delicate and more beautiful could be imagined. But this is only the best among a number of treats that I have had.

On the Sunday after my arrival, Paris celebrated the "restitution" of Alsace & Lorraine with a procession, & speech-making near the statue of Strasburg.[18] I did not get near enough to witness or hear either of these. The sound, not only on the Place de la Concorde itself, but also all the neighboring streets was tremendous. The only thing I saw was the air-planes which in great numbers

16. The "musique de scène" is the music accompanying the play.

17. The "conférence" (lecture) was delivered by Frantz Frunck-Brentano (1862–1947), who was a French historian and librarian (*Webster's Biographical*).

18. The "restitution" of Alsace and Lorraine was the return of these contested areas to France at the end of World War I. These areas would again be seized by Germany in World War II.

grazed the roofs of the houses and thrilled the crowd by "looping the loop" and doing other stunts. In the evening there was confetti-throwing on the boulevard. But I confess to having been bored by the proceedings. Standing around in a crowd does not appeal to me.

President Stevenson of the Seminary is in France. I had a pleasant conversation with him the other day. One of Army's friends among the old Benham men invited me to lunch a few days ago. His account of the splendid work in his Y.M.C.A. division made me feel keenly my own lack of success.

This letter will probably be the only Christmas present that I can send. But it is full of love for you, my dearest Mother, & for all at home.

Your loving son
Gresham

November 23, 1918

My dearest Mother:

Despite what I said in my letter of day before yesterday, I have sent you by American Express a little Christmas box, consisting of trifling articles made by wounded soldiers. The bead necklace (which naturally does not need to be worn as a necklace) is intended for you; the two little mats for Nena and Helen; and the toys and one doll for Tom & Louise. The toys are two in number, in order that if one is busted the other may take its place.

There is little to give except what I told you in my letter. But there is always lots of love. How I wish I could be in the Christmas circle! But I shall be there in spirit, & now that the joy of peace has come you will not feel my absence so much.

Your loving son
Gresham

Nov. 26, 1918

Dear Uncle:

Your letter of October 24 was certainly a treat; for although Mother has been a splendidly faithful correspondent it is good also to hear directly from others among the home folks. Mother will no doubt pass on to you some account of my experiences in the closing days of the war—experiences that I am not likely to forget. For nearly ten days, while getting settled in the "religious work" department, I have had a most delightful time in Paris. It seems strange to see the streets lighted at night, with lighted windows open in what would have been, a few weeks ago, a most reckless way. Paris seems to be nearly itself again. Only the piles of sand bags around monuments and in front of the facades of some buildings serve to remind us of the recent trouble. Your ancient home, the Bellevue, looks very cozy when I pass it at night. Evidently it has been used right along as a hotel.

I wish Aunt Bessie could have been with me last night at the Odéon where I enjoyed a most delightful rendition of "Le Bourgeoise Gentilhomme." This along with "Carmosine" ranks as one of the finest treats that I have had.

On Sunday I spoke at a camp about forty miles from Paris, and to-day I am to start on a preaching or lecturing trip in the central part of France. I have been transferred to the "religious work bureau," Paris being my station so far as I have any station. But probably I shall be in Paris only occasionally, to get orders.

I was glad to get a word of news (through you) from Loy and his family. What wouldn't I give to see that family as well as you and Aunt Bessie!

Meanwhile I can only beg you to give to Aunt Bessie my very best love.

Your affectionate nephew,
J. Gresham Machen

November 28, 1918

My dearest Mother:

Although I am in a very interesting city and have had time for nothing but a hurried glance at the cathedral, I am going to seize the opportunity of writing you a few lines, especially since a miserable steady rain puts rather a damper on sight-seeing. Your letter of November 5 arrived two or three days ago, before I left Paris. Let me say right off that the snapshot of the two kiddies with their grandmother on the porch of the little cottage at Seal Harbor is beyond question the sweetest thing I ever saw. I wouldn't take a thousand dollars for it, although it does make me terribly homesick. The kiddies are too sweet for anything, but the sweetest person of all is in the centre of the picture. The other snap-shot of Betty with the same two kids, is also a dandy. Tom certainly outdid himself as a photographer.

I am distressed to hear that Helen's recovery from her cold has not been as rapid as might have been expected, and eagerly await better news.

It was too bad that you got no letter of mine between Sept 14 and Oct. 17. At least two letters of mine, I should say, must be delayed or lost, and the worst of it is that I am afraid the lost letters contained the news of the most interesting part of my experiences.[19] I wonder whether it is now permissible to mention the names of the places where I have been. Restrictions have been removed at the present period, since the signing of the armistice, but as yet I have no definite information about the censorship of previous history.

On last Sunday, I went out to speak at Bourron, south of the forest of Fontainebleau.[20] The Ford that took me was scheduled to leave Paris at 8.30 A.M., but on account of some kind of trouble did not leave till about one. Then on the way out the chauffer proved to be incompetent; we ran out of gasoline; and so did not finish the forty-mile run till about six o'clock. I spoke at an evening service—

19. There is a letter of Oct. 3, 1918, included in this collection, so it arrived at a later date.
20. There is a "Bourron-Marlotte," which is about 38 miles E.S.E. of Paris and S. of the Fountainebleau Forest.

without, as far as I could see, any great response. Contrary to the original plan we spent the night at the camp, and limped along back the next morning. Danny drove the car in from the out skirts of the city.

On Monday evening there was a splendid rendition of "Le bourgeoise gentilhomme" at the Odéon. I had read the play over. It seems to me much the most delightful of the works of Molière that I have read so far. Although I was pretty tired, the evening was most enjoyable. The scene where the "maître de philosphie" sets forth the principles of elocution reminds me vividly of that London elocutionist who taught us to pop our p's.[21] But if I started calling attention to the things that made me chuckle particularly in that play there would be no time to give you any further news.

Before I left Paris I took occasion to stroll into a number of the churches like St. Eustache and St. Sulpice that I had never seen before.[22] The shortness of the days is certainly a hindrance to sightseeing. It gets dark about four o'clock or a little after, and even in the middle of the day (since the weather is always dismal) there is not a super abundance of light.

It was with great regret that I left my comfortable quarters at the Rue de Balois, and discontinued my delightful meals at the "Etablissements Duval." But the break had to be made and on Tuesday afternoon I took the train for Vierzon where I presented a letter of introduction at the "regional" office of the Y.M.C.A.[23] I was pleasantly received, and an itinerary of several months has been laid out for me in the Y.M.C.A. "region" that embraces a considerable part of central France. The first centre of my operations was to be Tours, and at Tours I am situated at present writing.[24] The regional director took me in a Ford (which happened to be going my way) as far as Blois, with its memories of Catherine de Medici. Fortunately I had some three hours before my train left, and you can be sure that I used them to obtain a hurried view of the château and the town. What a delightful place! I wish I could make a tour of the château. But travel is strictly regulated

21. A "maître de philosphie" is a master of philosophy.
22. Église Saint-Eustache is at the Place René Cassin, and the Église Saint-Sulpice is located on the Rue Palatine a couple of blocks N. of the Jardin du Luxembourg.
23. The town of "Vierzon" is located 117 miles S. of Paris and about 26 miles N.W. of Bourges.
24. "Tours" is located about 125 miles S.W. of Paris and about 83 miles W.N.W. of Bourges.

these days; whenever a member of the American expeditionary force like myself desires to travel by train he has to have a "movement order," which of course cannot be obtained without adequate motive for the journey. The only possible chance, therefore, for seeing any of the châteaux outside, perhaps, of a few of the large towns would come if I happened to be lucky enough to travel now and then by auto. But that is a very long chance indeed. Sightseeing and such will have to be postponed until the piping days of peace.

Meanwhile, however, I am at Tours, and since I am finishing this letter on the day after the day when it was begun I have already had time to see something of the town. Beyond question it is one of the most picturesque places that I ever saw. The narrow streets of certain quarters, with their bewildering wealth of solid old stone houses, are unsurpassed by anything that I have yet encountered in my travels. And the cathedral is magnificent; it is one of the things that I can unfeignedly admire. Admiration of Notre Dame at Paris for example is to me rather a duty than a spontaneous tribute. But it is different with the cathedral at Tours. Speaking of Notre Dame, by the way, reminds me that there the old glass has been removed in order to protect it from the bombardments, whereas here at Tours it remains in all its glory. The surroundings of the cathedral here are particularly fine—on the side the magnificent structure now used as a museum, on the other side the cloister, at the rear one of the most delightful quiet little ancient squares that could possibly be imagined. Yesterday afternoon, just when I wanted to prepare my talk for the evening, my room was occupied by the electrician who was making some repairs. In order to get out of the dreary wet I took refuge in the cathedral and in the fine interior of St. Julien. I do not know whether the surroundings helped my thanksgiving address, but the quiet opportunity of enjoyment was certainly refreshing.

I am to make Tours my headquarters for about a week, speaking at the numerous American camps in the vicinity. Last night (Thanksgiving) I made a beginning at a large camp in the outskirts of the city. Who should turn out to be the religious secretary at the camp but a Dr. Beatty, who was one of the charter members of the Benham Club—though it must be confessed a little remiss so far as visits to Princeton are concerned. He received me very cordially. In the evening

there was a good crowd of men at the thanksgiving service. Both
Dr. Beatty and I spoke. The Y.M.C.A. building is very large and well-
arranged, there being a fine separate room for the meetings.

I do not know where I am to go for to-night, since I have not
yet, this morning, been able to see the divisional secretary who has
me in charge here.

My, but the weather is dismal. A steady cold rain has been
falling since I arrived in this city. I should love to see something like
a stove where I could warm my feet. But Europe never was much on
stoves even in time of peace, and of course coal must now be saved
more than ever.

I do wish I knew more about French history. The taste for
history & biography, which should have appeared earlier, is just
beginning to be formed in my vacant brain. Also I shall really like
to know something about the history of architecture. Unless they
work me a little harder than they do at present, I think I shall look
up the public library here. Then maybe I shall give some lectures
on French history, they being much in demand in the camps!

Remember me (as well as giving my love to the members of the
family) to Betty. She does look too good for anything in that picture
with the kiddies. And she is good too. May she long be spared to be
a comfort to my dearest Mother.

Your loving son
Gresham

Dec. 5, 1918

My dearest Mother:

You can scarcely imagine my surprise and delight when I
received this afternoon three splendid letters from Mother all in
one blessed parcel. The letters were no. 43 of October 19, no. 45 of

Nov. 2, no. 48 of Nov. 12. I have already answered an un-numbered
letter of Nov. 5, which is probably no. 46. That leaves a possible
no. 47 unaccounted for, but I rather think that there was no such
letter. If not, the inadvertence as to the number is not surprising.
What is surprising is the accuracy with which you have kept up the
very useful system of numbering the letters. My own attempt at
reciprocation was an utter failure. The only question is whether a
letter is lost between number 43 and 45. My impression is that the
letter in question has already been answered. I did not bring all the
old letters with me from Paris. It would be a grief indeed to have
lost even a single one, since your letters are the light of my life.

What a wealth of thrilling news from home! Let me say first
of all that partly in view of the eccentric order in which the letters
came and partly in view of my own stupidity in reading, I did not
realize that Arly and Helen had actually had the dreaded "flu." I
tremble even now in retrospection, even though the danger—thank
God—seems to be entirely over. Think of my referring to Arly's
illness merely as a cold! At any rate I feel so close to you in sympathy
both for your terrible anxiety and for the relief which now seems to
have come. Pray God that Helen may now be getting along well, as
especially your last letter gives every reason to hope. Do not fail to
tell her and Arly, and also Tom and Nena, how eagerly I have been
listening to every bit of news that comes from any one of them.

As for the "flu" itself, it must have been terrible beyond
anything that could have been thought to be possible. When you
describe the closed theatres and schools and churches, the partial
cessation of business, the untended sick and unburied dead, I came
to believe that you in America have really witnessed greater horrors
than I who have been so near the battle front. The Black Death is
sometimes more horrible, with its stealthy search, than are all the
noise and smoke of battle.

But let me return to the happier news. And let me return again
and again to those Seal Harbor pictures. I really thought that the
former batch of them could not possibly be beat. But after receiving
the three contained in your letter of Nov. 13, especially the one
where you are sitting in the picture between the two kiddies, I am
no longer quite sure. That picture is just too sweet for anything. It

just seems to me that distance must be annihilated and that I just want to be able to give a good hug to the sweetest person that ever lived. If I don't by force of will put those five pictures out of my sight for a little while this letter will never get written. The temptation is to drop the pen every second or so and take a wondrous trip back into the dear sweet life of Seal Harbor, as Mother made it for all of her children both big and little.

I was intensely interested in your account of the rejoicing of Nov. 11. Really I believe America was more demonstrative in its joy than the supposedly "excitable" France. Remembering my own deadly weariness after a few months spent in the mere outskirts of war, with nothing that is nearest to home in any jeopardy, I sometimes try to realize what the French must feel after four years of the terrible struggle, with house and home as well as the lives of loved ones threatened at every moment even if not already reduced to melancholy ruins. Could you wonder if peace had been hailed with a very delirium of joy? But the truth is that some joys are too profound, or rather are too much sobered by irreparable sorrow, ever to be expressed by parades or shouting. Confetti-throwing at Paris, when it did come, seemed almost like a profanation. Self-control in danger and sorrow had been practical so long that the habit remains in time of joy.

I am delighted to hear that Lewis and Adine have a son. If possible I want to write to Lewis. I suppose "Legislative Bureau, Richmond" will reach him.

Your receipt of my letter of Oct. 4–6 gives me satisfaction, since apparently that letter was the one, along with the last two written before my final return to Paris, which described the things which will always stand out most clearly in my impressions of the great war. I have absolutely no diary, and for the most part could probably not fix the date of my journeys even within a week or so.

As for present news, I have to report since my last letter a rather easy and thoroughly delightful week at Tours. They have not worked me very hard—indeed I have not even had to speak every night. There was a change of schedule at the place where I was to speak last night, and the same thing happened with regard to to-night, except that this time I was given a few hours notice. It would be satisfactory to be a little more in demand, but I do believe that there are not so very many men who are delivering just the message that I am trying to deliver. For that reason it seems to me that the opportunities are worth waiting for.

Meanwhile I have been having a most delightful time. It is a measure of profound regret to me that my appreciation of the beautiful things of Europe and my interest in history have been awakened so late in life—after so many of the opportunities for enjoyment and enlightenment are past. This is the sixth time that I have been in Europe. Before this time I engaged in considerable sight-seeing, which I enjoyed and the memory of which will always be with me. But not till this time did the enjoyment of a good church become a passion, and never before did I feel that life was too short to read what I am eager to read. Along with a certain lamentable decline in "_____" and hopeful ambition, and the desire to do things, has come a new desire to receive—to receive an intellectual equipment which will never be of any immediate use. A perverse desire has come over me to steep myself in the history of the renaissance or of the "grande siècle" instead of preparing my Sprunt lectures.[25] But I am entirely ignorant, and in need of the most elementary instruction. I am just finishing the perusal of an "Esquisse d'une histoire de France" by Cavaignac, recommended by the intelligent matron who runs the leading bookstore of the town.[26] Dear me, before I read that book I hardly knew the difference between Saint Louis and Louis-Philippe! To-day I came away from the bookstore with "Le siècle de Louis xiv" by Voltaire and Brunetière's "Histoire de la Littérature française" under my arm.[27] I have not the slightest idea whether these

25. The "grande siècle" describes the Renaissance era in France. In 1915, Machen accepted an invitation from W. W. Moore, president of Union Seminary in Virginia, to deliver the annual James Sprunt Lectures at Union in January of 1921. The lectures were published in 1921 as *The Origin of Paul's Religion*. The book emphasizes the supernatural nature of Paul's teaching on the Gospel in opposition to the naturalistic and higher critical approach to Paul taught by the liberal scholars. As is seen in some of his WW I letters, Machen's concern for the supernatural was high on his list of attributes for biblical Christianity.

26. "Esquisse d'une histoire de France" (An Outline of the History of France) by Eugène Cavaignac, 1910.

27. "Le Siècle de Louis XIV" (The Century of Louis the XIV) by Voltaire, 1751, and Ferdinand Brunetière's "Histoire de la Littérature Française" (A History of French Literature). Voltaire is the assumed name of François-Marie Arouet (1694–1778). He was a writer with a particular fondness for satire, and his sharp wit landed him in the Bastille, 1717–1718, and again in 1726.

are the food I need. Probably I shall soon get hold of some stupid book, or my dinner will disagree with me; the spell will be broken, and if I get to see Chambord it will make no more impression on me than the Glen-Cove.[28] Meanwhile let me say that during the one sunny hour which we have had for the last four weeks, I went into the cathedral. The splendor of the old glass was almost unearthly.

At the beginning of Voltaire's history, in exalting the age of Louis xiv the author says that when Louis xiii came to the throne there were not yet four beautiful buildings in Paris, and as for the other cities of the realm they resembled those towns which are to be seen across the Loire. In short there was nothing but "grossièreté gothique."[29] Considering that France has passed through an age so sure of its inerrancy of _____ the only wonder is that there are any remnants of mediaeval splendor. The older things have been preserved almost by accident—like the château at Blois where the fortunate death of Gaston d'Orléans is commemorated by the ragged edge where he leapt off to destruction.

One afternoon I went out to Marmoutier across the river, with its memories of St. Gatien and Martin of Tours, and its remnants of the great monastery. Another day I visited Le Plessis-de-Tours, but the château and grounds are now used as a vaccine institute and strictly forbidden to all except physicians. I wanted to make the acquaintance of old Louis xi, as Scott introduces him at the beginning of Quentin Durward, which always seemed to me one of the most interesting scenes in all the range of the Waverly novels.[30]

When he left the Bastille in 1726, he went to England because his leaving the country was the condition of his release. He wrote tragedies, philosophical novels and poems, histories, philosophy, and generally raised the ire of any group he wrote about ("Voltaire," *Webster's Biographical*).

28. The Château de Chambord is a distinctively French Renaissance castle in the Loire Valley. It is located 224 miles S.W. of Paris and 28 miles S. of Nantes. There is a Glen Cove on Long Island, New York, across the Long Island Sound from New Rochelle, but Machen may have another Glen Cove in mind.

29. The words "grossièreté gothique" refers to the crudeness and vulgarity of gothic architecture, according to the assessment of some architectural critics.

30. Sir Walter Scott's (1771–1832)"Waverly Novels" include such recognizable titles as, *Rob Roy* (1817), *Waverly* (1814), and *Ivanhoe* (1819). The Waverly series numbered 48 volumes ("Waverly Novels," *Webster's Literature*).

As for reading, the question is where to begin. Shall I investigate Jeanne d'Arc, as she had her armor made here at Tours, or shall I assist in the murder of the duc de Guise in the château at Blois, or shall I sink myself in the "grand siècle" as I was anxious to do after reading "Le bourgeois gentilhomme?" My ignorance being equally profound at all points I cannot find a starting point. Yet I do not want to continue forever reading "esquisses."[31]

Once or twice I have visited the library here. The librarian is very kind about showing the manuscripts. But digressions with him are so frequent that it is hard to get anywhere. For instance when he started to show me a most interesting manuscript of the gospels he got started on John 9:2. How could that man's being born blind possibly have been a punishment for his own sins which had not yet happened if limited to this life. Obviously a previous existence is referred to! (The librarian is a crank on the subject of theosophy).[32] Or, to take another instance: When I was reading an innocent and most elementary encyclopedia article on Martin of Tours the librarian insisted on knowing whether I was interested in science. I was rash enough to pretend to some interest in it, especially since I did not know just what branch of science was referred to. That put me in his power. I was expected to read an article on $H2O$ and also to agree at once to the librarian's belief that there is only one element—namely "azote" whatever that may be. When I add that I am expected to translate frequently into English what the librarian is saying, you will understand that the path of learning at that library is a bit rough and thorny.

Night before last at one of the camps my talk was followed by a lecture by a Dr. Dewey, who for forty or fifty years has been Paris correspondent of the New York Evening Post. I rode in with him in an auto after his lecture. He proved to be a most entertaining and well informed man. It was a pleasure to observe his ability to interest the boys. Anecdotes and variety are absolutely essential. Meanwhile I have to plod along as best I can.

I was to speak during this week on "Bible Study," in connection with an effort to increase attendance in Bible

31. The word "esquisses" means "outlines."
32. "Theosophy" is religious philosophy or speculation about the nature of the soul.

study classes. In general I cannot say that there has been much cooperation or preparation for the meetings. But I cannot blame the hut secretaries. You see, I have been there now myself, and know something of the difficulties.

Last night a movie show was beginning just when I got to the hut where I was to speak. Naturally the talk was to be called off. It is unnecessary to go into the special reason for the conflict—electric current secured only for one evening, etc. etc. At any rate the opportunity was offered me of attending German entertainment in a large prison camp. Needless to say I accepted with alacrity. The evening was intensely interesting. The prisoners had manufactured violins and base viols themselves out of old boxes, etc.; and with such instruments rendered not rag-time but really good music. I did not know as I listened to the music that the string instruments were home-made. There was also good chorus-singing, a little one-act play, and funny songs and recitations. Some of the wit was not of the highest order, but in general the evening was most enjoyable— especially in view of the circumstances.

I was to be at Tours till Monday. Then I go to Saumur for a few days.[33] I hate to leave the nice room that I have here. My, how aged I am! I do so love to "stay put." The only discomfort here is the cold— the room is unheated. But my clothes are warm, and the weather— with unceasing mist or rain—is mild.

By the way it is awfully good of both you and Helen to knit things for me. I shall appreciate them deeply if the label enables you to send them—and indeed I shall appreciate your thoughts of my needs in any case.

In explanation of my hesitation about joining the crowd of secretaries who are besieging the authorities for permission to go home, let me say right off that it is not due to any luke-warmness of desire to see the home-folks and especially my dearest Mother. What wouldn't I give to be with you at this moment! But the opportunities for my kind of "Y" work are vastly greater now than when the war was going on. The men's minds are freer; they are bound to have more leisure; the need for the proclamation of

33. The town of "Saumur" is located 153 miles S.W. of Paris and 119 miles W.N.W. of Bourges.

the gospel is unparalleled. I don't suppose there ever was just such a need or just such an opportunity. As far as the Seminary is concerned, I don't see a tremendous amount of use in landing in the middle of the term. Of course I desire to work on my Sprunt lectures, and I don't suppose I shall be able to get down to that over here. But under the circumstances, especially since I do not know whether I could secure my release even if I wanted to, I think I ought to stick to my work here for the present. Of course any day may bring a fundamental change in the situation, which may hasten my home coming. Meanwhile I am eager for a chance at something other than the canteen service in which I have been engaged most of the time.

I feel sure, my dearest Mother, that you will appreciate the opportunities of preaching the gospel where there are so few to do this work. You know how well some of the sacrifices that you have made have turned out. And of course nothing permanent is determined. I shall be guided I hope rightly by circumstances.

I am signed up for the period of the war. The "Y" therefore can hold me. It would be a favor to release me. And I believe that the reasons for my going home at once are not quite as imperative as those that prevent the cases of the vast majority of the secretaries. For example the vast majority are married & have children; the vast majority have work that can be taken up equally well at any time of year; many are pastors—and you know the special danger of the protracted absence of a pastor. Furthermore I do not know that any secretaries—except those who were engaged only for a definite period—are being sent home as yet. So a little patience is needed.

Have you engaged your passage for the summer? This, I am afraid, is a joke. I fear it will be difficult to secure passports for European travel this summer. There are too many millions of soldiers to be moved. But before very long Europe will have need of the tourist industry again. What times we shall have!

Sometimes a longing for the mountains comes over me that is almost like a passion. I hate to see the best mountaineering years of my life slipping by unused. The passion grows on me, instead of diminishing, as physical vigor declines. Sometimes I imagine that

I am just starting up for some great peak on one of those frosty Alpine mornings. I tremble with delight at the thought of the joys above. But the subsequent plunge into the hindrances of mere lowland life is cruel deception. The air of the heights is to me more intoxicating than wine.

Home and the mountains—the account of early training the two will always be associated in my heart. I shall never stand on a great height without thinking of the times when we followed the shadow of the Castles or of Mount Madison up across the great ravines of the White Mountains.[34] The love of the mountains in me comes from the same source where I have derived every thing else worthwhile—namely from Mother.

Love to all
Your loving son
Gresham

34. The White Mountains are in E. New Hampshire and near the Machen's cottage in Seal Harbor.

12

THE "RELIGIOUS WORK"

December 17 to January 5, 1919

The following will review Machen's movements from Tours, to Saumur, to Angers, and to LeMans, and express his enjoyment of French theater in his hub of operations in Paris. There is hope that he will be going home soon, but he signed on with the "Y" for the duration. Joy is expressed in having the opportunity to proclaim "the gospel and the teaching of the Bible," but he is less than happy with the designation of such labors by the "Y" as "religious work."

Dec. 17, 1918

My dearest Mother:

How the days do slip by when there are no letters from home! Your letters are the landmarks of my life. Without them I am quite oblivious of the passage of time. The consequence is just now that I have allowed a good many days to pass without sending you a line. My last letter, I am afraid, was written about a week or so ago.

From Tours I went on Monday Dec. 9 to Saumur. On Monday night I spoke at the Y.M.C.A. theatre, as a curtain raises for the movies. Can you imagine any more difficult job? On Tuesday I did not speak at all. On Wednesday night I spoke to a good little group of men at a training-school, where men have been working to get commissions. This time I was repaid by some expression of interest on the part of several men, with whom I had satisfactory conversations after my talk. The two to whom I refer were thinking about entering the ministry. It was an encouragement to come into contact with some Christian fellows.

Saumur is an interesting little place, but the absence of a fine gothic church prevents residence in it from being delightful as it is at Tours. Of course I saw the château and went out to the "Dolmen." Also I had to go through the aromatic champagne caves in order to be with several of my Y.M.C.A. companions who were interested. There are some good old houses in the town, but in general the place is far less quaint than Tours.

The same is to be said for Angers, where I have been reading since last Thursday, though there are a host of interesting things here.[1] The château makes a fellow want to read Ivanhoe over again as much as anything that I can remember having seen. The big gateway, with its moat, though without its portcullis and drawbridge, is about the most realistic thing in the way of mediaeval architecture that I have yet encountered. The hôpital Saint Jean is intensely interesting, but unless you are lucky enough to get to it Sunday or Thursday you have to be shown around by the guardian, who is very learned and very obliging, but rather too talkative to permit much meditation on the part of the sightseer. The tapestries in the old bishop's palace converted me to tapestries. I confess I could never see anything in tapestries before. But these (the subject is the book of Revelation), instead of being jumbly, make the figures stand out like the best of the ancient painters. The cathedral is fine, and magnificently situated, but does not go to my heart at all like Tours. An enormous eighteenth-century altar reaches nearly up to the vaulting and effectually hides the splendid old stained glass of the choir. Let me confess my ignorance to a sympathetic ear. It does seem to me, my dearest Mother, that the early gothic architects had a lot to learn. It is the later stages of gothic architecture, when I suppose I ought to regard it as approaching its decline, that really, and truly appeal to me.

The sun is shining to-day. This is an event. During the past two months I do not believe that there have been in all more than

1. The town of "Angers" is 115 miles S.W. of Paris and 117 miles W.N.W. of Bourges.

ten hours or so of sunlight. I never dreamed that anything like
our weather was possible. Day after day and day after day, of mild
wet weather, with only a little struggling bit of light between nine
o'clock and four. But I rather like the mildness of the weather,
though my hotel room here, which is admirably comfortable in
every way, is actually heated when there is the slightest need of heat.

When I reported at Y.M.C.A. headquarters here I was greatly
disappointed to find that by mistake I had been assigned to
the educational department instead of to the "religious work"
department (I hate that expression "religious-work" so that I always
put it in quotation marks). So I had been booked to "lecture"
rather than to speak at religious meetings. The question then
became acute as to what I was to lecture about. I decided to lecture
about "The Spiritual Battle"—although usually I have succeeded
in avoiding any announcement of this theme, which I confess
would put me to sleep before the lecturer would have time to
begin. I discuss the spiritual resources of Germany in the present
war, the spiritual resources of the allies & the spiritual resources
necessary in the struggle which is going on after the war is over.
Well, surprising as it may seem, the thing doesn't seem to go so very
badly.

The first night I had by far the best audience that I have had
yet. The room was full, the colonel was sitting in the first row, the
chaplain conducted the proceedings in a dignified way, and the
crowd seemed to listen. On Sunday I preached on Rom 8:31, at two
different camps. In the evening especially there was a good big
crowd.

In general I feel somewhat more encouraged. There really
seems to be some response. Perhaps my trip is going to be worth
while. At any rate I certainly like the way things are done by the
Y.M.C.A. in this section. They are always expecting me wherever I
go to speak; the lecture is well announced; an auto calls for me at
the hotel to take me to the various places in plenty of time. Under
such circumstances a man feels encouraged to do better work.

I have continued my reading. Voltaire's book on the age of
Louis xiv (which I have finished) is certainly interesting. In the
incisive way in which he sizes people up he reminds me a little of

Macaulay though it is without Macaulay's mannerisms. Brunetière seems to have to be a bit lacking in a sense of humor, but I have been interested in his big history of classical French literature. I had to buy a volume of Corneille. It is great. I love to sit up in my room and spout it all to myself. When nobody is near to embarrass me by criticism it really seems to me that my rendition of heroic verse is fully as good as that of the best artists of the Comédie française! At any rate I take just as much pleasure in it. I have also been reading Pascal's "Provinciales." The edition of Pascal which I gave Loy & Arly some years ago is unfortunate, on account of the antique printing. The two-franc paper-backed copy that I am reading now is much better.

I am also trying to admire Bossuet, but find him rather tough.

In the words of the popular song of the American army, "Where do I go from here?" I am awaiting instructions. Meanwhile I send lots of love to all at home.

Your loving son
Gresham

Dec. 28, 1918

My dearest Mother:

After some three or four weeks of waiting, due to my vain efforts to have my mail forwarded in such a way as to reach me on my trip, I received to-day a packet of letters from home containing yours of Nov. 16 and Nov. 23 (numbers 48 and 49) and Arly's and Helen's of Dec. 1. These letters have been read and re-read, and they are going to be read and re-read again. Your letter of Nov. 12, to which you now refer, was received and answered three or four weeks ago.

Despite the courage and cheerfulness of your letters, I can see plainly, my dearest Mother, that there is still anxiety and suffering enough for you and for our family circle. I am thankful for the previous mercies of God and try to derive from them new confidence for the present and for the future. Your letters are just full of interesting news of various kinds, especially with regard to Dr. Patton and his lectures. Arly's fine letter deserves and will receive a separate answer.

And the presents contained in the Red Cross package deserve a separate paragraph at least, though what they really deserve is a good hug for the chief Santa Claus. The package got to Tours after I left, but I received the official American post-office notice about it, and hope to receive it itself before very long. On account of a sudden change of my orders the package like the letters has been following me over a considerable portion of France. I would not miss those "Vive-la-France" socks for anything. If only the military regulations would permit my displaying them on the streets of Paris, I should be proud to do so. But seriously it just warms my heart to think of the love and care of the folks at home that came with that package.

When did I write you my last letter? I wish I knew. Surely I must have written after I reached Le Mans, but to make sure I am going to begin my little narrative with the arrival there on Dec. 19.[2]

I certainly hated to leave that delightful room at Angers, which was only a few steps from the fine old Cathedral, on a nice quiet little street.[3] Angers was the pleasantest part of my trip, though Tours in itself is a more interesting place. The Y.M.C.A. people at Angers had everything arranged for me, and seemed desirous of having me stay just as long as possible.

At Le Mans, things were very different. I was not expected at the Y.M.C.A. office, no notice of my coming having come to them; because of the lack of transportation it was hard to arrange for me to speak; and the town itself was crowded and uncomfortable. The first night I had to stay in a very undesirable hotel, but the next night I got a fairly good room at a better house. The whole character of the town was different from that of Angers, where

2. "Le Mans" is located 120 miles W.S.W. of Paris and 122 miles N.W. of Bourges.
3. The town of "Angers" is about 115 miles S.W. of Paris and 117 miles W.N.W. of Bourges.

there was an atmosphere of quiet and gentility and moderate opulence.

The cathedral at Le Mans, however, is certainly magnificent, the choir with its old stained glass and with its grand proportions being the finest thing that I have seen on my present European tour. I suppose you have seen it. If not, something is left for next time, for it is certainly worth seeing. The only trouble was, I did not have the leisure and the inner repose which will make the cathedral at Tours linger in my memory beyond many superior sights. Somehow there was too much of a moving about at Le Mans.

As far as the work was concerned, Le Mans was rather unsatisfactory except for one splendid opportunity. On Friday night, Dec. 20, I spoke to a little group at the canteen in the town; on Sunday I spoke at two camps in the environs. The evening service represented the opportunity to which I referred. It was at a "forwarding camp," containing men from many different divisions, who as a result of wounds or for other reasons, have been separated from their original units and are being reassigned. The large room was full; there seemed to be no eagerness for mere amusement. I preached on Rom 8:31. After the meeting I talked for a long time to one fellow in particular who has been through agony of soul in his effort to find peace with God.[4] It made me think of Pilgrim's Progress. Well, I never knew before what the preaching of the gospel is. The Y.M.C.A. men who assisted me in the service thought I had missed a great opportunity in not calling for some kind of expression on the part of those who were touched by the gospel message. But when I was talking I did not know that it was anything more than an ordinary meeting, though I did get unusually good attention from the boys. There was certainly very little of mine in the sermon.[5] But the grace of God still finds an answer in the human heart . . . [a sheet of the letter is missing][6] . . . thought he

4. Rom. 8:31 reads, in the King James Version, "What shall we then say to these things? If God be for us, who can be against us?"

5. The "mine" would be his personality, delivery, and argumentation. It is interesting that he did not sense any particular special work of the Holy Spirit as he preached, but those present hearing his presentation of the Lord's message believed it a particularly powerful one. Could it be that when preachers feel "inspired" they are more full of themselves than the Holy Spirit?

6. The missing page is probably two sides of a sheet. This would mean that the pages numbered 6 and 7 in the transcription are actually pages 8 and 9 and the succeeding pages

was doing all right. I am supposed to be interested in theological education & I told him so when I saw him in Paris. But, oh dear, what a wretched job in every way this is for me!

The people who have been a little cordial to me in the Y.M.C.A. are just those from whom I expected it least.

The plan is to let American soldiers study at British and French universities while continuing to be connected officially with the army. The decision of the army has not yet been given us. Fortunately therefore not much is to be done for the present though a rush of work may come in any day. A lot of cards were sent out to the various Y.M.C.A. divisions the other day, to obtain information about the men interested in church service. I am interested in recruiting for church service; but only if I know that it is to be the gospel that is to be preached. My conscience troubles me about continuing to act in this particular movement.

What a joy it would be, on the other hand to continue the proclamation of the gospel and the teaching of the Bible!

If my conscience were quite at rest on the matter of principle, upon which Dr. Stevenson and I differ so widely, I should be happy now. I have drowned my troubles in a perfect debauch of classical French drama. Christmas day was typical. There was a magnificent offering at the Théâtre Français for the matinée and at the Odéon for the evening. On Dec. 24, I had a severe moral struggle. It had been reported that the Paris division wanted speakers for Christmas services. I did not want to miss the incomparable dramatic opportunities of the day. But even after I had my tickets I could not bear to think of a Christmas entirely selfish. Texts like "Woe is me if I preach not the gospel" kept coming back into my mind.[7] So about five o'clock I called at the office of the Paris division. I did so with fear and trembling. Just suppose I should have to miss "Esther"! What was my delight? The engagement that was given me was for

---

would be numbered accordingly. There is a break in thought between "in the human heart" and "thought he was doing all right." The lines on the top of page 7 are lined-out and written in the space between the lined-out lines is written "The missing page relates how he was suddenly recalled to Paris to take an 'office job' in connection with theological education for soldiers. M.G.M." "M.G.M." refers to Mary (Minnie) Gresham Machen, Dr. Machen's mother, so somehow these two sides were lost and she was summarizing her son's content to clarify why the letter did not flow well from page 6 to page 7.

7. "Woe is me if I preach not the gospel," is found in 1 Cor. 9:16.

the morning! Hurrah! Duty was combined with pleasure. So I spent my Christmas as follows:

In the morning I went out to a camp at Clichy and preached a Christmas sermon.[8] There was Christmas music by an informal choir of the men; the _____ was tastefully decorated; attendance was officially expected; the place was well filled, and the crowd seemed to be appreciative. My effort to help the boys, who had less opportunity than I for Christmas joys enabled me to feel a little tiny bit less selfish in the afternoon and evening.

In the afternoon beginning at 1.30 P.M. I had Racine—"Esther" followed by "Les Plaideurs." Madame Romano in "Esther" was simply superb; I do not remember when I have seen a piece of acting that impressed me more. And the choruses were beautifully rendered. I am just beginning my acquaintance with Racine, having read Bajazet, Esther, Les Plaideurs, and Bérénice. Les Plaideurs is a delightful little comedy (dear me, I didn't know a week ago that Racine ever wrote a comedy); and on Christmas it was most deliciously acted. On Christmas evening I continued with "L'Arlésienne" by Daudet at the Odéon. Do you know L'Arlésienne? If not, it is very different from what you might think it would be. It is a very tragic and very poetic little play in prose, not one bit like the books of Daudet about which I believe you have little enthusiasm. The "musique de scène," which represented a large part of the evening's feast, would have delighted you. As always at the Odéon, it was exquisite.

Well, that was sure some Christmas day—sermon in the morning and the entire rest of the day until late at night at the theatre.

Thursday was similar, my predecessor being still on the job at the office. In the afternoon I enjoyed Racine's "Bérénice" and Lesage's "Crispin, rival de son Maître" at the Odéon. The performance, as is usual at the Thursday matinées at the Odéon, was preceded by a conférence. This time the conférence was very sprightly. The conferencier, by the name of Navarre, took the position that in Racine the characters speak naturally

8. "Clichy" is an area of Paris that is just outside the current E05 beltway and N.W. of the center of Paris.

to one another whereas in "＿＿＿＿＿" for example they declaim with their faces to the audience. There may be some truth in it. At any rate the lecture was informing and amusing. Bérénice was glorious and the little comedy of Lesage very amusing indeed.

On Friday night I saw "L'Aiglon," which is being revived this year at the Théâtre Sarah Bernhardt. The chief subject of my disappointment was myself. How very little I could understand, even despite the fact that I had just read the play over with diligent use of Larousse! Here I have been a year in France and cannot understand the language much better than when I arrived last January. But if my disappointment concerned myself, it also concerned (to a lesser extent) the play. The part that is given on the stage is a fragment of the poem merely, and makes the impression of a fragment. For instance the whole of the scene on the battlefield of Wagram—which seemed to me as I read it the most poetic part of the whole work—is omitted.[9] It must be confessed that the rendition of so daring a piece of sentiment on the stage would be difficult. At any rate the progress of the action in the play is lost on the stage. A fine poem, but too long to be acted—that would be about my judgment about "Le Aiglon."

For next week a number of interesting things are in the offing—for example "Le Misanthrope." I wish Brunetière had let me enjoy Molière in peace. He says that "Tartuffe" is directed not at all merely against hypocritical professors of religion, but against such men as Bosseret or the noblest spirits of Post-Royal— indeed against religion itself—and that Molière's philosophy is an exaltation of "nature" as against all attempts at the heroic mastery of nature. I must say there is some truth in the latter contention at least. But meanwhile "Le Bourgeois Gentilhomme" is unquestionably funny—and innocently funny. It is too bad that Molière has to be taken so seriously.

Paris is terribly crowded these days. You can imagine, therefore, my delight when upon my arrival at help post eight

---

9. The Battle of Wagram, in July 1809, ended with Napoleon Bonaparte's forces defeating Austrian troops near Vienna. "Wagram" refers to the town near the battle site.

Monday evening I was put back into the most satisfactory room with bath, which I had on my last visit. My bags and baggage were all waiting for me in the room, in response to my telegram. It just seemed too good to be true. When that elderly landlady announced that she had given me my old room I came near hugging her. You will remember that I am at the Hotel de Palais-Royal, on the Rue de Valois.

I never appreciated before what a glorious privilege it is to be in Europe. It just seems as though every moment ought to be utilized. Sometimes on my previous trip I read nothing but silly stories. But now I regret the wasted years. Sometimes the realization comes over me afresh that this is really Paris and the river that I cross when I go over to the Odéon is really the Seine. It all seems too romantic and too wonderful to be true. I wish I had a dozen eyes and ears and brains in order to be able to take it in.

One thing that Europe has given me is good health. I don't know why it has done so, but the fact is there. For the first time in years I have really had a healthy appetite for days and weeks at a time. Not to-day, it is true, I am suffering a little with headache and indigestion. But the trouble is only momentary, and serves to set off all the more my customary good health.

All this does not mean that I am not crazy to see the folks at home. I sure am. And I do wish my dearest Mother could enjoy something of my good health.

This morning I heard a good sermon at the Temple du Saint-Esprit on the Ave. Roguépine—very different from the Monod variety, which I do not like.[10] The text was from the book of Revelation, the most striking idea being that the New Jerusalem comes from heaven—it is not a product of human civilization, but a gift of the grace of God. The sermon was more than good—in places it was really eloquent. And it was very timely in these days.

I took lunch yesterday with Aleck Thompson, one of the old Benham fellows. He has recently arrived in the service of the Y.M.C.A. He is singing for the American fellows & incidentally

10. The "Temple du Saint-Esprit" is at the corner of the Rue Roguépine and the Rue d'Astorg with its three green sets of double doors facing N. on the Rue Roguépine.

speaking to them. Aleck is just the best kind of fellow to have in the work. I was mighty glad to see him.

Love to all, my dearest, dearest Mother from
Your loving son
Gresham

Dec. 28, 1918

Dear Arly:

Really I do not know whether I should write first to you or to Helen, since if her note enclosed in your letter was only a "postscript" as she was modest enough to call it, it was a very delightful postscript. But I am going to take her at her word, and postpone my answer to her note until the next time. Mother tells me that the Christmas parcel, which is chasing me around France, contains a helmet knitted by Helen.[11] I am not going to wait until the arrival of the parcel to tell Helen that was simply lovely of her. As for the snap-shots of the summer home—they serve their purpose admirably. I seem to get a new idea of your life during the summer, of which, despite quarantine restrictions, I heard so much from Mother.[12] It must be a lovely place. The picture of you and Helen on the porch, with the dog between you is particularly good. Isn't it queer that I can't think of the name of that dog, though I remember that it was some very picturesque name? Well, those pictures are going with Mother's Seal Harbor pictures, to be looked over frequently when I need a little cheering up and a little reminder of home.

Naturally as February approaches you and Helen are constantly in my thoughts and in my prayers. I trust that not many

11. The "helmet" would currently be described as a tight-fitting stocking cap.
12. The "quarantine restrictions" would be those used to prevent the spread of the 1918 flu epidemic.

weeks after this letter arrives all may be over and all may be well. The news that you give of Helen's improvement since her recovery from the "flu" is reassuring.

The other family news—about Mother and about Nena—is not so good as I should like to have it. Things did seem to be going so finely for a time, but that I suppose was too good to last. I am glad that during the summer and during the autumn Mother was at least much better than we had feared she might be. And now I hope constantly for better news.

I am intensely interested in the criminal case that resulted so satisfactorily, and in what Mother tells me now and then about your busy professional life. There could scarcely be any better news than that you are thus winning a little something of the success that you so richly deserve.

The news of Mayor Preston's activities in Mount Vernon Place and on S. Paul and Courtland Streets is very interesting. Mount Vernon Place forms such a large part of our childhood that I can hardly bear to think of it being changed, even if the change is for the better, but I am inclined to rejoice in the other improvements. No doubt they serve to put-up the tax rate, but probably in the end they will pay. I am glad you like the new Confederate monument, and quite agree with you that the old one was not "monumental" enough. The sentiment in it is good, but somehow it always seems to me too delicate to be exposed to view on a public street.

It was mighty good of you to write me on the anniversary of your wedding, but what really ought to have celebrated the day would have been a letter of congratulations on my part. At any rate the congratulation is heartfelt. Nothing could possibly have exceeded my joy on the happy first of December 1917, and the joy has not been diminished by the year that has followed!

The report of Nov. 7 that peace had come was, as I can testify from personal experience, "grossly exaggerated," but the event of Nov. 11 was worth all the celebrating that could possibly be devoted to it.

Perhaps you think I ought to be agitating the matter of my return to America. Naturally I am longing to see you all at home, and also I am fully conscious of the duties of various kinds that await me. But the opportunities for service here are much greater than when the fighting was going on, and also the benefit which I am deriving from my stay is incalculable. Once back in America I shall not be able to return, the window of a move in these days of restriction upon travel must be well considered. I think I ought to be guided by circumstances. In a recent letter to Mother I set forth more at length the reasons for my present attitude, which may of course be modified at any time.

I have written Mother an immeasurably long letter to-day, which she will no doubt let you read in case you are interested. It seems strange that I should enjoy a stay in Europe so much more now even than in time of peace. One reason is, I think, that then there was an embarrassment of riches. One could go anywhere at will in the immense store-house of Europe, and the tendency was to hurry too much. Now when movements are regulated by military order, there is occasionally enough leisure at any one place (as at Tours) to prevent restlessness.

I am enclosing the English résumé of L. Aiglon enclosed in the theatre program. Let Uncle see it if it is convenient and give it to Mother to put into the archives of my letters. I really think it is something of a gem.

This afternoon I spent a little while in and around Notre Dame. It is finer than I thought it was. They are engaged in taking away the sand-bags from the portals, but the stained glass has not been replaced. The interior is practically invisible in winter; the struggling winter sun is quite insufficient to pierce the gloom.

One reason why I have met so few Baltimore people is that I spent most of my time with an Ohio division—the 37th. A Y.M.C.A. man whom I met a few days ago says that about thirty years ago he knew a Machen at the Baltimore City College. Did you ever hear of this Machen? For a few days when I first got into the American work I was with the 42nd division, where, it took me back to old times to hear about the Floyd Rifles and the Macon Volunteers. Unfortunately I did not meet the Macon fellows myself.[13] I was with

13. The Floyd Rifles and Macon Volunteers were units of the 2nd Georgia Infantry Battalion in the Civil War.

the 77th division—New York City national army[14]—for about a month. Then the 37th.

I understand the lid is off about mentioning places. If it really is I shall write a geographical letter telling about my whereabouts during the course of the year, though I had rather wanted to have the fun of tracing my travels on the map after I get home.

Remember me to Mr. Williams, and of course give my very, very best love to Helen.

Your affectionate brother,
J. Gresham Machen

Jan. 5, 1918[15]

My dearest Mother:

Your letter of Dec. 7 was sweet and lovely, and the news that it contained was fairly good, but I was grieved at the date and number of the letter (No. 51) for it indicated that one letter (No. 50) is still astray. The next time I take a trip away from Paris, unless I am to stay at some one place, I shall simply have my mail left here. As it is, although I wrote a packet of directions to the different places where I had been, I have not yet received either all of my letters or the Christmas package which I am so anxious to see. Since your letter No. 50 was probably the one where you mentioned receiving one of the most newsy letters of mine I feel particularly sorry to have lost it—even temporarily. Of course I still hope to get it in the end—if I did not my grief would be nothing short of intense.

But to return to the good news in your letter. I am delighted to hear that Helen is feeling better, and the thought of her going

14. Here, Machen may have been referring to the New York City National Guard. As much as 40 percent of the US military presence in France in the First World War was made up of National Guard units.
15. The transition to the next year is sometimes a problem even for the brightest of minds. The year should be 1919.

off cheerily to the movies with Tom certainly makes me wish that I could be one of the party. As for Nena, let us hope that Horton Manor will prove to be a great success.

Nothing could possibly delight me much more than the news of Arly's fine new case, and the professional success which seems to be gradually tending to approach what he deserves.

The news of Kirby Smith's death is very sad. He represented a type of scholarship which is none too common, and the personal loss to you added to your sympathy for Mrs. Kirby makes me grieve the more.[16]

I know how large a part of my life is made up of what the unsympathetic are induced to call "little" things. Hence I can sympathize with you very seriously over the loss of your Wedgwood medallion. Sometimes "vexations" are as hard to bear as sorrows.

[At this point, a section of the letter is missing. It may have been cut out by Mrs. Machen according to Dr. Machen's request in a later letter.]

At first I thought I was to be busy preaching in the "Paris division," but Mr. Edworthy of the religious work department seemed to feel that it would be more dignified for me to wait until he had written a letter about me to the Paris division. If such a letter has been written, nothing has come of it. My zeal has thus had a damper put on it in every direction.

[This is the reverse side of the portion that was cut from the letter.]

During the last few days there has been rather a lean and hungry time at the Théâtre Frànçais and at the Odéon, but the middle of the week was glorious. On Tuesday afternoon I had "Horace" and "L'Avare." It was a great afternoon. The comparison of "Horace" with the "Ariane" of Thomas Corneille, which I saw at the Odéon Monday night, made me appreciate the more the splendor of real genius.

"Tigres, allez combattre, et nous, allons mourir"—you just ought to have heard Mme. Silvain in that magnificent conclusion

16. Instead of "Mrs. Kirby," Machen should have written "Mrs. Smith."

of Scene vii in the second act.[17] In "L'Avare" the most striking thing was the acting of M. Féraudy in the scene where Harpagon thinks he has lost his money—a scene where what in itself would be merely comical becomes half tragic because of the degradation of human nature that appears. The actor won a great triumph in this scene; never before had I witnessed in the Théâtre Frànçais such a spontaneous burst of applause.

But Wednesday, New Year's day, was the greatest day of all. In the afternoon we had "le Misanthrope" of Moliere and "Il ne faut jurer de rien" of de Musset. The latter is not so exquisitely poetic as "Carmosine" for example, but is just a delightful and amusing little comedy.

In the case of "le Misanthrope" I confess that in order to attain the full comprehension of the play I needed the magnificent rendition of it on the stage. But now it has become a possession for life. It is different from such plays as "le Bourgeoise Gentilhomme," "Tartuffe," and "l'Avare" where a character is held up for pure ridicule or execration.[18] Here you smile at the dear old "misanthrope," but before the play is over you love him too. The words of Éliante in the fourth act sum up an impression already made upon the spectator by the masterly portrayal of the character:

Dans ses façons d'agir, il est fort singulier,
Mais j'en fais, je l'avoue, un cas particulier;
Et la sincérité dont son âme se pique
A quelque chose, eu soi, de noble, et d'héroïque;
C'est une vertu rare, au siècle d'aujord'hui,
Et je la voudrais voir, partout, comme chez lui.[19]

The affections of the spectator for the misanthrope become firmly fixed in the first act, where the "vieille chanson,"[20] in its

17. The French means, "Tigers, go fight, and we will die," from "Horace."
18. These three plays are by Molière.
19. The English is: "His actions are peculiar and extreme, but, I admit, I hold him in esteem, and the sincerity that is his pride has a heroic and a noble side. It's an uncommon virtue in this day which I wish others had in the same way" (Donald M. Frame, trans. and ed., *The Misanthrope and Other Plays, Molière*, Signet Classics [New York: New American Library, Penguin Group, 1968, 2005], 65). These translations taken from Frame's edition were written to rhyme in English, so there has been some artistic license used.
20. The French, "vieille chanson," means "old song."

contrast with the artificiality of bad poetry is a masterpiece of pathos.

> Si le Roi m'avait donné
>   Paris, sa grand'ville,
> Et qu'il me fallût quitter,
>   L'amour de ma mie,
> Je dirais au Roi Henri:
>   "Reprenez votre Paris;
> J'aime mieux ma mie, au gué!
>   J'aime mieux ma mie."[21]

I can still see M. Leitner as he recited these words and I believe the picture will remain during the rest of my life.

After the play was over I learned by heart some of the most striking things including these:

> Sur quelque préférence une estime se fonde
> Et c'est n'estimer rien qu'estimer tout le monde.[22]

and

> Montrer que c'est à tort que sages on nous nomme
> Et que dans tout les cours il est toujours de l'homme.[23]

In short I think you will agree with me that the eleven francs which I spent for my seat that afternoon was well spent. It not only gave me a new possession in the play itself, but it opened up to me an entire new realm, in which I can roam at will ever after.

On New Year's night I saw "L'Ami Fritz," also at the Théâtre Français. It is one of the prettiest little things I ever saw. I came

21. The English is: "If the king had given me great Paris for my own, and had said the price must be to leave my love alone, I would tell the king Henry: Then take back your great Paris, I prefer my love, hey ho, I prefer my love" (Frame, 36).
22. The English is: "Esteem, if it be real, means preference, and when bestowed on all it makes no sense" (Frame, 25).
23. The English is: "Proving that those who call us wise are wrong, and that mere human nature is too strong" (Frame, 82).

near disgracing the American Expeditionary Force by blubbering
too visibly at the pathetic places. Certainly Mme. Le Conte is a very
charming "ingénue." The play is Alsacian, but fortunately does not
introduce the subjects of the war or the German region. These
subjects were reserved for the poems which were recited after the
main attraction of the evening was over.

Yesterday I got the necessary letter from the American
consulate, and obtained a reader's ticket at the Bibliothèque
Nationale, in order to do a little reading in preparation for my
Sprunt lectures.[24] Unfortunately any lectures that I prepare now
will be out of date, because of the two and a half years that have
lapsed since we were cut off from the chief source of theological
supply. When we do get hold of the accumulation, it will come
in such bewildering quantity and will be so much in demand in
our Seminary library that digestion of it will be difficult. I envy
the "army of occupation." Think what a delight a few hours in the
bookstore of Berne, for example, would represent.[25]

To-morrow, if possible, I want to hear a lecture or two at the
Protestant faculty here. M. Goguel, the New Testament man, is, I
regret to say, a liberal.

This morning I attended the morning service at the Temple
de Pentemont, Rue de Grenelle.[26] In general I am impressed with
the thoughtful character of the preaching in the French protestant
churches, and with the combined dignity and force of the manner
of expression.

This afternoon I attended a conference at the "Eglise des
Batignolles," where a number of Protestant pastors gave some
account of their experiences during the four years of German

24. The "Bibliotheque Nationale" is the national library of France in Paris and it is currently located about six-tenths of a mile N. of the Seine at 58 Rue de Richelieu.

25. Machen may be referring to an inability to ship European theological journals and books to the United States during the war. There were so many foreign personnel in Europe during the war that their mail took priority over some of the mailings by the nationals. His envy for the "army of occupation" is that they will remain in the war zone and have access to the literature of the area.

26. The French Reformed Church (Église Réformée de France) congregation that used the property recently merged with another ERF congregation in Paris and no longer uses the building. At the time of the writing of this footnote, the façade of the church on Rue de Grenelle was undergoing restoration by the Paris City Council.

occupation.[27] I am sorry to say that my knowledge of French is so slight, and some of the speakers spoke in such a low tone of voice, that I missed a good deal of what was said; what I did hear was intensely interesting. The last speaker spoke the first Christian word, almost, that I can remember having heard since the armistice. "If you write to your friends in the army of occupation," he said in effect, "tell them first of all how profoundly grateful we are to them for having saved the cause of justice and liberty; but remind them also that God desireth not the death of a sinner but rather that he may turn from his worldliness and live," and also that while the guilty should be brought to justice there are also many innocent ones along the Rhine. In the desert of the newspapers, where with a deadly monotony and with an almost unbelievable poverty of thought the one plea for retribution goes on day after day and week after week, these simple words, from a man who has been through some of the worst of things, were wonderfully refreshing.

So far we have not had one single touch of winter. There has been practically no freezing weather so far as I can remember (except, I believe, a slight frost in November); and the temperature does not seem to be very much lower than it often is in summer. Just rain, rain, and, and then more rain—that is the European idea of winter.

And so it goes. I do hope that I shall receive that strayed letter. I wrote to Arly.

Love and more love.
Your affectionate son
Gresham

27. The Chapelle Descente du Saint-Esprit et Église Réformée is an attractive building located on the Boulevard de Batignolles. Above the entrance door is written, "Eglise Reformee de France." Since this is an ERF congregation, it is probably the same church that Machen described as the "Église des Batignolles."

13

A REVIEW OF PAST LOCATIONS AND MORE "Y" WORK

January 5 to February 7, 1919

With the relaxing of some aspects of censorship, Dr. Machen will use the new freedom to review his movements from his first post in St. Mard up to the current situation in the first letter below. He will be involved in a disagreement with J. Ross Stevenson, but will also realize he did not have the full picture. Use of the French theater will continue, but due to his study for the Sprunt Lectures, he will attend public lectures by some French scholars. His "Y" work will continue to revolve around Paris as he travels to different locations for services and lectures.

[In the following letter, Machen reviews his movements from his arrival at the front in St. Mard until the loosening of censorship after the war ended.]

Jan. 5, 1919

My dearest Mother:

You are mistaken in thinking that there is no more censorship. Letters are censored as before, at least in principle. But I understand that the restrictions about naming places have been relaxed. I am therefore going to supplement the ordinary letter that I wrote you to-day (in which I answered yours of Dec. 7) by satisfying your curiosity about the ancient history of my travels before the armistice.

The first town near the front that I saw was Soissons, where I reported to the original headquarters of the Foyers du Soldat, and incidentally saw the ruined cathedral. Thence I went to my first post, St. Mard, a little village about twelve miles east of Soissons and five miles north of Braisne. St. Mard is south of the Aisne. The French at that time were holding the heights along which runs the Chemin des Dames of sinister memory, the Germans being on the other side of the Ailette. I never saw the Chemin des Dames, but in that "quarry" which I described I suppose I was almost underneath it.

My next post, where I remained two months, was at Missy-sur-Aisne, about half-way between St. Mard and Soissons, on the north side of the Aisne but further from the front than St. Mard. From Missy I used to go on my bicycle frequently to Braisne, where the regional headquarters was moved after some three weeks of bombardment of Soissons. I also went once or twice to Soissons. On the afternoon just before the German advance began I took a walk with Montí up to the heights near the Fort De Condé, which is just above Missy. From those same heights, according to the papers, the Kaiser and von Hindenburg viewed the battlefield only a few days later. On the morning of my hurried departure I crossed the Aisne to Ciry Salsogne, where I joined my colleague of the Foyer du Soldat. After a night in a carrière just above Ciry-Salsogne we walked to the hamlet of Serches, and thence proceeded with the help of army waggons to Chacrise where we caught the last train. After spending a considerable part of a day between trains at Oulchy-le-Chateau, I arrived the same night at Meaux, where I reported to the regional director. Thence after a trip into Paris & back I went on a bicycle to Lizy-sur-Ourcq and May-en-Multrén. But that was only for a day. I returned to Paris, and was sent by Bobby Freeman for a Sunday at Valdahon, not far from the Swiss border. On the way, I had an interesting day at Besancon.[1] Then after having returned to Paris I was sent to Baccarat in French Lorraine.

1. This is the first time Machen has mentioned this village; it was not noted in his earlier marginal notes. The village of "Besancon" is located 210 miles S.E. of Paris and 115 miles N.N.E. of Lyon.

My first post (of any permanency) was "mud-camp" or "Camp de la Grande Voévre," near Brouville. Then I went to Pexonne, where I stayed about two months. From Pexonne I made one visit to the deserted Badonvillers, which was very near the front. Baccarat was our Y.M.C.A. divisional headquarters.

From Baccarat we went by train to Revigny, spending a night at Lunéville on the way, but merely passing through Nancy. At Revigny we had the job of getting some freight cars, and then proceeded north to Récicourt in the Argonne sector, some distance east of the forest of Argonne. Establishing our Y.M.C.A. divisional headquarters at Récicourt, a number of us went north (through the forest of Hesse) to the hideous mud and ruins of Avocourt, where I worked for several days in a dressing-station. On one day a party of us went to Montfaucon, where the evening's fire caused us to depart considerably quicker than we had come.[2] At Montfaucon, we were on epic ground. The little town, perched on top of a hill, and surrounded by open country, was a famous German position during the Verdun fighting, and was thought to be impregnable. It had been captured a day or so before we were there—exactly how I was never able to discover (that is I never knew exactly what part the French tanks had in the capture and what part our infantry had). When we were there the fighting was going on a mile or so to the north of the town.

From Récicourt we walked to Auzéville and there took the train for Bar-le-Duc, where we spent the night. From Bar-le-Duc we went to Commercy, and spent several restful days. From Commercy, spending a night at Toul, we went by train to Bernécourt and then by truck to Bouillonville, where we established Y.M.C.A. head-quarters. Four of us established ourselves at Thiaucourt, which is some twenty miles southwest of Metz. This region had been captured in the American drive when the St. Mihiel salient was wiped out.[3] The nearest I got to the existing front was a point near Jaulny.[4]

2. That is "fire" in the sense of shelling by the Germans and not a conflagration.
3. The "St. Mihiel salient" was the first major attack planned and carried out on the western front by the Allied Expeditionary Force. Though the significance of the effort had waned due to the long preparation time for Gen. Pershing's men, the attack was carried out in September when forces assaulted the southern face of the salient on September 12. The attack was successful and led to the liberation of Thiaucourt and liberation of several other locations ("St. Mihiel, Battle of," S. Pope and Elizabeth-Anne Wheal, *Dictionary of the First World War* [Barnesley: Pen & Sword Books, 2003]).
4. "Jaulny" is located 170 miles E. of Paris and 24 miles N.N.W. of Nancy.

When we moved from Bouillonville, I was lucky enough to catch an army truck going to Toul, where we spent several days awaiting orders. Then we were ordered to Paris.

Then I went, changing cars at Boulogne-sur-Mer and spending a night at Calais, to Dunkerque, where I spent about two nights. While at Dunkerque I took occasion to walk out to Malo-les-Bains, which I was unable to describe in my contemporary letter, since the mention of the sea would have revealed my whereabouts.[5] The place was very dismal, with its ruined casino, and the sand that in places had silted up almost to the second story of some of the fine villas. The beach was fortified by barbed wire, but beyond the barbed wire there was a magnificent broad expanse of hard beaten sand—I suppose about a quarter of a mile wide. It reminded a person a little of Cape May—except that the ocean swell was missing.[6] The North Sea is a poor imitation of the real thing. A small warship or two was riding outside the artificial harbor, and an air-plane was doing stunts for practice. (At Boulogne, by the way, I saw dirigibles flying so low over the town that when they came to an unusually high building they had to turn up a little in order to avoid hitting it. These were the only dirigibles that I have seen. I suppose they were intended to spot submarines. Dirigibles were unknown along the inland front.)[7]

From Dunkerque we went by train to Roulers, passing the former no man's land at Ypres.[8] Unfortunately it was getting dark at Ypres. In the abomination of desolation just beyond Ypres the train stopped for a considerable time. Apparently some German planes that were dropping bombs not very far away did not catch sight of us despite the distressing glow of our engine. After about two nights at Roulers—a considerable, but quite interesting town—I went to Lechtervelde, some miles north, where

5. "Malo-les-Bains" is on the beach on the N.E. side of Dunkerque.

6. "Cape May" refers to the resort town in New Jersey located at the S.E. tip of the state. This ocean-side village developed in the late Victorian period.

7. Machen saw the "saucisse" during the war, which were fixed position observation balloons. A dirigible is a self-propelled, directionally controllable lighter-than-air vehicle.

8. Dunkerque is on the coast of France and close to the Belgian border. It is about 150 miles due N. of Paris and 93 miles W.N.W. of Brussels, Belgium. Roulers is located in Belgium about 145 miles N.N.E. of Paris and about 55 miles W.N.W. of Brussels. Ypres is about 113 miles N.N.E. of Paris and 64 miles W. of Brussels.

I spent one night.[9] Then I secured French army trucks for our
canteen supplies and we pushed on east to Thielt where Y.M.C.A.
headquarters was established.[10] From Thielt, with out spending
a night there, we went to Dentergem.[11] From there the next day
we caught an ambulance to an advanced dressing-station near
Eyne on the Scheldt (Escaut).[12] The church spire of Oudenaarde
(French Ardenarde) could be seen almost a mile and a half away.
From that dressing-station I went the next day to a still more
advanced station in the town of Eyne (perhaps about a mile
from the other station). Parallel to the street of the village (upon
which was situated the convent occupied by the dressing-station)
and only perhaps about a hundred yards from it our infantry
were dug-in in a low railroad embankment. Beyond the railroad
was a field and then the river. Each man had his own little hole
scooped out—there was no continuous trench.[13] Some few had
taken caution of so digging themselves into the bank that there
was a little roof of earth above them. Some were over beyond the
embankment in a little crater or shell hole of some kind (which I
did not see). The man who helped me serve chocolate went over to
those men. I, who had taken my kettle in the other direction, did
not do anything so exciting.

It may be questioned whether this was the "front line," as a
medical captain called it or as one fellow called it only a "line of
resistance." The truth seems to be that our boys were across the
river to the left and to the right—but not immediately in front. The
Germans held the heights all along the other side of the river. This
was the situation after the Germans had been driven back from the
Lys to the Escaut, a day or so before I arrived in the region.[14]

9. Lechtervelde, Belgium, is located about 150 miles N.N.E. of Paris and 65 miles W.N.W.
of Brussels.

10. Thielt is in Belgium and is 150 miles N.N.E. of Paris and 45 miles W.N.W. of Brussels.

11. Dentergem is 151 miles N.N.E. of Paris and 44 miles W.N.W. of Brussels. It is about
13 miles E. of Roeselare.

12. Eyne appears currently to be a suburb of Oudenaarde. Eyne is located about 148
miles N.N.E. of Paris and 32 miles W. of Brussels. The river Scheldt, is know as l'Escaut
in French.

13. What Machen describes here is a "fox hole," which would become every soldier's best
friend and labor-intensive nemesis in World War II. In World War I, the fox hole was found
to be inadequate and was replaced by enough miles of trenches to circumnavigate the world.

14. The Lys is also know as the Leie.

From Eyne I marched with the battalion back to Olsene, a miserably ruined town on the Lys, where we spent the night. Thence I made my way back to Thielt. After several days there we went to east Deyuze on the Lys, where I spent one night.[15] Thence we proceeded to Synghem, several miles north of Eyne, and further from the Escaut than Eyne is. I spent the last night before the armistice in a little house perhaps three quarters of a mile west of Synghem.[16] The next morning, in the piping times of peace, I walked out across the Escaut.

Then I went back to Thielt and after a day or so secured my movement-order to Paris. Luckily securing a ride in an auto I went in fine style to Dunkerque—passing the ancient no-man's land at Dixmude.[17] Thence train to Calais, and thence sleeping car to Paris.

From there on I have already been able to mention names.

I had rather looked forward to pointing out these travels on the map after I got home, but no wonder you feel a little curious already.

To sum up, I saw something of five sectors of the front—Aisne, Lorraine, Argonne, Woëvre & Belgium.

Your loving son,
Gresham

12 janvier, 1919

My dearest Mother:

Your letter of Nov. 30 was received considerably later than that of Dec. 8, and I am not quite sure whether I have answered it. At

15. Deynze is located 150 miles N.N.E. of Paris and 37 miles W.N.W. of Brussels.

16. Synghem is in Belgium and is 147 miles N.N.E. of Paris and 30 miles W. of Brussels.

17. Dixmude is about 147 miles N.N.E. of Paris and 66 miles W.N.W. of Brussels, Belgium. In the letter's margin, Machen wrote, ""it was an ambulance," with reference to his comment that, "Luckily securing a ride in an auto."

any rate it deserves a far better answer than I can possibly give it. I am glad you received my letter of Nov. 7, for that along with the next one, which was written shortly after the armistice, contained an account of things which in themselves, aside from my feeble account of them, were undoubtedly interesting.

Your account of Arly's defense of the two young Hagerstown fellows is highly interesting and gratifying. I wish I could congratulate the successful attorney in person. And in particular I wish I could have been present at the trial, as I was during the week of that N.C.R.R. case, where Arly seemed to my mind to be handling the thing in a magnificent way.[18] It must be an intense satisfaction to be able to prevent injustice, as has been done in this present case.

You have already reviewed (before the arrival of the present letter), I hope, my little note apologizing for my criticism of Dr. Stevenson in two or three previous letters.[19] Really, my dearest Mother, I should be exceedingly grateful if you would find those letters and cut out the offending parts, or at least put right with them a reference to my note of apology. I have been exceedingly unjust, and Dr. Stevenson's present kindness makes me feel exceedingly mean. The reason for my being called up to Paris was not Dr. Stevenson at all, who was far away, but Dr. King, who had heard that my addresses were above the heads of the men and so (as well as perhaps for other reasons) was led to recall me to the office job. Dr. Stevenson has not attributed decisive weight to the criticism and says he will arrange to send me out again. I was pretty much discouraged day before yesterday, when I first heard of the criticism, and felt just like bending every possible effort to get back home and work on my Sprunt lectures. But the trouble is that my contract reads for the duration of the war, and besides I hate to feel that I have gone home just because I am no good here. So on the whole I am glad to have another chance for service in the midst of what means to me absolutely unparalleled opportunities.

18. Possibly, N.C.R.R. stands for Northern County Railroad, a former railroad of Maryland.

19. The only letter that appears to have been edited per Machen's request is the one of 1/5/1918 to MGM. If there were one or two others, they are no longer available. If the other letters were brief and contained no other information of significance, then maybe Mrs. Machen threw them out.

Dr. Stevenson arrived on Wednesday. The matter of theological education for American students is still largely in abeyance. I get something more of Dr. Stevenson's point of view about it. But still I do not want the job. It looks now as though someone else could be secured. At any rate, Dr. Stevenson is my friend after all.

Meanwhile, what a magnificent time I have had at Paris! At the theatre, "Le Cid" and "Le Marriage de Figaro" were the notable wants. The acting of the former at the Odéon, I must say, seemed to me to lack "verve," and the play itself seems to me to be far inferior to other master pieces of Corneille such as "Horace." The performance of "Le Marriage de Figaro" was typical of the kind of education that I have been receiving during the last few weeks. Before, Beaumarchais was a name to me and absolutely nothing more. But after reading over the play and the author's introduction to it and a brief account of the life of the author, after listening to the excellent preliminary lecture at the Odéon and then witnessing the play itself, a whole chapter of French literature and French history was opened to me.

One day I went to the French Protestant faculty, and attended two classes of Goguel, the New Testament professor. He is very wrong in his views, I regret to say. Among the students were two fellows just from Strassburg, where they had been students at the university before the German professors were deported. Albert Schweitzer, I understand, one of the most brilliant of all New Testament scholars, is at present at Strassburg, having returned from Africa, where to the surprise of everybody he went as a missionary. He is a kind of universal genius—physician, musician (of a very high order), missionary and New Testament scholar of an exceedingly radical type. He is an Alsacian.

What wouldn't I give for a few hours pillage in the theological bookstores of Strassburg? Absolutely no German theological works since the war are obtainable here, & we received in America only the books up to the early part of 1918. My Sprunt lectures will be out of date if I write them before I can get access to the current literature.

Yesterday morning I attended a lecture by the famous Loisy at the Collège de France. He is now no longer the Abbé Loisy, his connection with the Catholic Church having been terminated. And no wonder it has been terminated! It was rather interesting to see a man who has been so much in the public eye, and a man whose books are exceedingly important even though they are not true. He is a little wea___ old bit of a man, with a funny little stuttering voice. To get his permission to attend the lecture (which by the way proved to be unnecessary, the lectures at the Collège de France being public) I went up to his apartment on the Rue des Ecoles, where I was pleasantly received. The subject of the course was just what is most interesting to me at the present time, L'Apôtre Paul et la christianisme judaïsant.[20] I have been studying Loisy's recent book on Galatians, which I had not seen in America. Also, I attended a lecture at the Sorbonne (on a less interesting subject) just to see what it was like. I have a ticket to the Bibliotheque Nationale but have unfortunately had little time to make use of it, the library being open only during the few hours of daylight. I wish I could get to work on my Sprunt lectures.

And I wish I could see you, my dearest Mother. Perhaps I might make a move to get home, but I hate to do so till the troops return in large numbers.

Montí is in a hospital at Newilly-sur-Marne, some ten miles from Paris.[21] He is apparently suffering from nervous exhaustion, caused I suppose ultimately by the same effects of shell-fire that caused his deafness. This afternoon I made the long journey in the electric car out to Neuilly, but found that the patient was out, having been given leave for the day. Apparently therefore he is not very ill just now, but his trouble is of some months' standing and therefore gives room for uneasiness. It will be too bad if so bright a fellow is going to be permanently disabled. I had received several letters from him, which while entirely rational showed in handwriting as well as contents some effects of his nervous weakness. The hospital officials were even more unsatisfactory than the hospital officials usually are. When I tried to get access

20. *The apostle Paul and judaizing Christianity.*
21. About 16 miles due E. of Paris center.

to somebody who really knew something about the patient, so unprecedented a request was treated with scanty attention.

This morning I attended church at the Oratoire, being too late to go elsewhere. The preacher, I think, was Monod.[22] At any rate it was similar to the sermon by Monod that I heard some time ago. The text was from the Book of Revelation, but was in marked contrast to the sermon based on that book which I heard two weeks ago at the Temple du Saint Esprit. That other sermon was Christian. The crowd, I am sorry to say, was at the Oratoire.

How dreadfully poor the French Reformed liturgy is! Unlike the liturgy of the English Episcopal Church it seems studiously to avoid the great verities of the faith, notably the atoning death of our Saviour.

I hope you received my geographical letter, which I wrote you some week or so ago.

Give my very best love to all. You don't know how completely my heart is with you just now.

Your loving son,
Gresham

P.S. I have written several more letters to military post-offices about the Christmas parcel, but with out result yet. G. M.

Jan. 17, 1919

My dearest Mother:

With two splendid letters from home—number 52, of Dec. 17, which arrived some days ago, and number 54, of Dec. 29, which arrived to-day—I feel as rich as John D. Rockefeller.[23] Number 55

22. In an earlier letter to his mother, Feb. 5, 1918, Machen mentioned "M. Alfred Monod."
23. Dr. Machen had some acquaintance with John D. Rockefeller. On a few occasions, he preached at the Congregational Church in Seal Harbor, Maine, when John D. Rockefeller requested him to fill the pulpit.

is something to look forward to, and also, I hope, the Christmas package, though my fears are increasing with regard to that. It arrived at the post-office at Tours after my departure, and all efforts at getting hold of it have been so far unavailing. You can be sure that the efforts have not been spared.

Your anxiety before the arrival of my letter of Nov. 14 makes me penitent. Why in the world did I not send you a telegram? I thought of doing so. But at least I had not supposed that you would be anxious after the arrival of the letter of Nov. 7, for that was written when I was at the rear and not expecting to go to the front again.

I am delighted that you and the members of our circle have liked the letters that I wrote. It would have given me satisfaction if, as Arly and others wanted, extracts from the letters could have been published, but the instructions that we received some time ago were so explicit that I was obliged to write on the subject as I did. I suppose the regulations would not be so strict now, and I rather think it was a Y.M.C.A. regulation only that forbade the publishing of censored letters. At any rate no doubt it was well enough to be on the safe side. I feel deeply grateful for having the letters typewritten and sent to Bobby and Army.

Good for Helen! I am glad she made the family hang up stockings. She is entirely right. The custom ought not to be abandoned. Everybody should be a child on Christmas day.

Your letters are so full of interesting news that I cannot begin to comment on them adequately. I have read them over and over and over so many times that I have had to stop counting. Mr. Hodges says that the flu has broken out again in Millville, N.J. This news is distressing. I trust that the terrible times are not to be renewed. As for all that you say about Nena and Helen and Edgeworth and Tom and Arly, my heart is full of it. I feel thankful with you that the ones who are nearest to us have been spared by the flu, and that the family circle at Christmas was unbroken. Your letters seem to bring home very near to me.

As for the babies, I do hate to be missing so much of their company just at such a delightful stage. But since my time is limited to-day I must really break away from home, and give you a little bit of Paris news. As I have already written you, Dr. Stevenson was not at all responsible for calling me on to Paris and has acted as my friend. I was very much discouraged at hearing that some Y.M.C.A. men had reported to the authorities here that my talks were "too long and too deep," but conversation with Mr. Edworthy, whom I have mentioned several times as having arranged my trip, has served somewhat to mitigate my chagrin. He says that the criticism did not appear in any of the written reports, that some Y.M.C.A. men are not as good judges as they think they are, and that therefore he had not wanted to mention the matter to me at all. When I proposed breaking off and going home, he said that he was very much opposed to it, and that he wanted to send me out again to speak in the camps. So, insomuch as Dr. Stevenson has acquiesced very graciously and there does not seem to be much doing just now anyway about the religious education matter I am to leave to-morrow for the headquarters of the third Y.M.C.A. "region" at Vìerzon. After working for a few days in that region (the same region where I was before) I am to report to Paris and then go at once to engage in a distinctly religious "campaign" (if I may use an unsatisfactory and rather irreverent word) with a certain division that has distinctly asked for such service. This latter particularly ought to be quite an extraordinary opportunity.

Dr. Stevenson returned to Germany. Of course Germany is the post of honor, where everybody wants to be, but I have not felt like pulling wires to get there. As Bobby said in a recent letter it would be fun but "sad fun." Of course I would give several thousand francs for a chance at the bookstores, but even if I were allowed to find the recent theological works, I suppose I might not be allowed to take them away.

In the above I do not mean for one minute to hint that Dr. Stevenson had "pulled wires." That interpretation entered my head when the words came into my mind. Dr. Stevenson & Maitland Alexander & Reid Dickson are exactly where they ought to be. I only wish other portions of the American E. F. were as well served.[24]

24. "E. F." is the Expeditionary Force.

Dr. Stevenson turns out to agree with me in more ways than I thought.

What an idiot I was not to make better use of my educational opportunities here! During the past week I have dropped in at lectures at the Sorbonne and related institutions, and made acquaintances among the students, which if followed up earlier would have taught me some French and gotten me into the inside track. I have tried to work at the Bibliothèque Nationalé, the Bibliothèque Sainte-Genevìeve, and the library of the university, but have found them all rather unsatisfactory for my purposes.[25] If I only had more time, and if I did not want to do so many things at once!

In addition to two lectures by Loisy on Paul (at the Collège de France) I have attended two lectures by a certain Guignebert at the Sorbonne on Second Corinthians and on the teaching of Jesus. These last were both rather shallow and rather flippant. At one of them I made acquaintance with a long-haired but very kindly fellow, I think of Polish extraction, who took me in to hear Monsenior Dujardin, who it seems is a littérature of some distinction.[26] The lecture, delivered to about six people in École Pratique des Hautes Études[27] (all these numerous Écoles seem to be parts of what might be called in a general way the university) was on the subject of the origin of the Eucharist. Dujardin seems to have some wild idea about a pre-Christian "Jesus cult," after the manner of Drews or W. B. Smith. In addition to such lectures on the subject of religion, I have heard various lectures on Alsace & Lorraine, on de Musset, on German socialism, etc.

In general I cannot say that I am impressed. Guignebert for example seems to be a kind of eighteenth-century free-thinker, very different in spirit from twentieth century liberalism. There is a kind of jumpiness about the whole intellectual life of the university (as I have been able to observe it in two or three hours) which is almost weird. The contrast with the thoroughness of certain university

25. The Bibliothèque Sainte-Geneviève is four or five blocks E. of the Jardin du Luxembourg at 10 Place Panthéon. The "library of the university" would be that of the Sorbonne.
26. A "littérateur" is a writer.
27. Practical School of Higher Studies.

training that I enjoyed in my youth is nothing short of abysmal. While priding themselves on their cool intellectualism, the clarity of their intellectual powers, the French I must say seem to me to be sadly lacking in the very instincts of scholarship. Needless to say, this judgment is not final. I have certainly little opportunity of speaking on the subject with any authority.

At any rate the opportunities that I have enjoyed are broadening.

I have heard some more classical drama—for example the "Dépit Amoureux" and the "Amphytrion" of Moliere, and "Le Menteur" of Corneille. Two drawbacks emerge. In the first place the best classical plays are given on Sunday; it is tantalizing to read the Sunday bills. In the second place the Thursday classical series at the Théâtre Français turns over practically the whole house to the holders of season tickets. I don't quite understand that "abonnement" business. It seems to be a kind of closed corporation. But I did get a seat last Thursday through an outside agency. It was an exceedingly bad seat, but I did not want to miss "Le Menteur." Alas for the freedom & democracy of war times! That was the only benefit that I have yet observed in the war—you could always get a seat at the Théâtre Français.

The high-water marks for me were "Le Misanthrope"—"Le Bourgeois Gentilhomme"—with "Horace" & "Bérénice," etc., coming in only a little behind.

Alas, I have to give up my splendid room, where a mass of paper-bound & Hachette edition classics are a monument to a pleasant story![28]

My teeth are bad—very sensitive to heat—largely useless for chewing. But the dentists whom I have visited seem to think that I am mistaken in supposing that there is any trouble. Dentistry over here consists in treating a tooth when the jaw begins to swell and the ache becomes absolutely unbearable. As to what the French people think about Wilson. I cannot answer your question because I know nothing. Certainly I have wasted my opportunities. I ought to have been more sensible.

28. The Librairie Hachette or Classiques Hachette is an inexpensive series of French literary works.

The papers say only what it is politically pious to say. So not much is to be learned from them.

Montí, I am afraid, is in rather a blue way. I have had two rather discouraged notes from him.

You don't know how pleased I was at the special message that Betty sent me just as you were dispatching your letter. Give her my love in return.

As for the way I feel toward you all, and as for my eagerness for news from home, words cannot express what is in my heart.

Your loving son
Gresham

January 22, 1919

My dearest Mother:

On my way to the train on Saturday morning at Paris I stopped at 12 Rue d. Aguesseau to get my mail, and was gloriously rewarded by your letter no. 53, of Dec. 22. I had already received and answered no. 54, which arrived in almost record time. No. 53 is splendid. Naturally I share your trouble about Nena, but I hope for the best. All the other news is intensely interesting, and your saying that I am now the only one to whom you are first is absolutely true on the positive side. Certainly you are first to me, and anybody else would have to go some to usurp that position. But there are others to whom you are just about first, and at any rate absolutely essential!

Since last Friday, when my last letter, I think, was written, there has not been a great deal to tell. On Friday night I wound up my literary evenings at Paris with "Les Erinnyes" of Leconte de Lisle at the Odéon. During the day I accomplished a number of pieces of business, and among other things had my picture taken again. The old picture was all right except that the hat was arranged in such a bizarre way that I am ashamed of the unmilitary style in which

I appear. Of the new pictures the proofs are to be shown me on Friday; the making of the pictures will probably take some weeks after that.

I am now at Gièvres, where the great central warehouses of the U. S. army in France are located.[29] There is no town—or only an insignificant village—but an enormous camp with wooden barracks. I am living in camp with a crowd of Y.M.C.A. men. The absence of quiet and privacy makes me feel how very fortunate I have been during most of my year in France. It is a great blessing to be able to retire from the phonograph now and then. These fellows working in camp are the men who have really sacrificed themselves. I am afraid I have had rather an easy and selfish time.

Hardly a Frenchman is to be seen in the whole countryside. A more absolutely uninteresting place could hardly have been picked out in Europe, but the ground is sandy and well adapted to camp purposes. Big American locomotives pull the trains, which are composed largely of American freight cars. The other day I walked out to the central American lost-baggage office for all of France, in order to look for my lost suit-case. Nothing doing! But I am not going to give up my inquiries.

On Sunday morning I spoke at one of the huts on the subject: "The New Testament Account of Jesus. Is it True?" The character of the subject was not of my own choosing. A chaplain is conducting a series of discussions about the Bible, and did not want to break it up. Since it was rather in my line, I was glad to do what I could. But I think that chaplain is rather inclined to exaggerate the interest of the men in such subjects.

On Sunday afternoon I was to have spoken at the hospital; but there was a misunderstanding, and the service was not held. On Sunday evening I spoke at a very good little service at an officers' Y.M.C.A. hut. The chaplain in charge of the service was a fellow by the name of Laird, a Benham class-mate of mine at the Seminary, who left us after his first year to go to McCormick Seminary. I have not seen Laird since 1903. He is a very pleasant fellow. The Benham type of man is very refreshing when you do meet him in this army life.

29. "Gièvres" is about 115 miles S.S.W. of Paris, or halfway between Bourges and Tours.

On Monday night I spoke at a "Y" hut for the educational department on "Winning the Peace." It is a mistake to suppose that I ever intended to lecture on French history.

Last night, Tuesday, I had a religious service at another hut. The attendance was small, but the men seemed fairly attentive. After I got through an egotistical "Y" man, with our terminal facilities, talked and talked and counteracted any affects of what I said, if there were any effects.

To-night I am to speak again, and to-morrow I go to Paris, preparatory to going to Chaumont to help in a series of religious meetings which are to be conducted in a combat division.[30]

The divisional "Y.M.C.A." religious work director here is much more congenial than most of them, and I am having a fairly satisfactory time. But I wish I were home. After four days, a full year of service in France will have been rounded out.

At one of the huts here I met several Macon fellows who are working on the railroad.

You have asked what divisions I have worked with. In case I have not told you I may say now that for a few days after I got to Loraine I was with the 42nd division, Rainbow division, composed of National Guard from many states. I did not see the "Floyd Rifles" or the "Macon Volunteers," but heard about their being in the division. Then I was with the 77th division composed of New York City "National Army"—largely Jewish, Catholic and foreign. Then I became attached to the 37th division—of which the basis was Ohio national guard, but with other elements added to it. It was the 37th division with whom I traveled to the Argonne, Woëvre & Belgium.

Still there is no winter.

Love to all.
Your loving son
Gresham

30. "Chaumont" is about 140 miles S.E. of Paris and 53 miles N. of Dijon.

Jan. 25, 1919

My dearest Mother:

On my return from Gièvres to Paris yesterday, the Christmas package was waiting for me, and the Vive-la-France socks are at the present moment on my feet. Wasn't it remarkable? The splendid warm things came to hand on the very first cold day of the winter just when they could be most appreciated. The socks would be grand no matter who made them; because the purchased article always fails to stand the test. But last night when I got those socks out and looked at them in my room, and realized that Mother really made them, I could hardly keep from shedding a tear over them—tears of joy that I have such a mother and tears of sorrow that I am not with her at this moment. Just now, as I write, I have the second pair on my table just so I can put my eyes on it. How soft and well-made it is, and how eloquent it is of my dearest Mother's love and care!

I am going to write a little note to Helen about the helmet, which is lovely.

The cup of my joy was made full by a perfectly splendid letter (no. 55, of Jan. 4) which I received at the same time with the socks. I have already answered no. 54 and then no. 53. You speak of keeping up your diary. How unspeakably valuable it is and will be! I just love to read it over. There seems to be so much of Mother in it.

Joy is mingled with sorrow in the news which your letter contains. I am distressed beyond measure by your cold, and by Nena's poor health. Also Marie Buchanan Sullivan's attack is distressing. I hope to hear of her recovery.

I am very glad that Clare and Carrie are keeping you company from time to time. And what fun it must have been to see Loy! I wish I could have enjoyed his visit with you.

What you say about Dassy is just too sweet for anything.

I am glad you are getting my letters more promptly, and particularly glad that yours to me are also coming through so well. Those letters in the true old familiar 217 envelopes are the only things that keep me alive.[31] Aside from the mere joy of hearing from you, you have been writing such magnificent long letters recently. I feel almost selfish in taking so much of the precious energy which you can spare; but it is a joy.

A most satisfactory letter has just arrived from Army—expressing just that mixture of willingness to have me stay over here and warm desire to have me in Princeton which puts me most at my ease. If there is or ever was on this earth a better fellow than Army I have yet to hear of him!

I have already written nine letters to-day—until the worrisome things were off my mind I could not give myself the pleasure of writing to you—and there are more still to be done.

Very early to-morrow morning I start for Chaumont, on a ten days' speaking trip. Unfortunately I am to go with a certain Dr. Bell who rather riled me by thinking that I was Dr. Stevenson's private secretary. I tried to disabuse his mind on the subject, but I think the general impression, as obtained from the office here, remains.

I wish I could get home, see you, and then go to Princeton to get to work on my Sprunt lectures.

Love to all
Your loving son
Gresham

January 30, 1919

My dearest Mother:

My last letter was written about a week ago from Paris after I had received the long-expected Christmas parcel. Needless to say, I have been wearing the Christmas socks ever since, and the helmet is going to come in very handy also. The word "handy" may seem

31. The number "217" refers to the Machen house number on Monument Street in Baltimore.

to be somewhat "gauche" as applied to feet and head, but it conveys the idea. Of course I have received no letters since leaving Paris, since I am not going to make the grievous mistake of trying to have my mail forwarded. It is hard to wait till my return, but it is harder still to have my mail wandering aimlessly all over France.

I find it very difficult to write in my present situation, my room being entirely too cold to sit in. The company elsewhere is too good. There has been real winter weather for the first time this year. It has not been like American cold, but the ground has been white with snow and the thermometer, at least for a considerable portion of the time, below the freezing point.

I left Paris at eight o'clock last Saturday morning, with Dr. Bell of San Francisco Theological Seminary, arriving at Chaumont at about three in the afternoon. Chaumont, as you may know, is the headquarters of the American army in France. It is a fairly attractive town of about 15,000 inhabitants, magnificently situated on the edge of a plateau. We were soon instructed by the Y.M.C.A. man in charge as to the character of the campaign in which we were to engage in the 82nd division. A week of religious services, under the general charge of the division chaplain, is being undertaken by order (or with full endorsement) of the commanding general. The Y.M.C.A. of course is cooperating. The idea is that other activities in the division (entertainments etc.) are very largely to be called off, and that each speaker is to spend the week in some one place or at least within some single regiment, speaking at least once a day and trying to get personally acquainted with the men. The object is to secure the names of men who desire to unite with the churches of their choice, and in general to minister to the spiritual needs of the soldiers. Nothing of the kind, so far as I know, has ever been undertaken before, but it is hoped that the plan may now extend to many other divisions.

On Sunday Dr. Bell and I with some others were taken by auto some thirty or forty miles south from Chaumont to division headquarters at a small village called Prauthoy.[32] It was the very

---

32. Chaumont is about 140 miles S.E. of Paris and 53 miles N. of Dijon; Prauthoy is about 163 miles S.E. of Paris and 28 miles N.N.E. of Dijon.

coldest day of the winter, and we had an open car. My toes were
pretty cold, but I almost enjoyed the ride. On the way we stopped
for lunch at Langres, a very interesting town surrounded by its
ancient walls, and situated on the top of a lofty hill.[33] Naturally we
had no time to "do" Langres adequately, but I was glad to have even
a glimpse of so interesting a place and to enjoy the fine view from
the walls.

At Prauthoy we got into touch with the senior chaplain of the
division, Dr. Tyler, a Methodist who I have since heard had his last
charge in Baltimore. I rather guess that he is of Virginia extraction.
The division was at the start composed of Georgia, Alabama &
Tennessee national army men, although now it is known as the All-
American division and has altogether lost its specifically Southern
character, I have met a number of Georgia men in it, especially
among the officers. The Colonel, a West-Pointer, came originally,
I believe, from Mississippi. I am greatly impressed with these
Southerners—not only for personal reasons, but also because they
make the impression of being unusually energetic and efficient
officers.

My first assignment—to the 307th Engineers—proved to be
unfortunate because the chaplain of the Engineers had been told
that he was to have only one outside speaker and had arranged the
schedule accordingly. Dr. Bell, whom I got to liking very well, was
perfectly willing to yield to me; but, for various reasons, that would
obviously not do at all. Hence I had the chaplain get in touch with
Chaplain Tyler in order to have me reassigned. Meanwhile, however,
I had a very pleasant two days at Coublanc, the headquarters of the
Engineers.[34] Really, I never had been received in the army with quite
such hospitality as that. The colonel, (Colonel Finch), who is a most
delightful man, treated me as though I were an honored guest,
got me a nice billet, set me next to him at table, got me all the
transportation I wanted, and was good enough to say that he was
sorry I couldn't stay. The Lieutenant Colonel (Col. More) treated
me with exactly similar style, as did everybody with whom I came
into contact at Coublanc.

33. Langres is about 160 miles E.S.E. of Paris and 41 miles N.N.E. of Dijon.
34. Coublanc is located about 206 miles S.S.E. of Paris and about 37 miles N.W. of Lyon.

On Sunday evening the Colonel took me to speak to some colored troops who were gathered for a show. It was a new experience to me & was (if I may use an irreverent term without being misunderstood) considerable fun. I have often heard of darky meetings, but had never seen the real thing before. These were none of your sophisticated colored people, but the real country article from Georgia. One of them, in particular, did just about as much talking (simultaneous with mine) as I did. I did not know exactly what was up at first, but as soon as I located the talkative one & began talking to him it was all right. Afterwards they started a real darky song. If they had known that there was to be a real meeting with chance to say "Amen" I think they would have come in greater numbers than for an army show.[35]

On Monday evening I attended Dr. Bell's meeting at a neighboring village, and assisted by trying to play the piano. On a number of occasions over here, even my very slight ability to play has come in useful. The results of the meeting were good; a number of men expressed their desire to join the Church. Of course—I had nothing to do with that. Dr. Bell & the chaplain were in charge.

On Tuesday morning I went in by auto to division headquarters, and was sent out some eighteen miles to my present post at Bussières-les-Belmont where I am with the 320th Field Artillery.[36] The chaplain of the regiment who accompanied me, has since placed his lodgings with me & in general has treated me fine. It is he who has general charge of the meetings. We ate at the Colonel's mess (Col. Williams), and I have found the colonel & all the officers—nearly all of them Southerners—most delightful.

The services are being held in the room of the school-house which is being used by the Y.M.C.A. We had about sixty men present the first night, about sixty-five the second night, and about fifty the third night. Only a part of the regiment is quartered in this town: the attendance

35. The terminology used here to describe black people is currently unacceptable. However, to see Machen's words as intending to belittle the black people is unfair to the historical context and what he is conveying in this paragraph. After all, given that Machen collected his letters for posterity, why would he not have excised this paragraph if he intended to insult, demean, or ridicule? He had his mother cut out an earlier section that spoke negatively about J. Ross Stevenson, so the same could be done in the current case. Though it is not a popular principle currently, historical figures need to be understood in *their* context and not *ours*. It should be noted that Machen is giving *positive* comments about the service and not condemning the practices of the people.

36. Bussières-les-Belmont is about 172 miles S.E. of Paris and 38 miles N.E. of Dijon.

figures therefore are not discouraging. But unfortunately we do not seem to be reaching the men who are not already church-members. The fundamental purpose of the meetings is therefore hardly being attained. Perhaps, however, we are doing some good. Yesterday the chaplain & I went on an investigating trip to a neighboring town, & this afternoon we hope to go to still another town where a large part of the regiment is quartered. Probably we shall arrange for a service there—at least on Sunday. On Monday the series of services will be over. I may then be sent for a similar series in another division.

This is a very pretty country—with bold hills. The ground is still covered with snow, though the temperature has not been much below the freezing-point even at night. The industry of Bussières, which is an obscure village not even mentioned in my Guide Joanne, is basket-making. Bussières office-baskets for waste paper are sent all over the world, including America. It takes about an hour and a half to make a magnificent strong basket. The whole thing is done by hand, and almost without tools. It is a pretty sight—the skill of people who have been doing the thing all their lives. I enjoyed chatting with a family of the village this morning while they continued their work.

On Sunday I caught a bad cold, but it is gradually clearing up in a satisfactory way.

I wish I could see you all, my dearest Mother. As it is, I can only send my love.

Your loving son
Gresham

Feb. 6 and 7, 1919

My dearest Mother:

Since my last letter, about a week ago, I have still been passing through a lean and hungry time without letters from home. The uncertainty involved in having them forwarded from Paris is too great. But no one knows how I long to see the post-office at 12 Rue d. Aguesseau.

My last letter was written from Bussières-les-Belmont about a week ago. We continued the evening services every evening through Sunday, but on Saturday evening (and also on Sunday morning) I spoke at another village, Grenant, about four or five miles away, leaving a "Y" man and the chaplain to speak at Bussières.[37] The services at Bussières were attended fairly well—at least the attendance did not fall off appreciably—but we were weak in "tangible results." We did not succeed very well in reaching the men who were not already Church-members.

The five days at Bussières were very pleasant. The country is rather pretty, and the village itself fairly picturesque. Bussières, which is a small place, not deemed worthy of mention in Joanne, is the centre of the basket making industry. If I understood rightly, 95% of the office waste-paper baskets used in America (there is evidently some mistake here) come from Bussières, and the ware-houses of the place are stored with other baskets, cradles, etc. of every possible size and shape. Practically everybody in the village is engaged in this industry, which has been going on for generations. A most magnificently strong waste-paper basket can be made (practically without tools) in about an hour and a half. It is pretty to watch the skill with which the peasants work; they are not averse to chatting while they work. If I remained long at Bussières I might learn French.

On Saturday night I stayed at Grenant and pretty nearly froze. I had the choice of sleeping in the bed with the "Y" man, the bed being perhaps as much as three and a half or four feet wide or else of sleeping on his camp-bed. I tried the latter. It sure does take some blankets to keep one warm.

At Bussières I took my meals with the chaplain at the mess of the Colonel of the 320th Field Artillery. The Colonel and everybody else were very pleasant indeed. Major Harris of Atlanta, who is a lawyer in civil life, is a wide-awake fellow and knows Arly's book on Corporations. He told me to tell Arly that the lawyers are running the U. S. Army.

37. Grenant is located about 122 miles S.S.E. of Paris and 87 miles W. of Dijon.

On Monday, I made the eighteen-mile trip to Prauthoy, division headquarters of the 82nd division, on a truck, and after warming my toes a little at the Y.M.C.A. store was taken with other speakers and singers by auto about thirty miles or more to Recey-sur-Ource, Y.M.C.A. headquarters for the 6th division, among whom we are now working.[38] It was a pretty cold day for motoring. But at least I did not come as near freezing as I did that day when Arly took us out around Loch Raven.[39] That was the coldest experience of my life! The hardships of war are nothing to it! I wish, however, that I could repeat it, if I could repeat it in the same company.

After reaching Recey-sur-Ource, I came by auto along with a "singer" to the village where I am spending the week. Colmier-le-Haut is the name of the tiny little place (144 inhabitants).[40] It is finely situated on the very edge of a plateau (I think a part of the "Plateau of Langres") overlooking the Ource valley. The view is very attractive—especially before the snow was melted. This "Côte d'___" and Haute-Marne scenery (we are just on the border between the two "departments") is very attractive, with its pine woods, its rolling uplands, and its deep-cut ravines and valleys. The week has been fairly cold and bleak, but to-day the milder and wetter weather seems to be setting in again (Later. It is snowing again, I am sorry to say). I suppose this village must be a good 1,400 feet above sea level.

It is rather instructive to visit those parts of Europe which would never in the world be made the object of a sight-seeing journey. The church at Colmier-le-Haut is dishearteningly modern, and the scenery is not at all sensational. Yet the airy view constantly spread out before us is a joy; and it is interesting to live in peasant houses and get acquainted with the country-folks of France.

At Colmier-le-Haut I have a most delightful billet—the room of a lieutenant away on leave. There is a good cheery wood fire in the fireplace at this present moment. A most magnificent

38. Recey-sur-Ource is located about 141 miles S.E. of Paris and 34 miles N. of Dijon.
39. Loch Raven is a park on the N.E. side of Baltimore.
40. Colmier(s)-le-Haut is about 147 miles S.E. of Paris and 33 miles N. of Dijon.

manure-pile just a short distance from my window attests to the prosperity of the "patron," who is the owner of more than two hundred acres of land scattered in little patches throughout the surrounding country. But the house contains a tragedy. The only daughter of the patron and his wife, who are perhaps in their sixties, died a few weeks ago. She was about sixteen years old. It had been the ambition of these peoples' lives to give that girl a better education than they had enjoyed; all of their hard-working industry had been devoted to that one end, and now their interest in life is gone. Everything about the house recalls the daughter that they have lost. When the mother catches sight of my Larousse, she shows me the bigger Larousse that Madeline had used and the fine reports that she brought back from school. I can't even pet the family cat without recalling how Madeline had petted her. It is all perhaps a little more naïve than would be natural in America, but it is terribly sad.

At Coublanc I lived in the house belonging to two sisters, each with a young child, both of whose husbands had been killed in the war. Of course that kind of thing is the rule rather than the exception in France.

At Bussières I had occasion to go to see the village curé in order to ask him to let the Protestant chaplain have some of his wafers for the Sunday communion service.[41] When I went in he was engaged in teaching Greek & Latin to two little boys—the village school not providing the instruction in those languages necessary for the lycée of the collège.[42] It was like a picture out of countless French biographies & novels. The curé was very gracious about the wafers, but asked me how I interpreted "Hoc est corpus meum," and also why the clause, "He descended into hell" is omitted from the Apostles' Creed in a little book of devotion intended for the use of the American soldiers. About the latter point I could assure him that I disapproved as much as he did, of the mutilation of the creed.[43]

41. The "curé" is the parish priest.
42. The word "lycée" means secondary school, or high school.
43. The Latin, "Hoc est corpus meum," is translated in English, "This is my body," the meaning of which was a key point of controversy at the time of the Protestant Reformation. The question was, "In what sense must the elements of the Lord's Supper be called the body

But it is time to speak of my work. Beginning on Monday night I have spoken every evening during the week so far, and the series of services is to be continued through Sunday. The services are under the care of the chaplain, Chaplain Whyman, a Methodist minister, with whom I got along fine. Like Chaplain Williams, with whom I was associated last week, Chaplain Whyman believes in dignity in connection with religious services, and an avoidance of too much calling for a show of hands and the like. So far the services have been fairly well attended, but we have not succeeded very well in reaching the non-Church-members. This latter circumstance is of course a bit discouraging, but the chaplain agrees with me in exalting the function of conserving the spiritual life of the Christian men as the best preparation for future evangelization. He seems to think that I have been able to give the boys some of the solid instruction that they want & need. In addition to the evening service, we have started a little Bible-class which meets in my room in the afternoon.

Our singer is inclined to want to be a speaker in his own book, and contributes a little more fuss and "pep" than at times we might desire; but perhaps, rightly guided, it is all for the best.

Breakfast is at 6.15 A.M. That is the most military breakfast hour that I have yet encountered.

Don't imagine us as holding the services in a finely-equipped Y.M.C.A. hut such as you would find in the camps at home. On the contrary, we count ourselves unusually fortunate in having a shack with dirt floor, dimly lighted with candles and with just the edge taken off the chill by wood stoves. Life in the

---

and blood of Christ?" Protestant views developed the distinction between the sign—*the elements,* and what they signified—*grace,* in opposition to the Roman Catholic doctrine of transubstantiation. Three main views were drawn from the Bible by the Reformers. The Lutheran understanding designated consubstantiation, the Reformed view (Calvin), and those who held a memorial view (Zwingli). For a brief discussion of the debates with respect to Luther, see Steve Nichols, *Martin Luther: A Guided Tour of His Life and Thought* (Phillipsburg: P&R, 2002), 117-30. A. A. Hodge, *The Confession of Faith,* discusses some of the different views in his presentation of the *Westminster Confession of Faith,* chapter 29, "Of the Lord's Supper," pages 355-63, and Robert Shaw's, *An Exposition of the Westminster Confession of Faith,* on the same chapter of the *Confession* is also helpful. For discussion of the point Machen mentions here regarding the Apostles Creed, see, Herman Witsius's two volume work, *Sacred Dissertations on the Apostles' Creed.*

American army in these little villages is undoubtedly rough for the men in the ranks. But the boys are hardened to it.

My barrel contains only six talks. Yet here I have to speak seven times to the same crowd! Poor old Dassy!

You don't know, my dearest Mother, how my thoughts are with you just now. How I long for news.

Love to all
Your loving son
Gresham

14

GOING HOME!

The varied travels and duties will continue for Dr. Machen as he anticipates his return to the United States. He will lead special services, Bible classes, and preach in worship services. He is anxious to return to home and family and he expresses his joy at leaving France. The port of departure is Brest.

Wednesday, Feb. 12, 1919

My dearest Mother:

My last letter, I believe, was sent from Colmier-le-Haut on last Friday. The last two of our series of evening services were somewhat interfered with by a minstrel show which was put on after our Saturday service and an official memorial service for Roosevelt, which was placed before our service on Sunday.[1] The weather also was very much colder than during the early part of the week, the wood being just as scarce as ever and the tears in the paper of the windows just as numerous. The atmosphere inside the place was really almost too cold to support human life. Hence it is not surprising that the attendance on Sunday night was not so good as might have been hoped under better conditions. On Sunday

---

1. Theodore (Teddy) Roosevelt (1858–1919), the twenty-sixth President of the United States, died January 6 (*Webster's Biographical*).

morning I held a service at Buxerolles, a neighboring village, but
in as much as there was no fire in the wooden building and the
thermometer stood that morning at about 14 degrees Fahrenheit,
it was impracticable to keep the men for more than a very few
minutes.[2] The captain of the company at Buxerolles went with me
himself to the service. He is a South Carolinian with whom I spent a
pleasant hour after the service. He never goes to church for himself,
but says that over here the mothers of his men would like to know
that they were going to Church, so he encourages them to go in
every possible way. In fact he does everything except actually line
them up and march them to the services.

Perhaps the best feature of the week at Colmier-le-Haut was
the opportunity that I had, in the little Bible class in the afternoon,
of getting acquainted with a few of the Christian fellows of this
camp. Although "tangible results," in the shape of accessions to the
Church were practically nil, the Chaplain thinks, and I hope rightly,
that the week's work was by no means wasted. He believes that the
permanent results of such labor are often the results which are least
apparent at the time.

One disappointing feature was the total lack of interest on
the part of the officers. Even those with whom I was intimately
associated at mess failed to attend any of the services, and the
officers at the Roosevelt service, including the captain who spoke,
got up and left before our service began!

The wintry scenery was beautiful at Colmier-le-Haut during
the last few days especially. I took one or two beautiful walks! My
nice warm billet was useful for the purposes of the Bible class. The
last night I lost it & had to share the chaplain's bed, the lateral
cross-section of which is like this—U. The concavity threw the two
occupants into such proximity that when either one wiggled to the
slightest extent it woke the other.

On Monday morning we had a very long and cold auto ride
(of perhaps fifty or sixty miles in all—first by a round-about way
(picking up some other speakers)) to Y.M.C.A. headquarters of the
6th Division, & then to my new post in the 80th division, at a little
place called Nicey, which is about ten miles west of Châtillon-sur

2. Buxerolles is located 187 miles S.W. of Paris and on the N.E. side of Poitiers.

Seine.[3] The 80th is the "Blue Ridge Division" with troops from
the mountains of Virginia & Pennsylvania. In our village there is
a battalion of the 320th Infantry. I had rather hoped to get back
to Paris, since I have no news from home, no decent clothes, &
practically no shoes—my pair of shoes having been burned on
some stove. But when the arrangements were found to be all made
for me to go on to another division I could not very well back
away. The present kind of service is by far the best that I have had
since I arrived in France. I have the opportunity of preaching the
gospel in a far better way than when I was merely speaking one
night at each place. My experiences with the chaplain with whom I
have been associated have been very pleasant.

Nicey is a town of 700 inhabitants which seems quite
metropolitan compared with the tiny villages of the area that I have
just left. I have a nice room, but without any fire in it. There is ice
in my pitcher in the morning. A bouillotte (I am not sure about the
spelling), placed in the bed in the evening is a help. A bouillotte is
a jug filled with hot water—as you probably know.[4] I have not had a
bath for nearly three weeks! That is the greatest discomfort of all.

We are on the edge of a broad plain. The view from the hill
back of the village, which I enjoyed at sunset yesterday, was simply
lovely. The village church is old & picturesque. It is not mentioned
in Joanne. My landlady tells me that scarcely anybody gets to mass
here, even though the priest comes to this town only once in several
weeks.

Our services are being held in the Y.M.C.A. canteen. The
attendance is fair, but many of the men are present just in order
to read or write letters rather than to attend the service. They give
pretty good attention while the service is going on. At first I felt
greatly discouraged, but last night I thought there seemed to be
rather more response. On account of maneuvers we have not as yet
been able to organize a Bible-class in the afternoons, but I hope to
do so to-morrow.

3. Châtillon-sur Seine is 128 miles S.E. of Paris and 45 miles N.N.W. of Dijon; Nicey, as
Machen noted, is about 10 to 12 miles W. of Châtillon-sur Seine .
4. Maybe the word he was looking for was "bouteille," which means "bottle," but from
Machen's description, it must have been a hot water bottle.

My, I wish I could hear from home. I have asked a "Y" secretary who is going to Paris to bring my letters & telegrams. That method is more certain than ordinary forwarding, but it is exceedingly uncertain at best. I feel terribly anxious & eager for news.

The temperature at this side of the "Y" room is so frigid that I must bring my letter to a close & join the group around the stove.

Love, my dearest Mother, and more love to you & to all. I hope to see you before long. Pray God I may have good news soon.

Your loving son
Gresham

February 19, 1919

My dearest Mother:

Your letters, nos. 56 and 57, of Jan. 10 and Jan. 18, were awaiting me on my arrival last night. The cablegram, which was also awaiting me, I have already answered by wire to Arly. It is quite needless for me to say how I am thrilled by the news of the arrival of my new niece, but also how deeply anxious I am and how eager for further news of mother and daughter. Last week—that is, on Monday ten days ago—Dr. Pitman, the Y.M.C.A. religious secretary in charge of the region in which we were working, informed me that he would obtain my mail for me by a secretary who was going to Paris. Imagine my disappointment when, the day before yesterday, the plan proved to have come to nothing. I was so anxious, on account of the expected cablegram, that I asked for a movement order to Paris, which was granted. Having arrived late last night I obtained my three and a half weeks accumulation of mail this morning. Of course I was on hand, in my impatience, well before the opening of the Y.M.C.A. post-office. Along with your two letters, and the all-important cablegram, I received a particularly notable letter from Arly, which I am going to answer at once.

Your letters are if anything even finer and longer than usual, but my heart aches when I hear of all the manifold trouble and suffering that you have been passing through. The better news from Helen, especially in Arly's letter of Jan. 26—considerably later than yours—have comforted me somewhat, and given me some courage while I wait for further news of the baby. I hope the cables will be spared.

My week at Nicey with the 80th division was vaguely disappointing. The attendance kept up pretty well, but there were no very definite results, and interest seemed to be of rather a mild variety. On Sunday I walked seven miles to a village called Molesme, in which regimental headquarters and the first battalion of the 320th infantry were quartered—the same regiment in which (in the second battalion) I had been laboring during the week.[5] About twenty soldiers and not one single officer were present at the morning service that I conducted. The lack of interest everywhere on the part of officers is not only discouraging to me, but of gloomy omen for the future of our country. What will happen if the leaders of our people turn altogether away from God?

The walk over in the morning was pleasant, there being just the slight frost which was necessary to give some foothold instead of the terrific mud that had prevailed during the past few days of warm weather. The country is attractive, and on the way I inspected the rather unimpressive ruins of a Gallo-Roman town near the little village of Vertault.[6] The view from the site of the ancient town was much more attractive than the few remnants of a foundation in the place itself. That part of France is rather sparsely settled, and wild boars are said to be so plentiful as to become harmful to the crops. The Frenchman who pointed out the ruins to me was out with dog and gun for a morning's hunting.

On Monday I went to division headquarters, Ancy-le-Franc (no time to inspect the château), whence we proceeded by rail to Chaumont, breaking the journey by a night at Dijon.[7] Before I became acquainted with the Guides Joanne, the only thing that I

5. Molesme, is located about 118 miles S.E. of Paris and 55 miles N.W. of Dijon.
6. Vertault is just S. of Molesme.
7. Ancy-le-Franc is about 115 miles S.E. of Paris and about 50 miles N.W. of Dijon.

knew about Dijon was the "glorie" of it that made it famous in that
dear old rose-garden in Georgia, and always it will call to mind the
revered vision of my grandfather & my grandmother and still more
the dearest person of all who taught me its name.[8]

Joanne says that two days must be devoted to Dijon, but
unfortunately the orders of Joanne are not regarded as official
in the A.E.F. So we arrived after dark and departed by a seven
o'clock train the next morning. While hurrying to the train I had
a glimpse of the choir of the cathedral down a side street and of
the outside of the château that contains the famous tombs of the
dukes of Burgundy. It was rather a tantalizing experience—almost
comparable to passing by Chartres and Troyes without stopping,
under the impulsion of an inexorable movement-order.

When we arrived at Chaumont, after a sixty-mile railroad
ride that took most of the day, and when at Chaumont I had the
disappointment about my mail to which I have already alluded, and
when my request for a movement order to Paris was the more readily
granted because of some slight derangements of the further plans for
our party, I took a six o'clock train for Paris, arriving about 11 o'clock
at night. The Palais-Royal had not received my wire, and I had to
content myself for two nights with a bed in a room occupied by another
man. I think I have seldom been more miserable even in the war zone.
I was dirty, tired, and grouchy, and sorely needed to get my baggage
& settle down. But now my troubles are over. I have a delightful room,
and a much-needed bath has made me feel like a new man.

For some time I had been intending to apply very soon for
permission to go home, but had been retained by the opportunities
of the work. Every Monday, all was arranged for me to go to a new
place to preach the gospel. Had I broken away the place would be
vacant for the week. But the calls of home were very strong, and
when there came the slight derangement of which I spoke, I seized
the opportunity with avidity. I am anxious, not only to see you, my
dearest Mother (that is the supreme motive), but also to get to work
on my Sprunt Lectures. I feel that a long enough block of time has

8. The "gloire de Dijon" is a rose variety developed in France in 1853. The "dear old
rose-garden in Georgia" refers to the garden at Machen's mother's childhood home in Macon.
The home is currently a bed-and-breakfast.

already been taken from my real life work. And I am afraid I shall not be greatly missed over here by anyone.

Getting home is a much quicker matter than I had supposed. I am informed that it only takes some two or three days at Paris from the time the application is in, and a day or so at Brest, before one gets on the ship. We are sent, with the accommodations of officers, on transports. Although we are subject to duty on shipboard as "Y" secretaries, I suppose the work will be light if not altogether nominal for most of us. At any rate I hope so. I am not apt to be good for much on the ocean wave.[9]

At present I am still attached to the Paris staff, my application being delayed for a few days. A lot of things are to be done before I pull up stakes here—business correspondence, etc., purchase of baggage, disposal of equipment. When in my wire I said I would be home before April 1st, that of course was only a rough estimate. In what I have said above you have the same elements of calculation that I have. I do not know how long the voyage takes, or what delays may intervene. At any rate I am going to work hard to get home just . . . *[The remainder of the letter is missing.]*

Feb. 21, 1919

Dear Arly:

Your letter of Jan. 20 is one of the most notable that I have received for many a long day, but the cable of Feb. 10 because of its contents is the thing that first requires an answer. The cable arrived in Paris on Feb. 13, but for the reasons set forth in my letter to Mother I did not get it till the day before yesterday. I am overjoyed to hear that the baggage safely arrived, but a telegram is unusually enigmatic, and I have been trying to persuade myself that the laconic terms of this one do not hide anything particularly disquieting in the condition of mother or daughter.

9. An allusion to Machen's seasickness on the ship transporting him to France.

Unless I receive another cable, my approaching voyage will keep me without news for almost a month. It will seem longer than that, at any rate, to me.

As I have just told Mother, the encouraging news in your letter with regard to Helen's health have given me courage to hope for the best. What you say about Mother's poor condition is the more distressing because I had received a somewhat different impression about her. Her letters have been longer than usual and not lacking in vivacity. Of course they have been just lovely as they always are. But I realize now how large a part of their cheerfulness is to be attributed to Mother's desire not to worry me or interfere with my work. I wish I could have returned earlier. But at any rate I have now the satisfaction of knowing for a good many reasons that I am certainly wise in not postponing my voyage any longer.

The part of your letter which deals with architecture and with French literature is intensely interesting; I wish I had the resources for appreciation and enjoyment of my advantages that your reading have given to you. You can be sure that if I were not a member of the A.E.F. your advice that I take in Beauvais would not go unheeded.[10] But in order to travel over here it is necessary for me to have every time a military "travel-permit," which can only be obtained if the journey is strictly in the line of duty. The regulations are strictly adhered to; without the travel-permit signed by the provost-martial, it is impossible to get through the Paris stations. And I do not want to do what the head of our Y.M.C.A. division had to do when his papers were not in order on one occasion—spend a day or so in the guard-house. Traveling by rail is an official business which is by no means easy to arrange. Alas, I have had to pass by such places as Chartres, Amiens, Troyers a number of times without stopping.

As for what you say about French literature, I am afraid you exaggerate my attainments—which only seemed rather overwhelming to me because they have been built up within the past few months from absolutely nothing. I do not know whether I have seen any of the really great actors—certainly I have seen none so distinguished as Coquelin. The only one who might

10. Beauvais is 40 miles N. of Paris and 34 miles S. of Amiens.

perhaps almost be put into that category is Réjane, whom I regret to confess that I was so sleepy and tired as hardly to know what I was seeing. At the Comédie Française the leading female roles just now seem to be taken by Romano, who is "Esther," for example, was certainly superb. Among the men the acting of Féraudy (for example in "L.Avare" of Molière) seems to be among the most noteworthy.

I have just discovered that the apparent hospitality of the Théâtre Français to strangers was due only to the war and the German air-raids. The regular system of "abonnemonts" has now been set up again, and it is almost unbelievable in its anti-democracy.[11] So far as I can see, all of the classical performances come under the abonnements and due to the abonnements the entire house is taken by the holders of season tickets. The tickets cannot be secured by ordinary citizens, but are handed down from father to son for generations. Of course I have tried to get in through theatrical agencies, but although that succeeded once, it seems really to be quite impossible. You pay your money, on the chance that a ticket may be relinquished just before the performance. It seems to be a long chance. In short the subsidized French theatre, despite the nominally democratic institutions of the country is the very opposite of what a subsidized theatre might be expected to be—namely a means of popular education. The public is free to revel in the mud of modern comedy but acquaintanceship with decent drama is the privilege of a small clique. As for friendship toward strangers and allies, that is present when bombardments and air-raids make the strangers profitable. At other times it is mere newspaper camouflage.

You see, though I began with the friendliest feelings, I have gradually come around to the ordinary view. There are very nearly 2,000,000 Americans who think as I do now. For the sake of a little momentary spoliation, the friendship (which would have been much more profitable in the end) of a nation has been sacrificed. The closed doors and discourteous employees of the Théâtre Français, though perhaps trifling in themselves,

11. Machen mentioned "abonnemonts" with contempt in an earlier letter. The "abonnemonts" are subscriptions to the theater for the Paris elite.

in the midst of so much misery, are unfortunately typical of the selfishness of a whole people.

But why waste time with ill-natured words? Am I not soon going to be at home.

Your affectionate brother
Gresham Machen

P.S. How in the world did I forget to mention my interest in the thrilling account of your experience in the fire?

Feb. 25, 1919

My dearest Mother:

Your splendid letters nos. 58 and 59, of Jan. 30 and Feb. 3, have arrived in the reverse order. As trouble and sickness multiply, your letters seem to become longer and more lovely all the time. I read and reread them until I almost know parts of them by heart.

Certainly you have been passing through deep waters. I am grieved beyond measure at Catherine's death. Such sorrows are often the heaviest to bear, and they are the ones for which we receive the least sympathy. You relieve me somewhat about the kiddies, but I share to the full your anxiety about Nena in her attack of the flu. I am afraid I shall have to wait for better news until I get to America.

I am distressed to hear that you yourself, my dearest Mother, have been so far from well. Your letters are so brave and good that I am afraid I may not fully realize sometimes quite all that you have been passing through. But I sympathize most deeply, and long to see you.

The incidental reference to Summerville in your letter of Jan. 30, which arrived yesterday, caused me at once to send a wire urging you (through Arly) not to postpone the trip on account of any desire to see me in Baltimore. I can easily run down to

Summerville, and although the hotel may be crowded they will be able to put me up somewhere in an emergency. I have gotten used to sleeping in all sorts of places.[12] My main concern is that nothing should be allowed to interfere with your trip. Summerville in March & April is mere pleasure to you; it is the very hope and life of us all. For nothing else does you so much good, and your health is the thread upon which my life hangs.

When we get to New York we shall have to go to Y.M.C.A. headquarters to turn in our uniforms & transact other official business. If that letter got to you in time you might drop just a line to me at "Army Y.M.C.A. Headquarters," 347 Madison Ave., N.Y.[13] I hope they will not keep me long in New York. It is too bad that we cannot wear our uniforms at all ashore in America. I suppose I shall have to go at once to Brooks Bros. to fit myself out.[14] The Germans got my one civilian suit & I have none of the other articles of civilian attire.

I am to leave here on Friday night, Feb. 28, for Brest, whence I am to go as a "casual" on a transport to America. Going as a "casual" means that I am not to be given responsibility for secretarial duties on shipboard. I did not feel like tackling anything very much on the ocean wave.

The chances are that I shall go on a good big ship. I do not think it will be the "Leviathan"; but at any rate the voyage is not to be looked forward to with apprehension.[15] No submarines, no mines (since from Brest we do not have to traverse the channel or the North Sea), but possibly some "mal de mer."[16]

---

12. To say the least!

13. Currently located at 347 Madison Ave. is the entrance to an office building. The door is between a large "J. Crew" store at 349 and an entrance to a smaller office building at 345.

14. Brooks Brothers has been a famous clothier in New York since 1818. The store at 346 Madison Ave., directly across the street from the building where the "Y" headquarters was located, was opened in 1915. So, Machen could, if the current street numbering is the same as in 1919, purchase his new attire and then dispose of his YMCA uniform and equipment at the office in 347 Madison Ave (see: Brooks Brothers website).

15. When World War I broke out in 1914, the *S.S. Vaterland*, one of three huge German ships, was laid up in Hoboken, New Jersey, for about three years. In 1917 when America entered the war, the German monster-ship was seized and placed in service as the *USS Leviathan*. After the war, the ship was used from 1922 into the following decade as a merchant ship. The ship was moved to Scotland in 1938 where it was dismantled. The *Leviathan* was the world's largest ship until 1922 (United States Navy, the Naval Historical Center, http://www.history.navy).

16. "Mal de mer," is rough sea.

I forgot to tell you some time ago that on the train coming back from Chaumont, I met a young fellow (now an officer) by the name of Boyce, who is a relation of the Franklin St. elder.[17] He had heard me preach at Franklin St. He himself is not a member of our church.

Did I tell you that I had recovered my lost suit-case? It was reposing all the time in the office of the "Y" in Paris. I thought I had looked everywhere in France. The letter they wrote me about it went astray. But, alas, it was a most bitter disappointment. It contained almost nothing of the things that I thought I had put in it. My stubs of check-books (which I had for making out my income tax return), my address-book, etc., are gone.

How shall I spend my few remaining days in Paris? I have so much that I want to do that I shall probably end by doing nothing.

Love to all, my dearest Mother! And how I wish I could hear about the baby.

Your loving son
Gresham

Feb. 28, 1919

Dear Arly:

I am taking home my bank balances here in the form of New York drafts. In accordance with the advice of the bankers who sold me the drafts. I an now enclosing the receipt of the draft of the American Express Co. (1648.00) and a duplicate of the draft of Monroe & Co. (387.45). Please do not collect the duplicate draft, but simply keep both receipt & duplicate as a matter of precaution, in case the drafts in my possession should be lost.

I leave to-night for Brest.

17. "Franklin St." refers to the Machen's home church, Franklin Street Presbyterian Church.

You have no idea what the state of my mind is with regard to news from the baby & from Helen. It looks as though I must wait for news till I get home.

Your affectionate brother
J. Gresham Machen

P.S. Since I wrote the above, Mother's letter of Feb. 11, with good news about Helen and the baby, has just arrived. I feel profoundly thankful. J.G.M.

March 2, 1919

My dearest Mother:

In all probability I shall reach you as soon or almost as soon as the present letter, but my heart is so full of thankfulness for your splendid letters numbers 60 and 61 (the later of Feb. 11) that I do not want to postpone my answer until the happy moment when I arrive at home or at Summerville. Unfortunately I have not the former of the two letters with me as I write (I think I must have left it in my trunk), but I read it over many, many times. As for the letter of Feb. 11, it is cause for profound thanksgiving that I received that before I left. It came on my very last day in Paris. The reassuring news that it gives about Helen and the baby will serve to make the voyage a less anxious time for me. Also I was delighted with the encouraging news from Nena and the kiddies. How they must have grown up since I saw them! With the picture of them that I have in my mind I can hardly imagine them as making the observations which you record.

I trust you have received my cable urging you to go to Summerville irrespective of my arrival. I am eager for you to have the trip, as I explained in my last letter.

The Christmas package, I am afraid, must have been more trouble than it was worth. The American Express Co., through whom I sent it, did not seem to think that the customs-house would bother it. Your pleasure at the little trinkets pleased me greatly.

The last few days at Paris were pretty busy. I had to turn in equipment at the Y.M.C.A., give away old clothes, and do the thousand and one other things that crop-up when a person leaves a country where he has settled down for thirteen months. Having contributed very little money to any causes during the past year I decided to give 2000 francs to the McCall mission. I had wanted to contribute to the war-orphan work, but the secretary of the McCall mission seemed to think that what is needed most of all just now is aid to the work of evangelization. So my contribution is to be used as the authorities of the mission see fit—part to go to the evangelistic work properly speaking and part to the charitable work which is an adjunct and an aid to it. This seems better than simply giving through the Red Cross. I wish I had had time to inspect the work of the McCall mission—notably their school & their headquarters, to which I was cordially invited. I must say that the preacher at the station on the Boulevard Bonne Nouvelle, whom I have heard several times, does not impress me very favorably. The gospel in his preaching is too much chocked by a lot of stuff about social conditions. But the human instruments of preaching are never perfect, and I suppose on the whole that the McCall mission is doing as good a work as any agency in France. The present condition of the French nation is one gigantic tragedy of which the war is only a part.

By the way, I regret the ill-natured strictures in my last letter. My irritation got the better of me. I am thankful for the privilege of having lived in France, and I admire the real qualities of the French soldiers. Above all I wish I could help. It is a sad thing to be present at the dying of a people that might have been great. According to careful statistics published recently in one of the French papers the French population of France have diminished during the past four years by about three and a half million, being now only about thirty-five million. The birth rate has been only a little more than half equal to the death rate. These are surface indications of important facts. Resuscitation is not so easy a matter as some people

One of the YMCA services Machen mentions is providing soldiers with writing materials to keep their families informed about their lives. The soldiers were often reminded to "Keep Your Promise—Write Home."
Photo courtesy of Kautz Family Collection, University of Minnesota

think. It will not be accomplished merely by giving bonuses to large families. But who can tell what God may have in store? The wonders of His grace sometimes come when they are least expected.

At Paris, in the evenings I had time to go to the theatre a number of times. Cyrano de Bergerac at the Port St. Martin was fine.[18] On account of police regulations about the closing-hour, L.Aiglon had to be cut so ruthlessly as I saw it given that what remained was a mere fragment. But the performance of Cyrano was lovely. Aside from the fact that Cyrano is a finer play. Perhaps the most interesting contemporary play that I saw during the year was "Pasteur." It is a strange play. For example there is in it not a single female part. And the subject might seem to be dull. But the depicting of Pasteur's early struggles against incredulity and the first case of hydrophobia that he cured were quite thrilling.[19] No one could have supposed that the subject could be made so interesting.

18. The "Porte St. Martin" is the Théatre de la Porte Saint Martin in Paris on the Rue René Boulanger.
19. The disease "hydrophobia" is more commonly known today as "rabies."

I left Paris for Brest at eight o'clock Friday night, arriving Saturday morning after the usual uncomfortable night sitting up in a crowded compartment. During the morning hours, before we arrived, I had my first glimpse of Brittany. When we passed Morlaix on that high bridge I thought of you & of your automobile trip.[20] Morlaix is certainly a "trou," but a very interesting "trou," I should think.[21]

Who should prove to be the "personnel" man of the Y.M.C.A. who took charge of us on our arrival at the station but my friend Aleck Thompson, a chief of Benham Club who graduated from the Seminary in 1909. I am rooming with him at the Y.M.C.A. hotel here at Brest.[22] My name is not yet posted among those who are to report at once for the formalities of getting off, but Thompson informs me that it will be at the head of the next list. One cannot know ahead of time when the transports are coming in. But when they do arrive they only have to stay a day or so or a few hours in port. One has to be ready to go at very short notice. I may get off to-morrow or I may have to wait for days. The ships that have been used seem to be fine big boats—for example the Mauretania a few days ago. I am going to try to send another wire to Arly when I know what ship I am to take. If there is no chance to do so, the "Y" will notify Arly through the New York Office at 347 Madison Ave. about my sailing.

Yesterday afternoon I "did" Brest—which does not take very long. The bridge over the harbor affords an interesting view; the château with its ancient towers & its dungeons is interesting; and the interior of the cathedral erected under Louis XIV is really an impressive creation of a debased style. But the attractions of Brest are unworthy of the entrancing district of which it is the modern metropolis.

My dearest Mother, when shall I be able to see you? And when shall I be able to see the new baby? I grudge every minute that I have to wait.

Your loving son
Gresham

---

20. Morlaix is about 295 miles due W. of Paris on the N. side of Brittany on the road to Brest.

21. A "trou" is a hole. In what sense Morlaix is a hole is unclear, unless the town is situated topographically in the lowlands.

22. Brest is about 32 miles W.S.W. of Morlaix in Brittany.

15

LETTERS WRITTEN IN
FRENCH RECEIVED BY
J. GRESHAM MACHEN

June 5, 1918 to January 13, 1919

Translated by Kristi Wetzel

    Two correspondents wrote this small collection of fourteen brief letters in French to Dr. Machen—Montí, his YMCA colleague at Missy-sur-Aisne composed thirteen letters and V. Elie wrote one. As Montí mentions some "painful events" in the first letter, he is referring to the hurried withdrawal of Dr. Machen and himself from Missy-sur-Aisne as the Germans rapidly advanced. Dr. Machen recounted his experiences at Missy in a letter to his mother dated May 29, 1918. After fleeing Missy-sur-Aisne, Montí was re-assigned by the French army from his temporary YMCA work to military duty. He served with the 82e Regiment d'Artillerie Lourde (RAL). His return address in some of the letters indicates that his unit used "caterpillars" for the transportation of artillery. The "caterpillars" were trucks that had tracks similar to an earth-moving bulldozer and hauled artillery pieces onto their cargo beds for transportation much in the same way that broken-down automobiles today are moved onto flatbed tow trucks with a winch. As the war progressed, the military tank was developed, which married the separate canon and caterpillar driven chassis together in a single self-propelled unit.

301

[This letter was written on Le Foyer du Soldat, YMCA, letterhead stationery.]
  [Monti's return address is unclear, but he was with a unit of artillery caterpillars.]

June 5, [1918]

Dear Sir

  I hope you arrived in Paris without too much difficulty and that you have now put aside the shock that these painful events must have made you feel. After a painful retreat and some gloomy business, we somehow or other arrived yesterday at Nanteuil. We are going to stay there several days while waiting for a train that is to take us to the Mailly camp in order to repair our machinery. While beating a retreat, I met Mr. L___q, who was unhappy that you arrived in Chacrise too late for the last train. I take it upon myself to assure you of my deep appreciation for all the kindnesses and satisfactions you have so generously given to me, and I could never be able to thank you enough. I think that right now the YMCA is busy providing relief to the fate of the poor immigrants. How sad this exodus was! And the situation remains serious, but I hope we will soon come out of it.

  With the hope of having the pleasure of hearing from you, let me assure you of my best memories, and I remain respectfully yours,

Montí

[In the upper left corner of the page is a circular ink stamp mark indicating that the artillery caterpillars used by Montí's unit were built by French vehicle manufacturer, Renault.]

[undated][1]

Dear Sir

I am very annoyed because I am completely unaware if something unfortunate has happened to you after the sad events that displaced me from your friendship. I hope you have recently returned to Paris without any trouble and that the YMCA gave you a well-deserved rest. Our unit has returned to our attachment at the front, which is Mailly, the center of our group. We have a good month to repair our machines, and I assure you we have a serious job at the moment to restore them to their original condition. I believe that France must praise herself more every day for the American intervention because without the help of the United States, we would be definitely, without a doubt, lost. After four years of suffering, it has been sad and very humiliating. I hope now that the German flood has been stemmed, but I strongly fear for our beautiful Paris because of the vandals who always destroy with their cannons and gothas.[2] They will destroy some houses but not the Parisian soul. If you are still in the Paris area and you would like to get acquainted with my parents, it would be an immense pleasure for them to make your acquaintance, and this would equally be a great joy for me. In the eventuality, here is their address Avenue du Chateau, St. Gratien, _____, Gare du Nord [North Train Station], Chemin de Fer Ceinture [Railroad Beltway].

While assuring you once again of my best memories, I remain respectfully yours,

Montí

1. This letter follows the letter of June 5, which mentioned that Montí was anticipating being moved to Mailly. In this undated letter, Montí is in Mailly.

2. The Gotha was a German bomber that had sufficient range to fly bombing raids on England beginning June 13, 1917. Though the raids did not inflict much physical damage, the ability of the Germans to fly across the English Channel was a psychological coup. The G-4 Gothas were powered by two Mercedes engines, flown by a crew of three, carried three 7.92 mm machine guns, and could deliver an 1,100 pound payload. "Gotha" became a generic term used by the allies designating *any* German bomber, which is the way Montí uses it in this letter ("Gotha G Types,"*Dictionary of the War*).

"V. Elie," whose name does not appear in the Machen war correspondence and is of unknown identity, composed the following letter. From the information given in the letter, it is clear that the author and Machen were friends or acquaintances in Missy-sur-Aisne and their contact was probably through the YMCA. In Machen's May 29 letter, he told about his escape from the advancing Germans; "V. Elie" mentions suffering during the week of May 26 to June 2, which must refer to his own flight from the advancing army.

June 24, 1918

Dear Mr. Machen,

We received your charming letter dated June 12th with much pleasure. However, I was expecting a letter, and the previous evening, when we received it, I related to my friends that you most certainly would not have left us without news.

Indeed, this letter came to us at a moment when you would have been happy and content to be with us. For a few days, our meals brought us into a situation that left behind all the best moments of our stay in Missy. Moreover, we had great need to replenish ourselves because we suffered considerably during the week of May 26th to June 2nd. But in summary, apart from fatigue, a lack of sleep, and sometimes insufficient food—the fault of not having the necessary time to prepare and eat it—we are quite happy to be away from this business. Neither killed, nor wounded C.H.R.[3] Only the two horses of the colonel were killed by the same shell during the night of the 26th or 27th of May. Following the fatigue of this retreat, I developed an attack of nerves and I am now in a hospital in Beauvais. If I were still at C.H.R., I would look into this matter of your suitcase and I would make an effort to get it to you. So then, I can only advise you, if you don't receive a response from Sergeant Major Aube, then write to either Lieutenant Potrel or Lieutenant Desert who will do their utmost possible to get it to you if it is still in our care, which I cannot assure you.

Mr. Machen, please believe that we have the best memories of the good relationship that existed between you and us during your

3. The meaning of this abbreviation is unknown to both the editor and the translator.

stay at Missy. And allow me to say also that I was particularly happy to see the wonderful resistance, which has permitted once again the stop of the German invasion. Perhaps it will one day be possible for you to tell us a definite, fixed location where you are, and during the course of my placement, we would have the opportunity to pass through the same region, and it would be a pleasure to go tell you "hello," and perhaps also seek out the pleasure of tasting a cup of your excellent (hot) chocolate.

And in closing, my comrades and I remain devotedly yours.

V. Elie

Mentioned in three letters to his mother dated July 4, 8, and 13, Machen commented that Montí had not yet received in the mail the new uniform he purchased and mailed to him. In the July 4 letter, Machen commented that the uniform was a "costly" purchase made in Paris. The concern over the uniform continued into August when on the 15th, Machen commented that, "Several letters have come from Montí. He has never received the fine uniform which I had sent him from Paris some two months ago." Beginning with the letter below, Montí tells Machen of his efforts regarding the wayward uniform.

July 17, [1918]

Dear Sir,

I am back here from leave, as you must think. I spent happy days with my dear parents. During my stay with my loved ones, we spoke at length of you and your kindnesses of which my parents and I are so appreciative. I passed by North Aguesseau[4] to see, by chance, if you were in Paris at the time. Regrettably, they said "no." I was amazed at the extent of the buildings that the Y.M.C.A. occupies. While in Paris, I stopped by on the 4th of July, and I noted with pleasure that the rapport between the French and the

4. This is the street location of the YMCA offices in Paris.

Americans has improved. I am once again in Mailly. Upon my return here, I found a good letter from you for which I want to thank you very much. Unfortunately, I have not yet received the uniform you so generously offered me—but I am not worried—I do not expect it before a month. I wrote to _____ and asked him under what conditions the mailing took place, and these _____ are quite serious about having taken guarantees for the arrival of the package. Murillan has moved up to *brigadier*, which means corporal.[5] He asked me to mention his respect and appreciation. Please be assured that the two of us will often have fond memories of our little time in Missy, and above all, our very good Director, because, as for me, I owe you such appreciation that thoughts of you will never leave me.

    While hoping for the pleasure to hear from you next, I am respectfully yours,

Montí

July 30, [1918]

Dear Sir

    I am allowing myself to write you a few lines to find out your news, which I hope is still good. I think my last letters addressed to Rue d'Aguesseau have been received. When receiving your last letter, I was very shocked to see American stamps on it. I am hoping however that you are still in France and that this circumstance is due to your stay in an American sector. Quite frankly, the military operations are now turning to our advantage and the last German offensive attempt ended with great failure. Thanks to the intervention of the United States, I hope we will see a victorious end to this war next year. I must give my compliments on the value

5. The editor does not know the identity of Murillan. It is clear from the context of Montí's comment that he and Machen were familiar with Murillan and had some experiences together.

of the fighting spirit of your fellow countrymen whose praise is on everyone's lips. As for me, I am still at Mailly. We are continuing our repairs; I think we are here for two more months. I am temporarily spending my time removed from the front line, but I have the hope of being useful soon because certain units rendered enormous service in the latest battles. Unfortunately, the gift you have sent me has not reached me yet, but there is still no reason to worry, and if it is not stolen, it will eventually arrive here.

Now and then, it would be so kind of you to share your news with me, which I will always receive with great pleasure because it is with emotion that I recall your warmth and your kindness.

With assurances of my appreciation, I am respectfully yours,

Montí

Please write me at the following: St. Gratiens du Chateau ____ Oise

September 8, [1918]

Dear Sir,

While waiting for news from you, I am allowing myself to go back to corresponding with you. I am hoping you are still in good health, to the satisfaction of the Poilu whose morale you know how to raise so well with your devotion.[6] I hope you have received my last letters. I am announcing the receipt of the package, of this superb uniform that you sent to me. I still insist on thanking you a thousand times and expressing all my appreciation.

At this time, the caterpillars are working some from all sides. My section is still in Mailly but our departure is pending, and I

6. As was seen in the Machen letters, "Poilu" is the French slang for a soldier in the way "Doughboy" was the common term for the American soldier. The translator adds that "poilu" is a term normally applied to animals and its application to the French soldier describes him as a "hairy beast." These hairy beasts must have picked up their name due to the lack of opportunities to shave while fighting for their lives at the front.

expect we will be leaving the camp in just a few days. It is a matter of leaving for an American sector, but. . . .[7]

The news and communications continue to be excellent and the Germans are really being hammered. It is unbelievable to have succeeded with a stroke of genius after the two awful failures at the beginning of the year. The name of General Foch will be immortal. I believe when the hour calls, your fellow countrymen will be giving the final blow, and the German beast will no longer wag his tongue. You will find here a group of comrades from Missy who appreciate you and remember you with great pleasure.

Respectfully yours,

Montí

[in sequence but undated][8]

Dear Sir

What a joy it was yesterday to receive your generous gift of a uniform! I do not know how to thank you. It really is too much for me. I could never be appreciative enough of all your kindnesses. The uniform fits me admirably well; one would say it is custom made. I am not going to dare to put it on for fear of ruining it because it is so fine. The package went on quite a trip to reach me. Finally, it was necessary to expedite it to the _____ who did not understand much. But having seen my address on the first paper, he called me in and it all became clear. Unfortunately, we are still in Mailly. It is a bit shocking to stay idle for some time when all the other poor souls are crying out unceasingly.[9] I hope you are in good

7. The implication is that what will really happen is up-in-the-air.

8. The previous letter and this letter both tell Machen of Montí's having received the uniform. It may be that Montí believed the first letter did not get through for some reason. The editor believes this undated letter is the second in the sequence because Montí tells Machen that he has tried it on and it fits, etc.

9. The sense here is that the "unfortunates" are crying out, i.e. they are doing their part, yet there is no relief (translator's note).

health and shielded from all danger. I must go now because the work hour is approaching.

Once again, dear sir, please accept my most sincere thanks and appreciation.

Most respectfully yours,

Montí

September 20, [1918]

Dear Sir

It is with lively pleasure that I read your charming letter of August 19 & 20 that just arrived yesterday. As busy as you are, I thank you for thinking of me and for setting aside your precious time to write to me. However, I do not understand why your letters take so long to reach me. Almost a month. But the essential thing is that they arrive, for the most part. Your service sounds very interesting but must give you plenty of trouble to direct. It is true that you must be rewarded for your efforts by the satisfaction you get out of your work. As for me, I am obligated to tell you that I am still at Mailly. We have had several orders to leave with counter orders that followed. It has also been necessary for us to go into the American sector to participate in their attack. Effectively, my division sent fifty something machines, but the ones from my section were not included, and only my lieutenant and his chauffeur gave their help, replacing the head of the Section who is on leave now. I must send you my sincere congratulations on the success accorded to your fellow countrymen who have really had a good _____. Thanks to the valiant American troops, the St. Mihiel's Salient,[10] which was a continual menace for us, has been completely

10. Montí's French original "Les Saillant du St. Mihiel" refers to the American troops' involvement in this battle with the Germans, September 12–16. "Saillant" means "bulge," which in this case referred to the bulge in the trench-lines in a southwesterly direction that

taken out at last. In addition, more importantly, the lot of prisoners and equipment is not to be scorned. Additionally, the Germans are now harassed from all sides and don't know where to turn their head because of the battering given to them on all sides by the Allies. My brother is enlisting to be a soldier. He is in the 20th class. He would then be leaving in a month for J;[11] but preferring to choose his area of service, he is anticipating his orders and is joining the artillery. Since the uniform is too nice to wear here, I sent it back home where I will find it brand new for my next leave one month from now. These ten blessed days are always anticipated with impatience, I assure you. My parents have asked me to express their appreciation to you for all your kindnesses on my behalf, and naturally, I am sending mine. I sent you a little photo card about 8 days ago; I hope you have received it.

With the hope that my letter will find you in good health, I am respectfully yours,

Montí

November 7, [1918][12]

Dear Sir

I've been deprived of your news for a very long time. All the same, I hope that you are still in good health and that you were spared this awful illness that caused such trouble. After having done an assignment of 15 days in the American sector, we have returned to Mailly. Since the happy events of my last letter _____ Germany is now completely _____, ____[indiscernable]_____

---

peaked at St. Mihiel from the major line running northwest to southeast between Verdun and Nancy ("St. Mihiel, Battle of" and Map 3, p. 539, *Dictionary of the War*).

11. An abbreviation that had meaning for both the sender and recipient but none for the editor or translator. It may be an abbreviation for the French term for what Americans would call "boot camp."

12. This letter was written in haste, on a small piece of paper, and many of the words are faint yielding several un-translated words in the English rendition.

and unerringly lost _____ in a struggle without end and that she will not delay in disarming and completely evacuating our dear France. What is left at this time is to show more and more honor to the courage and valor of your fellow countrymen _____ appreciate the _____ qualities _____.

Montí

———— ⬦⬦⬦ ————

December 2, [1918]

Dear Sir

    I assure you it was a great pleasure to receive your letter of November 18th. This last Sunday, having come to spend 2 hours back home, I received news of you. I am happy to hear that you are in good health and are safe & sound. I heartily congratulate you for the comfort and the services you have rendered to the French soldiers. Please excuse the disjointedness of my letter. I am doing poorly. For a month, I have had different tremors that have weakened me, and I have had several fairly strong attacks of nerves that have worn me out. Consequently, they had to evacuate me, and since yesterday, I am in the hospital at Fr____. I am not terribly sick, but I am concerned about getting well so that these nervous crises do not come back anymore. I would have greatly insisted on seeing you, but Sunday, I was only able to stop by my home, and I was not able to make inquiries about you with so little time. I would have wanted so much to shake your hand. Moreover, I hope that you will not leave France right away and perhaps when I am recovering, I will have the pleasure of seeing you. I would like to talk about some serious things regarding the post-war. In fact, I am not aware if the work of my father will resume after the war, and only with great difficulty will I be working in my trade with others, having not been raised with this goal. So, if later on I have need of your support and recommendation, and if you have knowledge of some kind of employment I could fill alongside your friends who are staying in France, I will be very appreciative if you think of me and inform me. Please excuse my boldness, I beg you. I am taking the liberty of this approach knowing the amiable friendship you have toward me, and I am sure that you will not be offended. Perhaps my father had the pleasure of seeing you. I know he was supposed to go to the Rue d'Aquesseau to try to see you and to thank you for all your kindness on my behalf.

I would be so appreciative if you would continue to send me your news, which I advise you to address to St. Gratien.

Respectfully yours,

Montí

January 3, 1919

Dear Sir

On the occasion of the New Year, please permit me to send you my most sincere wishes of happiness. The year 1918 finished long years of misery, of suffering, and of worries. So it is with a smiling eye that we can welcome the New Year, which announces itself with radiance. I hope this letter will find you in good health. Maybe you are no longer in France. As for me, I am still in the hospital, and I have successively been evacuated to Troyes, Limoges, Paris, and now I am finally at Neuilly-sur-Marne. In short, what I have is weakness, and it will take some time to recover. I would be very happy if I received your news because it is always with appreciation and emotion that I think of you. Once again, dear Sir, Happy New Year.

Respectfully yours,

Montí

January 11, 1919

Dear Sir

Having received a visit from my father on Thursday, I've had the pleasure of receiving the letter you sent to my home. I am happy to know that you are still in France and especially in Paris. I think then I will be able to shake your hand one day. I am actually in the military hospital in the town of Evrard. It is next to Neuilly, about a half an hour from Paris by train. I feel better. I even believe I have recovered, and I hope these accidents will never reoccur. But it was just 3 weeks ago, I was in pitiable condition, always hurting and having more nerve attacks. Here I can see my family now and then, and I hope to go on leave during the day tomorrow on Sunday. The hospital of the town of Evrard is a former insane asylum. Moreover, there is bloodletting in some of these buildings. In my building, there are those who are seriously wounded and some with illnesses like mine. It pains me to notice the poor consideration they give to the foreign wounded. The draconian regulations, as they were in the days of the insane asylum, are still in place, and we are completely deprived of freedom. I would have believed that after 4 years of battle, we would have the right to some gratitude or at least a little comfort. It is not just me. You could see this for yourself if your _____[13] would allow you to come up here. I am happy to hear that Paris pleases you and am content to see you appreciating literature and French theater. I regret that they changed your post if your former one suited you better. However, I am sure that your presence is as useful for the public good in this service as well as it was in the other, no harm intended.

While hoping to see you soon, I remain respectfully yours,

Montí

13. Montí may be referring to someone or something that is necessary for Machen to have in order to visit him, such as a leave from a superior and/or an official document granting him permission to travel. Due to the limitations of the rail service, the relocation of troops, and other post-war logistical problems, personal travel was greatly limited.

[January 13, 1919][14]

Dear Sir

I learned this morning that unfortunately, you troubled yourself for nothing.

I deeply regret it. It is really a case of bad luck because it is the first time I went out of this cursed hospital. And you wouldn't believe how much I regret that I did not see you. I dare to hope that you will want to do this little trip a second time. I am unbelievably bored here. In addition, this feeling of always being cooped up is very painful.

While hoping to see you shortly, would you please allow me to shake your hand warmly?

Montí

February 7th, 1919

Dear Sir,

I am currently recovering and completely regaining my health. I hope you will soon be returning to Paris, and I intend to come to your hotel shortly. I hope to have the pleasure of finding you in good health and spending a few good moments with you. In the end, being back with my family is completely restoring my health, and I hope that under their watchful eye, I will eventually get through these painful events. While hoping I will soon have the pleasure of seeing you, I remain respectfully yours,

Montí

FINIS

14. This date is the day before the stamped cancelation date on the accompanying envelope.

SOME CLOSING THOUGHTS

GIVEN THE GREAT AMOUNT of correspondence written by J. Gresham Machen during his war experience, it is appropriate to draw out some reoccurring themes and points of particular interest. It should be remembered that, with a few exceptions, these letters were written to family members and they contain some of Machen's thoughts that he might not express to more casual correspondents or professional associates. The letters reveal his thoughts about the war, the "Y," the church services he attended, his return to his work at Princeton, his thoughts about those with whom he worked, his frustrations, and his concern for the spiritual welfare of the soldiers of the AEF. However, as mentioned in the introduction to this letter collection, Dr. Machen meticulously collected his own correspondence for posterity; Machen may even have published his own correspondence if he had been providentially granted a longer life. With respect to the war letters, the editor believes that due to the encouragement of his family regarding the letters it is almost certain that he wanted them published.

Dr. Machen wanted to take advantage of his opportunity to learn the French language and enjoy as much of the national literature as possible when he had breaks from his "Y" responsibilities. He was a scholar and New Testament Greek was the language he used constantly in his profession, so the acquisition of French in the land of the French was a wonderful opportunity to expand his linguistic abilities. Coupled with his desire to learn the French language were concerns that he should be sensitive to the French culture and people. During his initial time in Paris, he pointed out to his family the lack of concern of the great mass of Americans in the war to learn even a few words of French. Machen sought as many opportunities as possible to immerse himself in the French language and its culture as he awaited his first YMCA assignment in Paris, and he continued to study and acquire

315

the language as he had time during the remainder of his "Y" service. After the war ended in November 1918, he remained in France with the "Y" for several months and continued to study French, learn from the Paris academics as he worked on his James Sprunt Lectures, and imbibe as much of the culture as he could. Though he became a vendor of snacks, toiletries, and hot chocolate as part of his "Y" work, he continued as a professional to learn when and what he could.

During the First World War, J. Ross Stevenson was a member of the YMCA Religious Work Bureau that was responsible to decide how the organization would handle the spiritual side of its program overseas.[1] Stevenson had introduced Machen to "Y" work and encouraged him to join in its labors.[2] During a visit by Stevenson to France, November 1918, Dr. Machen had the opportunity to meet with him, but his letter home recounting the event does not mention the subject of their discussion.[3] By the end of December, he commented to his mother, "If my conscience were quite at rest on the matter of principle upon which Dr. Stevenson and I differ so widely, I should be happy now." The "matter of principle" to which he referred involved curriculum changes that Dr. Stevenson desired for Princeton Seminary. There was a move to ease the biblical language requirement and then fill the open slots with English Bible and practical theology courses. Further, there was, according to some faculty, a movement to turn from the seminary's Reformed heritage and diminish the teaching of Calvinism as it was taught by Samuel Miller, the Alexanders, the Hodges, and B. B. Warfield. A few months before Dr. Machen's departure for France, B. B. Warfield had written in *The Presbyterian* that, "What we need in our pulpits is scholar-saints become preachers. And it is the one business of the theological seminaries to make them."[4] The Ken-

---

1. The other members included Ralph W. Harbison, Chairman, Clarence A. Barbour, Bishop Charles S. Burch, Walter Kidde, W. Douglas Mackenzie, William B. Millar, John D. Rockefeller, Jr., Robert W. Spear, and Bishop Luther B. Wilson. See *Service with Fighting Men: An Account of the Work of the American Young Men's Christian Associations in the World War*, vol. 2, William Howard Taft, Frederick Harris, Frederic H. Kent, and William J. Newlin, eds. (New York: Association Press, 1922), 560; the official YMCA history of its work during the First World War, including history, maps, photographs, descriptions of the varied fields and types of "Y" work, floor plans of "Y" installations, and several lists including a causality list. See also Stonehouse, 212, regarding Stevenson and his work in the YMCA.

2. Stonehouse, 212.

3. MGM, 11/21/1918.

4. Nov. 22, 1917; reprinted in, J. E. Meeter, Vol. 1, *Selected Shorter Writings: Benjamin B. Warfield* (Phillipsburg, NJ: P&R, 1973), 378.

tucky theologian believed it was essential for ministers to be thoroughly equipped for the ministry, and his colleague and protégé, J. Gresham Machen, was likewise concerned that seminary students have the tools to minister the Word of God accurately.[5] The division at Princeton over the curriculum was indicative of problems that would develop over the next decade as the seminary moved to a more inclusive, less Calvinistic, and more practical theology oriented program.[6] As he had mentioned in an earlier letter to his mother, Machen's article, "The Minister and his Greek Testament," had been published since his arrival in France in 1918.[7] In that brief article, he contended that the minister must be a specialist in the Bible, and that for one to be a specialist or expert in the Bible it is necessary to know the languages of the Bible. So, Dr. Machen thought that due to his opposition to the curriculum changes at Princeton, J. Ross Stevenson, in his administrative capacity with the YMCA, had blocked or delayed him from serving in the religious work and that he was responsible for Machen's being posted in Paris rather than with the troops. However, he found out that he had drawn the wrong conclusion from the evidence, and that it was instead Dr. King and not Dr. Stevenson who had him moved to Paris due to rumors that Machen's sermon/ lecture content was "too long and too deep."[8] Whatever Machen said about Stevenson to his mother has been lost because he asked her to snip the comments about Stevenson from the letters he sent home. Later, Machen mentioned seeing Dr. Stevenson in France again and said that he better understood Stevenson's views on theological education for American students, though he did not agree with his perspective. He added, "At any rate, Dr. Stevenson is my friend after all."[9] Though there was peace in the mind of Machen at this point, his assessment of the situation with Dr. Stevenson would change over the course of the next decade.

5. Benjamin Breckinridge Warfield was born in Kentucky. For an interesting biographical article on B. B. Warfield, see Bradley J. Gundlach, " 'B' is for Breckinridge: Benjamin B. War- field, His Maternal Kin, and Princeton Seminary," in, Gary L. W. Johnson, ed., *B. B. Warfield: Essays on His Life and Thought*, Phillipsburg: P&R, 2007, 13-53.

6. See, Hart, 119-28, for his analysis of how the desire for curriculum changes contrib- uted to the events leading to Machen's resignation from Princeton and founding Westminster Theological Seminary.

7. Letter to MGM, 3/7/1918; *The Presbyterian*, 88 (Feb. 7, 1918) 8-9; reprinted in J. Gresham Machen, ed. by D. G. Hart, *Selected Shorter Writings* (Phillipsburg, NJ: P&R, 2004), 210–13.

8. MGM, 1/12/1919; 1/17/1919.

9. MGM, 1/12/1919.

While serving with the YMCA in France, Dr. Machen attended Sunday services whenever he could at the place available to him whether in urban Paris or near the trenches. In some cases, he attended French Protestant services as he had done while awaiting his orders in Paris after arriving in France. Mme. Lalot and Machen heard Alfred Monod preach on "give us this day our daily bread," about which he commented, "I was disappointed. It was all perfectly good in its way. But it was not at all the bread of life."[10] Later in the month he found services on his own as he "attended the French Protestant service at the church near the Etoile in the morning, and in the evening went to the McCall Mission at 8 Boulevarde Bonne Nouvelle. The McCall Mission was interesting."[11] Not long before his departure to return to America, Machen gave 2000 francs to the McCall mission. Initially, he wanted the funds to be used to help the mission's ministry to war orphans, but the director encouraged him to give the money to the evangelistic ministry instead. Machen commented to his mother:

> This [giving to McCall] seems better than simply giving through the Red Cross. I wish I had had time to inspect the work of the McCall mission—notably their school & their headquarters, to which I was cordially invited. I must say that the preacher at the station on the Boulevard Bonne Nouvelle, whom I have heard several times, does not impress me very favorably. The gospel in his preaching is too much chocked by a lot of stuff about social conditions. But the human instruments of preaching are never perfect, and I suppose on the whole that the McCall mission is doing as good a work as any agency in France. The present condition of the French nation is one gigantic tragedy of which the war is only a part.[12]

Surrounded with the death and destruction of war, J. Gresham Machen wanted to do something to relieve the misery of France's condition while remaining true to his commitment to biblical and

10. MGM, 2/5/1918.
11. MGM, 2/14/1918.
12. MGM, 3/2/1919.

confessional Christianity.[13] By giving to the McCall Mission, he made the best selection he believed he could make in his current situation. He was not completely satisfied with the preaching at the mission, but his desire to donate funds to help the French people led him to give to the organization he thought was most in accord with his own theological commitments. With respect to Sunday worship, he found himself making compromises so that he could worship with other Christians. In some cases, he could not worship at all due to the intrusion of the war.

Sometimes the best Dr. Machen could find for a Sunday service was one led by a Roman Catholic. While he was working in the "Y" in "Camp de la Grande Voivre" ("Mud Camp"), he attended the services of the camp's Roman Catholic chaplain. He commented to his mother that:

> This morning the chaplain of the regiment, who is a catholic, has just held a general service & is now celebrating mass as I write. The general service was frankly supernatural—the loaves and fishes—and satisfactory. The reading of the Gospels was urged, & the moral exhortations were good. As hymns we had "Onward Christian Soldiers," "Lead, Kindly Light." I was pleased with the service. It was far, far better than what we get from the Protestant liberals.[14]

Dr. Machen praised the "general service" because it was supernatural. The biblical texts containing accounts of the loaves and fishes tell of the feeding of thousands with only a few fish and pieces of bread. However, though Machen praised aspects of the chaplain's service, when it came time for the sacrifice of the mass, he chose to write his mother a letter. Insofar as the chaplain was consistent with biblical, supernatural Christianity, Machen believed he could benefit from the service, but when the proceedings turned to transubstantiation, and the sacrifice of the mass, it was time to write a letter. The final

13. In the letter to his mother written Aug. 1, 1918, he commented that his participation in the "religious work" of the YMCA was not as difficult for him as it had been because, "The confessional barriers between myself and the men who live here are no longer so serious."
14. MGM, 6/29/1918.

comment in the quoted portion above says that the general portion of the service was better than "what we get from the Protestant liberals," and it was better because it respected the miraculous, the supernatural, the ministry of Christ as he overruled the laws of creation by greatly multiplying a few bits of food into a feast for thousands. The supernatural gospel would be foundational to Dr. Machen's teaching. He would go on in his James Sprunt Lectures to affirm the supernatural origin of Paul's teaching, and then in *Christianity and Liberalism* he would define liberalism as another religion due to its opposition to the supernatural.

Dr. Machen tried to organize Bible studies with the troops and later in his "Y" work led services during his association with the "religious work." Though he found the term "religious work" objectionable, he believed it was the work for which he was most suited.[15] While he was working in the Foyer du Soldat program with the French, the mass of people he made contact with were French Roman Catholics. The sense one gets as the YMCA war literature is read is that the leaders of the American "Y" were worried about how their predominantly Protestant program was going to mesh with the almost totally Catholic constituency of the "Y" in France. There is an air of "don't step on any toes" in the instructional literature about the content of speeches and lectures to be delivered by YMCA speakers.[16] Machen commented while he was awaiting his first "Y" assignment that, "All my training is for Bible teaching and the like which is not done in the slightest among the French troops, and indeed for certain reasons must be carefully excluded."[17] In June, early in his work with the American "Y" program following his hasty exit from Missy-sur-Aisne and its Foyer du Soldat program, he expressed his frustration over having to piece together services for the troops. At one point, he found a chaplain to lead the evening service and Machen was going to lead the morning service. However, the morning service ended up being the reading of a Bible chapter and praying with "six or eight men."[18] By the end of the month

15. MGM, 12/17/1918; Machen was not fond of the term "religious work." He commented, "I hate that expression 'religious-work' so that I always put it in quotation marks."

16. See the booklet *Suggestions for Speakers Concerning Y.M.C.A. War Work*, published by the YMCA, regarding how YMCA speakers were expected to behave and contour their speaking.

17. MGM, 1/29/1918.

18. MGM, 6/23/1918.

of June, he held a service during the week with but a few men present. On that Sunday, he held a Bible study with about a half-dozen men before the morning service was led by the chaplain.[19] Machen commented later in the summer, "This afternoon, for example, I hope to get two or three men together for prayer and Bible reading. We may find a comparatively quiet place at the edge of camp."[20] Even when he was working in the "religious work," he found it difficult to lead the soldiers in services, organize Bible studies, and have prayer. Given that Sunday was often payday for the troops, when sporting activities were enjoyed, movies were shown, song and dance shows performed, and when special meetings were held, Machen's complaints about the difficulty of serving the soldiers' spiritual needs can be easily understood—it seems as though the military leadership, in some situations, intentionally organized events to conflict with the "religious work." Though the YMCA provided a vital service by having a library, selling snacks and sundries, and giving out writing paper, the "Christian" part of the organization's name became lost in its ambiguous branch designated the "religious work." One has to wonder, given that the American troops had chaplains, why the "Y" tried to have "religious work." It may be that the "Y" leadership believed the military chaplains would not be able to handle the theological opposition presented by a Roman Catholic country. It should be remembered that in the later decades of the nineteenth century and into the early years of the twentieth there were strong anti-Catholic sentiments in America due to the influx of immigrants from southern Europe. By the time of the Second World War, the military would take over the responsibilities that had been addressed by the "Y" in the First World War. As Machen went through his months of service he expressed disenchantment with the YMCA and commented on the "immense superiority of the opportunity offered by the chaplaincy" and that the "deeper elements of the [YMCA] work are crowded out in one way or another."[21]

As Dr. Machen's YMCA responsibilities lessened later in his time of service, he took advantage of the educational opportunities available in Paris. During the course of his letter writing, he expressed con-

19. MGM, 6/29/1918.
20. MGM, 7/8/1918.
21. Ibid.

cern about the Sprunt Lectures he was scheduled to deliver at Union Theological Seminary, Virginia, in 1921. He felt that the months with the "Y" had caused him to fall behind in his reading of contemporary scholarship. Though the French theologians in Paris would not be as beneficial for his purposes as the German theologians, he took advantage of what was available and looked for lectures. He began by attending two classes taught by a New Testament professor on the Protestant faculty, Maurice Goguel. Machen commented briefly and to the point, "He is very wrong in his views, I regret to say."[22] His next choice to hear lecture was Alfred Firmin Loisy, who had been excommunicated by the Roman Catholic Church for his views. Machen described him as "a man whose books are exceedingly important even though they are not true." The course Machen attended for two lectures was on Paul and Judaizing Christianity, a subject that would contribute to his Sprunt Lectures and their publication in *The Origin of Paul's Religion*.[23] Charles Guignebert offered lectures on 2 Corinthians and the teaching of Jesus at the Sorbonne, Machen attended and described them as "rather shallow and rather flippant."[24] The final venture into the world of French Protestant theological professors took place when he heard Édouard Dujardin lecture on the origin of the Eucharist. Once again, Machen provided a succinct perspective when he commented, "Dujardin seems to have some wild idea about a pre-Christian Jesus cult, after the manner of Drews or W. B. Smith."[25] All in all, Dr. Machen did not think much of what France had to offer in New Testament studies. The only Paris theological academic mentioned in *The Origin of Paul's Religion* was Loisy due to, as Machen said, the importance of his books.[26]

War provides an opportunity for people to do things that they would never choose to do on their own. Though J. Gresham Machen's service was that of a non-combatant, he was still faced with conditions that required a considerable ability to adapt to dangerous and culturally different situations. In France, Machen worshipped God as he had

22. MGM, 1/5/1919; 1/12/1919.
23. MGM, 1/12/1919.
24. MGM, 1/17/1919.
25. Ibid.
26. J. Gresham Machen, *The Origin of Paul's Religion* (New York: Macmillan, 1923; reprint, Birmingham: Solid Ground Christian Books, 2006), 47, 76, 229, 262.

the opportunity in churches and special services. Surely, he would rather have been home in a Presbyterian Church, but he made do with services offered by everything from the McCall Mission street preacher to a Roman Catholic chaplain. He was well educated and enjoying the fruit of his academic labors as a professor at Princeton Seminary, but his "Y" work would not at first allow him to use his gifts for the "religious work." In the States, he enjoyed the privileges of his family estate as he traveled to Seal Harbor, Maine, for his summer vacations, and his finances were sufficient that he could shop at Brooks Brothers and have his suits tailor-made. Machen was always well dressed in his homeland. In France, he spent months in a wet wool uniform, the odor of which was further enhanced by his own filthy body that had not been bathed in months. When he began work with the YMCA, his whole world was turned upside down just as were the worlds of the other countless AEF personnel and support organizations. Instead of riding a bicycle through the quaint village of Princeton, he was grabbing rides on ambulances, military trucks, trains, camionettes, and "Fords." Machen enjoyed sports, but the sport he adapted to in France was trapping and killing rats. Instead of teaching Greek and New Testament studies in the classroom, he created opportunities, with varying degrees of success, to minister the Word of God to the soldiers. It must have been quite a scene to behold Dassy standing over a hot cauldron of chocolate in his matted and filthy uniform, greasy hair, and at times, unshaven beard. In all of this, Machen had adapted to a desperate situation in the hopes that by doing his bit and helping the soldiers in the First World War, the allied victory would deliver Europe from oppression and provide for a lasting peace.

GLOSSARY OF PEOPLE, PLAYS, LITERATURE, AND OTHER WORDS OF INTEREST

NAMES MENTIONED IN THE letters, such as "Arly" or "Cousin Saida," are listed in the glossary as Machen wrote them. The editor is especially thankful for the information about Dr. Machen's family provided by Grace Mullen. Machen family entries that have no documentation cited were provided by her.

Adine: the wife of Lewis H. Machen.

Arly: see Machen, Arthur W., II.

Army: William Park Armstrong (1874–1944), a graduate of the College of New Jersey, Princeton Seminary, who received degrees from the universities of Marburg and Berlin in Germany. He was the Professor of New Testament Literature and Exegesis at Princeton Seminary, 1903–40, and he became the Graduate Professor of New Testament Exegesis, 1940–44. Army was Machen's closest friend on the Princeton faculty. See O. C. Hopper, *Biographical Catalogue of Princeton Theological Seminary 1815–1914* (Princeton: The Theological Seminary of the Presbyterian Church, 1955), 227.

Aunt Bessie: see Johnson, Elizabeth.

"babies": mentioned several times beginning with the letter of June 29, 1918. At the time of Machen's YMCA work in France, Tom and Nena Machen had two children, Mary Gresham and Arthur W. Machen, III. Machen's mother is mentioned in the letters as caring for the "babies." Machen also used "kiddies," which may or may not refer to the same children.

Balzac, Honoré de (1799–1850): a prolific French novelist. His greatest work is *La Comédie humaine* (1829–1847, *The Human Comedy*), which is a huge work containing interconnected novels and short novels that provide a picture of French society in his era. Some of his other works are

La Cousine Bette (1847, *Cousin Bette*), and *Le Cousin Pons* (1847, *Cousin Pons*). See *The Columbia-Viking Desk Encyclopedia* (New York: The Viking Press, 1953, 1960, 1968); *Merriam Webster's Encyclopedia of Literature* (Springfield: Merriam-Webster, 1995).

Beattie, Lee William (1858–1937): a graduate of Union College, Schenectady, New York, '79, whom Machen describes as "Dr. Beatty." He completed his divinity degree at Princeton Theological Seminary 1879–80 and 1881–83. See *Princeton Biographical*, 105; *The Benham Club of Princeton, New Jersey* (Princeton: Benham Club, 1912), 55.

Beaumarchais, Pierre Augustin Caron de (1732–1799): began his vocational life as a watchmaker. He invented a watch escapement mechanism but controversy over its patent led to litigation. He turned from the mechanical world of watch making to writing dramas. He produced *Le Mariage de Figaro* (1784, *The Marriage of Figaro*) and *Le Barbier de Séville* (1775, *The Barber of Seville*), which became sources for operas for Rossini and Mozart respectively. He also published the first complete works of Voltaire (*Columbia Encyclopedia*; *Webster's Literature*).

Benham Club: a dining club for students in Princeton. J. G. Machen was a member of the club and made several friends during his years at its table. The club was started in 1879 by the widow Anna Amelia Benham (*Benham Club*, 3–4).

Bérénice: see Racine, Jean.

Bernhardt, Sarah (1844–1923): the stage name of the French actress, Henriette-Rosine Bernard. She performed at the Odéon Theater, 1866–72, at the Comédie Française, 1872–80, after which she toured Europe and the United States. In 1899, she leased the Théâtre des Nations, which was renamed the Théâtre Sarah Bernhardt where she played in Rostand's *L'Aiglon* (*The Eaglet*) in 1900. She made two silent films in 1912 and even continued acting after having her leg amputated in 1915. She was known for her remarkable voice and her controversial personal life, which she revealed in her memoirs, *Ma double vie* (*My Double Life*) in 1907. See *Columbia Encyclopedia*; *Webster's Literature*).

Bernstein, Henry-Leon Gustave-Charles (1876–1953): a French playwright who gained his early fame for writing melodramas, but who later turned to more serious subjects. His first play, *Le Marché* (*The Market*) was produced in 1900 at the Théâtre-Libre in Paris. In 1907, he wrote *Samson*, which was a violent and fast-paced drama. The play that Machen saw on February 9, 1918, *L'Elévation* (*The Elevation*), was first performed at the Comédie Française on June 6, 1917. In America *The New York Times* reported that Bernstein had written the play while recuperating in a hospital from wounds he received as an aviator for the Saloniki army. This play shows the uplifting influence of war on the leading characters. *The Times* concluded its report by saying, "Profound emotion, which gripped actors and audiences alike, marked this premiere as unforgettable" (*Webster's Literature; Columbia Encyclopedia*).

Betty: a household servant who was particularly helpful to Dr. Machen's mother. Machen sometimes greeted her in the letters he wrote to his mother.

Bird, Brooke: a relative of Machen who went to France to fly in the war.

Bossuet, Jacques-Bénigne (1627–1704): the Roman Catholic bishop of Condom, France. He was known for funerary orations, prose, and theological tracts (*Webster's Biographical*).

Bourget, Paul-Charles-Joseph (1852–1935): a French critic, poet, and novelist. *Le Disciple* (*The Disciple*) was published in 1889 and showed a change in Bourget's thinking as he moved towards conversion to Roman Catholicism in 1901. Bourget prefaced this novel with an appeal to the youth to abide by traditional morality. Thus, Machen's positive comment that it was a "remarkable novel" may reflect his own theological interests (*Webster's Biographical*).

Brunetière, Ferdinand (Vincent de Paul-Marie-Ferdinand) (1849–1906): became professor of literature at the École Normale, Paris, 1886, then he went on to be a lecturer at the Sorbonne in 1893. Some of his published works are, *Études critiques* (1880–1907, *Critical Studies*), *Le Roman Naturaliste* (1883, *The Roman Naturalist*), and *L'Évolution de la poésie lyrique* (1894, *The Development of Lyric Poetry*) (*Webster's Biographical*).

Carrie: see Hammond, Carrie Machen.

Charlie: Charlie Buchanan, mentioned in Dr. Machen's letter to "Miss Marie" dated March 18, 1918. The letter mentions that Charlie served in the First World War. He was a close childhood friend of Dr. Machen.

Clare: Clare de Graffenried, Minnie Machen's friend from her childhood days in Macon, Georgia. She lived in Washington, DC, and held a position of responsibility in the Bureau of Statistics. Visits were exchanged frequently and she was a close friend of the family.

Corneille, Pierre (1606–1684): considered the creator of French classical tragedy. His first play, *Mélite*, was a comedy that was first performed in Paris in 1630. His tragi-comedy *Le Cid* (1637) is considered by many the most significant play in the history of French drama, which was followed by his Roman tragedy *Horace* (1641), then his *Cinna* (1643), and his fourth classical work was *Polyeucte* (1643). Corneille turned to comedy in 1644 with *Le Menteur* (*The Liar*) (*Webster's Literature*).

Corneille, Thomas (1625–1709): the younger brother of Pierre Corneille. Thomas was a successful dramatic poet in his own right. The younger Corneille produced no less than sixteen tragedies between 1656 and 1678. His finest work is the tragedy *Ariane* (1672, *The Labyrinth*) (*Webster's Literature*).

Coquelin, Benoît-Constant (1841–1909): known as Coquelin Aîné (Coquelin the Elder), he was an actor with the Comédie-Française (1860–92). His most famous role was playing Cyrano in *Cyrano de Bergerac*. Ernest-Alexandre-Honore, known as Coquelin Cadet (Coquelin the Younger), was a comedian and actor like his older brother Benoît. However, since both actors died in 1909, either Arly did not know the Coquelins had died or there was another Coquelin (JGM to Arly, 2/21/1919; *Webster's Literature*).

Coquelin, Ernest-Alexandre-Honore (1848–1909): see Coquelin, Benoît-Constant.

Cousin Kensey: Johns Hammond Kensey, who was the husband of Machen's cousin Carrie.

Cousin Saida: the daughter of William Edgeworth Bird and Sarah C. J. Baxter. Sarah was Minnie Machen's aunt, so Saida was Minnie's cousin and the second cousin of J. Gresham Machen.

Cyrano de Bergerac: see Rostand, Edmond.

Dassy: a nickname for Dr. Machen. He was also called "Das." Hart has traced the origin of the nickname to the German *das Mädchen* (the article plus the noun), which means "the maiden." The nickname plays on the similarity between "Machen" and "*Mädchen*" and the German article *das*. The nickname poked a bit of fun at Machen while being a term of endearment (D. G. Hart, *Defending the Faith* [Grand Rapids: Baker Books, 1995], 130–31).

Daudet, Alphonse (1840–1897): a French writer of novels, short stories, and plays who is best known for his portrayal of life in southern France. The play *L'Arlésienne* (1872, *The Woman of Arles*) was a failure when first performed but it was acclaimed when it was revived in 1885. Alphonse's son, Léon (1867–1942), was a French journalist and writer of books on psychology, medicine, politics, and literary criticism, and wrote some novels (*Webster's Literature*).

Dickson, Reid Stuart (1885–1959): studied at Princeton Seminary, 1907–10, was ordained June 21, 1910, and then pastored at New Providence, NJ, 1910–13, until he moved to pastor a church in Lewistown, PA, 1915–23. He then served several positions with the Presbyterian Church boards before becoming an assistant pastor in Pasadena, California, 1950–59. He served with the YMCA, 1917–19. In the Machen war letter of June

7, 1918, Reid is described as "one of the Benham boys," which refers to the student dining association called the Benham Club (*Benham Club*, 5, 59; *Princeton Biographical*, 351).

Drews, Arthur (1865–1935): a German philosopher and professor at Karlsruhe. In the letter to his mother of Jan. 17, 1919, Machen referred to Drews's view of a "pre-Christian Jesus cult." Drews published the book, *Die Christusmythe* (1909, *The Christ Myth*)(*Webster's Biographical*).

Dujardin, Édouard Émile Louis (1861–1949): perhaps the "Dujardin" Machen mentioned in his Jan. 17, 1919, letter to his mother. He was a French journalist and author. He wrote poetry, plays, essays, and novels, and one of his theologically oriented plays is *Le Mystère du Dieu Mort et Resuscité* (1923, *The Mystery of God's Death and Resurrection*)(*Webster's Biographical*).

"Fat Axford": probably John Hall Axford (1889–1929). Rev. Axford served in Alabama churches for his brief ministry, except during the period of his war work with the YMCA (*Princeton Biographical*, 363).

Féraudy, Maurice de (1859–1932): a notable French stage and cinema actor and director. In 1919, he appeared in the film version of René Hervil's play, *L'Ami Fritz* (*Webster's Literature*).

Freeman, Robert (1878–1940): a member of the Princeton Seminary Class of 1907, who was born in Edinburgh, Scotland. He was ordained in a Baptist Church in Buffalo, NY, in 1900. He then served in three other pulpits until he went to Pasadena, CA, to serve the same church from 1911 to 1940 (*Princeton Biographical*, 327).

Gardiner: a contact in the YMCA leadership whose help Machen sought to get him into the religious work. He is described by Machen as the "late assistant pastor of the First Church of Princeton" in his letter of Oct. 31, 1918.

Gilbert and Sullivan: the common designation for the teaming of the playwright Sir William Schwenk Gilbert (1836–1911) and the composer, organist, and choirmaster, Sir Arthur Sullivan (1842–1900). In only two weeks, Gilbert wrote *Dulcamara, or the Little Duck and the Great Quack*. The famous team of comic opera writers began their work together with *Thespis, or the Gods Grown Old* (1871) and then *Trial by Jury* (1875). Their success continued with *H.M.S. Pinafore* (1878) and then *The Pirates of Penzance* (1879). The play mentioned by Dr. Machen, *The Mikado* (1885), is Gilbert and Sullivan's famous opera that tells the story of a man from Japanese royalty who is romantically interested in a woman who is the ward of a small-town tailor (*Webster's Biographical; Webster's Literature*).

Gilman, Daniel Colt (1831–1908): served for twenty-five years as Johns Hopkins University's first president. Before Johns Hopkins, he was a professor of geography at the Sheffield Scientific School of Yale, 1861–1872, and then president of the University of California, 1872–1875 (*Webster's Biographical*).

Goguel, Maurice (1880–1955): Professor of Exegesis and New Testament Criticism in the Faculty of Free Protestant Theology (Paris). Three of his books are *Jésus de Nazareth, Mythe ou Histoire* (*Jesus of Nazareth, Myth or History*, 1925), *L'Apôstre Paul et Jésus Christ* (*The Apostle Paul and Jesus Christ*, 1904), and *Vie de Jésus* (*Life of Jesus*, 1932) ("Goguel, [Henry] Maurice," Raymond W. Albright, in Douglas, ed., *New 20th Century Encyclopedia of Religious Knowledge*, 2nd ed. [Grand Rapids: Baker, 1991]).

Gresham, LeRoy (1871–1955): a first cousin of Dr. Machen and the son of Thomas Baxter and Jessie Rhett Gresham. Dr. Machen and Loy grew up together and were as close as brothers. Loy was a PCUS pastor serving in Salem, Virginia, from 1909 until he retired in 1946. Before entering the ministry, he practiced law in Baltimore, 1896–1903 (E. C. Scott, *Ministerial Directory of the Presbyterian Church, U.S. 1861–1941* [Austin: Order of the General Assembly, 1942], 50).

Gresham, Thomas B.: Minnie Machen's brother, who Dr. Machen referred to as "Uncle." The Machen and Gresham families lived near each other in Baltimore and spent considerable time together. The Greshams had moved to Baltimore in 1887. "Uncle" was an elder in the Franklin Street Presbyterian Church where Dr. Machen's family were members. Thomas had two sons by his first wife, LeRoy ("Loy") and Abbot, who were like brothers to the Machen boys. Elizabeth Johnson was Thomas's second wife.

Guignebert, Charles (1867–1934): had several of his books published in English including: *Jesus* (1935), *The Jewish World in the Time of Jesus* (1939), and *Christianity, Past and Present* (1927)(*Webster's Literature*).

Guitry, Sacha: Alexandre-Georges Guitry (1885–1957), who was born in St. Petersburg, Russia, and became a prodigious French playwright that often acted in his own productions. Some of his plays are *Petite Hollande* (1908, *Little Holland*), *Le Scandale de Monte Carlo* (1908, *The Monte Carlo Scandal*), and the play that Machen saw, *Pasteur* (1919). He wrote, acted, and directed in motion pictures such as *Roman d'un tricheur* (1938, *The Story of a Cheat*). His autobiography, *Mémoires d'un tricheur* (*If I Remember Correctly*) was published in 1935 (*Webster's Literature*).

Hammond, Carrie Machen: Dr. Machen's first cousin and the daughter of his uncle James Machen. Her husband was Kensey Johns Hammond (Cousin Kensey). She visited the family in Baltimore frequently, especially before she married Kensey. Carrie was older than the Machen boys because she often stayed with them when the parents traveled.

Hampden-Sidney: a college in Prince Edward County, Virginia, near Farmville. It traces its history to its organization by Hanover Presbytery as an academy in 1775. Union Theological Seminary was established as a distinct institution on the Hampen-Sidney property in 1823, but its history can be traced to as early as 1806. Union commenced its programs in the current Richmond location in 1898 (Walter W. Moore and Tilden Scherer, *Centennial Catalogue . . . Union Theological Seminary in Virginia* [Richmond: Whittet & Shepperson, 1907], 6–19; the articles on Hampden-Sidney and Union Theological Seminary in Alfred Nevin, *Encyclopedia of the Presbyterian Church* [Philadelphia: Presbyterian Encyclopedia Publishing Co., 1884].)

Helen: Helen Woods Machen, who was the wife of Arly.

Hodges, Richard (died 1933): an alcoholic who lived in southern New Jersey and was financially supported by J. Gresham Machen for over twenty years. Hodges was unable to keep a job and he needed to live in a dry town to assist him in resisting the temptation to drink alcohol. For a study of the friendship between Hodges and Machen, see the editor's, "Mr. Machen's Protégé," *Westminster Theological Journal* 71, no. 1 (Spring 2009): 21–51.

Hugo, Victor (1802–1885): a poet, dramatist, and novelist who is best known to Americans for his *Notre Dame de Paris* (1831, *The Hunchback of Notre Dame*) and *Les Misérables* (1862). He was elected to the Académie Française in 1841 after three unsuccessful attempts. In his later years, Hugo was a politician and noted political writer. Hugo's *Marion de Lorme* is the play that Machen saw with Mme. Lalot in Paris while awaiting his orders for his first YMCA assignment (*Webster's Literature*).

Joanne: not a person, but a published travel guide that Machen used in France. Machen would have preferred a "Baedeker," which was probably not available due to its publication in Germany. The Baedeker guide series was started by Karl Baedeker (1801–1859).

Johnson, Elizabeth: "Aunt Bessie" and the second wife of "Uncle," Thomas B. Gresham.

kiddies: see "babies."

Kirk, Harris Elliott (1872–1953): the pastor of the Franklin Street Presbyterian Church, Baltimore, where the Machens were members. Kirk served the church from 1901 until he died. Kirk was a graduate of both the Southwestern Presbyterian University and its Divinity School that were both located in Clarksville, Tennessee. The divinity school was open from 1885 to 1917. Southwestern University moved to Memphis in 1925 and is currently named Rhodes College (*Dictionary P.C.U.S.*, 379; W. R. Cooper, *Southwestern at Memphis 1848–1948* [Richmond: John Knox Press, 1949]).

Laird, Melvin Robert (1877–1946): attended Princeton 1902–1903, but completed his divinity education at McCormick in 1905. He was the president of Lincoln College, 1917–18; a chaplain in the US Army, 1918–19; and the pastor of Westminster Presbyterian, Omaha, Nebraska, 1919–24. He apparently left the ministry in 1924 and lived in Marshfield, Wisconsin, until his death in Rochester, MN (*Princeton Biographical*, 312).

L'Aiglon: see Rostand, Edmond.

L'Ami Fritz: *Friend Fritz*, a novel written in 1864 by Émile Erckmann (1822–1899) and Louis-Alexander Chatrian (1826–1890). The dramatic version was first performed in December 1876 at the Théâter Français in Paris, which was the same theatrical company that produced the performance viewed by Machen in January 1918. *The New York Times*, Dec. 25, 1876, commented that the first performance was well attended and that standing room for the debut sold for 50 to 100 francs. The play is based on the Bible text, "Be fruitful and multiply and replenish the earth" (Gen. 1:28)("Erckmann-Chatrian," *Webster's Literature*).

Lamartine, Alphonse de (1790–1869): a French poet and statesman. His first collection of poems *Méditations Poétiques* (*Poetic Meditations*, 1820) established his reputation as a poet. The year following his election to the Academie Francaise in 1829 saw the publication of his two-volume work *Harmonies poetiques et religieuses* (*Poetic and Religious Harmonies*). Following the publication in 1839 of *Recueillements Poétiques* (*Poetic Contemplations*), he became greatly involved in politics and served as head of the provisional government following the revolution of Feb. 24, 1838 (*Webster's Literature*).

Lesage, Alain-Rene (1668–1747): a French novelist and satirical dramatist. The play that Machen saw, *Crispin, rival de son maître* (*Crispin, Rival of His Master*) was first performed in 1707. Lesage composed over one hundred *comédies-vaudevilles* for the Théâtre de la Foire (*Webster's Literature*).

Les Butors et la Finette: *The Pig-headed Ones and Finette* ("Finette" is a woman's name), written by François Porche in 1918. The play is an allegorical history of the First World War. It was first performed on November 29, 1917, at the Théâtre Antoine. Machen viewed the play February 10, 1918 (Albert Schinz, *French Literature and the Great War* [New York: D. Appleton, 1920], 349).

Lewis: see Machen, Lewis H.

Lisle, Leconte de: Charles-Marie-René (1818–1894), a French poet and served as the Senate librarian in Paris. He is considered a poet of disillusionment and skepticism who found his inspiration in the works of the ancients. Under the pseudonym of Pierre Gosset, he published *Histoire du Moyen Age* (1876, *History of the Modern Age*) ("Leconte de Lisle," *Webster's Literature*).

Loisy, Alfred Firmin (1857–1940): a Roman Catholic priest until he was excommunicated in 1908 for his views presented in the books *L'Evangile et L'Eglise* (1902, *The Gospel and the Church*) and his defense of those views in *Autour d'un Petit Livre* (1930, *Around a Small Book*). Loisy was a French linguist, biblical scholar, philosopher of religion, and professor of the history of religions at Collège de France (1909–1926) (*Webster's Biographical*).

Loy: see Gresham, LeRoy.

Macaulay, Thomas Babington (1800–1859): an English writer and politician. He served as a Member of Parliament, 1830–34, 39–47, 52–56. Machen referred to Macaulay's five-volume *History of England* (*Webster's Biographical*).

Machen, Arthur Webster (1827–1915): J. Gresham Machen's father. He is not mentioned in the letters in this collection but his relation is provided here for information.

Machen, Arthur W., II: Dr. Machen's older brother and Helen's husband. Arly followed in his father's footsteps and was a successful attorney in Baltimore. He was the person that Machen corresponded with during the war regarding business and finance matters. In the letter of Feb. 6 & 7, 1919, Machen notes that "Major Harris of Atlanta" was familiar with "Arly's book on corporations." The book referred to is *A Treatise on the Modern Law of Corporations*, 1908; Arly also published the title, *A Treatise on the Federal Corporation Tax Law of 1909*, (Hart, 175fn20).

Machen, Arthur W., III: the second child of Arthur W. Machen, II, and a nephew of Machen.

Machen, Betsy: Elizabeth Palmer Machen, who was the third child of Arthur W. Machen, II, and one of Dr. Machen's nieces.

Machen, Cornelia Burton: married to Thomas Machen on Dec. 30, 1913. Nena appears to have suffered from a weak constitution because she was often ill during the time of these letters. She was the mother of the "babies."

Machen, James: Dr. Machen's paternal uncle and the father of Carrie Machen Hammond and Lewis H. Machen.

Machen, Lewis H.: the son of James Machen.

Machen, Marie Gresham: the daughter of Thomas and Nena Machen.

Machen, Mary (Minnie) Gresham (1849–1931): J. Gresham Machen's mother. Machen's maternal ancestors were from Macon, Georgia. Mrs. Machen's father, John Jones Gresham (1818–1891), was a prominent and wealthy figure in Macon. Mrs. Machen published *The Bible in Browning with Particular Reference to the Ring and the Book*, 1903. She commented that, "no modern poet has manifested such intimate acquaintance with the Bible as Robert Browning" (p. 1). Dr. Machen inherited his wealth from his maternal grandparent's estate through his mother and the legacy left to him by his father (Hart, 13).

Machen, Thomas: J. Gresham Machen's younger brother. Tom was married to Nena and their children included the "babies," Marie Gresham and Arthur W. Machen, III.

Maitland, Alexander (1867–1940): one of the descendants of the first president of Princeton Seminary, Archibald Alexander, Maitland received his divinity degree from Princeton Seminary in 1892 and pursued most of his ministerial years at the First Presbyterian Church, Pittsburgh, serving there from 1899–1929. He was awarded honorary doctorates by Lafayette College (PA), the University of Kentucky, and the College of Wooster (OH). He moderated the PCUSA General Assembly in 1914 (*Princeton Biographical*, 173).

Martin of Tours (c. 316–397): a convert to Christianity who served in the Roman army before becoming a monastic. He founded the first monastery in Gaul and is the patron saint of France ("Martin," *Webster's Literature*).

Mikado: see Gilbert and Sullivan.

Miss Marie: perhaps a member of the Buchanan family. One of Dr. Machen's friends from his childhood was Charlie Buchanan. Dr. Machen wrote Miss Marie on March 18, 1918. Sometimes when she is mentioned in the letters she is included with Mrs. Buchanan. Miss Marie and Mrs. Buchanan gave Machen a sweater and some wristlets to provide some winter comfort.

Molière: Jean-Baptiste Poquelin (1622–1673), an actor and playwright considered by many to be the greatest of all writers of French comedy. He traveled with a theater group and wrote plays from 1645–58. His first great success was after his return to Paris when he wrote *Les Précieuses Ridicules* (1659, *The Ridiculous Young Ladies*). Molière remained in Paris and soon had his own theater. During a performance of his last play, *Le Malade imaginaire* (1673, *The Imaginary Invalid*), he collapsed on stage and died later that night. Machen, who seemed to be particularly fond of Molière, mentioned in his letters the plays *La Jalousie du Barbouillé* (50, *The Jealous Husband*), *Le Dépit Amoureux* (1656, *The Amorous Quarrel*), *Le Bourgeoise Gentilhomme* (1670, *The Would-Be Gentleman*), *Le Misanthrope* (1666, *The Misanthrope*), *Georges Dandin* (1668, *The Confounded Husband*), *L'Avare* (*The Miser*, 1668), *Amphitryon* (1668), *Tartuffe* (1669, *The Impostor*) and *Les Fourberies de Scapin* (1671, *The Mischievious Acts of Scapin*) (*Webster's Literature*).

Montí: a French soldier who was assigned the task of assisting Machen at the Foyer in Missy-sur-Aisne as part of his military duty. His letters to Machen have been translated into English and are included in this book preceding the glossary.

Mrs. Buchanan: the mother of Charlie Buchanan, mentioned in the company of Miss Marie in the letters.

Musset, Louis-Charles Alfred de (1810–1857): a romantic poet, dramatist, and fiction writer born in Paris. His first work was *Contes d'Espagne et d'Italie* (1830, *Stories of Spain and of Italy*). The plays mentioned by Dr. Machen were the comedies *On ne Badine pas avec l'amour* (1834, *No Triffling with Love*) and *Il ne faut jurer de rien* (1836, *It Isn't Necessary to Promise Anything*). *Carmosine* was written around 1850. He was elected to the Académie Française in 1852 (*Webster's Literature*).

Nena: see Machen, Cornelia Burton.

Pascal, Blaise (1623–1662): a French philosopher, mathematician, scientist, theologian, and general genius. His work *Pensées*, which was published posthumously from his notes, and his *Provinciales 1656–1657*, show the breadth of his intellect and his theological interests (*Webster's Biographical*).

Pasteur: see Guitry, Sacha.

Patton, Francis Landy (1843–1932): one of Machen's colleagues at Princeton Seminary as well as a good friend. After leaving the presidency of Princeton University in 1902, he became the first president of Princeton Seminary serving until his retirement to his home in Hamilton, Bermuda, in 1913. David B. Calhoun's, *Princeton Seminary, 1869–1929*, 1996, 522 fn 12, notes that on Patton's eighty-fifth birthday, the city of Hamilton, reported by *The Royal Gazette*, unveiled an official portrait of Patton titled "Bermuda's Grand Old Man."

Pollard, John Garland (1871–1937): born in Virginia, served as Virginia's Attorney General from 1913 to 1918, and resigned to serve with the YMCA in Europe during the First World War. In 1921, he accepted a position as professor of constitutional law and history at the College of William and Mary. He was elected governor of Virginia in 1929 and when his term ended he became the chairman of the Board of

Veterans Appeals (see The Library of Virginia online catalog entry for "Pollard, John Garland").

President King: Henry Churchill King (1858–1934), the President of Oberlin College from 1902 to 1927. President King was for several months the Director of the Religious Work Department of the YMCA in France. Some of King's published titles are *Reconstruction in Theology, Theology and the Social Consciousness, Rational Living,* and *The Laws of Friendship, Human and Divine* (for a biography of King see www.oberlin.edu /archive/holdings/finding/RG2/SG6/biography.html).

Racine, Jean (1639–1699): a French dramatist who was raised from the age of nine in a Jansenist convent. *Esther* (1689) was one of two religious tragedies he wrote for a girls' school during his later years. The other tragedy, which Machen mentions, was *Athalie* (1691). Other works by Racine include *Bajazet*, which was about recent Turkish history (1672); the only comedy by Racine was, *Les Plaideurs* (1668, *The Litigants*) (*Webster's Literature*).

Ranigan: the man who handled the distribution and accounting of the expenses fund provided by Machen for his alcoholic friend, Richard Hodges.

Robinson, Bobby: Harold McAfee Robinson (1881–1939), a close and lifelong friend of Dr. Machen. They established their friendship through the Benham Club at Princeton. He served pastorates in Pennsylvania at Milroy and Germantown, and he taught at Lafayette College, Easton, PA. He also worked for twenty years for the PCUSA Board of Publications, then the Board of Christian Education. It is in the latter capacity, as Hart points out, that the Machen-Robinson friendship was tested during the theological controversies of the 1920s (*Princeton Biographical*, 300; Hart, 130).

Robinson, Mary: the wife of Dr. Machen's friend, Bobby Robinson.

Rostand, Edmond (1868–1918): the author of the play *Cyrano de Bergerac*, first performed in 1897 and published the following year. The play tells the famous story of a man who feels that no woman can ever love him because of his enormous nose. Other plays by Rostand include, *Le Gant rouge* (1888, *The Red Glove*), *L'Aiglon* (1900, *The Eaglet*), *Chantecler* (1910), and published posthumously was his *La Dernière Nuit de Don Juan* (1921, *The Last Night of Don Juan*) (*Webster's Literature*).

Sand, George: the pseudonym of Amadine-Aurore-Lucile (Lucie) Dudevant (1804–1876), whose original surname was Dupin. Her first use of "George Sand" was as the author of the novel *Indiana* (1832). The play that Machen saw in February 1918 at the Odéon was *Le Marriage de*

Victoriae (1851, *The Marriage of Victoria*). Her plays often exemplified her own romantic promiscuity as they followed the theme "love transcending the obstacles of convention and class." However, in her later life her novels and plays displayed "impeccable morality and conservatism" (*Webster's Literature*).

Schweitzer, Albert (1875–1965): of German descent and born in the Alsace. The missionary work Machen mentioned in his letter of Jan. 12, 1919, involved the founding of Lambaréné Hospital in French Equatorial Africa (1913). With respect to Schweitzer's musical interests, he wrote a monograph on J. S. Bach (1905) and published a critical edition of Bach's organ works (1912–14). A few of his theological works were *Von Reimarus zu Wrede* (1906, in English published as, *The Quest of the Historical Jesus: A Critical Study of Its Progress from Reimarus to Wrede*, 1910) and *Die Mystik des Apostels Paulus* (1930, in English, *The Mysticism of Paul the Apostle*, 1931). He is probably best known for receiving the Nobel Prize for peace in 1952 (*Columbia Encyclopedia; Webster's Biographical*).

Smith, Kirby Flower (1862–1918): Professor of Latin, 1889–1918, at Johns Hopkins University (Kirby Flower Smith Papers, online catalog entry at Johns Hopkins University libraries).

Smith, William Benjamin (1850–1934): a professor at Tulane University. The theme of his teaching on Christianity involved tracing its roots to a pre-Christian Jesus cult. *The Birth of the Gospel; A Study of the Origin and Purport of the Primitive Allegory of the Jesus*, was published posthumously.

Seal or Seal Harbor: a coastal town in Maine where the Machens vacationed in a cottage at the Seaside Inn.

Stevenson, J. Ross: became the president of Princeton Seminary in 1914 and continued in that office until 1936. Stevenson's openness to modernism and ecumenism contributed to the reorganization of the seminary board in 1929 to create a theologically more inclusive seminary. In 1929, Dr. Machen left Princeton to found Westminster Theological Seminary due to the board reorganization and a weakened commitment to the inerrancy of the Bible. In the letter of Dec. 28, 1918, Dr. Machen mentioned that there was some tension between them in France *(Princeton Biographical*, xiii, xix, xxii, xxiv).

Tartuffe: see Molière.

Thompson, Aleck: Alexander Thompson Jr. (1882–1957), a graduate of Hamilton College, Clinton, New York, 1906, and Princeton Seminary, 1909. He was a pastor in Little Britain, PA, 1909–1914, Westfield, NY, 1915–1921, and North Church in Geneva, NY, 1921–1953. He was given

the Doctor of Divinity by both Hamilton College, 1940, and Hobart
College, 1944 (*Benham Club*, 79; *Princeton Biographical*, 396).

Tom: see Machen, Thomas.

Uncle: see Gresham, Thomas B.

Vigny, Alfred-Victor de (1797–1863): a French poet, playwright, and novelist.
The poem collection mentioned by Dr. Machen in his letter of February
28, 1918, may be this author's *Poèmes Antiques et Modernes* (1826, *Poems
Ancient and Modern*)(*Webster's Biographical*).

Wanamaker, John (1838–1922): known for starting a men's clothing business
in Philadelphia at 6th and Market Streets in 1861. Within ten years,
Wanamaker's was the largest retail men's clothing store in America.
He expanded the location into a department store beginning in 1877.
He was the US postmaster general, 1889–1893, during the administra-
tion of the US President and Presbyterian elder, Benjamin Harrison.
Wanamaker was a member of the Presbyterian Church (USA) (*Webster's
Biographical*).

William: a family servant. He was a general helper around the house who
handled the heavier tasks of running the household and errands and
assisted Dr. Machen's mother when Betty could not.

INDEX OF SUBJECTS
AND NAMES

339